SPECIAL OPERATIONS SERIES

Project Editor by Éric MICHELETTI

Special Operations Series

Project Editor by Éric MICHELETTI

© Histoire & Collections, 1999
5, avenue de la République - 75841 Paris Cedex 11 - France
ISBN : 2 908 182 947

Paul GAUJAC

SPECIAL FORCES IN THE INVASION OF FRANCE

Translated by Janice LERT

Histoire & Collections

To Sergeant Camille A. Barnage, to First Sergeants Lucien J. Bourgoin and to Lewis F. Goddard, who fell during the liberation of Provence, August 7-11, 1944, and were laid to rest in the U.S. military cemetery in Draguignan, France.

Forward

During the year 1944, nearly 170 Allied Special Forces teams were operating in occupied France. Their general mission was to help the Resistance movement, carry messages to them from the Allied command, and participate in the fight against the occupying forces. These teams were made up of officers and specialists and took various forms depending on the job assigned to them: liaison detachments and interallied Jedburgh teams, British Special Air Service parties, American Operational Groups, French Counterscorch Groups.

Their story is not well known. Even though the prestigious SAS fascinates historians and novelists, Jeds and OGs only rarely appear in books dealing with the actions of the intelligence services or the Resistance movement [1].

It is not so much a question of lack of interest as it is a lack of the documents needed to undertake a serious study or a historical account. Moreover, the secrecy surrounding the special services and the later careers of many of the participants are not conducive to revelations.

The aim of this book is to present the action of the members of the Allied special forces who were parachuted into France on missions dictated by the Allied command. We have excluded the comparatively better-known SAS. In an effort to avoid errors and stick strictly to the detailed account of each team's operations, we have chosen to base our work on written reports of the time, rather than on later testimony.

---

1. One exception is the book *Hidden Ally* by Arthur L. Funk, dedicated to the French Resistance movement, special operations and the Allied landing in Southern France in 1944.

Henri Amouroux in one of his books underlines the importance of these documents:

"The reports of the French, English and American Jedburghs were written up immediately on returning to London and are particularly instructive concerning the number of guerilla fighters, their weapons, the German opposition and the results of the operation. For History it is unfortunate that this material has not been put to better use.

They also furnish important information about the political situation. Here are the French French as seen by the London French. Their view can be quite interesting" [2].

The quality of these reports depends largely on the person who wrote them. They are often prolific, sometimes elliptical, but have the advantage of being fresh from the scene of events and show real spontaneity, even if sometimes the opinions expressed are blunt: double-talk wasn't the preferred language of the Special Forces. However, they contain information or indications which were clear to the participants at the time but must be "decoded" for today's reader. Or at least placed in the context of the time. This is often a difficult task, for the necessary archives are not always available and some of the events related require a certain confidentiality ...

The decision to engage special forces on a large scale came late in the war, at the time of the invasion of Normandy. Beyond the fact that it was at that time considered very dangerous, if not suicidal, to operate in uniform behind the German lines, the Allied command doubted the existence and the effectiveness of the interior resistance movement. In June and July of 1944 about one third of the teams were parachuted into France. Those remaining in England and Algeria were sent over in August and September, at the time of the landing in Provence and the push toward the Rhine. Thus it is clear that their participation was closely linked to the operations undertaken by the regular Allied forces. Nor can this engagement be considered apart from the action

2. *Joies et douleurs du peuple libéré*, published by Robert Laffont, 1988. In our study we will follow the anglo-saxon custom, rather than that of H. Amouroux, and use the word Jedburghs in its plural form.

of the secret services connected to the underground networks and resistance movements.

Along with the fact that the Special Forces teams received missions that were strategic to the war effort, the converging interests of the regular and special forces required that the activities of the latter be placed within the framework of the operations being conducted by the Allied command and the different organizations involved with intelligence gathering and special action.

The extraordinary, sometimes even comical, adventures that the team members experienced, must also be set in the general context of the time. Among the Free World forces, relations were complicated by conflicts of interest, and disputes between the Allies and Resistance groups inside and outside occupied France. On the German side, the situation was just as complex, with troops separated into occupation and field forces, the antagonism between the police or intelligence services of the Wehrmacht and those of the SS and the proliferation of paramilitary organizations among others.

The plan that we have chosen for this tale of the special forces is based on geographical divisions such as those used in the history of the French Forces of the Interior (Forces Françaises de l'Intérieur - FFI) published in 1945.

After all, the principal mission of the special forces was to bring aid and support to the FFI. However, chronologically speaking, this period is also marked by three important events: the invasions of Normandy and Provence, and the Allied pause in the march on the Reich in October of 1944.

And even before the "Battle of France" was over and Liberation completely achieved, another battle was shaping up in the northeast and around the pockets along the Atlantic coast, where special forces and guerilla fighters played a new role. The FFI were progressively transformed into "regular" troops, while the paratroopers of the Special Forces prepared for new adventures in Germany or the Far East ...

As far as the text is concerned, we have chosen to simplify by using certain conventional expressions and abreviations. Thus, as commonly used, the abreviation FFI refers not only to the French Forces of the Interior but also to their troops. The same can be said of SAS, which refers to both the organization and the men.

Concerning Allied abreviations, Anglo-Saxon usage has been adopted. Anglo-Saxon and French military ranks have also been preserved to distinguish the Allied soldiers from their French counterparts.

When speaking of missions, the code name is frequently used to refer to the whole team. This is in keeping with the mentality of the time.

Finally, the story of the adventures of the Special Forces teams has been volontarily limited to operations directed against the German occupiers. While certain politico-military aspects are mentioned — especially personality conflicts and in-fighting between factions involving people who were often drawn into a situation unawares — it is only to clarify the development of events or the behavior of the different participants. Another whole book could be devoted to this aspect of the conflict.

Thus the reader, while discovering the atmosphere of the times inside and outside France, will be able to appreciate in depth the courage, enthousiasm and spirit of sacrifice which inspired these men — British, Canadians, New Zealanders, Americans, Belgians, and French — these Special Forces parachuted to participate in the Liberation of France.

Translator's Preface
to the English Edition

The English translation was conducted in constant collaboration with the author, who based his original French edition on certain reports in English written by members of the Special Forces teams. Parts of these reports have been reproduced as written or slightly modified for a better comprehension.

The Allies as referred to in the book are essentially the US, Great Britain and other Commonwealth countries, and the term Allies is often used in opposition to the French.

Most of the action is situated during the last months of the war, and in an occupied country, France, whose population was consequently divided: some backed the Vichy puppet regime, some wanted to fight it, many just didn't want to get involved. We as readers are forced to deal with the complexities of the political situation. The race was on inside and outside France among individuals and political movements to fill the power vacuum created by the withdrawal of the German forces.

The arrest of certain members of the Resistance immediately replaced by others, each with an alias or code-name, movements annihilated and reborn under a different name, or fusing together, or taken over by umbrella organizations, may seem confusing to the modern reader. They certainly were more so at the time and the author's talent in dealing with these questions is a tribute to the authenticity of his work.

He attempts to put a name and face to each individual member of the Special Forces teams and in so doing has created a memorial to their action: France owes much to this handful of soldiers who believed that she could and should help free herself.

Janice Lert, May 1999.

Glossary

ABTF	Airbornew Task Force.
Abwehr	Amt Auslandsnachrichten und Abwehr (counter-espionage bureau of the German Armed Services).
AFHQ	Allied Forces Headquarters (Algiers).
AFN	Afrique Française du Nord (French North Africa).
AK	Armeekorps.
AMF	'North Africa' section of the SOE.
Anvil	First code name for Allied invasion of Provence.
AS	Armée Secrète (secret army - French Resistance fighters).
ATS	Auxiliary Territorial Service (female).
BAR	Browning Automatic Rifle.
BBC	British Broadcasting Corporation.
BCA	Batallion de chasseurs alpins (Mountain Infantry Battalion).
BCRA	Bureau Central de Renseignement et d'Action (central intelligence and action bureau).
BCRAA	BCRA in Algiers (or BRAA).
BCRAL	BCRA in London (or BRAL).
BLO	British Liaison Officer
BOA	Bureau d'Operations Aériennes (French airborne operations bureau)
Btl	Batallion
CA	Corps d'armée.
Caïman	Plan of operations to be carried out by the FFI.
CCS	Combined Chiefs of Staff.
CDL	Comité de Libération (liberation committee).
CFL	Corps Francs de la Libération (Resistance movement including armed formations of MUR).
CFLN	Comité Français de la Libération Nationale (acting government of the French Republic formed in Algiers in 1943 and headed by De Gaulle and Giraud).
CFP	Pommies Corps Franc (independent group).
CIC	American Counter-Intelligence Corps.

CNR	Conseil National de la Résistance (created in Paris in 1943 by Jean Moulin, uniting resistance movements and labor unions).
COMAC	Comité Militaire d'Action (Paris - CNR).
COMIDAC	Comité d'Action en France (Algiers - CFLN).
COPA	Centre d'opérations de parachutages et d'atterrissages (parachuting and landing operations center — replaced by SAP).
CP	Command post.
DB	Division blindée (armored division).
DBLE	Demi-brigade de la Légion étrangère (French Foreign Legion Half-Brigade).
DCA	Défense contre avions (anti-aircraft artillery).
DF	SOE 'underground communications' section.
DGSS	Direction générale des services spéciaux (French special services headquarters).
DMD	Délégué militaire départemental (départemental military deputy).
DMN	Délégué militaire national (national military deputy).
DMOS	Délégué militaire pour le théâtre d'opérations sud (military deputy for Southern theater of operations).
DMR	Délégué militaire régional (regional military deputy).
DMZ	Délégué militaire de zone (military deputy for the zone).
DMZN	Délégué militaire pour la zone nord (military deputy for the Northern zone).
DMZS	Délégué militaire pour la zone sud (military deputy for the Southern zone).
DR	SOE section for 'Netherlands, France, Fighting France'.
Dragoon	Second code name for Allied invasion of Provence.
DSR-SM	Direction des services de renseignement et de la sécurité militaire (intelligence and military security headquarters).
DZ	Drop zone.
EM FFI	Tripartite (USA, GB, France) FFI headquarters in London.
EMN FFI	National FFI headquarters in occupied France.
ETOUSA	European Theater of Operations, US Army.

F	SOE 'France' section (Buckmaster).
FANY	First Aid Nursing Yeomanry (female).
FFC	Forces Françaises Combattantes (movement created in 1942 with the purpose of symbolically uniting the efforts of the Free French and the Resistance movements)
FFI	French Forces of the Interior (combined Resistance movements).
FFI-EM	FFI headquarters in London.
FFL	Forces Françaises Libres (Free French Forces - Armed Forces present with De Gaulle in England.) FILA Forces de l'Intérieur - Liaison administrative (FFI-EM bureau in London).
Flak	Flieger Abwehr Kanone (German anti-aircraft artillery).
FLN	Front de Libération Nationale (Aslgerian national liberation front).
F/Lt	Flight Lieutenant
FN	Front National (Northern zone Resistance movement - Communist).
FTP	Francs-Tireurs et Partisans (communist Resistance movement).
FTPF	Francs-Tireurs et Partisans Français (military Resistance organization).
G-2	American 2nd bureau (intelligence).
G-3	American 3rd bureau (operations).
Gestapo	Geheime Staatpolizei.
GFP	Geheime Feldpolizei (secret field police).
GMR	Groupe Mobile de Réserve (mobile reserve group).
GPRF	Gouvernement Provisoire de la République Française (provisionary government of the French Republic).
HMSO	Her Majesty's Stationery Office (publisher).
HQ	Headquarters.
lc	Intelligence officer of a German staff.
ID	Infantry Division
Jedburgh	Tripartite liaison mission (shortened to 'Jed').
JMO	Journal des marches et opérations (journal of marches and

operations). Massingham Code name for the SOE/OSS base in Algeria.

MI 6	Military intelligence 6 (secret intelligence).
MI 9	Military Intelligence 9 (escape and evasion).
MLN	Mouvement de Libération Nationale (Southern zone Resistance movement).
MNPGD	Mouvement National des Prisonniers de Guerre et Déportés (National movement of POWs and displaced persons).
MOI	Main d'oeuvre immigré (immigrant labor).
MUR	Mouvements Unis de Résistance (Southern zone federation of Resistance movements, later becomes MLN).
NAP	Noyautage des administrations publiques (political infiltration of public services).
NCO	Noncommissioned Officer.
Neptune	Code name for the Overlord operations planned in 1944.
OB West	Oberbefehlshaber West (Commander in Chief, Western Front).
OCM	Organisation Civile et Militaire (Northern zone Resistance movement).
Oflag	Offizierlager (officers' prison).
OG	Operational Group.
OMA	Organisation Métropolitaine de l'Armée (independent military organisation).
ORA	Organisation de Résistance de l'Armée (military Resistance organisation).
Orpo	Ordnungspolizei (police charged with maintaining order in occupied France).
OSS	Office of Strategic Services (U.S.).
OSS/SI	Intelligence branch of the OSS.
OSS/SO	Special operations branch of the OSS.
OT	Organization Todt.
Overlord	Invasion of North-Western Europe across the English Channel.
POW	Prisoner of War.
PWE	Political Warfare Executive.

RAF	Royal Air Force.
RF	SOE 'Free France' then 'Allied France' section.
RI	Régiment d'Infanterie (french infantry regiment).
SACMED	Supreme Allied Command, Mediterranean.
SAP	Service d'Atterrissage et Parachutage (landing and dropping service).
SAS	Special Air Service.
SD	Special Detachment.
SF	Special Forces.
SF Det	Special Forces Detachment.
SFHQ	Special Forces Headquarters (London).
SFU	Special Forces Unit.
SHAEF	Supreme Headquarters, Allied Expeditionary Forces.
Sipo-SD	Sicherheitspolizei und Sicherheitsdienst (SS security organization).
SIS	Secret Intelligence Service (British).
Sked	Radio time slot.
S/Ldr	Squadron leader.
SOE	Special Operations Executive (British).
SOL	Service d'Ordre Légionnaire (French 'Legion' service in charge of maintaining order).
SPOC	Special Projects Operation Center (Algiers).
SR	Sicherungsregiment (security regiment).
SR	Service de Renseignement (intelligence service).
STO	Service du Travail Obligatoire (mandatory work service for Frenchmen in Germany).
STS	SOE Special Training School.
USAAF	United States Army Air Forces.
ZNO	Zone nouvellement occupée (newly occupied zone).

Chapter I

Jumping into occupied France...

On April 11, 1944, around 21: 00, a bomber is getting ready to take off from England, heading towards the east into the darkness. On board there are no bombs, just an advance echelon participating in Operation Citronelle, an interallied mission scheduled in the north-eastern part of occupied France.

The engines churn with a roar as the mechanics give the crew the ritual good-luck sign, thumbs raised ... Then the plane starts to roll toward the end of the runway as the hulking camouflaged hangars fade away into the night.

The flight, slightly disturbed by flak fire as they pass over the coast, lasts for almost four hours in complete darkness. So the three officers are relieved when the trap door finally opens and cold air rushes in.

"Action station", commands the dispatcher.

The first jumper of the stick moves toward the hole, grabs the edges with his two hands and swings his legs to the side, then lets them dangle in the air. The second crouches behind him, his knees pressing against his companion's back.

"Number One, Go!"

On the order, Commandant De Bollardière, leader of the mission, tumbles out. His American adjutant follows, then the French radio operator. Their silk parachutes automatically burst open with a dull thud and start in to vibrate like wild pendulums. As he descends, the American drifts slightly off target: beneath him he can't make out even the faintest glow of a lantern, just a checkerboard of dark and light shapes that he takes to be bushes and fields.

After he hits the ground, he rolls up his parachute, takes off his boots and waits patiently for the reception committee to arrive. Twenty minutes later he can hear female voices at a distance: in the dark he moves toward them and finds the reception committee, four women and two men, busily talking.

The drop has actually taken place on the outskirts of the German training camp in Mourmelon, more than a mile from the intended site. But contact has been established: Mission Citronelle is in the field.

The Interallied Mission Citronelle

It all began during the first months of 1944, after the Allied secret networks in France were destroyed by German police. In London, the RF section in charge of the Free French at the Special Operations Executive (SOE) — the British special operations office — and the Bureau Central de Renseignement et d'Action (BCRA) that it supported, were trying to reknit the broken strands connecting them to the armed Resistance movement. In preparation for the invasion, several "interallied" missions were thus sent out to make contact with the French underground. The first team, dropped in January of 1944, met with leaders of the Lyon region and the Vercors maquis, then was picked up during the first days of May.

The next five missions were organized along the same lines: in April in the Ardennes, the following month in the Cantal, and three more in June to the maquis in the Morvan, Savoie and Lozère regions.

In January of 1944, the mission to the Ardennes received the code name Citronelle, first in the series of herbs and fragrances ascribed to the interallied missions. Initially the mission included Commandant Jacques Pâris de Bollardière [1], Captain D.E. Hubble of the Royal Artillery, First

---

1. Named "Companion of the Liberation" on June 23, 1941, as a member of the 13th DBLE.

Lieutenant Victor J. Layton, a reserve officer with the US Army, and Flight Lieutenant Whitehead of the RAF, who, from February on, worked together on preparations for their coming action. They each received a code name: Prisme, Bissectrice, Triedre and Parabole.

After studying the available intelligence reports, they soon came to the conclusion that the situation in the Ardennes was unique. The population had been evacuated in 1940 and found themselves, when they came home, in a forbidden zone strictly controlled by the Germans. And even though the density of German troops was considered low [2], enemy counter-espionage was particularly active: numerous foreigners working in diverse organizations such as the Todt, were often used as informants.

Under these conditions, the team realized that it would be useless to draw up plans like those used in zones that were well-controlled by the local maquis, such as Savoie.

"In the Ardennes, commented the leader of the mission, the only way to survive is to maintain high mobility and excellent security".

Consequently he asked that an intelligence officer be assigned to him to keep track of the activities of the Gestapo, especially actions apt to be taken against the partisans. This officer [3] was soon designated and would prove extremely useful.

"I also hope, Bollardière continued, that the partisans can be equiped to be able to move out on short notice. Without changing the basic contents of the containers, we must insure that the supplies dropped are well adapted to the situation. Every drop should include food rations for two weeks".

For security reasons it was important that the guerilla fighters not depend on any of the few local farms, and that they be completely free to move. Of course all this was assuming that there actually existed guerilla fighters in the Ardennes region !

2. Only one territorial battalion, the Landesschütze-Btl. z.b.V. 581 in Charleville. The Ost-Btl 680, part of the Eastern contingent, is also mentioned in Mézières from November 1, 1943 on.

3. Capitaine Carrière (Jacques).

After a long wait, an answer finally came back from France: there did exist a core group of 800 resistants in the area, but no suitable drop zone could be found nearby. Follow-up messages confirmed this information and it began to appear that the mission might not be carried out after all.

It would later turn out that there was, in fact, no organized armed maquis whatsoever and that, on the other hand, there were at least 60 possible sites where men or supplies could be dropped.

As it seemed impossible to find a drop zone in the area, it was decided to send an advance team to locate the partisans along the border and furnish them with weapons.

Once slated for departure, the three parachutists [4] were given specially prepared civilian clothes with no indication of their origin. Commandant De Bollardière also received a work "agreement", including most importantly the pre-arranged sentences necessary for liaisons via the BBC or to check as to whether the team was still free or had fallen into the hands of the German police.

The drop finally took place on the edge of the Mourmelon training camp, more than a mile from the designated DZ east of the city of Reims.

And it took a long time for the reception committee to find the two other jumpers who had drifted toward the east. They then had to wait for daybreak to pick up one of the packages which had fallen almost a mile away.

They arranged to have a messenger sent to Paris to obtain the names of the necessary contacts in the Ardennes.

Then after emptying two bottles of champagne, the three officers left in a gasogene truck for Hope Farm (la ferme de l'Espérance), located near a crossroads. That was where they see "their" first German, coming to buy eggs.

In the evening they reached Mourmelon where a man hid them for a week. Finally, instead of the messenger from Paris, they met Planète, the military delegate (Délégué militaire régional - DMR) for

---

4. Bollardière, Layton and Lieutenant Gérard Bréaux alias Blanc (a Senegalese), the radioman.

Region C [5], who confirmed the absence of an organized maquis in the Ardennes.

The parachutists then travelled to Renwez, halfway between Rocroi and Charleville, where they were met by the chief of the local gendarmerie [6] who had intended to shelter them in an empty house hidden in the woods on the edge of a swamp. On the way there they learned that the house had already been searched several times by the Germans looking for réfractaires [7]. They decided it was wiser to move to the other side of the swamp. They set up the radio in a hut and sent their first messages to London. And they used their three-day supply of emergency rations sparingly until a strong liaison could be established.

Meanwhile in Charleville, André Point, alias Commandant Fournier, FFI leader for the département [8], had been informed. He came to give his advice about the possibility of building up a maquis and how to go about it. Two days later he took the team in a panel truck to an underground shelter near Laifour, where the Meuse River forms an impressive loop under a 900-foot-high cliff. Even though it was only a few miles from Monthermé, the spot seemed safe: during their four-week stay a couple of poachers would be the only visitors to disturb their tranquillity.

"What have you got for weapons?" asked Fournier.

"All we have, replied Layton, are our own: six Stens with ammunition, twenty Mills defensive grenades, and just about all our radio gear".

"Good! As far as the men for the maquis are concerned, I'll round them up. I've brought you some food. I'll keep you supplied until you are able to fend for yourselves".

Relations with the resistants were cordial from the start and would remain so until the end. But the Resistance leaders had a hard time understanding the relationship between this mission and others

5. Named DMR in February 1944, Colonel Gilbert Hirsch-Ollendorf, alias Grandval (Planète) was accompanied by his chief of staff, Commandant Aubusson (Nérot), and two messenger-body guards.

6. Translator's note. French police force in charge of small towns and rural areas.

7. French rebels fleeing from STO, mandatory work service in Germany. TN.

8. French territorial administrative division. TN.

scheduled or already in operation in the area, and consequently they remained cautious. And agreements reached during meetings were not always carried out.

What the members of Mission Citronelle didn't know was that there existed another plan, Plan Paul, with almost the same objectives as their own!

In March of 1944, after the meeting of regional maquis leaders in Paris, the leader of region C was informed, as well as his comrades from the Côte d'Or and Brittany, that some of their départements were of interest to a certain Commandant Millet, alias Régis or Paul, who had arrived from London:

"We want to create in each département well-organized formations having at their disposal one or more sites where paratroopers can jump, and a drop zone for supplies in containers. When the time comes, these zones will be used by the Jedburgh teams, composed of officers or NCOs, bringing with them special anti-tank weapons. Their action may start either before the invasion or simultaneously with it".

The Ardennes and Meuse départements seemed to be particularly appropriate and so on March 30th Régis and Aubusson [9] went to Charleville "where a series of important arrests was underway". They met Fournier there, and he confirmed the situation as described in Paris:

"The Ardennes partisans are not organized in groups, as London seems to believe. The known and registered réfractaires still live with families or on farms. They can easily be contacted and summoned. But they are in need of training, which is hard to provide under these conditions".

In each département a leader was chosen whose job it was to organize the volunteers into hundred-man units, and, with local help, look for suitable drop zones.

And from the BOA in Toulouse came an officer in charge of aerial operations who took over his job on May 15th. But his first interview

9. Commandant Aubusson took part in the meeting as regional "maquis" leader and AS (Armée secrète) Chief of Staff for region C.

with the DMR went badly: the officer sent from the BOA refused to place himself and his men under Planète's command [10].

This helps to explain the lack of drop sites and the fact that local leaders hesitated to let go of their men; they needed them for other plans. It is nonetheless surprising that Commandant De Bollardière was sent to the Ardennes without any knowledge of Plan Paul.

De Bollardière was only interested in getting his own mission underway. He suggested that some réfractaires be sent to him so that he could organize the embryo of a guerilla group which he would then furnish with weapons.

Aubusson agreed:

"Fournier will take care of recruiting the fighters and getting their pay to their families. He will stock food at different places around the département, will get any information about the Germans to you, and will act as agent to your group. We will give your maquis the code name Prisme".

On April 25, as the first recruits were arriving, a message was dispatched to London asking for the necessary arms and supplies to equip the maquis being formed. The answer came on May 7, when the BBC broadcasted a message for a drop site already under use with the code name Bohémien.

The Manises maquis

So the team left the Laifour dugout around 22:00 and moved out onto the neighboring Hauts-Buttés DZ, a plateau covered with scrub oak and mud holes. This high swampy moor looked like it belonged in the Arctic. The Croix-Scaille electric line had been cut for the occasion. In the bitter cold the hours seemed endless as the reception committee, directed by farmer Machaud, got ready. Everyone strained their ears ...

The drone of an engine grew stronger in the calm of the night and, at 02:30, the plane flew over the site. From the ground it was clearly

10. For reasons both technical — vis-à-vis the Allied services — and political — control of the interior Resistance groups — the BCRA preferred to maintain control over the air operations teams in France.

visible, passing twice over the lights. A flashlight flashed out the pre-arranged Morse code signal letter. The plane answered and with this the last doubts vanished and the red lanterns were lit on the ground. On its third run, the plane headed straight toward the red glow and dropped fifteen containers and four packages. From the sky it looked as if giant mushrooms had popped up all at once: they were the different-colored parachutes bursting open one after the other in the air. Below, the reception committee was trying to count them so as not to forget any in the field, which could have dire consequences. They floated slowly down: then with a metallic clank the containers hit the soil.

The men on the ground were amazed: for a moment they forgot their warnings about caution, and danced around shrieking with joy. Then in the blink of an eye every item was recuperated and camouflaged on the spot. The parachutes were unhooked and carefully rolled up. Then teams of four men, armed with large wooden sticks, carried the containers into the woods nearby and concealed them in crannies.

During the following night the material was carried to a prepared hideout and then at dawn the men gathered round for the moment they had all been waiting for: the containers were opened and the contents inventoried.

As the covers were ripped off their hearts sank! The containers contained almost nothing of what had been requested: no equipment whatsoever and only enough weapons for about sixty men, along with six large lamps but no batteries, picks and shovels, some cans of corned beef ...

What would Fournier think? He had seen the message sent to London asking for 180 sleeping bags and knapsacks, canvas pails and other material needed in the harsh Ardennes climate. Even though it was May, water in the pails was often still frozen in the morning and it rained two or three times a day.

With the new equipment five groups of ten men each were created, along the lines which had been decided on during previous discussions in London. But only two of the squads could be correctly armed.

Around May 25, the Special Forces team with about thirty poorly-equiped men moved two miles to the north into the Manises woods, still on the right bank of the Meuse and close to the Belgian border. Tents were made for the recruits out of parachute material, while the paratroopers, who had better equipment, slept outside. Contact was made with pro-Resistance farmers to insure regular food delivery. And over the camp floated a blue, white and red banner with the cross of Lorraine embroidered on it, a contribution of the ladies of the area.

On the 28th, the BBC broadcasted another personal message announcing a drop on a newly approved site called Astrologie near Thilay. This time the committee was beefed up by adding fifteen men from Capitaine Levert's Monthermé border group. The group had no idea how many planes might be involved and counted mainly on its radio equipment — S-Phone and Eureka — to insure a successful drop.

The weather was clear, and the members of the reception committee were barely ready when they noticed a plane approaching the DZ. On the radio, Lieutenant Layton had a hard time guiding it to the lighted strip: there were two other planes circling overhead and they kept interferring with reception. The first drop finally took place beyond the lanterns and the two others crosswise. By dawn 45 containers and 40 packages had been picked up and camouflaged in the surrounding woods.

Hardly had the material been gathered and the men hidden away in a clump of fir, when an enemy fighter plane came hedge-hopping over the DZ, probably looking for traces of nighttime activity. So the team remained hidden until nightfall when they found their way back to Laifour. Three days later, when things had quieted down, the reception committee carried the material to the hideout.

Even though the contents weren't as disappointing as before and included weapons and field gear [11], they didn't exactly correspond to what had been requested.

11. 90 rifles, 18 bazookas, Mills and Gammon grenades, Stens, 18 Brens, explosives, 60 knapsacks, 88 backpacks, 110 collections of ponchos, sweaters and wool gloves, 88 leather vests, 30 sleeping bags, 40 blankets.

"We got the impression, Layton said later, that things were packed haphazardly, without reference to our needs, and that all the requests for equipment that we had taken such pains to write, had hardly been read".

That was really unfortunate because the men were so poorly clothed that they couldn't even stay outside all night, let alone participate in sabotage action:

"Recruits should report in their oldest clothes and with a minimum of equipment, Fournier had told local leaders".

It was also impossible to give the same equipment to each man, which was hard on discipline. Finally they decided to send scouts into Belgium to search out and buy shoes and clothing.

On June 5th, the BBC broadcasted a new message: "King John is wise, five friends will visit him tonight!" So five officers were going to jump onto the Astrologie site. At nightfall an American four-engine plane took off from Harrington, the Carpetbaggers' base in England. The crew of the B-24, who were old hands, easily found the drop site after a flight lasting only an hour and a half, and without any reaction from the German flak.

On the ground Layton had battery problems with the S-Phone and Goetchebeur landed in a swamp. But when the eight containers were finally buried nearby, everybody headed toward the Fontaine farm in Vieux Moulins de Thilay for supper:

"The dining room was decorated with the interallied colors, recalled one of the members of the reception committee. Ten officers took part in the meal, some in uniform and all bearing weapons: the five newcomers [12], Commandant Prisme, American Lieutenant Victor, Lieutenant Pierre [13], and two US Air Force Lieutenants who had bailed out and been picked up".

Everyone enjoyed a lavish meal. When the champagne was uncorked, Captain Hubble warmly thanked his hosts for the

12. Captains Hubble and Carrière (Point and Jacques for the partisans), the intelligence officer, Flight Lieutenant Whitehead and two sabotage instructors : Sous-lieutenants Goetchebeur (Echardonnette) and Racine (Brabant).

13. Layton and Bréaux were known to the partisans as Vic.

wonderful welcome that his team was receiving. Layton translated, then announced the great news from London:

"The Allied invasion starts today !"

Just before dawn, the mission returned to the Manises woods and the intelligence officer went to Charleville to meet the partisans that he had been in contact with from London. One of the two homing pigeons that had come over on the plane was released with a message telling of the safe arrival of the other members of the mission. While tents were being made out of the parachutes from the second expedition, Hubble asked by radio for an emergency supply of pants, shoes and warm clothes.

This was all the more important because new recruits were arriving every day. Actually of the 230 recruits, only 160 could be readily equiped from head to toe. This brought to 190 the number of armed men, as well as two French officers, one active and one reserve, and eight Allied aviators having escaped through Belgium on their own since the break-up of the organized escape route.

The drop site Astrologie could no longer be used for security reasons. So Layton and Hubble left on the morning of June 12th to reconnoiter a zone two miles to the north that they had spotted on the map.

As they were coming back after noon near Vieux Moulins, dressed in civilian clothes with pistols in their belts and rifles slung over their shoulders, they heard gunfire coming from the direction of the camp. They quickly ducked into a trail on the north bank of the Manise. While they were discussing exactly where the camp was, a German soldier suddenly jumped out from behind a bush, pointing his gun at them.

"Halt ! Hände hoch !"

Layton was the first to react: he jumped to his left toward a row of fir trees, followed by a volley of bullets. Then, because he heard automatic gunfire and had lost track of Hubble, he hurried back to camp to warn the others.

But everyone was already at his station and the watch guards had taken up their positions. Patrols had been sent out to get information, and they reported that the Germans had barred the roads leading out of Revin and were patrolling in cars along the roads in the valley and on the hilltops.

Around 16:00 an enemy patrol approaching the camp was turned back by the resistants, who lost several men during the fighting. Sporadic gunfire lasted until nightfall, while the partisans who had no combat station were busy digging holes to bury food and ammunition.

"We will move out at 23:00, decided Commandant De Bollardière, who had been wounded in the thigh. Each officer will take command of a group. Try to get through the German blockade at different points. That will get them mixed up and they won't be able to tell which direction we are taking. Try to get to Six Chenons".

That would have been a difficult plan even for experienced fighters. It was all the more complicated for these new partisans and for the aviators who hardly understand French. Around midnight, an hour late, 250 men were finally assembled in single file in the dark.

Since the column didn't seem to be advancing, Captain Layton went up front only to discover that Bollardière had already left with fifty men. The only information that Goetchebeur could give him was the rally point. Layton then took charge of a hundred men and disappeared into the dark. It was hard going, and the column finally reached the road from Monthermé to Hargnies around 03:00. Then German machine guns opened fire and the men scattered in every direction. Finally Layton and the fifteen men remaining with him hid themselves in the tall ferns.

The whole maquis was now divided into small groups, hiding in ditches at a stone's throw from the Haybes road. Only four men — Whitehead, an American pilot and two young partisans with an automatic rifle — managed to get through the German blockade that night. But since they had no backpacks, they were forced to bury the radio set, including the Eureka, and that slowed them down. Just before dawn, after reconnoitering their surroundings, the team crossed the road under a shower of bullets that mortally wounded one of the young patriots. That brought to four the number of partisans killed.

Actually only the groups led by the paratroopers and the veteran maquis leaders were able to get through the blockade the following night and regroup on the Belgian border. Layton's group remained hidden in the ferns the whole day of the 13th, in the rain, without food or water, trying to avoid detection. Around 18:00, the sky cleared.

A patrol with dogs was coming closer so the group formed a circle, ready to fire. But when the enemy finally came into view, the rest of the group suddenly disappeared, leaving Layton alone with a single Resistance fighter! To avoid being captured, they crawled to a denser clump of bushes where they came across a sixteen-year-old boy, unarmed and terrified, who had become separated during the night from Commandant De Bollardière's column.

At 21:00, taking advantage of the pouring rain, the three men started out toward Les Hauts-Buttés, where they thought that the blockade might be weaker. They crawled through a swamp alongside the road leading to the hamlet, then crossed through the village and walked south looking for a place where they could build a fire and dry out before going to Six Chenons.

The next day they found no trace of De Bollardière at Six Chenons. A visit to the village of Linchamps for information and food — they hadn't eaten anything in two days — was just as fruitless. Layton then decided to go to Charleville to warn London and recontact his chief through Fournier. He sent the boy home, and the two men, with pistols and grenades hidden in their clothing, safely crossed the Semoy River and took the road to Nouzonville.

Suddenly a patrol appeared, forcing them to run for cover, first into the woods, then down onto the banks of the Meuse. There they had to hide in a culvert to escape German soldiers patrolling along the railway which had been sabotaged recently.

Layton saw only one solution: swim across the river. With his two haversacks around his neck, papers and documents under his beret, he dived in, followed by his companion. There was a strong current there and the Germans on the bank were firing in his direction. Nevertheless he finally arrived safely on the opposite bank, but without his companion, who hadn't followed him across.

In the fields peasants were quietly working, acting as if nothing has happened:

"Can you show me a place where I can change my clothes? asked Layton".

"Walk on a little further to Joigny, one of the farmers answered. There's a small hotel there".

To the couple of innkeepers on the porch of the inn, Layton preferred to announce with a deep American accent:

"I'm an American pilot being chased by the Germans. I need some food and dry clothes before I can go on".

Once he had changed he continued on to Charleville, sticking to forest paths. But time was running out and if he wanted to get to Charleville before nightfall, he realized he would have to take the main road.

That was when he came upon a bicycle patrol stopped on the roadside. It was too late to turn back: one of the German soldiers was getting up, intending to ask him for his papers. Layton took a chance and asked him point blank:

"What's the matter with your bikes? Do you need a hand to help with repairs?"

The ploy worked so well that once the bicycles were fixed, the soldier offered to take him to Charleville on his baggage rack.

So that was the way he entered Charleville. He could finally eat, wash and change clothes at the home of some friends he could trust who took him in.

Arrival of Jedburgh Team Andrew

In Charleville, Layton contacted Commandant Aubusson and sent a message through to London: five FFI had been killed, 140 captured, and the group dispersed. There were maybe 100 partisans remaining.

Five days later, having finally heard from De Bollardière, he met him in Belgium, two miles from the border. All that was left of the Manises maquis was about thirty men. Then Layton learned from partisans and the intelligence officer the circumstances surrounding the German destruction of the maquis.

According to information received by Oberst Grabowski, chief of the Feldkommandantur 684 in the Ardennes — certainly from the Saint-

Quentin Gestapo whose sixty policemen covered the Aisne, Oise, Somme and Ardennes départements — many young men from Revin had been disappearing into a maquis in the Manises woods.

Not that the Germans deserved any credit for uncovering this "secret": the whole business was taking place in broad daylight and with plenty of whoopla.

"Like their fathers in 1914", said Whitehead later.

The two hundred men were allowed to join up without first being tested. This was contrary to orders. And thus the maquis was soon invaded by young men unprepared for living off the land. It was then decided to send them home and to change the camp site.

But before these plans could be carried out, the Germans intervened. The action was launched by 300 German soldiers assisted by Ukranian volunteers [14]. They were guided by a young boy who had been caught in Revin after secretly leaving the camp. One of the agents recruited by Carrière was aware of the attack being prepared, but he had no contact to whom he could relay the information.

Grabowski was persuaded that the maquis was based in the village of Revin. He [15] therefore neglected Les Vieux Moulins de Thilay and Les Héez d'Hargnies, allowing the older partisans led by the officers to escape from the net and regroup in Belgium. Thus when the forest was scoured on the morning of the 13th, 106 young men, each fending for himself, were captured. After they had gattered as much equipment as possible, the Germans turned their attention to their prisoners. Some woodcutters, wrongly arrested and then released, would later testify: the soldiers tortured them, then finished them off with machine guns and hid the bodies in the Bear Pit, near Linchamps.

14. In his report Captain Layton spoke of 4000 volunteers coming from neighboring regions. Their losses were estimated at 40 killed and 90 wounded. The Ukranians probably came from the *Freiwilligen* (Ost) *Stamm-Regiment* 4, which had settled in Namur since February and had become a training station for Russian and Ukranian volunteers from the Eastern troops.

15. On July 27, 1944, the mission members asked London to denounce Grabowski as a war criminal on the BBC. The next day the announcement was made on the radio by the Fighting France spokesman.

Captain Hubble, dressed as a civilian and carrying nothing but his dog tags, was among the captives. Twice on June 13th he was taken by car to Charleville to be brutally interrogated. A month later he was seen in the Saint-Quentin prison, walking with the condemned inmates, with a cross drawn in white chalk on his back. A short time afterwards, a peasant reported having seen an American or an Englishman surrounded by German officers on reconnaissance south of Hargnies. It was supposed that he was being interrogated as to the place where he was parachuted and was showing the Germans a false DZ. After that all trace of him was lost.

The Prisme maquis was finally reunited on June 16th at Franc Bois, between Willerzie and La Croix-Scaille. The radio officer came in with his group of guerilla fighters and contacted London again. Finally Layton, who was believed to have been shot by the Germans, reappeared on the 24th.

Without their rucksacks, the men had had to abandon their personal belongings to carry military supplies. There was no more parachute material for tents, no more group equipment. So they started in from scratch again in the woods, and built huts out of branches. Transporting food took too much time, and the two available mules weren't much help: no pack-saddles! Carrying water for cooking and washing was risky: too much coming and going could give away the maquis hideout. Commandant De Bollardière was very firm:

"We cannot under any circumstances stay more than five days in the same camp! And it is out of the question to camp beside a river: it would be too easy for us to be spotted".

For the Germans were still just as zealous. Besides the attack on the Manises, they were also crowing about the arrest of the Charleville sector chief on June 9th (he would be shot on July 1st), then the breaking-up of the group protecting the Paul site in Hautes-Rivières, and the destruction on June 18th of a maquis east of Sedan.

It was now clear that dispositions such as those previously taken could only lead to a repetition of the Manises tragedy: the only solution was to organize a completely independent maquis. So Commandant De Bollardière decided to create supply dumps all over the département and to recruit new candidates among the people that were being refused by certain FFI leaders: school teachers, policemen, customs officers, poachers, who proved to be excellent guerilla fighters. And thanks to Capitaine Levert's border patrol which was able to recover some hidden weapons, about one hundred men could soon be equiped.

Contact had been reestablished with Planète and Aubusson, and they agreed to these arrangements, as long as they didn't create a rival organization. And they repeated the instructions previously given to Fournier. However since relations between Fournier and Bollardière were a bit tense, Aubusson asked Marcel Dupeyron, the head of the Nousonville sector, to serve as go-between and get the pay to the recruits' families.

Liaisons between the command post, the maquis annex where newcomers were trained, and the exterior, were handled by customs officers and smugglers who knew the woods well. Moreover from time to time Capitaine Carrière brought information obtained by his network. Contact was made with the Belgian maquis who had a very efficient intelligence-collecting organization. Their area of operations was in the territory controlled by the Dînant Kommandantur, whose chief was on poor terms with his Charleville colleague. The latter thought he had finished with the Prisme maquis, but he learned through the BBC [16] that it had been built up again: he was worried about maintaining safe transportation routes throughout his region, and kept requesting reinforcements to mount a new attack. He got no answer.

Little by little small groups of fighters began to gravitate around Prisme in order to get weapons, and two parachute drops were organized: one for the Givet sector and one for a group of independent Francs-Tireurs et Partisans. (FTP). Sabotage teams from the outside came for three to four-day training period, and everyone received weapons and night combat instruction.

At the Prisme maquis a sabotage platoon and an anti-tank platoon armed with bazookas were created. These weapons were used for the

16. Some say that the message revealing the reconstruction of the maquis was part of an undercover plan designed to foster doubt and paralysis in the German ranks.

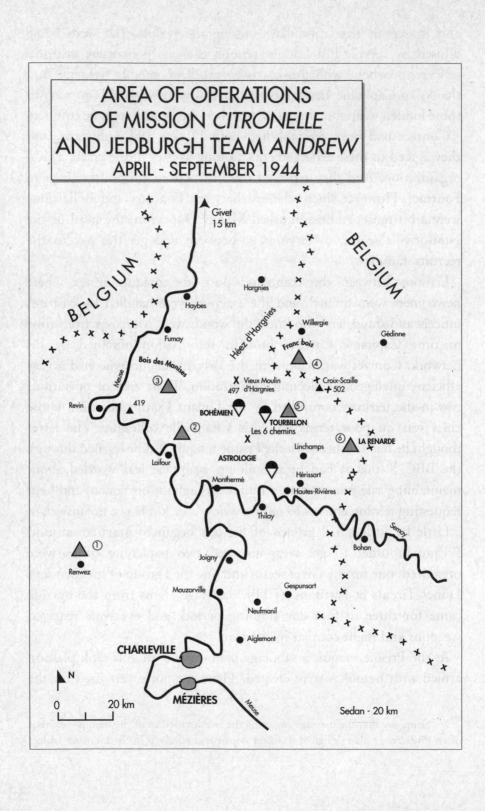

AREA OF OPERATIONS
OF MISSION *CITRONELLE*
AND JEDBURGH TEAM *ANDREW*
APRIL - SEPTEMBER 1944

Givet
15 km

BELGIUM

BELGIUM

Hargnies

Haybes

Willergie

Fumay

Héez d'Hargnies

Franc bois

Gédinne

Bois des Manises

④

③

Vieux Moulin
d'Hargnies
497

Croix-Scaille
502

Revin

419

BOHÉMIEN

⑤
TOURBILLON

Linchamps

⑥
LA RENARDE

②

Les 6 chemins

Laifour

ASTROLOGIE

Hérissart

Monthermé

Hautes-Rivières

Thilay

Semoy

Bohan

①

Joigny

Renwez

Mouzorville

Gespunsart

Neufmanil

Aiglemont

CHARLEVILLE

N

MÉZIÈRES

Meuse

0   20 km

Sedan - 20 km

first time on July 20 to attack the fuel depot in Aiglemont. Even though the fuel tanks were not destroyed, the action undertaken by the FTP created quite a stir: the enemy and the local population were convinced that 400 men with 75-mm cannon took part.

At the end of July, the maquis relocated five miles north-east of Astrologie, on a spot where eight forest-fire trails met.

One night a messenger arrived in the camp:

"Capitaine Jacques has sent me to warn you. The Jerries plan to attack your camp tomorrow morning at 05:00".

At the appointed hour the men heard gun fire in the distance: a patrol sent out to get bread must have run into the Germans ... A little later, German soldiers advancing along three of the fire trails were greeted by heavy Bren automatic fire. After a try at outflanking, they finally made it into the camp, only to find it abandoned. The partisans — including a group in training and three Allied aviators — had filed out in good order toward La Croix-Scaille.

For his attack, Oberst Grabowski, who had information about the partisans being sent out to Hargnies for food, had been able to assemble a thousand men — flak crews, railroad guards, etc — and obtain permission to operate inside Belgium. His attack had been launched from the Gedinne-Willerzie road while another column advanced from Monthermé toward Hargnies. It had cost him dearly: two officers and 52 soldiers killed for only one partisan killed and two wounded. The wounded were taken in and cared for by Belgians.

A new camp was installed near an approved DZ and while the men were waiting for a scheduled drop, they prepared caches for the material. But the moon changed and nothing happened. Things were getting critical and three false alarms didn't make matters any better: everybody was touchy. That was the moment Bollardière chose to resign his command.

For security reasons, the maquis moved to the Camp de la Renarde, five miles further south. London then announced an operation on Astrologie, with five officers for the mission. The drop zone was three hours away, so the designated reception group started out immediately. They waited at the site until 04:00 and finally gave up: it was clear that no plane would be coming that night.

Four days later, August 15, the signal message was broadcast again. The night was pitch-black and an East wind was blowing at more than 40 mph. A plane arrived around midnight. As soon as the parachutes — eleven in all — had touched ground, the oil lamps were blown out. But in the western sky the airplane was still circling. The stick had been blown way off target. And the first parachutist, found in a mud hole, declared himself to be a British subject, but spoke with a strong foreign accent. After searching for two hours Bollardière and Layton finally found someone who could give them some information:

"I'm Captain Rankin, part of Mission Noah !"

The day was spent trying to find the seven other Belgian members of the Special Air Service [17] and their two packages, then to get them back to camp. This was when Lieutenant-Colonel De Bollardière — he had been promoted on August 5 — learned that five other officers were in the plane: three members of a Jedburgh team and two for Citronelle.

Three days later a runner arrived from Revin:

"Five paratroopers, found in the woods a mile-and-a-half east of the village, request a contact with Colonel Prisme".

When they arrived in the camp, these officers identified themselves as those of the second stick which had been blind- dropped over the Manises woods.

During the action the Jedburghs had lost their radio set, and the two supplementary Citronelle officers [18] all their personal equipment. Neither group was capable of telling Bollardière what London expected him to do! On the other hand, all information concerning the enemy was given to the Belgians of Mission Noah before they left for the border maquis. Moreover, it was agreed that Bréaux would act as radioman for the three Jedburghs.

17. The SAS Noah party included about 40 paratroopers and a few Jeeps from Captain Blondeel's Belgian company. Its mission was to send back information on enemy movements and to set booby traps.

18. Captain Ruffey (Masse) and Sous-Lieutenant Codart (Courbette).

Jedburgh team Andrew [19] had been called up on August 8 and briefed two days later in London. Its mission: make contact with Citronelle and assist it in the organization and support of the FFI, now estimated at 150 men in the area, after the loss of 200 during a skirmish with the Germans.

Its chief, Major Coombe-Tenant, had been made prisoner in Boulogne in 1940, escaped two years later from the Westphalia Oflag and made it back to England via the Belgian escape circuit. After a turn on the SOE staff, where he helped create the instruction program for the Jedburghs, he had joined them at Milton Hall.

The two bombers left England with thirteen paratroopers and forty-eight containers. Above France the wind had reached storm level and the flight was bumpy, but there was no flak. Finally over the DZ east of Revin, the lanterns were clearly visible and the SAS were the first to jump.

But on the second run, the lights had disappeared. The men had to choose, either go back to England or jump blind!

Coombe-Tenant decided to jump.

As the radioman was descending, an exceptionally strong wind pushed him towards a particularly steep, deep canyon:

"I took a hard blow when I landed, Sergent Harrison told the partisans sitting around him. First I tried to untangle my parachute which was caught in a tree. Then I took off in the direction that seemed to me to be the right one, only to discover, at dawn, that I was walking in circles ! So I decided I'd better wait for daylight and look for a safe house".

Towards 09:00 he noticed a house and decided to approach it carefully. When he showed his ID card as a member of the FFI staff, he was hidden in the attic with a basket of food. And the farmers went out looking for the two other officers, who arrived during the evening, safe and sound. The Major's bag was brought in, but the radio set and

19. Team No. 37 - Major A.H.S. Coombe-Tenant (Rupel), of the Welsh Guards, Lieutenant Edouard d'Oultremont (Demer), Belgian Army and Serjeant Frank Harrison (Merxe) of the 2nd Northants Yeomanry.

the operator's gear couldn't be found. Just to be on the safe side, they decided to sleep in the woods about a mile from there.

After two days in the woods, a lieutenant came to meet the team and led them, after plenty of detours and a six-hour walk, to the maquis.

"I couldn't understand very much of the first discussions, Harrison continued, except that you were in dire need of weapons and ammunition after the attack of the week before.

Actually not only was the radio set lost, but also the quartz crystals and maps that had been attached to one of the containers, because the knapsack in which they were supposed to be carried was too heavy. Bréaux sent two messages in code Andrew and got no answer, so the Major decided to send them in code Citronelle. Several days later, while he was out reconnoitering two DZs with the officers of the interallied mission, London finally acknowledged receipt of the messages.

From August 20 on, the Belgians undertook a series of guerilla actions under orders from their commanders. On the 23rd one of their groups attacked a German convoy near Hérissart. But the target was too big for them and the guerilla fighters soon needed help. Sixty Prisme men with three Brens were sent out. When they arrived on the scene an hour later, they found no sign of the Belgians, and the Germans were in position around their trucks. Through his binoculars Bollardière saw two women in the convoy and sent out orders not to attack. But it was too late: a stray shot was fired ... In ten minutes twenty Germans were killed and two prisoners taken. During the assault, Lieutenant Granier, a cavalry reserve officer from Sedan who had joined up at the beginning when the Prisme maquis was first created, was critically wounded leading his platoon.

Unexpectedly a Kriegsmarine company based in Belgium intervened early in the afternoon of the 24th. The Germans surprised the partisans who began to scatter. Bollardière ordered the men back to their stations. The assailants set up two 60-mm mortars, and shells were soon bursting in the branches over their heads. Many men were lost. Lieutenant Codart was critically wounded.

Then Lieutenant d'Oultremont was hit in the back and leg by shrapnel. Bollardière and Layton were also hit. For some reason the enemy decided not to persist [20], and withdrew just as the partisans retreated with their weapons and ammunition, with ten wounded and two prisoners.

Joining up with the New Jersey Scouts

They all made their separate ways back to a camp previously occupied, south of the Tourbillon dropping zone. A doctor was sent for and emergency care was given to the wounded before turning them over to the nuns at the Hauts-Buttés Hospital. Bollardière continued to give orders from his stretcher. During the night a squad was sent out to recover equipment and bury the six dead. Then the maquis set up camp around the DZ, waiting for the next drop. The resistants were even talking about a whole batallion of paratroopers dropping out of the sky!

A message came through on the BBC, but no plane appeared. The situation was getting drastic:

"With the remaining ammunition, said Layton, 30 rounds per rifle, 100 rounds for the automatics and 800 for each Bren, we can't do anything until we get supplies by air".

Another BBC message came through, but it was for Astrologie, where two BCRA agents and two Citronelle officers [21] arrived.

On August 29th, Bollardière decided to go to Linchamps where the men were able to get some of the khaki uniforms used by the Armistice Army. Although the uniforms did not necessarily ensure better treatment in the event of being captured, at least they made the officers and troops look better. Captain Layton even got his first change of socks since he had jumped on June 12.

Gunfire could be heard to the east and to the west, so Bollardière took his troops to Nouzonville to secure the bridge and facilitate the Allied advance. By September 2 the Americans still had not arrived, so

---

20. German losses were estimated at 60 killed and 60 to 70 marines wounded.
21. Sous-Lieutenants Schlitz (Tetraèdre) and Alix (Crystallisation).

they continued ambushing retreating enemy convoys and armored vehicles. The only good this did was to attract the attention of the Germans. Every German vehicle going through woods started firing plentifully and haphazardly into the ditches.

The mission still hadn't received any instructions as to how to contact the Americans, what action to undertake, which bridges to blow up or to protect ... Messengers were sent to the Belgians and to Sedan without any result.

Finally on September 5, after moving to Gespunsart, two platoons were sent out to attack a stalled German convoy and lay an ambush near Neufmanil for the retreating enemy vehicles — 40 Germans were killed. It was at this moment that, near the camp, the Resistance fighters saw two armored cars with a white star on them. When Captain Layton approached, the patrol leader declared that he belonged to the 102nd Reconnaissance Squadron of the New Jersey National Guard.

Layton was immediately put at their disposal to supply guides and information about the region, to go with them into Belgium to interrogate German prisoners and insure contact with the SAS Mission Noah operating east of Gedinne. Then he gave the necessary information to the V Corps G-2 and turned Lieutenant Schlitz over to them. He was in a hurry to fulfill the mission for which he had been parachuted into the Ardennes: go on into Luxembourg.

From the explanations he was given, Layton began to unravel the circumstances surrounding his chance encounter with the New Jersey cavalry. On September 2, while Gerow Corps (V Corps) was progressing toward the north and the city of Valenciennes, the Americans decided to pause and wait for fuel before continuing through Lorraine towards the Rhine.

This was why Citronelle got no information about what they were supposed to be doing. Two days later, while the 4th Infantry Division was clearing out the last pockets of resistance in the region around Saint-Quentin, V Corps turned toward east and sent its cavalry and tanks toward the Meuse to fill in the void left west of

Sedan. The 4th Infantry Division followed behind them on a forced march as fast as their limited means of transportation would allow. Their movement and assembly in the area around Charleville were preceded and covered by the 102nd Mechanized Cavalry Group of which the New Jersey squadron was a part.

While this was occuring, Lieutenant-Colonel De Bollardière, in Nouzonville, was preparing to demobilize his maquis:

"Our men were decent and discrete, said Squadron Leader Whitehead. But in Charleville a crowd of rookies were strutting around like old veterans. Every officer had at least Captain's stripes, and every soldier was at least a sergeant. A stranger would have thought that Hollywood was making a film about the French Revolution and that the scene was set for the storming of the Bastille".

Some suggested to Bollardière that he take command, but he preferred to avoid getting involved in the confusion, and requested to be assigned to the Special Air Service (SAS). He advised the young fighters who could not follow him to the paratroopers, to sign up instead for the FFI regiment being formed.

Whitehead got the radio equipment together, had the wounded transported to hospitals and the dead decently buried. Then he went to Saint-Quentin and Nancy looking for Captain Hubble. He learned that Major Thackthwaite, designated by the Special Operations leaders to undertake an inquiry, had found his name scratched on a cell wall at the prison at Fresnes [22].

Then the members of Mission Citronelle and Jedburgh team Andrew went to Paris for the flight back to London or — for the two Jedburgh officers — back to their regiment in Brussels.

Later Commandant Lejeune of the G-3, FFI Headquarters, would praise the Citronelle members:

"Of all the missions, this was the group which carried out its job in the most difficult circumstances".

---

22. After the war it was learned that Captain Hubble had been sent to Buchenwald concentration camp in September of 1944, along with 36 Allied agents assembled at Compiègne. From there he disappeared altogether.

These events in the Ardennes are caracteristic of the life and activity of the Allied Special Forces teams parachuted into occupied France, with their tragedies and disappointments, but also with their moments of victory and glory.

Chapter II

German order and National Revolution

On the morning of June 17, 1940, Marshall Pétain announced over the radio to the French people that contact had been made with the enemy to end the fighting. On the 20th a delegation went to Compiègne where an armistice was signed with the Germans in the evening of the 22nd. Two days later the ceremony was repeated in Rome for the Italian armistice. Fighting thus stopped on June 25 at 12:35.

The truce stipulated that German troops would occupy a large fraction of continental France, that the French Armed Forces would be disarmed and demobilized, except for a contingent needed to maintain order inside the country, and that Axis control commissions would check that the truce was being observed.

The French government settled in Vichy, where the pace of events quickened. On July 4, diplomatic relations with Great Britain were suspended. On the 10th the Assembly voted to give Marshall Pétain full powers to create a new constitution. On the 11th, constitutional bills defining the new French state were voted: the spirit and the letter of these acts were in deliberate contradiction with the preceding parliamentary system.

France was divided into two zones with different statutes, separated by a "demarcation line": in the north German order ruled, in the south Pétain's National Revolution reigned supreme.

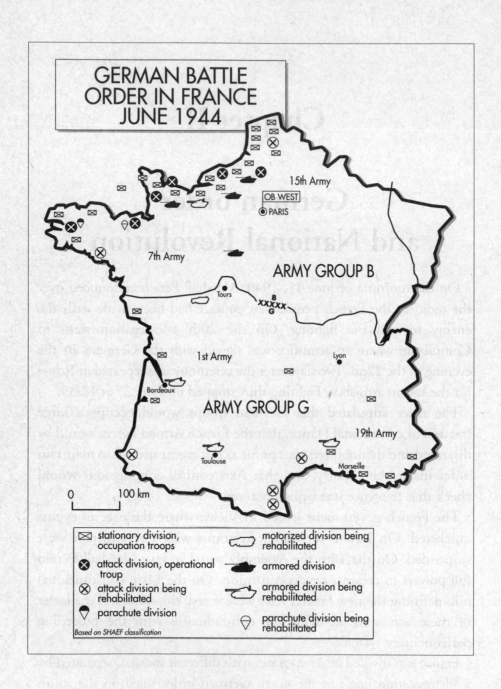

GERMAN BATTLE ORDER IN FRANCE JUNE 1944

15th Army

OB WEST

PARIS

7th Army

ARMY GROUP B

Tours

B
XXXXX
G

1st Army

Lyon

Bordeaux

ARMY GROUP G

19th Army

Toulouse

Marseille

0   100 km

⊠	stationary division, occupation troops		motorized division being rehabilitated
⊗	attack division, operational troup	▬	armored division
⊗	attack division being rehabilitated		armored division being rehabilitated
▽	parachute division	▽	parachute division being rehabilitated

Based on SHAEF classification

The administration and the occupying troops

Alsace and Moselle were progressively Germanized and integrated into the Reich, while the Nord and the Pas-de-Calais regions became restricted zones and fell under the control of the German command in Brussels. Beyond these border zones, two other zones, restricted in the north and reserved in the east, where residents and French civil service agents had to abide by strict rules, completed the security zones of the Reich. Likewise travel was strictly controlled in a stretch of land 10 to 20 miles wide up and down the Atlantic coast.

The German Forces stationed in France were placed under the orders of the Commander in Chief, Western Front or OB West. During the spring of 1944, the greater part of his 58 available divisions were stationed opposite England along the Channel coast from Brittany to Flanders. Elsewhere, and especially south of the Loire River, there were only a few large units, most either being formed or re-formed.

The services of the *Militärbefehlshaber* in Frankreich controlled the administration and milked the economy for the benefit of the Reich. In the départements the Kommandanturen [1] served as intermediairies between the German high command and the French administrative services and population: it was forbidden for German troops to deal directly with local authorities.

There was therefore a big difference between operating troops, made up of large mobile units, and "occupying" troops or Besatzungstruppen. The latter were attached to a region and included security troops who, above all, maintained order and protected military installations.

But the complexity of the German war machine in France did not stop there.

There were also, of course, elements of the two other services, i.e. Kriegsmarine and Luftwaffe, and their combat and support structures

---

1. *Oberfeldkommandantur* for the region and *Feldkommandantur* for the département.

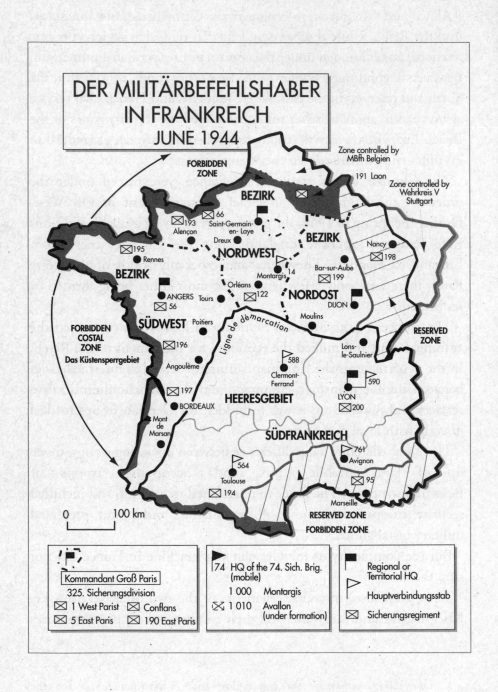

DER MILITÄRBEFEHLSHABER IN FRANKREICH
JUNE 1944

Zone controlled by
MBfh Belgien

FORBIDDEN ZONE

191 Laon

Zone controlled by
Wehrkreis V
Stuttgart

BEZIRK

66

193 Alençon

Saint-Germain-
en- Laye

Dreux

BEZIRK

Nancy

198

195

Rennes

NORDWEST

Montargis 14

Bar-sur-Aube

199

BEZIRK

Orléans

122

NORDOST

ANGERS

56

Tours

DIJON

SÜDWEST

Poitiers

Moulins

196

FORBIDDEN
COSTAL
ZONE

Das Küstensperrgebiet

Angoulême

Ligne de démarcation

588

Clermont-
Ferrand

Lons-
le-Saulnier

RESERVED
ZONE

197

BORDEAUX

HEERESGEBIET

590

LYON

200

Mont
de
Marsan

SÜDFRANKREICH

761

Avignon

564

Toulouse

95

194

Marseille

RESERVED ZONE

FORBIDDEN ZONE

0   100 km

Kommandant Groß Paris

325. Sicherungsdivision

1 West Parist   Conflans

5 East Paris   190 East Paris

74 HQ of the 74. Sich. Brig.
(mobile)

1 000   Montargis

1 010   Avallon
(under formation)

Regional or
Territorial HQ

Hauptverbindungsstab

Sicherungsregiment

each had different systems of command. Party organizations were also distinct bodies. Then the Waffen SS, even though placed under control of the Army for military operations, remained under their own administration for everything else.

Next came the Organization Todt, which provided construction services for the Wehrmacht. It employed mainly foreign workers, and managed important fortification and transportation projects. The Reichsarbeitdienst, mandatory work service for young men before they joined the military, also participated in these projects.

Other organizations with armed and uniformed personnel were also present: the customs service, the *Arbeitseinzatz Frankreich*, in charge of organizing the STO, mandatory work service for the French, the railroads, the postal service, etc.

In November 1942, after the Allies invaded North Africa, the Axis forces took over the southern free zone [2]. Then when the Italian armistice was signed with the Allies in September 1943, the Germans occupied the whole of France.

The former free zone was placed under the territorial authority of the military Commander in Southern France based in Lyon. But the Germans took care to maintain fictive "French sovereignty" and preferred to install — instead of the *Feldkommandanturen* as in the north — "liaison staff" with the mission of "representing" the Wehrmacht and insuring its interests and those of the war vis-à-vis French services. Thus in every regional capital a *Hauptverbindungsstab* controlled the *Verbindungsstäbe* of the départements within its territory.

An exception to this system was the creation in February 1944 of a reserved zone made up of the seven départements along the Mediterranean coast.

To insure the security of military installations and prisoners of war, the territorial command had at its disposal, not only detachments of MPs, but also a few territorial units of limited combat value: older personnel, few vehicles, varied weapons taken in part from the depots

2. A restricted zone or no man's land along the Spanish border was then created.

of the armistice army, etc. It also controlled security troops (*Sicherungstruppen*), 85 battalions in all — 66 regimental and 29 independent units —in June 1944 [3]. Along with the build-up in the number of units, efforts were made to give greater mobility to possible reserve forces for interventions.

In the Paris region the 325th security division obtained a fourth regiment with a battalion better equiped to handle "gangs". And in the south the best-trained battalions were regularly rotated to where they were most needed in the Massif Central or the Northern Alps. The territorial command could also call on local operational troops which could be used for a single mission or a limited time.

The creation of a motorized brigade was undertaken in Montargis by Generalmajor Jesser, with equipment obtained from the police or made available after the conversion of infantry divisions into armored tank units. Nevertheless the second regiment intended for Avallon could never be formed because of equipment shortages [4].

This delay was all the more annoying because the German command had placed great hopes in this brigade to intervene in the mountains south of the Loire River, where the "gangs" were particularly active. So, to add strength to the liaison staff, a security regiment from Marseille was moved to Brive and two batallions from Toulouse were transferred into the southern Alps.

Six batallions of *Osttruppen*, composed of volunteers recruited among the Soviet POWs, were put into action after April 1944 against the "gangs". It was also decided to give a priority mission to two large units — the 157th mountain division in the Alps and the 189th division in the Massif Central — to combat the maquis,

3. The occupying troops were approximately for each département 1,000 civil servants and 700 soldiers, including MPs and a security battalion.

4. Theoretically it included a reconnaissance batallion and two security regiments composed of two batallions and three heavy companies.

5. In October 1942 several training and mobilisation units based inside the Reich were rebaptized "reserve divisions" and transferred into the occupied territories to be used exclusively for instruction and thus relieve the *Ersatz Armee*, which took charge of recruitement and basic training in Germany.

instead of their usual training mission of instruction [5]. Finally mobile task forces, made up of the two armored divisions of the Wehrmacht stationed in southern France, were engaged in the Massif Central and the Rhône River valley to assist the harder-pressed garrisons. And the elements of the Das Reich SS armored division, used for training in the Toulouse region, were often solicited for local actions.

Police and Intelligence Services

Concerning police and intelligence-collecting, seven services, controlled by two rival authorities, the Armed Forces and the Party, were operating in France. The *Sicherheitspolizei und Sicherheitsdienst* (Sipo-SD), the SS security organization, theoretically limited to search and suppression of "Anti-German activities", was actually in open competition with the *Amt Auslandsnachrichten und Abwehr* [6], the intelligence service of the Wehrmacht.

Up until 1942, the Abwehr network was organized with different satellite agencies gravitating around bases in Münster and Stuttgart, and a centralizing station for the different activities in Paris, known as the *Abwehrleitstelle* or *Alst Frankreich*. In 1943 this network was reinforced in the north and extended to cover the south, following the reorganization of the operational troops.

But the Abwehr also had to adapt its means and its structures to the increase and diversification of Resistance movements and of Allied secret services activities. In 1944 this resulted in the creation of three coordinating agencies, each under direct control of its corresponding central bureau in Berlin.

The first, known as *Meldeleitkommando West*, took charge of military intelligence missions. The second controlled sabotage, subversive activities and agent recruiting. The third coordinated the fight against the maquis and the Allied services, as well as unit (Map coordinate locating).

6. Foreign information and counter-espionage bureau of the combined armed services, otherwise known as the Abwehr.

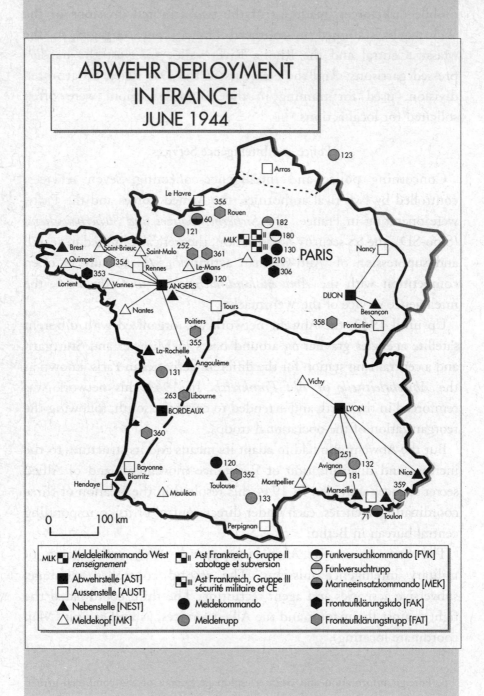

ABWEHR DEPLOYMENT IN FRANCE
JUNE 1944

123

Arras

Le Havre

356
Rouen
60
121

Brest
Saint-Brieuc
Saint-Malo
252
MLK
182
180
Quimper
354
361
130
Nancy
353
Rennes
Le-Mans
210
PARIS
Lorient
Vannes
ANGERS
120
306
Nantes
Tours
DIJON
Poitiers
Besançon
355
358
Pontarlier
La-Rochelle
Angoulême
131
Vichy
263
Libourne
BORDEAUX
LYON
360
251
132
Bayonne
Avignon
Nice
Biarritz
181
120
Montpellier
359
Hendaye
352
Marseille
Mauléon
Toulouse
71
Toulon
133
Perpignan

0   100 km

MLK	Meldeleitkommando West renseignement		Ast Frankreich, Gruppe II sabotage et subversion		Funkversuchkommando [FVK]
	Abwehrstelle [AST]		Ast Frankreich, Gruppe III sécurité militaire et CE		Funkversuchtrupp
	Aussenstelle [AUST]		Meldekommando		Marineeinsatzkommando [MEK]
	Nebenstelle [NEST]		Meldetrupp		Frontaufklärungskdo [FAK]
	Meldekopf [MK]				Frontaufklärungstrupp [FAT]

These were areas that the Sipo-SD would have liked to control and where it was continually meddling.

The territorial system, considered too rigid, was progressively replaced by a more flexible system based on *Kommandos*, mobile units placed at the disposal of the operational troops to carry out their missions. Each Kommando could control several Truppen who could operate independently in any given area. Some of these Kommandos were adapted to operational troops at the army or army group level, through the intelligence officer (Ic) belonging to their staff. Others units were responsible for border control, training language-qualified agents and other specialized activities. To carry out their missions, the different units employed various agents, especially Frenchmen belonging to collaborationist parties, who received special training.

Military Intelligence was entrusted to the *Meldekommandos*. In early 1944 five of these groups were operating in France: one for each service — the Army and the Navy — in the north (including Belgium) and in the south, the fifth being a Luftwaffe group based in Saint-Cloud for radio and coordinate location. The other missions were performed "by advance intelligence and reconnaissance detachments" or *Frontaufklärungskommandos* (FAKs). Sabotage and counter-propaganda were the specialty of the Vaucresson FAK who coordinated a dozen units spread out over the entire country. A FAK in Paris for the Western region and two *Frontaufklärungsleittruppen* for the North-East (Dijon) and Southern France (Lyon) took charge of counter-espionage and the fight against subversive and armed underground movements.

Lastly a company from the 3rd Brandenburg regiment, composed of French-speaking volunteers and attached to the 19th Army, was operating in the South-East. This company was particularly dangerous: it infiltrated networks, movements and maquis, preparing their destruction. It also furnished interpreters for major operations against the "gangs".

The Abwehr worked in close collaboration with the secret field police or *Geheime Feldpolizei*, a sort of military security squad for the armed forces. The GFP did not only protect troops; it constituted the

SIPO - SD LOCATED IN FRANCE JUNE 1944

The GREPO, located on the Pyrénées border, was deployed in the following towns, from east to west: Cerbère, Banyuls, Le Perthus, Le Boulou, Prades, Bourg-Madame, Font-Romeu, Ax-les-Thermes, Saint-Girons, Bagnères-de-Luchon, Argelès-Gazost, Oloron-Sainte-Marie, Tardets, Cambo.

0   100 km

- Befehlshaber der Sicherheitsdienst und des SD [BdS]
- Kommandant der Sipo (SD) Kommando [KdS]
- Aussendienstelle [ADST]
- Aussenpost [AP]
- GrenzpolizeitKommissariat [GREKO]
- Grenzpolizeitpost [GREPO]

Abbeville · Le Havre · Amiens · ROUEN · SAINT-QUENTIN · Charleville · Briey · Morlaix · Saint-Lô · Caen · Beauvais · CHÂLONS-SUR-MARNE · NANCY · Brest · Saint-Brieuc · Evreux · PARIS · Reims · Bar-le-Duc · Quimper · Alençon · Versailles · Melun · Troyes · Epinal · Belfort · RENNES · Chartres · Le Mans · ORLEANS · Auxerre · Chaumont · DIJON · Vannes · ANGERS · Tours · Bourges · Nevers · Montbeliard · Nantes · La-Roche-sur-Yon · Châtellerault · Blois · Besançon · Niort · POITIERS · Châteauroux · Moulins · Châlons-sur-Saône · La-Rochelle · Montluçon · LIMOGES · VICHY · Cluses · Saintes · Angoulème · Clermont · LYON · Annecy · Périgueux · Tulle · Chambéry · BORDEAUX · Cahors · Saint-Etienne · Grenoble · Agen · Rodez · Mende · Valence · Gap · Montauban · Nîmes · Avignon · Digne · Bayonne · Pau · TOULOUSE · Draguignan · Menton · Hendaye · Tarbes · Carcassonne · MONTPELLIER · Nice · Foix · Perpignan · MARSEILLE · Cannes · Toulon

repressive auxiliary needed in the fight against the Resistance groups. The GFP could be part of either the territorial or the operational forces. Its territorial groups progressively lost their importance, as the Sipo-SD requested and obtained police control in the countries occupied by the Wehrmacht. In 1942 five or six groups stationed in the capital were dissolved and their personnel absorbed into the Sipo. This didn't cause much of a problem since many of the GFP officers were originally recruited from the State Police. In spite of this the GFP continued to provide security to troops and military installations.

The latent conflict between the Wehrmacht and the SS finally came to a head in June 1944 when all military services, in the Reich and the occupied territories, were put under the control of the head of the secret police, the *Reichsführer SS und der deutschen Polizei*.

The *Sicherheitspolizei und Sicherheitsdienst*, the Sipo-SD, improperly called the Gestapo by the French, was a political organization, with the triple role of police, intelligence gathering and counter-espionage activities. Once it got a foothold in France, it grew by leaps and bounds, due to its natural dynamism.

Under pressure from the Party, it first obtained the almost complete dissolution of the GFP, then the establishment of three regional offices: Angers for surveillance of Brittany and the South-West, Dijon for the East and Rouen for the zone stretching from the Ardennes to the Loire River. The Abwehr had created different institutions on either side of the demarcation line, but the Party security leaders seemed to have considered France as wholly occupied even before November 11, 1942. Agents infiltrated the free zone on different missions and after France was completely occupied, offices were created forming a close network of seventeen Kommandos with branches in outlying cities and on the borders, especially in the Pyrenees mountains.

. Organization was extremely flexible, to be easily adapted to the necessities of the moment. The whole outfit was coordinated by the Sipo-SD command in Paris, under the orders of *Gruppenführer und Generalleutnant der Polizei* Oberg, *Höherer SS und Polizeiführer*, and *Reichsführer* Himmler's representative in France.

In the offices, missions were allotted to the different bureaus modeled after the administrative bureaus in Berlin. Section IV, or Amt IV, in charge of repression of political opponents, handled both intelligence and counter-espionage activities. Its scope included diverse opposition groups: Communists, Gaullists, terrorists, the church, etc.

Counter-espionage, except for cases involving military establishments or personnel which came under the jurisdiction of the Abwehr, was dealt with by Section IV E. Its activities included penetrating underground movements, intercepting parachute drops, and border control. The bureau was helped by numerous French agents, employed individually as informants, rabble-rousers, infiltration agents, interpreters, recruited among petty delinquants and hit men belonging to fascist-type parties. As *Standartenführer* Knochen, chief of the Sipo-SD stated:

"These assistants must participate in risky police action against pockets of enemy resistance, in searches and arrests. Their service can in no way be compared to that of a simple escort".

Amt IV also had important means devoted to find Resistance radios including vehicles and central stations. Amt V sometimes lent a hand for search and arrest missions.

The increase in the activity of armed groups and maquis resulted in considerable development of Section IV in the various branch offices, often assisted by Sonderkommandos or special mobile units made up of policemen, SS, Wehrmacht soldiers and French agents — especially militiamen.

For the same reason the Sipo-SD decided to organize teams also made up of Frenchmen belonging to collaborationist parties, in charge of helping maintain order and protecting railroads and other installations vital to the German occupiers, and also infiltrating the maquis.

The SD advised close cooperation with the Wehrmacht, but it was they who defined the objectives, in collaboration with the intelligence services, and took direct control of the troops who, in some places, maintained alert squads ready to intervene on call.

The mission of Section VI was technical, basically directed against the Allied intelligence services, with, among other things, detection of underground radios and persuading radio operators to turn traitor, a part of Funkspiel or wireless games. With more personnel in Paris than in the provinces, it pretty much followed its own rules, in close contact with Amt VI in Berlin. Originally it was a political information and infiltration organization, but its activities soon came to include not only military espionage, rivaling the work done by the Wehrmacht, but also searching for suspects and infiltration of the maquis groups, a job theoretically entrusted to the 4th bureau.

The police responsible for maintaining order or *Ordnungspolizei* were composed of militarized units of 400 men each, located in Paris and in each region. These squads took charge of opposing the Resistance forces in the field and nothing except their repressive nature distinguished them from the regular army.

Lastly a police regiment controlled by the Orpo and linked to the SS was on permanent operation in France. These policemen in feldgrau uniforms, who had nothing to do with the SS beyond their name, primarily took part in raids designed to apprehend the enemies of the Reich. They also executed special missions given to them by the branch agencies of the Sipo-SD.

Partisan Militia and Peace-Keeping Forces

At Vichy the situation got more serious and complicated as the years went by. The spreading of the conflict, with the USSR entering the war, occupation of the free zone, the Italian desertion, the German requisitions of economic means and manpower, the increasing importance of the Resistance movements, the creation of the "maquis", drew the government into an irreversible process of radicalization.

7. The number of employees in each office varied : 400 in Paris, 120-30 in Lyon or Toulouse, 90 in Orléans, for example.

To maintain order and public security, the French State had inherited the Gendarmerie and police from the preceding government. The Gendarmerie was part of the War Department and had survived many an upheaval. It was not about to change. However in June 1942 after the return of Pierre Laval to power, the Gendarmerie was placed under the direct authority of the leader of the government.

The Garde, created from the mobile Republican Guards and detached from the Gendarmerie after November 1940, was first organized in two brigades composed of three thousand-man legions each. In September 1942 to "avoid confusion between the legions of the Gendarmerie, subject to the head of government through the general director of the national Gendarmerie, on the one hand, and the Garde legions which were part of the army, on the other", the latter received the name of "regiment". But in April 1943, the Garde was put under the control of the Interior Ministry to participate in operations of public security, especially those concerned with maintaining or reestablishing order. The Germans however didn't have much confidence in this contingent and rejected Laval's request to increase the personnel to 25,000 men.

The police organization was more deeply transformed. An intendant was dispatched to each regional prefect and several special departments were created to police Jews, secret societies, communists, antinational activities and economic matters, etc. The two main innovations were the creation of guard units for the transportation and communications networks, whose job it was to prevent and detect sabotage on lines, bridges or train stations, and Reserve Mobile Groups (Groupes Mobiles de Réserve - GMR) put at the disposal of the regional prefects.

The communications guards were organized, like the military, in units with vehicles. In November 1942 its men numbered 3000 in the occupied zone and 2900 in the free zone. To deal with the increase in sabotage actions, the French government at that time asked the German authorities for better weapons, including automatic rifles, and 2600 more men. This guard body should not be confused with the civil service of railway guards, created in 1943 under German pressure.

The GMR were made up of policemen in uniform and had their own administration. They were organized into 57 groups of about 200 men each, on foot or mounted, and established in both zones: 16 in the north and 41 — including four mounted units — in the south, for a total of 10,000 men. The intention was to increase the number of groups to 118, including nine mounted units. Even though they normally worked in the region where they were stationed, they could exceptionally be called into a neighboring region.

In August 1940 the National Revolution government established a special program aimed at young people, the Chantiers de la Jeunesse, designed to replace military service for young men aged 18 to 22, who were not allowed to serve in the two 100,000-man armies permitted in mainland France and in North Africa by the armistice commissions. These Chantiers were placed under the direction of a commissary general from the Army. Fifty groups were formed of about 1,500 men each, covering the whole of the free zone.

The young recruits received military-style instruction while carrying out public work projects. The same type of program also existed in the Navy and the Air Force, and there were officer-training schools established by the Education Ministry.

One last group was the Compagnons de France, a squad exclusively made up of volunteers, working hand in hand with the Chantiers. However from 1943 on these organizations gradually lost their importance, as they had become suspect to the German authorities and to Vichy.

Moreover the Chantiers were disorganized by the departure of 16,000 young men and 400 of their leaders for Germany.

After the German invasion of the free zone, the Chantiers still remained as a territorial administration dealing with of everyday problems of personnel and supplies, as well as guards and fire-fighting formations on the Mediterranean coast including many seamen, and units of foreign workers. It is true that demobilized Indochinese, Madagascan and Senegalese infantry personnel were kept in France as unarmed workers. Organized into "groups of native colonial soldiers eligible for repatriation", they were allowed to keep their uniforms for reasons of prestige. In August 1944 more than two thirds of them — 4,800 with the organization Todt and 6,400 with the operational troops — were participating in emergency work in Lorient, Cherbourg and Calais.

Along with these groups, other various formations were constituted, including the 1er Régiment de France, authorized by the Germans in June 1943 for the purpose, as the Vichy government saw it, of replacing the armistice army.

In June 1941 the Légion Française contre le Bolchevisme (French anti-Bolshevik Legion), which was to become first Tricolore a year later, then the Légion des Volontaires Français (French Volunteers - LVF) in January 1943, was created. This formation was used to fight with the Wehrmacht on the Eastern front. A French contingent of the Waffen SS was recruited beginning in July 1943 and made up a Sturmbrigade that was also destined for combat in the East. However certain members of all these units participated individually in operations against the maquis.

The creation of these units, extremely limited in manpower, illustrates both the failure of the Vichy government to obtain from the Germans the possibility of creating a French army capable of defending the interests of France, and the German failure to direct the warlike instincts of the French toward the creation of important legions useful in Russia.

The diverse political parties in the northern zone were also disappointed. The Parti Populaire Français, the Rassemblement National Populaire, Francisme and the Mouvement Social Révolutionnaire, created along with the Ligue Française as anti-Bolshevik action committees, supported the LVF and worked in favor of an anti-Gaullist, anti-communist and anti-semite state with an authoritative system based on secret police intelligence-collecting and direct action by paramilitary militiamen. Since they couldn't do otherwise, each party possessed its uniformed legionnaires or free guards, who were often potential informants or police auxiliairies.

In the free zone, a unique association was formed after the defeat, which would become the major support group for the new regime. It was baptised Legion Française des Combattants and would be later completed by the Volontaires de la Révolution Nationale, thus outwardly affirming its role as the party of the government.

After Laval returned to Vichy, this group was reorganized and placed directly under government control.

Among the various organizations created by this Legion appeared the Service d'Ordre Légionnaire (SOL), created in January 1942 by Joseph Darnand in the Alpes-Maritimes, that progressively grew to cover the whole southern zone. In January 1943 the SOL separated from the Legion and stepped out as a paramilitary group, limited in manpower but with strong political ideals. Coming under Laval's direct authority, it became the Milice Française (French Militia) and was controlled by the Interior Ministry.

In Laval's mind this "modernized" SOL would be able to counter the ultras in Paris. For Darnand, the militia's role was "propaganda, vigilance and security", a reminder of the original role of the SS in Germany. The Militia soon had its own intelligence service, a regular army — the Franc-Garde (Free Guards) — and an officers' training school. But its numbers were limited: excluding the thousand men split equally between the 2nd Service (the "police") and the Free Guards (the soldiers), there were hardly more than 10,000 active militants — 6,600 in the southern zone and 3,800 in Paris — mostly unarmed.

By constituting the French Militia, Pétain and Laval created an instrument of civil war. Local militia leaders, in exchange for weapons needed after their units suffered a series of attacks had no qualms about exchanging information about Resistance movements with the German police, against Darnand's orders.

Thus started a true collaboration which was enhanced in January 1944, under German pressure, by Darnand's promotion as head of all the forces insuring the security of the public and of the State:

police, gendarmerie, mobile guards, mobile reserve groups (GMR), fire-fighters, communications guards, etc. After attacks by Resistance groups on militiamen the month before, that had left 52 dead or critically wounded, the Militia got involved in a vicious circle of revenge actions.

The climate of civil war was aggravated by a Franco-French tragedy taking place in the Alps during the first months of 1944. The Vichy government was getting worried about the increase in bloody attacks in the Haute-Savoie region, and the German threat to intervene and destroy the "terrorist hideouts" by their own means. So they assembled in that area various formations in charge of maintaining order, with the idea of undertaking wide-spread action against the maquis. A police superintendant, Colonel Georges Lelong, was chosen to be their leader and installed his offices in the town of Annecy. He had at his disposal 9,000 guards and GMR, and soon 900 militiamen, also theoretically placed under Lelong's orders, arrived to join them.

On January 31 the Haute-Savoie was decreed to be under a state of siege and notices were posted warning the population of the coming operations. In London, the English had just decided to arm the partisans. Pressure from the Vichy government was such that 600 Resistance fighters gathered on the Glières plateau to provide security for a drop zone. A few inconclusive skirmishes took place, with some men killed and others taken prisoner. Lelong was then chastised by Darnand for not being more agressive, while the massive arrival of German reinforcements served to underline the failure of the Vichy troops.

On March 20, the militiamen attacked. Then on the 26th 6,000 Austrians and Bavarians from the 157th division launded an assault. During the night, after a combat in the snow at a ratio of one against fifteen, the resistants finally withdrew: 145 were killed during the battle or executed afterwards. The enemy lost 450 men, killed or wounded, a third of whom were members of the French peace-keeping forces.

The Glières tragedy was a prelude to the events that would soon be taking place in the French theater of operations, with the principal actors from both sides: Frenchmen supporting one side or the other, Germans at bay, skeptical British and Americans ... It also illustrates the recklessness of the Vichy regime towards the end, the complexity of interior resistance, the ambiguities of outside help, the differences in the aims and the means granted by the Allies.

Chapter III

Fighting France and the Allies

For a long time, in continental France, the Resistance movement was limited to a small number of men and women whose living conditions were very different according to whether they were operating in the occupied zone or the free zone. Moreover the various movements and itineraries, often created spontaneously and in a variety of forms, were built up little by little by people who had varying motivations, activities and aims.

The situation was complicated by outside events : the invasion of Russia and the engagement of communists in the Resistance movement [1], the entry of the United States into the war, the occupation of the free zone, the transformation of North Africa into a base of operations, the instauration of mandatory work service, the increasing radicalism of the Vichy regime.

But, especially under pressure from the French Committee in London and because the movements and circuits were harrassed by the Germans, an embryo of unification appeared and the different British, French and American agencies, sometimes associates, sometimes rivals, decided to work together for greater effectiveness.

---

1. After the war the Organization spéciale was nevertheless officially recognized as a 'fighting unit' from October 1940 on. The Front National, its follow-up, and the FTPF were officially recognized from May 1941 on.

However oppositions and rivalries didn't just disappear, not even during the summer of 1944, when it was thought that the war would be over by Christmas.

Movements, maquis and circuits

In the beginning, the 'soldiers of the shadows,' military or civilian, belonged to 'movements'. In the occupied zone the most important of these was the Organisation civile et militaire (OCM), created by uniting officers of the 2nd bureau with civilian leaders, and which, at one time, had hoped to federate all the organizations in the northern zone. In the southern zone, some soldiers with Capitaine Frenay at their head created the Combat movement, made up mostly of technical officers : career officers, engineers, industrialists, civil servants, intellectuals, etc. Its main job would be to train officers and constitute the organizations which would furnish the models for Resistance groups.

After the attack on Russia and the political turn-around of the Communist Party, the communist-oriented Front National was organized in the northern zone and tried to penetrate into the south. This group favored immediate action to a fault. In January 1942, General De Gaulle designated Jean Moulin to coordinate the activities of the movements and group them under his leadership. Moulin applied the orders he had received and started by trying to separate political action from military action. The Service d'Atterrissage et Parachutage (SAP) in the south and the Bureau d'Opérations Aériennes (BOA) in the north controlled and centralized operations, with the help of specialists dropped by parachute inside France.

A year later, the military unification of the three main movements in the Southern zone — Combat, Franc-Tireur and Libération who joined together under the title of Mouvements Unis de Résistance (MUR) — was completed.

The first maquis were started by groups of volunteers dedicated to immediate action, belonging to movements or circuits. But their numbers sharply increased after the Germans decided to install mandatory work service for Frenchmen in Germany. This measure, far from producing the intended effect, resulted in the exact opposite: not only did Germany still lack the necessary manpower to keep its factories and farms producing, but also the number of 'réfractaires' increased: the threat of being deported to work in Germany turned thousands of 'spectators' into active resistants.

The réfractaires hid in isolated regions and turned into fighters, whenever existing Resistance formations were able to provide them with subsistance, training and arms. Thus in March 1943, the requisitioning of men for Germany provoked the creation of a Service National Maquis in the southern zone. Its job was to take in and train the réfractaires, thus completing the military organization surrounding the Armée Secrète (AS) and its raiding squads (Groupes Francs) in charge of sabotage [2].

Changes within MUR were not to the liking of the local leaders of the Combat Arm, who had difficulty accepting directors named by the higher authority. Some left to join the Organisation Métropolitaine de l'Armée (OMA), which was suspected of "giraudism" because it naturally joined General Giraud. This group was against premature action and refused to take part in any federation of movements. It considered itself an advance echelon of the African Army and took charge of preparations for its invasion of southern France.

In the northern zone the attempts at unification met the same obstacles. The OCM, the most important and best organized of the movements, didn't appreciate being obliged to play second fiddle in an umbrella organization.

Even though attempts were made to keep the movements and circuits secret, even from one another, in the end they couldn't help but intermingle, because they were all recruiting from the same pool of men. Itineris had by definition ties to the exterior, but movements

2. At the end of 1943, the number of members was estimated at 50,000 Resistance Fighters: 30,000 in the south, 20,000 in the north, plus 7,000 FTP belonging to the Communist Party.

'lived' in a closed atmosphere, even though they had to seek outside help to furnish them with the money and weapons they so drastically needed. For this reason some of the movements decided to cooperate with the Allies, even accepted to fight under their banners, which was not exactly to the taste of the services of Free France (France Libre) in London.

The itineries, whether they were devoted to escape, infiltration, information or action, needed means — radio equipment, arms, money, schools, planes, boats, submarines — that the Free French did not have. They depended entirely on the Allies, especially the British, who thus had a direct influence on the interior Resistance.

The secret war in France was normally controlled by the British Intelligence Service, and specifically by the 'information' branch, the MI 6 or Secret Intelligence Service. But once France had been invaded, the SIS was particularly hard put to intervene on the continent. This helplessness, coupled with Winston Churchill's insistence, brought about the creation of a new organization in July 1940. The 'sabotage' section of the SIS was transformed into a new agency baptized Special Operations Executive, whose job it was, according to the Prime Minister, to 'bring fire and blood to Europe'.

The SOE rapidly diversified its missions from industrial sabotage to recruiting partisans, including, if necessary, luring away Frenchmen who came to England to serve with De Gaulle. The SIS had done the same.

The SOE took charge of secret armed action, sabotage and destruction of military installations and enemy industrial potential in the occupied territories. Its F Section, directed by Major Maurice Buckmaster, formerly a Ford manager in Paris, was aimed at non-Gaullist Frenchmen. Even though its orgainzation was strictly British, it employed many Frenchmen whom it recruited directly [4]. Its goal was to establish small groups of specialists who, when the time came, would be able to undertake the destruction necessary to insure the success of the Allied invasion. Under its influence paramilitary groups were

4. Fifty "Buckmaster" circuits would be officially recognized as "fighting units" after the war.

created, sometimes by luring away patriots who had been recruited by Resistance movements. Moreover, more out of pragmatism than political calculation, it maintained relations with Vichy and its army. Thus, thanks to a mission sent to London, the OMA regularly received money, weapons and ammunition from the SOE through the Buckmaster organization. This was not at all to the liking of the Gaullist Bureau Central de Renseignement et d'Action (BCRA).

The France Libre section of the SOE also furnished operational and material supplies to the BCRA. Originally a purely military organization, little by little the BCRA's main job became supporting activities in France.

It had few contacts with the American Office of Strategic Service. The latter was on the contrary in close contact with the heads of the armistice army [5] in mainland France and in North Africa, and was well-placed to take advantage of the privileged position of accredited American diplomats at Vichy. The Americans were opposed to De Gaulle and tried to create a third French rallying point for those who favored neither Vichy nor De Gaulle: their choice finally settled on General Giraud and they helped him escape from France. Giraud was installed in Algiers in January 1943, and worked toward resuming the war against the Germans. But at the same time he was not really opposed to the principles of the National Revolution and thus attracted the ill will of the Free France movement which accused him of fostering "dissent within dissent".

The same accusation was leveled at the Vichy government special services, whose leaders escaped to French North Africa when the free zone was invaded, leaving behind them the secret services that had been set up "under the nose" of the Germans. Their activity progressively resumed from Algiers where the Direction des Services Spéciaux was soon created.

For the France Combattante, the summer of 1943 was marked by the agreement reached between Generals Giraud and De Gaulle and

5. Army of 100,000 men authorized by the armistice signed with Germany in June 1940. TN.

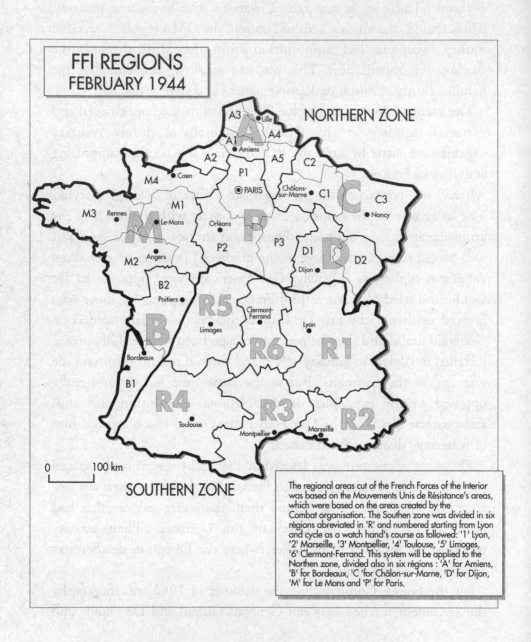

FFI REGIONS
FEBRUARY 1944

NORTHERN ZONE

A3 · Lille
A1
A · Amiens
A2
A4
A5
C2
P1
· Caen
M4
Châlons-
sur-Marne · C1
C
C3
· Nancy
M3 · Rennes
M1
M · Le-Mans
· Orléans
P
P3
D1
D
D2
M2 · Angers
P2
· Dijon
B2
· Poitiers
R5
Clermont-
Ferrand ·
B
· Lyon
· Limoges
R6
R1
· Bordeaux
B1
R4
R3
R2
· Toulouse
Montpellier ·
· Marseille

0   100 km

SOUTHERN ZONE

The regional areas cut of the French Forces of the Interior
was based on the Mouvements Unis de Résistance's areas,
which were based on the areas created by the
Combat organisation. The Southen zone was divided in six
régions abreviated in 'R' and numbered starting from Lyon
and cycle as a watch hand's course as followed: '1' Lyon,
'2' Marseille, '3' Montpellier, '4' Toulouse, '5' Limoges,
'6' Clermont-Ferrand. This system will be applied to the
Northen zone, divided also in six régions : 'A' for Amiens,
'B' for Bordeaux, 'C 'for Châlon-sur-Marne, 'D 'for Dijon,
'M' for Le Mans and 'P' for Paris.

the fusion of their armies. Once was over the tumult caused by the quarrel between Algiers and London, the interior and exterior Resistance movements were finally consolidated in spite of persistant hard feelings.

Travel now took place in both directions, via Spain or Switzerland, in motorboats, submarines, by parachute drops or light planes specially equiped for landing on short temporary airstrips. Teams spotted the landing strips, guided the planes and evacuated equipment or men under armed protection. But the French still depended on their Allies to train agents and furnish the necessary supplies to the resistants. And the British needed to know the political color of the itineries involved before they decided to drop arms.

Weapons dropped by parachute were generally distributed to the maquisards, who lived sparingly, hiding in the forests or in the mountains. To obtain supplies, they raided the Vichy administration's depots or instated a system of requisitioning, which the population didn't always appreciate. Very few of them had weapons. And the containers dropped by parachute usually contained only explosives, Tommy guns or automatic rifles, rarely heavier machine guns or mortars. Often the partisans were forced to avoid fighting.

The German operations directed against these "gangs" started in July 1943 with the break-up of two maquis in Haute-Savoie. In Corrèze, the fighting lasted from September to November. In February 1944 came the episode in Glières, then, the following month, one in the Ain.

At the beginning of 1944 itineris and armed groups started to take on more and more importance for the German occupying forces. They instigated more action against the clandestine organizations and maquis, and the maquis increased in numbers accordingly. The arrival of hoards of volunteers — men escaping from itineris being tracked by the Germans, réfractaires refusing mandatory work in Germany, career soldiers — in isolated areas, forced each movement to constitute a guerilla army.

There was constant debate among the armed movements as to whether to undertake immediate action or to wait for the intervention of the regular Allied forces. There was also quarreling over whether to form small groups of guerilla partisans or larger maquis. Then there was the opposition between the Allied military and the Resistance leaders about repeated massive bombing raids.

The German offensive against the maquis obliged the leaders, in spite of their differences and rivalries, to coordinate their action. In the face of danger the AS and the FTP worked together in the regions being threatened. Likewise the Gaullist Resistance and the OMA cooperated effectively, but with some difficulty, stemming from the Gaullists' fear of being put under the orders of career officers, too convinced of their own technical superiority.

Outside France in November of 1943, the Direction Générale des Services Spéciaux (DGSS) was created. Then, in January 1944, a Comité d'Action en France (COMIDAC) was created at government level to control operations in the occupied territories. Jacques Soustelle was named secretary general of the COMIDAC and director of the DGSS. He had at his disposal bases in London and Algiers,[6] combining the necessary intelligence, action and counter-espionage elements, and assuming complete responsability for liaisons with the Resistance movements.

In occupied France Jean Moulin had likewise created a centralized organization. The movements had to go through him, first to get money, and then for means of transmission which were controlled by a liaison officer from the BCRA. And the air and sea operations service, composed of officers trained in England and organized by the Royal Air Force and the SOE, had a monopoly on pick-ups, landings and parachute operations.

In the same vein, under orders from General De Gaulle, the Organisation métropolitaine de l'Armée became, at the beginning of 1944, the Organisation de Résistance de l'Armée (ORA). It was to be integrated into the Resistance movements, and the latter could do nothing but accept.

6. The London BRAL office bore the seal of the BCRA of Free France, and the Algiers BRAA that of the SR of the armistice army.

This idea of a centralized command in the occupied territories was sharply criticized by some. When General Delestraint and Jean Moulin were arrested in June 1943, the centralizing tendancy was momentarily forgotten and the Committee in London came up with a compromise. The British certainly had something to do with this sudden change. So many itineris were destroyed that the SOE, fearing that unless drastic measures were taken immediately the French Resistance would be useless on D-Day, demanded that the French decentralize their secret organizations.

Therefore twelve regional military delegates were named. They received radio equipment to keep them in contact with the unified staff headquarters and the two BCRA bases. They were under the orders of three top-level delegates: the national delegate in Paris whose job it was to arbitrate conflicts between delegates and movements, and two DMZs, one for the northern zone and the other for the South. Finally in February 1944, the Forces Françaises de l'Intérieur (FFI) united ORA, FTP, Corps Francs de la Libération, itself made up of all the armed formations of the MUR.

A regional organization, modeled on that of the Secret Army, was decided on. The north zone was divided into six regions: A with its center in Amiens, B - Bordeaux, C - Nancy, D - Dijon, M - Le Mans and P - Paris. The southern zone was also divided into six areas: R.1 - Lyon, R.2 - Marseille, R.3 - Montpellier, R.4 - Toulouse, R.5 - Limoges and R.6 around Clermont-Ferrand. On the local level, peculiarities often remained, but the départemental and regional administrations gradually came to include all parties, under the control of the national FFI staff. The Coordination Committee became the military action committee or COMAC. It now considered to consider that its role had changed from that of a liaison structure to that of a collective command structure.

From Special Forces Head Quarters to FFI Head Quarters

The final step was taken in April 1944 when General Koenig, military delegate of the CFLN and commander-in-chief of the French Forces in Great Britain, arrived in London:

POSSIBLE MAQUIS STRONGHOLDS MAY 1944

Strongholds

Natural borders limiting a stronghold's zone of influence

Probable limits of influence of a stronghold without natural borders

Estimated number of soldiers in each possible stronghold

/ / Total effectives/armed soldiers/potential fighters

1a	6 000/4 000/12 000	4	5 000/3 500/8 000
1b	2 500/1 000/5 000	5	3 000/300*/8 000
1c	3 000/1 500/5 000	6	3 000/2 000/5 000
2	8 000/5 000/12 000	7	2 500/500/4 000
3	2 000/2 000/5 000	8	400/100/2 000

* Plus 800 French-made weapons with little ammunition

Map labels: 8 ARDENNES, PARIS, Seine, Nancy, BRETAGNE 7, Rennes, Troyes, VOSGES 6, Tours, Auxerre, MORVAN 4, Dijon, JURA 3, Rhin, Loire, Clermont-Ferrand, Limoges, 1a, Saône, Lyon, 1c, Bordeaux, MASSIF CENTRAL, 1b, ALPES 2, Garonne, 5 PYRÉNÉES, Pau, Toulouse, Rhône, Marseille

0 100 km

"Your mission, General De Gaulle told him as he left Algiers [7], is to represent the French government at the supreme Allied command. It is your job to prepare for military action by Resistance forces during the Allied invasion".

At the same time, the Conseil National de la Résistance, which controlled COMAC, believed that the insurrection should be led from France and not from London. Consequently they assigned the direction of the French Forces of the Interior to the National Staff of the FFI in occupied France. Thus, as the invasion neared, two rival organizations were vying for command.

In the beginning, to insure, on the military level and in liaison with the Allied high command, that the CFLN decisions concerning the interventions of Resistance movements behind the enemy lines were carried out, Koenig had a staff at his disposal under the direction of Colonel Ziegler (Vernon). Ziegler's job was to harmonize the activities of the French and Allied secret services, then coordinate the operations of the interior forces with those of the invading troops.

On May 1st, Koenig was named military delegate for the northern zone of operations, and a new structure, baptized FFI General Headquarters (EM FFI), was created. This occured a week after General Cochet was named to the same position in the southern zone, thus aligning the French structures on the pattern of the two Allied commands, in Western Europe and the Mediterranean. On June 1st, Koenig became commander-in-chief of the interior forces, recognized by SHAEF [8]. SHAEF gave him his orders through Special Forces Headquarter (SFHQ), a structure conceived to take command of the French sections of the SOE and the OSS.

The plan started in North Africa, where a common British-American base was established in Guyotville, near Algiers. It received the code

7. Where he had been working since October 1943, as deputy chief of general staff for the Army, on the delicate question of trying to unite the FFL and the African Army into a single corps.

8. General Dwight D. Eisenhower's Supreme Headquarters Allied Expeditionary Forces in London.

name Massingham, and operated under the auspices of the Inter-Service Signals Unit 6. Then in May of 1944, in preparation for the invasion of Provence, its elements were regrouped in a Special Projects Operation Center, to which the French were admitted a month later.

In London, since March 1944, SHAEF had responsability for all secret service activities linked to Operation Overlord, the invasion of north-west Europe via the English Channel. And on May 1st, SOE/SO became SFHQ, a cover agency aimed at insuring secure relations between the Center and the military formations engaged on the continent. Then the separation between the two rival 'French' sections within the SOE, F section and RF section, disappeared. Unlike the situation in Algiers, the French were not admitted to SFHQ; the Allies were reluctant to include them for security reasons.

But Koenig was dissatisfied with his fictional role as 'commander-in-chief'. He met with the heads of the two Allied services to convince them to create a new headquarters including both the BCRA and SFHQ. On June 20th, once the success of the invasion was insured and distrust had been dissipated, the Allies finally agreed to the principle of creating an 'FFI Headquarters'. And on July 10th, when Eisenhower was finally convinced of the military benefits of the Resistance movements, he gave the green light.

"Considering the development of the French Resistance forces, he decided, I request that responsibility for matters concerning the FFI be progressively handed over from SHAEF to the reinforced FFI headquarters".

But two more weeks went by before the FFI command status was known; henceforth it would be placed under the orders of SHAEF and take charge of supervising the work of the underground units.

Colonel Vernon was flanked at that time by two Lieutenant-Colonels: Buckmaster from the SOE and Van der Stricht from the OSS. The same triple structure was adopted in each of the sections or bureaus set up during the last two weeks of July. An important segment of SFHQ, dominated by the British from the SOE, left to join the French staff. But SFHQ retained responsibility for support: air and sea transport, supplies of weapons, food, clothing, radio equipment etc.

Finally on August 22, the 300 persons working in the offices scattered throughout London moved into Bryanston Square to the offices of ETOUSA, the American command in Europe.

The FFI Headquarters were made up of the usual four bureaus as well as a fifth in charge of transmissions and a sixth taking responsibility for training the special units. The 2nd and part of the 3rd were manned by the F section of the SOE, which was careful to keep part of its personnel separate from the FFI staff: they were necessary to deal with its 'anti-Gaullist' (Buckmaster) agents and to insure that they remained safe in case of leaks that might allow them to be identified by the BCRA. The RF section (Free France) took charge of the 6th bureau. The rest of the staff came from BRAL.

It was soon clear that this latest merger was chaotic. Even though some members of the OSS gave the structure their total support, others questioned the effectiveness of the headquarters staff, who looked like members of a 'political group'. As far as the British from the SOE were concerned, they found the FFI staff 'inconsistant' and had trouble accepting the presence of French officers arriving from Africa that they called 'turncoats'.

The FFI headquarters was truly in a difficult position. First it had been subordinated to SHAEF and SFHQ. Now — even after uniting with SFHQ — it still could not send a single agent or parcel by air without the assistance of a British or American squadron, and it had no authority over them. Moreover, any initiative with political implications was likely to be vetoed by one of the three allies.

Fortunately among the subordinates work was too absorbing and pressure too great for the men and women to be affected by the turbulence at the top. Everyone tried to get his job done without worrying about questions of politics or personalities.

Little by little the rough chaff wore away and work got done quickly and easily. Nevertheless, agents were sometimes sent to the wrong spot and requests for weapons sometimes got no answer. And the men who lived in the field in extremely difficult conditions where the least mishap could have dire consequences, were aware of the uneasiness spreading through the London bureaus at times.

When he arrived in London, General Koenig was briefed in the BRAL 3rd bureau by the Bloc Planning officers:

"The note about military action by the Resistance groups that we drafted last March, said Colonel Combeaux, provides for a sabotage zone and a retreat zone, in the mountains and in the Paris region, where the maquis can concentrate their efforts".

For the Allied planners, the problem raised by the use of armed movements was particularly complex. It was not simply a question of political implications, but also stemmed from the fact that, at that time, no one really had a precise and realistic idea of what kind of help the interior Resistance groups could give to the regular forces.

However in January 1944 the planning for the invasion brought to light the importance of an interior force whose action could facilitate the landing and the advance of assault troops. Nevertheless only the British were really interested in the interior Resistance forces, and the RAF participated in ten times the number of flights than the USAAF: Roosevelt was still just as opposed to General De Gaulle, and the American airmen were more interested in their bombing missions. When March came around, Eisenhower admitted in a top-secret memorandum that he would registre... need the help of the Resistance groups in France, and he put his support behind the OSS projects.

The planning section of the BCRA in London, created to analyze the military problems raised by using the French Resistance groups, started a study about certain aspects of the Battle of France fought by the Allied invading armies, which showed how much help the guerilla fighters could bring to the invading forces. In February this study was completed by a detailed investigation of the use of the French interior army.

In the north of the country, there were only three regions where creation of maquis groups could be considered: Brittany, Swiss Normandy, and the triangle formed by the Jura, Morvan and Vosges regions. In the south the mountain terrain was favorable to implanting maquis for thousands of patriots, with large strongholds: Massif Central, Alps and Pyrénées mountains. Even though it was of less strategic importance, the south became interesting when one considered that strongholds created there could represent a threat to the German forces in the north and a support for any Allied operation launched in the south.

In this analysis the enemy counted for little. It was true that the German operational troops were lined up along the English Channel facing toward the invasion and their density was inversely proportional to the zones of possible maquis action. So it was reasonable to think that armed movements operating behind the lines would be mainly opposed by occupying troops.

This was the conclusion reached by the representatives of SFHQ and the FFI headquarters, meeting in London on May 20, 1944, to examine the possible support and use of Resistance forces after D-Day. For them, once the invasion had begun, the zones where effective resistance was possible would be the ones where the German forces were the weakest.

The different operating zones were defined according to the nature of the land and their position relative to the regions that were crucial to enemy operations and communications.

The maquis-held strongholds could evolve into the control of firmly held airstrips that could be the starting point for Allied large-scale air lifts. For this reason the Massif Central was of strategic interest both from a military point of view — possibility of intervening in neighboring regions — and from a psychological one. Conveniently located in the center of France, with a weak enemy contingent, it had in its favor excellent communications and optimal conditions for receiving supplies by air.

The Alpine stronghold was the most favorable region, in spite of the fact that German troops were as numerous there as anywhere, and that conditions in the mountainous sections were difficult for air drops. Here the maquis were well organized, with plenty of combat experience, their morale was good, and because of this they could be put to use first as a strategic base to be developed later. The retreat in the Jura, next to Switzerland, offered the same possibilities with limited enemy troops.

The Pyrénées mountains, a natural mountain stronghold bordering Spain, had great potential value with weak German forces and good possibilities of bringing in supplies from North Africa. The partisans in this area were quite well organized.

The Vosges could be placed in the category of zones under maquis influence. The possibility of transforming the area into a stronghold was not excluded, in spite of the difficulties of getting supplies in because of the distance and the weather. The armed groups in the area were scattered and not well organized.

The Côte-d'Or and the Morvan were typical behind the lines terrains. Brittany and the Ardennes were classified as battle zones, in which small group action was well adapted, but they could evolve into rear action zones: supply conditions were normal, but the enemy presence was powerful.

The resistants in Brittany were eager, but Brittany was in need of important air support to be useful. Concerning the French Ardennes, the conditions of security were difficult and the region was of no interest except if the members of the maquis were armed.

Basically, then, the leaders participating in the May 20th meeting believed that certain zones, if they were correctly reinforced with men and supplies after the invasion, could be taken over by the patriots and become strongholds.

"It is clear, concluded Colonel Robin Brook, chief of the Western European division of the SOE, who was presiding over the meeting, our present resources limit the number of strongholds that can be developed. And as long as the guerilla fighters haven't proven their capability after D-Day, no request for air transport will be justified."

This hands-off attitude, motivated by military considerations, also had political overtones. The Allies knew all about the oppositions within the ranks of the Resistance fighters; this conflict had seeped through into their own organizations. Thus the SOE usually refrained from helping elements who might, after the war, act against their interests, while the OSS supported anyone who wanted to fight Germans. In spite of this the OSS leaders were far from unanimous about the way to proceed; this was similar to the attitude of the

American government, wanting to postpone purely political considerations until the end of the war.

Neither was political afterthought absent from discussions among the French as to the choice of regions and ways of intervening.

Political and Military Stakes

At the end of the meeting, it appeared that the mission that could be entrusted to the maquis was to assist in extending the beachhead into enemy-held territory, by delaying arrival of reinforcements and creating diversions in distant zones, while at the same time preparing to support a secondary invasion. SFHQ would support the Resistance movements with specialized or conventional troops dropped by air, with liaison teams and in some cases direct air support.

But beyond the purely military aspects of the mission, General Koenig could not ignore the basic controversy, necessarily political, gnawing away at the interior and exterior Resistance forces: after D-Day should they favor popular insurrection, or prefer mass mobilization of all able-bodied men to fight alongside the regular invading forces?

At one time the MUR had drafted a note about an insurrection taking place on D-Day with the double purpose of helping the invading forces and driving out the Vichy authorities. The CNR, which adopted in March 1944 the Resistance action program, followed the same line of thought, as did the COMAC two months later when it talked about preparing the French people for insurrectionary mass action.

Along with sabotage and harassment activities planned by the Allies, which continued to have priority, the FFI would have to mobilize and direct the masses to insure that power remained in the hands of the Liberation committees, representative and administrative structures on the regional and departemental levels.

On the local level, a variety of behaviors seemed possible. In fact, the theoretical unification of the movements had taken place only on paper, far from the groups concerned; certain movements and their troops really maintained relative independence. This was partly the case for the ORA, which continued to think of itself as part of the regular army. And it was particularly true of the FTP, who were in favor of general strikes and national insurrection, immediate action and guerilla warfare. Since the Communist-oriented Front National, could not control the FFI, they tried to replace it by the Milices patriotiques [9].

Differences concerning the best way of continuing the combat — armed insurrection or maquis, immediate action or waiting for the invasion — were even creating cleavages within each separate movement.

In the orders it gave to the COMIDAC in April 1944, the CFLN reiterated the military interest and moral importance of a general uprising, while at the same time insisting that it must be controlled and staggered timewise.

COMIDAC itself, in its note concerning the use of the partisans in May, no longer spoke of insurrectionary actions but rather of large scale actions.

SHAEF, in addition to carrying out the different sabotage plans approved by the Allied command during the spring of 1944, expected that the resistants would undertake guerilla operations. Should they, in this case, order an insurrection in France?

While a large scale action might confuse the enemy as to the intentions of the Allies and delaying movements of its reinforcing troops, it could, on the other hand, result in certain destruction of maquis and itineris.

The Allied planning group decided to opt for partial operations, consisting of a mobilization of Resistance forces, zone by zone, according to need and without revealing Allied intentions to the Germans. The first area of operations to be chosen was Brittany. However the situation was complicated by the suspicion surrounding certain French staffs and services. This had forced the Allies to take precautions that, they realized, would have political consequences [10].

9. In theory the Milices patriotiques, patriotic militia, were an auxiliary force available to the CDL and reserves for the FFI.

To insure the secrecy of the operation, strict orders were given so that neither the RF section of the SOE, nor the BCRA were informed. General De Gaulle himself, who was deliberately excluded from the planning of Overlord, was informed only the day before that the invasion was about to take place. Moreover General Koenig and his staff were subject to the ban imposed by SHAEF: travel to foreign countries prohibited, radio liaisons controlled, etc.

In Algiers on May 16, 1944, De Gaulle — concluding a memorandum written by the COMIDAC concerning the use of the French Forces of the Interior — complained to the Allies of the 'suppression of direct communications between French the various headquarters in London (which) makes work practically impossible. If this measure is maintained the use of the Resistance forces will be jeopardized. It is clear that the French command will not accept to engage them under the circumstances.'

This document addressed to the Allies was part of an ambitious French project put together by the BCRA in London and approved by General De Gaulle. The aim of this project, code-named Caïman, was to define the conditions for engaging the interior Army in generalized military action under De Gaulle's orders, in coordination with the Allied invasion. Creation of zones of operations was proposed in regions where the maquis was well established and where occupying forces were weak, especially the South-West and the Sisteron-Grenoble-Besançon corridor.

The first instruction pamphlet, thirty pages long, defined the general conditions for the military use of the Resistance forces during operations of liberation.

The second, intended for the Resistance movements, dealt with targets and defined the conditions for carrying out sabotage attacks. It

10. "The security service of SHAEF suspected General De Gaulle's headquarters in Algiers of being infiltrated by the German secret services... At the end of the war, when the Allies got their hands on the SD archives, they found that the only absolutely correct report that the SD had received about Neptune came from a Colonel belonging to De Gaulle's staff in Algiers." (Anthony Cave Brown, *The Secret War*).

confirmed the concept of direct intervention starting at the beginning of the invasion, in connection with the Allied forces and aiming at liberating entire regions. The note sent to the Allies was a summary of these two documents and a request for the necessary means and material.

This project provided for sabotage of communications lines in the north; local insurrection — particularly in Paris — or general uprising could only be considered in exceptional cases. Two main zones of action were defined, with specific targets. First the city of Paris, where armed intervention should not be launched except if the German troops were deeply demoralized or attempting a rapid withdrawal. The targets to be taken were those crucial to transportation and communications: bridges, electric plants, public services, ministries, etc. The second zone of action was Brittany, to open up the ports of Saint-Malo, Brest and Lorient.

In the south-east the constitution of a normal sabotage efforts was advised in the valley of the Rhone River, with, when possible, operations designed to liberate the Savoie, Dauphiné and southern Jura regions.

The South-West and Center regions, defined by the quadrilateral La Rochelle - Clermont-Ferrand - Foix - Bayonne, were not included in the main operations, but the FFI could hope to become an essential element in the liberation of this zone. The final sentence tells us that operations concerning the liberation of territory in the South-West-Center zone and the Jura-Savoie-Dauphiné area were outlined in a plan code-named C.

The air support necessary to Resistance fighters, from D-Day on, was significant. All French units of paratroopers were designated as part of the first echelon. Then as airstrips were captured, other Allied airborne troops would follow with anti-tank and anti-aircraft weapons, reconnaissance and transport planes, etc.

Actually the available means were extremely limited and speaking about general insurrection seemed a bit exaggerated. This was already pointed out on May 27 by a well-informed leader who had seen the plan:

"This plan is based on a historical error. The men who thought up Plan Caïman must believe in the open revolution theory but prefer Gambetta's method to Carnot's ..."

The plan was delivered to Wilson, Supreme Allied Commander in the Mediterranean, who turned it over to Eisenhower in London.

The following analysis of the plan appears in the SHAEF War Diary:

'On May 16, 1944 the Chief of Staff, SACMED, transmitted the French plan, signed by General De Gaulle (unaware of Operation Overlord). More interested in the help to be furnished to the Resistance than the help the resistants can furnish to our operations. Ambitious. Counts on political as well as military advantages for De Gaulle.

The De Gaulle plan — De Gaulle, as president of the CFLN Comité Français de Libération Nationale — must authorize any operation aimed at liberating any part of the territory of France. Every decision has to pass through the Action Committee (Algiers)'

'The plan is not supported by SHAEF. Largely replaced by an agreement between General Koenig and SHAEF. According to the terms of this document, Koenig accepted nomination as Commander in Chief of the FFI under the direction of the Supreme Allied Command. Nomination announced on June 23, 1944 by letter from SHAEF.'

On June 5, after debating the idea of launching operations simultaneously over the whole territory, Eisenhower decided in favor of the invading forces in spite of the risks that the patriots and the population were apt to encounter. The head of the OSS in London and the chief of the SOE came to ask General Koenig if he had any objection to the BBC's sending out coded messages that called for destructions and a general uprising. The visit was a simple formality: the decision had already been made and orders given!

General De Gaulle, who arrived on the 4th from Algiers where the CFLN had just declared itself the acting government of the French Republic (Gouvernement Provisoire de la République Française - GPRF), could only repeat the call in the name of the GPRF. On June 6, D-Day, he settled, at least on the national level, the question of nationwide insurrection or general mobilization and spoke to the population by radio:

" The final battle has started ... France will fight with furor. She will fight in good order!"

In France this broadcast was understood by some as a call to insurrection and by others as a call to mass mobilization. Finally on June 25, General Koenig gave the order to demobilize: it resulted in the armed groups suffering huge losses. This was just when the Allies finally consented to organize massive drops of weapons and missions.

- The FFI, General Eisenhower finally recognized, can play two major roles in the plans outlined by SHAEF. Their action can be important by creating strategic diversions outside the battle zones and through tactical cooperation in or near these zones.

The controversy with SHAEF was soon complicated by a quarrel, of which Koenig was the instrument, between Algiers and Paris. In Algiers in May the COMIDAC, part of the Comité Française de Libération Nationale in Algiers, decided that the COMAC, an organization of the Comité National de la Résistance, would not be placed in command. But the CNR in Paris had already given COMAC the supreme command of the FFI for a certain number of missions.

The problem was brought to the attention of the CNR which decided on June 17 in favor of COMAC. All that was needed was the authorization of the president of the acting government (De Gaulle). That authorization would never come ...

Actually, until they met up with the invading forces, the troops of the Forces Françaises de l'Intérieur fought region by region, sector by sector, but always under the orders of the regional military delegates and the officers of the interallied missions. To help them, officers, soldiers, instructors, arrived by parachute.

At the end of the meeting between SFHQ and the FFI staff on May 20, 1944, the French participants [11] should have been satisfied: certain points had been clarified and SFHQ decided to accept all the

11. Colonel Robin Brook, chief of D/R (France-Netherlands section of the SOE), accompanied by Brigadier Edmund Myers of the SOE, who came as a 'neighbor' bringing with him his experience in the Balkans, and Major Paul Van der Stricht, DR/US. Colonel Vernon, Lieutenant-Colonel Combeaux, Commandant Lejeune, from the EM FFI.

conclusions concerning, in particular, the airborne troops and special units, in England and in North Africa, who could work with the partisans and furnish them with strong leadership if necessary.

But the three available Allied airborne divisions were scheduled to be engaged in the first phase of the Allied invasion, and the Polish brigade was kept in reserve for special use. So was the French 1st Parachute Regiment, which at one time had been programmed to jump onto the island of Elba and was more or less implicated in the invasion of Provence: they were to be grounded by the CFLN, kept in reserve to maintain law and order in liberated France. As for the Shock Battalion, where some of the soldiers also obtained their airborne qualifications, we will see the job they were to be given during the invasion in Southern France.

The accumulation of Special Organizations

Besides the airborne troops, for the Resistance to be effective it also needed weapons, ammunition, advisers and radio gear, communications, all to be sent in by air.

Among the special units were the liaison personnel, organized into Jedburgh Teams and Special Allied Missions, and the American Operational Groups, trained to operate behind enemy lines. SFHQ also included in the list the British Special Air Service, but this group remained under the control of SHAEF through the commanders of the British Airborne Forces Command.

Moreover SFHQ had no monopoly over operations in France. The Special Intelligence Service had also created, along with the Special Operations branch of the OSS, an information-collecting project, effectively excluding the SOE, especially the F section (Buckmaster). The project had received the code name Sussex and was supervised by an intelligence officer from each of the three countries concerned (USA, Great Britain and France). The idea was to drop by parachute, in preparation for D-Day, about 60 teams across northern France from Brittany to the Belgian border, at a distance of 40 to 60 miles back from the coast. Their mission was to obtain tactical information about the enemy, then meet up with advancing Allied troops.

The first team was parachuted in February to reconnoiter possible dropping zones in the region around Châteauroux. Two months later other missions infiltrated the occupied territory and, at the end of the month of August, 52 intelligence teams were in the field [12].

In the end, about ten different secret organizations, not all of them controled by SFHQ, were working for Allied forces engaged in the battle of France. In addition to the itineris of SIS agents, reinforced by the Sussex teams that we have just mentioned, were:

- The escape itineries organized by the DF section of the SOE or the MI 9;
- About 100 groups that the RF section of the SOE was able to equip at the last minute with radio sets;
- The 25 regular itineris of the F section of SOE;
- Squadrons of the SAS regiments;
- Jedburgh teams and OSS operational groups.

The SAS brigade included four British and French regiments, a company of Belgians and a Phantom signals squadron, a total of about 2,500 men, more than two-thirds of whom were to serve in France. The difficulties that its leader, Brigadier R.W. McLeod, met illustrate the complexity of employing special units, exacerbated by rivalries between organizations.

From the beginning of 1944, the use of SAS troops was under consideration, either in independent groups or as support for Resistance organizations. In the latter case, its basic mission was to make contact with the maquis and organize bases capable of receiving parachute drops of light motorized units, whose mission was to create havoc in the enemy rear lines over a wide area. The regions preferred by SHAEF were, in order of priority: Brittany, the Orléans forest, the Morvan and the département of Vienne.

Operation plans had to be approved by the Special Operations bureau of SHAEF, which was created to insure liaisons between the 21st Army Group and the British airborne forces.

12. Only three teams would be captured by the Germans — their six American members, including the only female agent, would be killed.

But the SAS brigade was also subordinate to Special Forces Headquarters, which rightly considered itself as having the final authority over the Resistance movements and the maquis. For SFHQ, the most important job was to reinforce the maquis by turning them into properly equiped disciplined troops.

The quarrel with the SOE, brought about by a reciprocal impression that Jedburghs and SAS were both carrying out the same mission, came to a head after the first days of the invasion on the continent.

On June 17, McLeod sent a bitter report to the airborne headquarters:

"I don't think, he wrote, that the strategic use of the SAS has been correctly assessed. These are troops that should not be used for political tasks."

He then complained about the objectives that had been assigned, on short notice, to the teams in the field.

"Certain requests certainly originate from SOE suggestions, and I feel that we are considered as a military accessory by the SOE, to execute the missions they are incapable of assuming. It appears that the policy of using the SAS is a short-term one, largely dependent on the whims of the SOE. A grave danger therefore exists that the SAS will be used according to the views of SFHQ rather than those of the chief of the Airborne Troops ..."

Four days later, to clear the air and establish long-term goals, SHAEF sent a memorandum about operations to Airborne Headquarters, providing for, first and foremost, furnishing the resistants with a core of disciplined troops, and executing guerilla attacks. Six bases of operations were designated: Brittany, Indre and Morvan, already established, and the Massif Central, Savoie-Jura and Vosges.

Confusion still existed however concerning the preparation and the execution of missions. Preparations were hardly helped by multiple trips back and forth to attend meetings, whereas normally it was the SAS officers who were responsible for liaison within SFHQ. Finally on August 5th, things would be brought back to normal by the suppression of the independent control allotted to the SAS. When the FFI headquarters were created, a liaison officer was detached to the section in charge of special units. This 6th bureau, directed by Lieutenant-Colonel L.H. Dismore and supervised by the RF section of the SOE, had its main offices — chairman, administration, security, SF Rear Line Section, operations room — located in Duke Street, between Hyde Park and Regent's Park, near the headquarters of the SOE and the OSS.

The Jedburgh and OSS Training Sections worked at Norgeby House. Not far from there, in two annexes, various offices dealt with agents embarking on and returning from missions, especially the OG's Conducting Officers and the Return of Field Personnel. And in Milton Hall, Northamptonshire, resided Major Henry B. Coxe of the OSS, in charge of Jedburgh training.

Theoretically he had about forty men and women at his disposal:

	British	Americans	French	Total
Senior officers		4	2	1	7
Juniors officers			9	2	3	14
NCOs		—	—	4	4
Civilians and secretaries		7	2	3	12
Total		20	6	11	37

At the beginning of August, most of the FFI staff was installed in Bryanston Square, where two buildings of the Camp were reserved for the 6th bureau.

It appears that plotting within the various services mentioned above didn't, after all, poison the atmosphere of the sections in charge of the special units. Perhaps this was because they were relatively homogenous, the British preponderance being evident.

When officers parachuted into France, they concentrated only on their mission, unconcerned with quarrels and rivalries among those they scornfully called deskmen. Their only significant feeling was exaperation when their radio messages went unanswered or when their partisans waited in vain for a parachute drop.

Weapons from the sky

Supplying weapons to the maquis was one of the main tasks of the teams parachuted into France. Their prestige vis-à-vis the guerilla fighters grew with their success at obtaining the arms awaited for so long. Arms drops were an encouragement to the maquis to continue the fight, and a tangible sign of the confidence placed in the movements by the commanders. But the drops depended on both the available aircraft in the Air Forces, and the priority accorded by SFHQ.

The Allied airmen were at that time giving priority to the air offensive against the Reich, and Air Chief Marshall Sir Arthur Tedder, Eisenhower's deputy, went so far as to express serious doubts as to the real nature of the requests of the SOE/SO and the effectiveness of that organization.

Churchill fiercely defended the role of the French in the liberation of their own country. He insisted that the Resistance, in spite of political antagonisms, be included in the invasion plans. But in May 1944 the most optimistic reports spoke of 85,000 armed Frenchmen and only 10,000 truly equiped and trained: therefore, to be effective, the Resistance movements had to be reinforced by massive drops of weapons, ammunition and supplies.

The Allied command was, in fact, hard put to satisfy all the requests from the different services with the means at its disposal.

At the beginning of 1944, SHAEF expressed concern about the lack of adequate aircraft for the program of arming the Resistance fighters. The Americans in particular were somewhat embarrassed about the difference between their support and that of the British — 85 RAF planes for 14 from the USAAF — and thought that this could be interpreted by the French as simple indifference. General De Gaulle, unaware of the real causes of the lack of planes, had complained to

Washington. The State Department then warned Eisenhower that the whole business could be interpreted as American opposition, for political reasons, to arming the Resistance movements.

In spite of these considerations, priority was maintained for standard warfare operations. Finally on May 26, preparing for an increase in requests after D-Day, two additional squadrons of Liberators were devoted to special operations. Or perhaps the Secretary of State had had his way and Eisenhower had decided that it was time to protect the Resistance operations from diplomacy!

There were now 115 available aircraft — 22 Stirlings and 57 Liberators in England, 18 Halifaxes, 15 B-24s and three B-17s in North Africa — to which could be added about 15 Lysanders, Hudsons, Mitchells and Dakotas, that could be used on rudimentary airstrips. But it was only in July, with the massive support of the U.S. Eighth Air Force, that things finally got rolling.

The rate of success of the parachute drops, depending on the quality of the airplane crews and the efficiency of the reception committees, progressed steadily: 50% in April, 75% in July. On the other hand, tries at daylight drops and higher altitude drops did not produce the hoped-for results.

The Lysander, a single-engined plane normally used for army support, was the first aircraft to be used for pick-up missions, that is, recovery and dispatching of agents in occupied territory. This plane could carry from two to four persons and, stripped of all unnecessary equipment and supplied with an extra fuel tank, could land on a 500-yard long grass strip, 500 miles from its home base. Once it was proven feasible to land a plane in the countryside on nights with a full moon, larger double-engine planes were used: Lockheed Hudsons armed in 1943-44 and Douglas Dakotas desactived after D-Day.

- The strip is lighted by three flashlights forming an L turned towards the wind, the head of the reception committee, trained in England, reminded his fellow teammates. Once recognition signals have been exchanged, the plane touches down, taxies back to the base of the L, discharges its passengers and packages and picks up the return passengers ... I shout OK! and the plane takes off again two or three minutes after having landed.

Parachute drops were the job of bombers adapted to special duty missions, baptized Carpetbaggers by the USAAF. The British Halifaxes MK II and V — obtained from the Bomber Command which kept a jealous eye on its four-engine aircraft — underwent some modifications: the dorsal turret disappeared, a re-inforced steel nose was added, the exhaust ports were camouflaged, the back wheel was made retractable, a trap door was installed for the parachutists, fuel tanks were added, etc. The normal load was 15 containers: nine in the bomb compartment and three under each wing.

The basic American plane was the B-24 Liberator, model H or J, painted black and stripped of some of its weapons. The pilot's cockpit had better visibility and the navigator's compartment was large and insulated.

All the four-engine planes were equiped with a Rebecca ground-to-air directional guidance system and an S-Phone emitter-receiver. Through a hole cut in the floor of the fuselage — the Joe-hole — jumped the agents of the OSS, the SOE, the BCRA or SHFQ. The crew called them all Joe, as much by affection as to preserve their anonymity.

Load capacities varied with the aircraft: 18 to 24 containers weighing about 200 lbs each for the Stirlings, 15 for the Halifaxes, 12 for the Liberators and the Flying Fortresses. Moreover to make maximum use of the craft, specially wrapped packages that could be dropped without parachutes along with the containers, were added. They weighed about 90 lbs and contained non-fragile material, such as uniforms or boxes of rations.

Each drop was specially adapted to the circumstances, while taking into account the standardization of material and loading procedures. The parcels were packed in two OSS and SOE packing stations that worked around the clock. More than 800 people took part in these operations: 350 in the English packing station, 325 for the Americans from February on, 50 to transport the material, 25 liaison officers at the different airfields, 65 people at SFHQ, etc. The same system was used in North Africa, but with less personnel.

The drop order was prepared by both services in liaison with the partisans in the field who sent in the request, and always taking into account tactical considerations and quotas established by SHAEF giving priority to their own needs. Once the request was granted, a personal message was put out over the airwaves by the BBC. It included the code name of the DZ chosen among several suggested by the petitioners. It had to be at least one thousand yards long on each side. Once confirmation was received from France, the four-engine aircraft handled the drop. They were guided toward the zone, even in clouds or fog, by the Rebecca unit which began receiving the reception committee's ground-installed Eureka signal from sixty miles out. The reception committee chief used an S-Phone with an 80-km range, allowing him to talk to the plane crew and deal with last-minute problems.

SHAEF was impressed by the results obtained by the FFI during the week following D-Day and decided to make an all-out effort. They estimated the number of maquisards at 32,000 of which 16,000 were armed, and the number of those ready to take part in combat at 100,000. They decided to equip as many men as possible so that they could take part in two important missions: covering the break-through north of the Loire River and the invasion of Provence. As a result, some Eighth Air Force aircraft were taken off the bombing campaign to participate in massive daylight parachute drops. On June 15, 75 B-17s were made available to SFHQ and, three days later, from 180 to 300 planes were promised. Once the crews had been quickly trained in Carpetbagger methods, five squadrons of thirty-six B-17s, each one capable of carrying equipment for 1,000 to 1,200 partisans, were committed to the project and four massive drops took place between June and September.

The first, code-named Zebra, was carried out on June 25 by 180 B-17s, after waiting three days for the weather to improve. Four of the five designated zones — Limoges, Vercors, Dijon and Haute-Savoie — were served. The fifth zone, situated in the Cantal, lacked a reception committee. The second drop and the largest, Cadillac, took place on July 14 with nine squadrons escorted by five hundred fighter planes: 500 tons of equipment were dropped in the Vercors, near Châlon-sur-Saône and in the Limoges-Brive region. The third, Buick, took place on August 1st with five squadrons, in the region of Chalon, in the Jura and in Savoie. The last of the series was carried out with 72 B-17s south of Besançon on September 9.

From May to September 1944, 350,000 men were thus equipped with weapons sent in by air.

The total tonnage of supplies sent into France in 1944 was:

	Great-Britain		Mediterranean	Total
	RAF	USAAF		
Jan-March 1944	693	73	172	938
April-June 1944	1162	733	794	2689
July-Sept 1944	3223	1925	1100	6248
Total	**5681**	**2731**	**2074**	**10486**

During the same period nearly half of the 7,000 missions flown for the two theaters were in support of OSS and SOE Allied organizations. The remaining half went to various other services: 37% for the BCRA, 9% for the SAS, whose men finally entered massively into the fight, and only 8% for SPOC in Algiers. In spite of what is commonly believed, it is evident that the French did not get the lion's share of supplies. The small share received by SPOC was due to the limited stocks available in North Africa and the fact that in the Mediterranean region priority was given to the maquis in the Balkans.

It is interesting to study the inventory of weapons dropped by parachute during the month of July 1944, for example, which is the month of Operation Cadillac:

	Night	Day	Total
Explosives (pounds)	234,000	14,350	**248,350**
Rifles	46,000	3,650	**50,210**
Bren automatic rifles	9,900	650	**10,550**
Bazookas	690	690	—
PIAT anti-tank grenade launchers [13]	290	87	**377**

13. Projector, Infantry, Anti Tank; British weapon weighing 30 lbs, only effective at a distance of 100 yards but capable of firing explosive and smoke shells.

Mortars	—	—	—
Stens	39,070	2,220	**41,290**
Grenades	177,600	2,750	**180,350**
Pistols	9,480	435	**9,915**
Ammunition(thousands of rounds)	31,396	6,230	**37,626**
Tonnage	2,135	512	**2,647**

The paucity of mortars — 47 in August and 123 in September — dropped late in the war, is symbolic of the Allied distrust of the maquis:

The Allies, worried about the partisans' intentions and their lack of training parachuted neither officers nor mortars. A Sten Tommy-gun and a handful of plastic explosive would have to do [14].

These arms deliveries had, it is true, certain consequences. They resulted in bitter debates concerning both the distribution among the different maquis and the types of weapons dropped.

Nevertheless parachute drops in the dark, in constant danger of interception by the Germans, had a strong emotional impact on the life of the maquis groups and the Special Forces teams that lived with them. These Allied parachutists — who had little information about the situation they would be encountering on arrival, who could not understand the rivalries within the ranks of the Resistance movements, and who were unaware of maquis prejudices against them — were plunged, as soon as they touched French soil, into the very particular atmosphere of the maquis, completely different from that of the London offices or the training centers in the lush British countryside.

Interallied Missions and Jedburgh Teams

In preparation for the Allied north and south invasions and the paths they later followed, assistance brought by the Allied special forces to the Resistance movements was not limited to simple arms drops.

About twenty interallied missions were dropped from January to September 1944 in areas with dense maquis groups situated in strategic zones. The French sometimes call them maquis missions, including

14. *Histoire militaire de la France* (Military History of France).

them in the larger group of parachuted missions aimed at transmitting orders from London and providing the unity to the movement when, in a given region, a conflict broke out between Resistance leaders. The officers of these missions acted principally as advisers, sometimes took command of a local group, or were sent to get information for the Allied staff. Each one of these teams included a French representative and a representative of the Allies, but other than that they varied enormously in size and importance according to their assigned job.

To start with, Mission Xavier was sent to Region R.1 during 1943. It included a delegate from the BCRA and one from the SOE. There was no cohesion between these two officers in the beginning because they had no precise mission, so they soon ended up isolated from each other, each one remaining in direct contact with his own service which sent him orders, money and parachute drops.

The first three-way mission sent into France at the beginning of 1944 had a symbolic name, Union [15]. For the first time, this group had a mission worked out in common by the three Allied agencies (SOE, OSS, BCRA), but its terms were still imprecise, for the agencies were still ill-informed as to the importance and organization of the maquis. Once in the field, each member of the team took charge of a département in R.1 and each did a good job, but without any real coordination.

The second interallied team sent into occupied France received the code name Citronelle. It would serve as a model for later missions. Its area of operation, distinctly smaller than that of the preceding mission, was limited to the Ardennes département, chosen by the Americans, even though they had almost no accurate information about the Resistance in that region.

But for the SOE the major problem before June 1944 was to decide whether, in preparation for the invasion, it was more important to

15. Directed by Colonel Pierre Fourcaud, one of the first BCRA agents, and including Lieutenant-Colonel Sir James R.H. Hutchinson, head of the RF section, Captain H.H.A. Thackthwaite, RF (L) chief, U.S. Marine Corps Captain Peter J. Ortiz, who had served in the French Foreign Legion, and a French radio operator, C. Monnier.

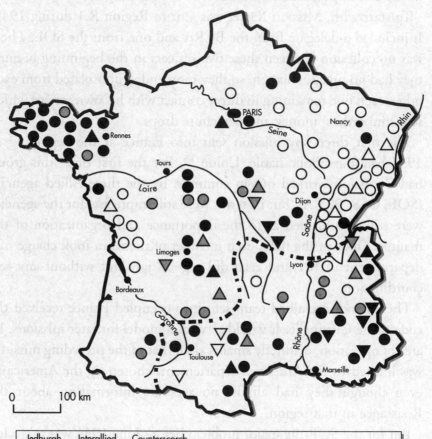

JEDBURGH TEAMS AND INTERALLIED MISSIONS

PARIS

Nancy

Seine

Rhin

Rennes

Tours

Loire

Dijon

Saône

Limoges

Lyon

Bordeaux

Garonne

Rhône

Toulouse

Marseille

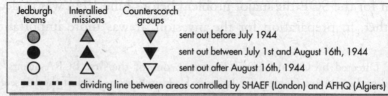

0   100 km

	Jedburgh teams	Interallied missions	Counterscorch groups	
sent out before July 1944	● (grey)	▲ (grey)	▽ (grey)	
sent out between July 1st and August 16th, 1944	● (black)	▲ (black)	▼ (black)	
sent out after August 16th, 1944	○	△	▽	

–··–··– dividing line between areas controlled by SHAEF (London) and AFHQ (Algiers)

concentrate efforts on circuits located in urban zones with minor sabotage actions executed on request, or develop its ties with the rural maquis and equip them hoping that, at the appropriate moment, they would be able to keep the enemy occupied far from the beachhead.

It was considered that sabotage activity might have some effect on the German war machine in France, but would not significantly influence the outcome of the conflict. On the other hand, guerilla actions, especially if they lasted over a period of time, risked turning to the enemy's advantage. The Germans could use their tanks and aviation against adversaries who were ill adapted to standard warfare, underequiped and undisciplined. The result might be heavy losses among the resistants and the civilian population. It is easy to imagine the political consequences.

A solution was found at the late of the summer of 1942 by Major General Colin Gubbins, then deputy executive director of the SOE, shortly after the failure of the landing at Dieppe. The idea was to parachute behind the enemy lines, simultaneous to the continental invasion, small groups of officers and men with the mission of rousing and arming the civilian population to execute guerilla attacks against enemy communications lines. The operating code name suggested for this personnel, recruited and trained by the SOE, was Jumper.

In July 1942 the project was baptized Jedburgh, from the name of a small town in Scotland situated on the English border. It was to be made up of seventy British and American teams.

On December 24, several important decisions were made affecting this project. The teams would be uniformed and one of the two officers would be a national from the target country. Thus Belgians, Dutch and Frenchmen were recruited. They would be parachuted into safe areas and met by SOE agents. Each team would have only one or two missions, and they would not be part of the tactical strategy of the regular forces, because of the time — 72 hours — necessary to get the mission onto the site and operational.

In March of 1943 the opportunity to test the idea come up during Exercise Spartan, constructed around the theme of a continental invasion by Allied forces advancing towards the north from a fictive conquered beachhead in the Salisbury plain. Eleven jumpers trained by the SOE took part, along with six agents equiped with radio sets emitting to a receiving station in Scotland. When the exercise was over, the SOE concluded that it would be necessary to drop the teams more than forty miles behind the lines in order to effectively attack enemy communications lines, and to make available to the army and army group staffs, signals and liaison detachments in contact with the special forces.

In July, Lieutenant General Frederick Morgan, in charge of planning the invasion, recommended that the SOE propositions be adopted. Liaison detachments would control the Resistance groups and the teams, in England, would constitute until D-Day strategic reserves, designed to command and equip Resistance groups as necessary. Then the British and American Chiefs of Staff gave their authorization.

In October, SOE and OSS each agreed to furnish the necessary personnel to establish thirty-five teams, as well as fifteen reserve teams, for a total of 100 teams and 300 men.

In Washington the project was greeted enthusiastically by General William J. Donovan, head of the OSS, who gave it absolute priority and put the Western Europe office of the SO Branch in charge of prospecting in the military camps in the south of the U.S. to find the fifty American officers necessary. Actually the whole country was crisscrossed to find the rare birds with superior intelligence capable of dropping behind the enemy lines, skilled at using light weapons and, especially, who spoke perfect French.

The recruits trained in the U.S. were then sent to London where they went through a selection process and more intense training. Of the 55 chosen candidates, only 35 would be accepted, so they had to call for additional volunteers serving with army units based in Great Britain. Most of them were to join up in February 1944, a month after the beginning of training. In the end less than one out of two candidates would pass the tests, but this ratio was better than that of the British, whose candidates were mainly recruited from infantry and artillery units.

The SOE also had trouble finding the necessary personnel. However they found a solution thanks to the BCRA. General De Gaulle, contrary to all expectations, accepted the principle of a tripartite organization designed to mobilize and control the maquis. Eighty officers, mostly regular, and sixteen radio operators were thus recruited in North Africa by the two missions led by Commandant Saint-Jacques of the BCRA. They all volunteered to parachute into France and join up with the maquis France. After a grevling testing period, several candidates were selected.

The Spartan experience resulted in the drafting of a first document which was distributed in December 1943 and became the basic manual of the Jedburgh teams. At that time it was decided to create 300 teams before April 1, 1944. This overly optimistic objective proved impossible.

Finally the creation of about one hundred teams was programmed by the Allied command, who defined the composition and role of the team.

'The Jedburghs are specially-trained teams of three men. They will be parachuted onto previously chosen sites behind the enemy lines in France, Belgium and Holland, starting on D-Day. Each team will include two officers and a radio operator. One of the officers must be a native of the country in which the team will operate, the two others are British or Americans. The members of the team are soldiers and must arrive on the scene of action in uniform. They will establish contact with Resistance groups, bring instructions from the Supreme Allied Command, insure radio transmissions for the group, and, if necessary, take command.'

Each team member was to be trained in guerilla warfare and exercising command, as well as in the use of explosives. Having no cover story the Jeds, if captured, were to give only their name, rank and serial number, and request to be treated as prisoners of war in accordance with international conventions.

The creation of these teams actually solved two problems. In case of a break in communications between the underground organizations and London, SFHQ needed to have ready a certain number of trained groups that could be immediately sent out to an organization that was isolated or had lost its leaders. Moreover, since for security reasons it was impossible to give special information about D-Day long in advance, SFHQ believed that the arrival of Allied officers in uniform, with quasi-permanent contact to London, and bringing supplies and precise orders, would have considerable effect on the morale and discipline of the Resistance fighters.

In December 1943, the French, British and Americans, physically fit, speaking French, and volunteering for a risky mission, were assembled in England. The group was a collection of strong men, easy-going and often boisterous, including some former parachute jumpers, adventure-seekers from before the war, and a variety of intellectuals. In contrast to the ease of the American and British volunteers, the French, including a number of career officers haunted by the memory of 1940, seemed sad and austere [16].

Majors Henry B. Coxe of the OSS and Combe-Tennant of the SOE took charge of the future Jeds while a training program was being drawn up by the SOE. It began with a complete psychological interview with three psychiatrists in Peterfield, south of London, followed by rigorous physical training in Scotland. After two weeks, the volunteers were divided into three groups who rotated between the three SOE Special Training Schools: No. 6 at Wokingham in Berkshire, No. 41 at Market Harborough, Leicestershire and No. 45 at Fairford, Glouchestershire.

The radio operators, including sixty-six American NCOs, received intensive training at Henley-on-Thames. And, like their officers, they also went through psychological testing and rigorous physical training, practice shooting and close quarters combat.

At the end of January, all the candidates took a five-day test in the field in a simulated situation, at Horsham in Sussex. Then in Cheshire, where the Americans — used to the six-week training sessions of Fort Benning — were surprised at how short the course was: three days with a daily parachute jump from 500 feet up. Their first balloon jump through a narrow trap door, and the absence of a central

16. *US Army Special Operations in World War II* - CMH, Washington, 1992.

parachute were other surprises!

After February 1944, the trainees were taken to Milton Hall, a magnificent 17th-century property located ten miles from Porterborough in Northamptonshire.

The terrain around the property was perfect for preparing the agents for their missions.

Milton Hall became the main instruction center for the Jedburghs, baptized ME 65, and the SOE had the upper hand there. The commander was Lieutenant Colonel Frank V. Spooner, with Major O.H. Brown as training director. Bill Sykes, a former Shanghai policeman, directed a team of twenty-three instructors, including eight Americans, who took charge of the trainees, organized into three companies.

Operational training started on February 21 and, since the date of the invasion was unknown, the initial formation of the teams was set at six weeks. It included technical training (sabotage, guerilla warfare, weapons, close quarters combat, signals, survival training, airborne operations), tactical training, including guerilla warfare, commandos, forced marches, escape and evasion. The training also included lectures on the organization of the Resistance and French language courses.

The last French volunteers arrived at Milton Hall in March after a recruiting campaign in the Far East organized by SOE/SO. In April 1944 the actual training phase was completed by a three-day exercise, the chosen members of each team, at Horsham.

Even though the teams were originally formed by friendships and affinities within the group of candidates, it was the new commander, Colonel George Richard Musgrave, who, after consulting the chief instructor Major McLallen, made the final decision.

"To form the teams, says General Ausarresses who participated in the Chrysler team dropped over the Ariège, the British colonel used a method that the French army of the time wasn't familiar with. He asked each officer to name the Allied officer with whom he would prefer to be parachuted, either as chief or as adjutant. The teams were thus somewhat like 'mariages', and the designated officers then joined a radio operator in a room to get to know each other better."

Actually training continued right on up to D-Day, except for the teams sent by boat on May 2 to North Africa in preparation for the invasion of the south of France. Thus from May 31 to June 8, several teams participated in the last major exercise, Lash, in Charnwood forest north-east of Leicester. The exercice included mission preparation, contact with the partisans, and attack on targets communicated by radio messages. The exercise was a success, although SFHQ found fault with participants' decision moves by large groups in broad daylight and vague orders given to the resistants.

During these five months of training, changes affecting the Resistance movement significantly modified the intended missions. Initially, the project was presented to the French authorities as simply destroying military targets with the help of resistants, or creating groups for guerilla warfare. The French officer would manage liaison between the resistants and the Allies.

These missions were progressively enlarged and in their final stages, on D-Day, it was intended that these teams operate somewhat along the lines of the interallied military missions. They would be parachuted to FFI leaders to insure regular contact with London, and they were to report on the precise situation in their sector, then help with the arming, organization and training of the maquis. They also directed guerilla operations as requested by FFI headquarters.

While they were waiting for departure, the teams continued to train. When called up, after being put on alert, the Jeds were generally quarantined before going to London where, in a protected spot, they were briefed by the ad hoc section of the SOE on the important aspects surrounding their mission. Then during the days preceding their departure, they were taken to the Eighth Air Force Carpetbagger base in Harrington or the base of the RAF 38 Group at Tempsford. Equipment generally arrived from Area H, checked by SFHQ in Holme.

Of the total of one hundred teams planned in 1943, 94 became

17. Including 94 French, 49 British and 40 American officers, 14 French, 38 British and 36 American radio operators.

operational [17]: thirteen were dropped in June 1944, eighteen in July, seventy-two others followed in August and September.

On arrival in France they contacted the local head of the Resistance, established a liaison with SFHQ in London, and prepared to arm and equip the maquis located in their operating zone. The Jedburghs did not command, but informed, suggested, helped with preparations, took part in sabotage actions against lines of communication and depots and provided liaison with troops advancing toward the maquis zones.

Each team had a unique experience because each region and each maquis was different. German strength and proximity to battle areas also influenced the atmosphere and the operating conditions of the teams in the field.

Teams disregarded the manual. Often left without precise instructions from their superiors, the Jeds had to improvise, but without going overboard on conformity. Once in France, just like the SAS, they ignored SOE-recommended segregation policies; they gave weapons to anyone who was ready to fight, regardless of his political color.

Their only contact with the outside world was the radio station Charles. The operators were versatile in using the technique of call signs and requests or frequency changes. Two contacts per day were authorized, at different times on odd and even days. The frequencies could be changed on demand, but not the time slots or explain, to avoid saturation, of course. Nevertheless a message could be sent outside of the allotted sked, on one of the two emergency frequencies open 24 hours a day. The Charles station, with American and British personnel, thus insured liaisons from 64 Jedburgh teams and 24 mobile stations to the armies deployed north of the Loire during the summer of 1944.

It is true that north of the Loire River teams placed at high-ranking staff headquarters bridged the gap between regular forces and the underground. The creation of Special Forces Detachments requested from September 1943 on by the SO Branch of the OSS, was finally authorized by SHAEF in January 1944. The SF Dets were attached to

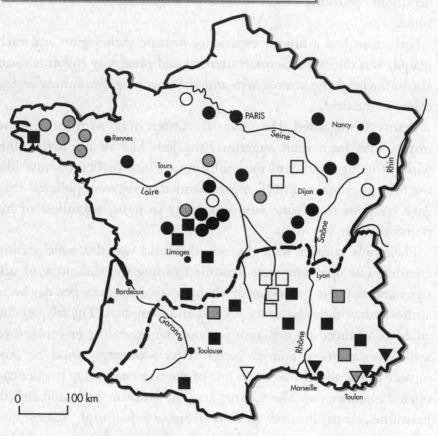

SAS PARTIES AND OPERATIONAL GROUPS IN FRANCE
JUNE-SEPTEMBER 1944

PARIS

Rennes

Nancy

Seine

Tours

Rhin

Loire

Dijon

Saône

Limoges

Lyon

Bordeaux

Garonne

Rhône

Toulouse

Marseille

Toulon

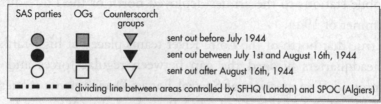

SAS parties	OGs	Counterscorch groups	
● (grey)	■ (grey)	▽ (grey)	sent out before July 1944
● (black)	■ (black)	▼ (black)	sent out between July 1st and August 16th, 1944
○ (white)	□ (white)	▽ (white)	sent out after August 16th, 1944

■ ■ ■ — dividing line between areas controlled by SFHQ (London) and SPOC (Algiers)

0   100 km

army or army group G-3s, and controlled by SFHQ. Their role was to inform SFHQ as to the capabilities — or perhaps the lack thereof — of Resistance movements, transmit information, relay requests for assistance, help recover agents or resistants who had been overtaken by the regular forces and other duties. Occasionally they could transmit details about sabotage or counter-sabotage actions to the underground, thus insuring and facilitating the progression of the Allied forces.

Nine teams, each composed of a dozen officers and twenty subalterns, were created by SFHQ from June to August 1944, including six OSS groups for the American forces: SF Detachment 12 (Yalelock) for the 12th Army Group, SF Det 10 (Yankeedoodle) for the 1st Army, and SF Det 11 (Underfoot) for the 3rd Army. At the top level, Colonel Sir Robin Brook, in charge of the advance echelon of SFHQ, played the same role at advanced headquarters of SHAEF.

These detachments created, at one time, problems with the FFI Headquarters, who made a show of susceptibility to force themselves on their partners. The FFI requested that elements working under its command be known as EM FFI (Etat-Major FFI) Staff Detachments. SHAEF was not opposed to the idea, but considered that this modification would simply create more confusion, so decided that units would continue to operate under their original titles.

In the south of France it was decided to engage two special types of teams, adapted to special local needs. On the Italian border, British Liaison Officers, accompanied by French and Italian officers and with radio contact at their disposal, were designed to help Italian partisans intensify the guerilla fighting in the Alps. The aim of the SOE was to close all the mountain passes to the Germans, while at the same time allowing Allied troops to pass so that they could reinforce the troops coming up through central Italy. In Mediterranean ports — Marseille, Toulon and Sète — marine paratroopers from the so-called Counterscorch Groups, were sent in to oppose destruction of harbor installations and blockading of approach lanes.

The Operational Groups

The territory south of the Loire was the special domain of the Operational Groups, which can be considered the American counterpart of the SAS: they used almost the same arms and similar training and tactics.

But their mission was strictly limited to supporting armed Resistance organizations, and they differed from the SAS by the high proportion of French-speaking soldiers in their ranks, the absence of vehicles, standardized organization and control by SFHQ.

The OG Branch of the OSS was created in May 1943, nine months after receiving approval for the formation of guerilla warfare units, requested by AFHQ [18] for the Western Mediterranean theater.

Without waiting for this decision, a recruiting program had been launched to fill the 540 authorized positions:

- The OSS brochure distributed in various army barracks, said an officer eating his heart out in a Louisiana camp, made you think of what you heard in some radio programs that make chills run down your spine: We are looking for volunteer officers ... Secret and extremely dangerous overseas missions ... Close quarter combat ... Job similar to that of operational commandos ... If interested please fill in the enclosed application form [19].

The candidates, whose profile was similar to that of the Jedburghs, were first chosen among infantrymen and engineers, except for radio operators and medics who were specialized professionals. After an inital screening for physical condition and fluency in French, they were questioned, first as a group and then individually, about their motivations in volunteering for a dangerous mission behind enemy lines. The OGs came from the Army and had already gone through basic training, so the emphasis was put on specialized techniques: destruction, American and foreign light weapons, reconnaissance, first aid, security, survival training, close quarter combat, topography, amphibian and airborne training, etc. Most of the exercises took place

18. Sir Maitland Wilson's Allied Forces Headquarters in Algiers.
19. Roger Hall, You're stepping on my cloak and dagger, translated into French as: *Les paras terribles* - Fayard, 1964.

at night, with parachute drops, mountain climbing and landings by sea.

From the beginning it was decided that OSS-type instruction would not be used for the OGs, since they were to work in uniform, within well organized and disciplined units, and not individually or in small teams.

"A group normally includes four officers and thirty NCOs, Major Van der Stricht explained to Colonel Vernon during the meeting on May 20. It is commanded by a Captain with a Lieutenant as second-in-command. It can be divided into two sections of sixteen men each, including a radio operator, or six squads, each with a radioman. They are well armed [20] and have specific means of liaison with the central station. The OGs can be engaged as a group or as separate squads to destroy of specific targets, or reinforce and train guerilla groups. Once their mission is over, they must remain in the field to help the FFI as long as necessary."

In April 1943, recruiters visited American camps and chose 200 candidates. In June officers were selected and, in August, after some administrative problems involved with getting the men assigned to the OSS, the first group left for Algeria.

In September two officers and thirty men were transported to Corsica to participate in the liberation of the island. They constituted A Company, and remained in Bastia afterwards to participate in operations in Italy. Recruitement of French OGs was then at its height.

After airborne maneuvers in North Carolina, the first group including thirteen officers and 83 NCOs arrived in North Africa where A Company was reassembled in February 1944. Six other groups — two Italian and four French — formed during the winter of 1943, arrived in March 1944, followed four months later by a German OG attached to A Company.

The first group based in England, in spite of the reticence of the

20. Garand rifles, Thompson Tommy guns, M1 carbines, 30 cal. machine-guns, bazookas, explosives, mines, booby traps, etc.

SOE, was made up of Norwegian-Americans, ten officers and 69 NCOs. After going through preliminary training, including mountain climbing, skiing and amphibian operations in Colorado and Massachusetts, the Norwegians went to Inverness, Scotland in January 1944. There they took part in an intensive course of instruction in the SOE and OSS schools: destruction of bridges, railways, electric plants, telephone lines, map reading, Morse code, reconnaissance, close combat, parachuting, assaults by sea, etc.

Two raids in Norway had to be abandoned for lack of sea transportation, refused by the SOE. Then the Norwegians were transferred in May to the command of operational groups linked to SFHQ to operate in France. At that time two French OGs came from Algeria to join them.

On their arrival, to complete the limited specialized instruction they had received in the U.S., the men took a complete course on special techniques — demolitions, radio procedure, foreign weapons — except for airborne training which had already been taught in Algeria at the OSS jump school. Eight OGs were finally available — two French and the two Norwegian groups in Great-Britain, four French groups in North Africa — plus a Polish OG trained by the SOE to be dropped near Lille.

Finally, fourteen sections of fifteen members each, including a radioman and a medic, were parachuted from Algiers into France between June 8th and September 2nd. In close cooperation with the maquis they protected the flanks of the landing forces, disrupted enemy columns, destroyed depots and paralyzed communications routes, while at the same time organizing arms drops and training the resistants.

Between August 1st and September 9th seven sections also left from London to harass the enemy and prevent the destruction of infrastructure that would be needed by advancing Allied armies.

In October 1944 all the teams had been overtaken by the advancing Allied troops, so they made their way home to England, with, for

21. The official OSS account speaks delicately of "British restrictions vis-à-vis Norway".

Chapter IV

Isolating the Normandy Beachhead

When on June 5, 1944, the Allied command gave the signal for the start of Operation Overlord, only seven officers of the special forces — belonging to Mission Citronelle in the Ardennes and Benjoin in the Cantal [1] — were operating in France.

In the London headquarters they truly believed that it would be suicidal to send men speaking French with a heavy Anglo-Saxon accent into territory occupied by the Germans. This belief persisted until it became clear that these highly visible foreigners could count on massive popular support to protect them from danger.

A month later, once the restrictions had disappeared, more than thirty liaison and combat teams were engaged in Brittany, in the Morvan and in the territory south of the Loire River.

According to a map drawn up on July 5, 1944 by SFHQ, four départements were at that time considered to be under the control of Resistance organizations: Ardèche, Drôme, Savoie and Jura. There were five zones in which the Resistance had organized activities: Morbihan, Indre-Vienne, Haute-Loire, Hautes-Pyrénées and the Vosges.

---

1. Mission Union which had been working in the south-east from January on, was taken out of operation in May.

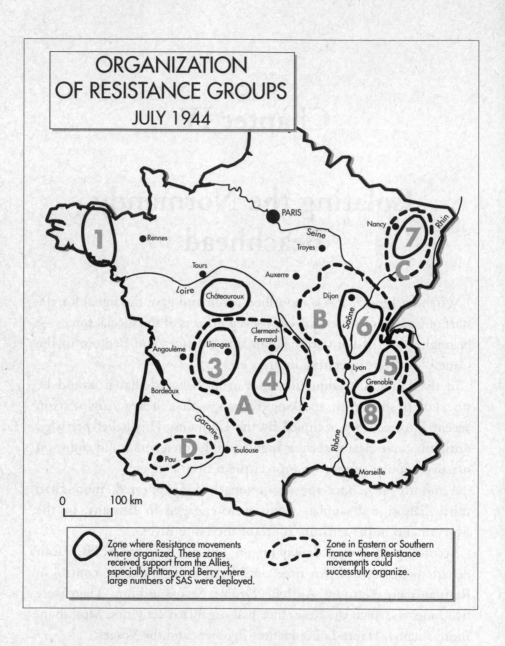

ORGANIZATION OF RESISTANCE GROUPS
JULY 1944

Zone where Resistance movements where organized. These zones received support from the Allies, especially Brittany and Berry where large numbers of SAS were deployed.

Zone in Eastern or Southern France where Resistance movements could successfully organize.

0   100 km

Curiously these regions did not exactly correspond to those — Brittany, Berry and Morvan — receiving Allied support.

Jed Team Harry in the Morvan region

On another map drawn up at the same time, this one by FFI Headquarters in London, the situation was about the same except that the zones were separated into two categories: those where the Resistance was being organized and those where it could be successfully organized. And the Morvan wasn't shown at all!

The Morvan isn't exactly mountainous terrain. It is composed of wide hills, sometimes appearing almost flat. Access is easy and major roads cut through it in all directions. At the BCRA in London it was believed in the spring of 1944, that the maquis established in the region would be playing an important role. When General Koenig received Colonel Viat, chief of the French participation in the interallied mission, in charge of coordinating maquis action, he was categorical:

"The region called Morvan is an area of much strategic importance, because the retreating German troops will have to go through there one day. The zone is particularly well-adapted to guerilla warfare. Consequently it is vital to control the main roads as tightly as possible, since the retreating enemy will have to use them."

Actually the favorable hilly terrain is surrounded by the cities of Dijon, Beaune, Le Creusot, Autun, Château-Chinon and Saulieu. So it was decided to avoid assembling large groups of men with a centralized command, but to encourage independent maquis of 300 to 500 men. The same type of organization was advised further north, to provide cover for the Morvan retreat.

After receiving orders from London in preparation for D-Day, the authorities of Region P and the FFI chiefs of the three départements concerned — Aube, Yonne and Nièvre — withdrew to the Nièvre to organize the Morvan retreat. Thus at the time when the first of the three special forces teams arrived in the region, all the FFI leaders were already on the site.

In London the mission code-named Verveine was waiting impatiently to be sent out into the field. It had been created at the beginning of May and included three officers and a radiowoman, who had tried to study in detail the geographic, political and military documents available at the BCRAL and in the London information services. The Allies sent in an officer with his own radio operator, intended as chief of the British part of the mission, code-named Isaac.

It was however a Jedburgh team which got to the Morvan first. Between June 2nd and 4th, the three officers of Team Harry [2] were briefed about their mission: installation of English bases while maintaining liaison between the Resistance groups and the High Command. At that time the team was introduced to the two advance scouts of the SAS mission Houndsworth, who would be going with them. On the 5th, since no reception committee could be mobilized, the operation was delayed. Then it was finally decided to proceed without a committee.

On that same day, Hastings, the chief of Mission Isaac, and his radioman were being briefed in London by SFHQ. First of all they were to ascertain whether the Morvan mountains were, as hoped by the bureaucrats, conducive to guerilla warfare, evaluate the local maquis and the possibility of increasing the number of fighters with, if necessary, outside assistance to bring in men and equipment.

"Your mission is to advise and train Resistance fighters, said the officer in charge of the briefing. You will transmit to their leaders the orders of the Allied command and coordinate their activity with the SAS. You will also have to check out possible zones for landing aircraft and gliders".

"How big is the maquis in this region?" asked Hastings.

"We really don't know. Here is a list of the Resistance leaders in Regions D and P; some of them are attached to the Section F organization. Jedburgh team Harry and an SAS advance party will go in before you: they should be able to furnish us with contacts and a reception committee."

- And how big a zone is the Morvan?

2. Team No. 46: Captain Duncan D. Guthrie (Denby) from the Duke of Cornwall's Light Infantry, Lieutenant P.E. Rousset alias Dupont (Gapeau) and Sous-Lieutenant Couture alias Legrand (Centime) from the BCRA.

"I've prepared a photo layout for you showing the suggested limits. It covers almost all of the département of the Nièvre, the north of the Saône-et-Loire, the west of the Côte-d'Or and the south of the Yonne."

In the evening of June 6th, the Jeds piled into a two-engine Hudson from Squadron 161 of the Royal Air Force. Along with them, the two SAS officers and a radio liaison patrol from the Phantom unit also climbed in. Just as Jed chief Captain Denby was closing the door, the text of the briefing intended for Isaac was handed to him. But since the pilot wanted to take off right away, he could only give it a glance.

The flight was normal, no flak, even though searchlights swept the sky every now and then. But when they arrived near the drop zone, the plane started turning in circles. Three quarters of an hour went by and the dispatcher finally informed Denby that the pilot couldn't find the DZ and intended to return home.

"Does he at least know where we are? asked Denby."

"Yes. But he can't pinpoint the exact spot."

The Jed chief went to talk to the pilot:

"It doesn't matter because we were supposed to jump blind anyway. If you can drop us within ten miles of the designated DZ, and let us know exactly where we'll be landing, then we're ready to jump."

"OK, answered the pilot. I'll drop you between Rouvray and Saint-Léger-Vauban. Go out slowly. Once on the ground, make the letter G with your flashlight and we'll send down the three baskets."

The jump was indeed very slow, because the SAS were hindered by their knapsacks attached to their legs. Outside the sky was black and it was raining hard. From the ground Denby sent back the signal, and the Hudson came around again.

Even though the stick was scattered over more than a mile and some of the men took a bad jolt, Denby had everyone assembled by dawn, except the Jeds' radio operator. They ate a snack under the trees and released two carrier pigeons for England.

With the first rays of dawn, they began looking for the packages. The one containing personal equipment and 150 first-aid packs was in good condition, but the two others had crashed — their parachutes had roman-candled — and the radio sets were lost. At noon they decided to bury the chutes and the packages and determine where they were, then wait for dusk before starting out.

At nightfall the paratroopers thus left from the neighborhood of the village of Bussières, and took the road south through the Saint-Léger forest towards a rendez-vous with a fellow named Louis, to take place early the following morning, on a bridge over the Cure River. Progress was very slow. The knapsacks were heavy, especially those of the SAS. And the American maps, drawn to a scale of 1/100,000, turned out to be inaccurate. When they were five miles from the bridge, Denby realized that the men were worn out and wouldn't be able to reach it in time. He decided to leave them there and go ahead, empty-handed, with Lieutenant Wellsted of the SAS. They walked as fast as they could and arrived at the bridge on time for the meeting. But no one was there waiting for them.

The afternoon went by. The radio operator Centime joined them and the approved drop zone near Le Vieux-Dun was reconnoitered. During the night, spent in a hut in the woods, the SAS took up positions around the DZ in case a plane appeared.

On the morning of June 9th, they tried again to make contact with Louis. Without any luck and not knowing what else to do, Denby and Wellsted decided to try the impossible: they sent Lieutenant Dupont to Le Vieux-Dun dressed as civilian-looking as possible. The first person he met was a peasant woman:

"I'm a French paratrooper and I'm looking for the maquis."

"Wait for me here, Mon bon Monsieur, answered the woman. I know a man who is about to take a Belgian refugee to the maquis."

The three men first went back to the hut and then the whole group, guided by the young peasant, left for the Chevrière forest maquis where they were warmly received. They were in luck: the regional military delegate Lieutenant-Colonel Lemniscate [3] had installed his headquarters there. After they had made themselves known, Captain Denby requested authorization to use the partisans' radio set to send

3. Jarry alias Lemniscate. DMR of Region P.

a message to London using Jed code. Then the newcomers were invited to sit down to a copious meal."

The Jeds had come across the Camille maquis, also known as the Lormes maquis, considered to be the best in the region.

"The maquis, Denby told the interallied mission five days later, is made up of 120 to 150 men, including a small company of Spaniards. Grandjean, [4] its leader, a former NCO in the French army, has a strong personality and is very popular in the area. He makes a point of honor of paying cash for all the food or tobacco he requisitions and thus gains the respect of the local population. Lemniscate's headquarters on a farm just a few miles away means that he can get money quickly and regularly."

Confidence was so high that soon after the arrival of the Jeds and the SAS Lemniscate decided to move inside the area controlled by the maquis.

"His staff, continued Denby, includes his wife, as well as Pair and Ratissoire of the BOA, plus Commandant Defoe, maquis inspector, whose exact role it is hard for me to understand ... Several girls work as secretaries or in codes. And of course liaison agents stop by from time to time."

The SAS were upset at being cut off from their base. In the Peirouse woods they found a patch of ground that could be used to receive a reconnaissance team. The first try during the night of June 9 to 10 was a failure. Denby came to the DZ too: a plane appeared but it didn't respond to the signals flashed from the ground [5].

Two days later Major Fraser, the SAS party leader, arrived in camp. He and his men had actually been dropped two nights before, but so high up that they were scattered in the trees.

He had waited in vain for his two officers, and had finally decided to set up his operations base in the Peirouse woods: this would be

4. Commander Lonohy (Grandjean) was the départemental maquis chief. The Camille maquis, part of Libération-Nord, was actually led by Captain Bernard (Camille).

5. When he got back to camp he learned that it had been determined that the Belgian refugee was tried a Gestapo spy and shot.

accomplished four days later when the twenty-two parachutists were finally reunited. As for Lieutenant-Colonel Hastings and his radio operator of Mission Isaac [6], they joined up with the Camille maquis on the 14th.

From mission Isaac to mission Verveine

Before leaving London, Hastings had spoken twice with his French counterpart, Colonel Viat alias Dubac (Diagramme), to compare their viewpoints about the best way of carrying out their mission. They found themselves talking the same language. And since an SAS team was about to jump in the area, they joined up with them to facilitate their contacts on arrival.

The drop was scheduled for the night of the 10th to 11th. Hastings met the SAS recce party at the Fairford airstrip. At 21:30, the two four-engine Stirlings from Squadron 132 took off. The silence in the planes was disrupted for a minute over the Normandy beachhead. Then everyone settled down to a snooze until the dispatcher gave the order to get ready, 25 minutes before jumping.

The pilot in Hastings' and Fraser's plane could not really see the ground. The dispatcher, beside the hole, yelled:

"Four minutes to jump!"

Then three, then two, then one minute:

"Go!"

Hastings jumped No. 11, behind the SAS and the Phantom patrol who were carrying in their backpacks two SF sets for the Jeds instead of their personal equipment. At the same time containers were dropped and two baskets with the Isaac radio sets. The men waiting on the ground couldn't see any parachutes pop open and Hastings couldn't make out even a faint flicker of light beneath his feet! This was because his parachute opened in the clouds nearly 1000 meters up. The descent was unending, and a strong wind mades the parachute vibrate and pushed it off its target.

6. Sir J.R.H. Hutchinson alias J.L. Hastings (Télémètre), a Glasgow shipowner who had fought in Gallipoli in 1915, chief of the RF section in 1942 which he left, in October 1943, at age 50, to undertake training as an agent. His radioman was the Canadian Sergeant John Sharp.

When he bumped down, Hastings felt a sharp pain in his hip. He sat down in the grass and whistled softly to try to attract his companions' attention. No one answered. Just a herd of frightened cows galoping every which way. Finally day broke and the stick, minus Major Fraser and an SAS trooper, could assemble. The radio sets couldn't be found. They were probably hanging in a tree somewhere. The best thing to do was to take cover in nearby woods and rest until nightfall.

During the day, they saw, through their binoculars, trucks carrying men dressed in blue — perhaps militiamen — who were scouring the countryside and gathering the scattered containers. So the paratroopers decided to leave the woods at nightfall, cross the road and lose themselves in a deep forest. Gunshots could then be heard in the direction of a village, which proved to be Lormes, at ten miles from the point where the sticks were supposed to have been dropped.

On the morning of the 12th, Hastings made his decision:

"We will meet, he told the SAS chief, at the point fixed with Major Fraser. It's about twelve miles from here. You go one way. I'll go another way with my radioman and an SF set, to try to contact the maquis. If I haven't arrived within a week, rendezvous each day at 02:30 on the rally point."

The two men disappeared into the forest, guided by their compasses and picking wild strawberries to complement the single can of rations that they had had to eat since they jumped. During the night they dared to walk out in the open to go faster.

Early in the morning of the 14th, they were noticed by a miller's wife who, when she learned who they were, invited them into her house, gave them something to eat and a chance to wash up, then informed the local Resistance leader.

Two hours later a car arrived from the nearby maquis and took them to the camp. There Hastings met Fraser and Denby, who handled introductions. He learned that the trucks he had seen that morning belonged to the maquis. During conversations with Lemniscate, Grandjean and Defoe, he received confirmation that Colonel Moreau,

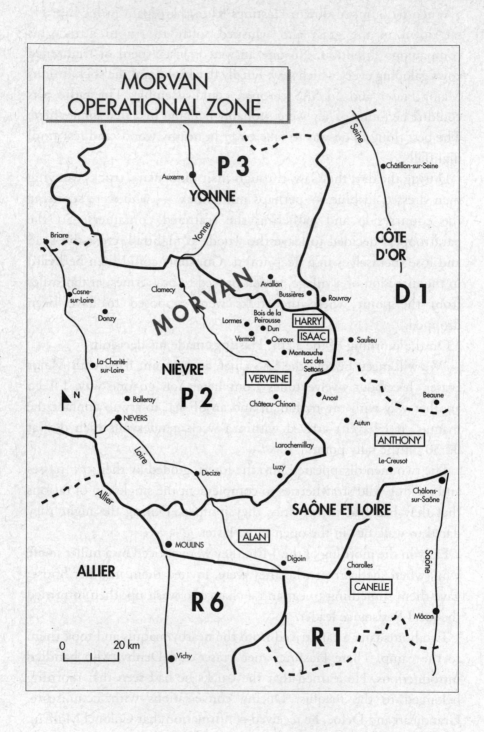

MORVAN
OPERATIONAL ZONE

P 3
YONNE
Auxerre
Seine
Châtillon-sur-Seine

Briare
CÔTE
D'OR
D 1

Cosne-sur-Loire
Clamecy
Avallon
Bussières
Rouvray

MORVAN

Donzy
Lormes
Bois de la
Peirousse
Dun
HARRY

La-Charité-
sur-Loire
Vermot
Ouroux
ISAAC
Saulieu

NIÈVRE
Montsauche
Lac des
Settons

VERVEINE

P 2
Balleray
Château-Chinon
Anost
Beaune

N

NEVERS
Autun

ANTHONY

Loire
Larochemillay
Le-Creusot

Decize
Luzy
Châlons-
sur-Saône

Allier
SAÔNE ET LOIRE

ALAN

MOULINS
Digoin
Charolles
Saône

ALLIER
CANELLE

R 6
Mâcon

R 1

0   20 km
Vichy

FFI chief for the Nièvre [7], was in the Montsauche forest, ten miles to the south.

"The fact that the départemental head and his staff were in a different maquis from that of the DMR, said Hastings, unnecessarily complicated things: all the coming and going were risky business, and the few vehicles that we had were kept busy all the time.

Once Hastings had sent a message to London to report his arrival and ask for replacements for the lost equipment, he organized job-distribution: he himself took charge of relations with the FFI and he gave Captain Denby the mission of assisting the SAS. They were preparing for the arrival of the main body of the detachment. But, because of bad weather, the drop was put off night after night. One of the consequences was food rationing. Denby managed to overcome this problem by organizing a trade off between Camille and Fraser: food for weapons and ammunition.

It rained continuously and when there was no rain it was foggy. The men were soaked and, to make matters worse, one of the SAS who had been hurt on landing, needed an operation on his arm. He was taken to the field hospital recently created by Camille in the Château de Vermot, in spite of Denby's objections. Denby thought that the hospital was too dangerous, located on the edge of the forest and near a road. Since it was the only suitable building available, it had to do, but several teams with Brens were posted around as lookouts just in case.

During the night of the 21st to 22nd, the last paratroopers of the 1st SAS finally landed at Dun or at the Vellottes, with several losing their way or hurt and taken immediately to the hospital.

Meanwhile Hastings informed SFHQ on June 16, that, because so many new maquis groups had sprung, it had become impossible to supply them all, so he had decided to concentrate his efforts on the nine main groups, eventually distributed throughout the Nièvre region and consequently able to serve as nuclei for the other smaller groups.

7. Colonel Roche (Moreau) was the former military chief of Libération-Nord.

In his message he stated that all the maquisards had undergone a baptism by fire. They had vehicles and plenty of food, but needed fuel, compasses, camping supplies, boots and other equipment.

"Morale is high but the quality of the leaders varies, and the level of training is quite low because of the lack of weapons. Jedburghs could be sent to the maquis that need them."

On June 21, Hastings protested the decision of SFHQ not to carry out any operations during the June-July moon period, which was contrary to what had been promised before he left [8]. In the same message he reported the lack of contact with the DMR of Region D and gave the location of main enemy detachments in the Nièvre [9].

That same day Hastings was contacted by Colonel Dupin [10] who presented him with an order signed by the Action Committee in Paris, appointing him to the field command of the six départements: Aube, Yonne, Nièvre, Haute-Marne, Côte-d'Or and Saône-et-Loire. Reporting to SFHQ, Hastings noted that this command was absolutely necessary and that the départements could in no way be directed from London.

The Allied mission chief was far from imagining then what a kettle of fish he had fallen into! For the moment he reached a modus vivendi with Lemniscate, Crespin, Moreau and Dupin, forcing the latter to recognize that orders from the high Allied command took precedence over those from Paris.

"Actually we never had any direct contact with Crespin, Hastings said later. He was supposed to be the sub-regional head [11] but he was never more than a dark shadow in the background."

And London still did not react to the agreement between the Resistance leaders, nor to the request for Jedburgh teams or drops of

8. Hastings thought this decision was absurd, because the SAS continued to receive air support in full view of the members of his own mission.

9. The département was controlled by the *Feldkommandantur* 568 in Nevers, with annexes in Clamecy and Château-Chinon.

10. Colonel Dupin, known in the Cher under the alias Benoît, was arriving from that département. His 'adventures' are related in Chapter 7.

11. Actually he was the FFI chief for Region P.

No. 38 radio sets to keep the different maquis groups in touch with each other. This silence was all the more disturbing because Hastings was an SOE insider.

On June 23, he reported that the region was filling up with German troops and that an attack on the Vermot maquis seemed imminent. The next day the SAS laid a nighttime ambush against a convoy on the Château-Chinon road: four trucks were destroyed and a Russian officer captured. In revenge, the Germans attacked the two Montsauche [12] maquis and burned the village.

Then, on the 26th, it was Vermot's turn. Vermot was defended by the Julien maquis, from Libération-Nord, who had about a dozen Brens.

Around 15:30, the hospital guards sounded the alarm and held the attackers back, thus allowing the patients and medical personnel to be evacuated. But the building was finally occupied by enemy soldiers who set it on fire. As the partisans watched them from the forest, the Germans seemed particularly hesitant and inexperienced, charging in without looking, then taking up positions on the outskirts; they didn't look like they had any real desire to go deeper into the woods.

Denby then asked Major Fraser to counter-attack on their flank. Under a heavy rain, a confusing battle ensued. At midnight the SAS broke camp, while shots could be heard in the dark. Then the 150 men of the Camille maquis, along with the Jeds who had continued to encourage them and lead the attacks, left by the road, with their equipment in ox-carts, towards the north and the Iles-Ménéfrier. Hastings joined them two days later with his sergeant carrying the radio sets.

Early in the morning, the Germans forced their way into the woods and destroyed the equipment left at the campsite. Then they left the zone, burning several villages along the way and shooting about thirty hostages. The operation, organized by the Château-Chinon Kommandantur captain, supposedly involved 400 men of the 654th

12. ORA Bernard maquis and FTP Joseph maquis.

battalion of the Russian Liberation Army, made up half of Germans, half of so-called white Russians [13].

When Hastings asked Lemniscate and Grandjean to come to the Montsauche départemental headquarters, they promised him that they would think about it.

A certain tension was perceptible among the leaders. During the preceding week, Hastings had run into the hostility of the maquis leaders when he insisted that they accept the help of qualified officers:

"How do you expect my men to take orders from a fellow who has just arrived in the maquis?" one of them answered.

Hastings deplored that so few officers had joined the group. He suggested they be used as adjutants, advisors and instructors. Denby however, who sympathized with the partisans, thought the opposite. Therefore when he visited the large Bernard maquis, he regretted that there were so many career and reserve officers joining up for one reason or another and hoping to take over command.

"Even though they recognize their technical inferiority to real officers, Guthrie (Denby) explained, those who have been in the Resistance for several years have a hard time accepting the newcomers!

Lieutenant-Colonel Hastings' departure for Montsauche reignited the tension between Colonels Dupin and Moreau. Moreau, the FFI chief, was unanimously preferred over the départemental staff by the men of the maquis. And to make matters worse, London still gave no sign of life."

Finally on July 3, SFHQ woke up.

"You must deal with Colonel Dupin no further nor consider appointing anyone to a command position over the départemental chiefs!"

Hastings protested, arguing that a common command structure in the Morvan was necessary and inevitable, which had been, by the

---

13. Some even speak of 800 men. They were from the *Ost-Bataillon* 654, transferred into the south of France in October 1943, then assigned to the occupying troops and moved to Châlons-sur-Marne.

way, the aim of Mission Isaac. In the meantime this mission — and it would be Hastings only victory — had been renamed Verveine. He suggested waiting for the arrival of Colonel Diagramme, but insisted that introducing a few competent officers into the military hierarchy could only have a positive effect on scheduled operations.

Two messages came back from London on July 5:

"Don't compete with Lemniscate", said the first.

And Hastings noted:

"That advice is purely theoretical. It shows that London is not conversant with the instructions which they had given me in my mission."

The second message was even more surprising. He was requested to cease all activity until the arrival of Dubac.

Thus precious time, needed to organize and prepare the camp, would be lost.

That didn't keep him from accepting the services of Lieutenant Jean Lebaudy (Lefaure), who arrived in the maquis with Dupin, and to entrust him with the recruitment of twenty men and women to act as liaison officers or agents, with a couple of cars and some bikes at their disposal.

During the nights immediately following the reception of the messages from London, the French participants in Mission Verveine were dropped in the Nièvre and the Ain départements: during the night of 5 to 6 July Lieutenants Lemaître and Michon with their radio operator, Miss Heim [14], were met on a DZ west of Donzy, then Colonel Dubac the following night on a zone near Oyonnax.

Jed Teams Hugh and Hamish in Berrichon country

Further west, beyond the Loire River, in the northern part of Region R.5, two other Special Forces teams were dropped in the Indre just after D-Day.

14. Respectively known as Quartier, Physique and Danubien in messages sent to London.

Jedburgh team Hugh [15], dropped first, was to contact the resistants, prepare for the arrival of the main contingent of the SAS Mission Bulbasket, and reconnoiter the areas where this contingent was to operate. While waiting for the Bulbaskets, it would lend its radio material to the SAS advance echelon, and carry out operations against the Limoges-Châteauroux and Bordeaux-Tours railway traffic.

After the briefing on June 3rd in London, departure was scheduled for the evening of the 5th. The plane took off at 23:00 from Tempsford, the carefully camouflaged airbase west of Cambridge, with the three members of the team and two SAS officers. The flight was exhausting: the paratroopers were cramped in the aircraft and there was flak as they flew over the French coast.

They were dropped around 01:30 in correct order: first the SAS with their leg-bags, Captain Crown, the radioman Sous-Lieutenant Mersiol then Captain Legrand. Their arrival on the edge of the forest north of Saint-Gaultier could have been better: they were blind dropped and the DZ was not the best. A short time elapsed before the reception committee arrived and helped to recover the containers and packages scattered around in the trees over a radius of more than a mile. Then at 10:30 radio contact was made with London.

During the afternoon of the 6th, they made contact with the FFI chief Surcouf, and Samuel of the Buckmaster section [16] arriving from Vienne, who advised setting up camp in a safer place. In the evening, the SAS and the Jeds moved closer to Châteauroux and participated in the reception of a parachute drop for Samuel.

---

15. Team No. 4 - Captain then Major William Crawshay alias Crown (Hugh) of the Royal Welsh Fusiliers, arriving from the Yugoslavia section of the SOE in Cairo; Capitaine then Commandant L'Helgouach alias Louis Legrand (Franck alias Scipion) from the Infanterie ; Sous-Lieutenant R. Meyer alias Mersiol (Yonne) of the BCRA. The unusual presence of two Frenchmen shows the lack of available personnel in the OSS around the middle of June.

16. Surcouf was Commandant Mirguet, from Lorraine, sector chief of the Le Blanc AS, named at the end of May, 1944, after several arrests, as head of the FFI in Indre; Samuel was Commandant Maingard alias Dédé or Philippe from the shipwright circuit of the SOE.

On June 7, Hugh inspected several groups being established in the La Châtre sector. The result of these first contacts was the impression that the region was full of possibilities, but that the lack of cadres and weapons meant that the men were better off dispersed for the moment. He wrote his first report:

"Contact established with head of Resistance Indre area. Already toured 60 mi without sight of enemy. Population enthusiastic. Existing maquis groups have doubled in 48 hours. Reports show enemy may be leaving Châteauroux. Can ensure permanent cut Toulouse railway by maquis. Will require Jed teams soon."

The answer arrived immediately from the base:

"Your number one excellent work. Agree most important task permanent cutting Toulouse railway. Have earmarked Jed team but shall not dispatch until need confirmed by you."

The visits to the various maquis groups continued, then Jeds and SAS approached the Le Blanc AS. Samuel decided to entrust the Indre to the Jedburghs and return to his troops in the Vienne. As for the SAS, they were placed under the protection of a maquis near Lussac, well situated to carry out raids on the Bordeaux-Poitiers line.

On June 9, London asked how job-distribution was being planned with the future team and a possibly unified command. Hugh, in agreement with the chief of the SAS detachment, suggested that his team take charge of organizing and arming the Resistance fighters in the Indre:

"Three thousand in maquis. Morale good but depends on rapidity of invasion. Can one count on eventual arrival of paratroops. Propose organizes area as follows: Hugh remains with départemental chief FFI and organizes reserve striking force. Three Jed teams in three chief sectors. Hugh could thus ensure control over local command and coordination of work in sectors and recce further areas. Can now guarantee permanent cutting of all railway lines. Will work up to efficient ambushes [17]."

17. The Germans considered the situation sufficiently alarming for the staff of the 196th security regiment and the 960th Flak battalion to be sent to Châteauroux to "clean up the region".

Once again the answer came back the same day:

"In reference to paratroops the answer is no except SAS whose plans you can obtain. In reference to proposed organization remember your briefing. Before any question of control by you is raised you must get agreement local FFI chief, also that of Samuel to whom you are accredited, and London headquarters. Cheerio."

And the on-the-air dialogue continued the 12th and 13th:

"From Hugh. No. 13. Surprised at your message number 15. Proposals put forward were results of discussion between Samuel, FFI chief and us. Perfect harmony between Samuel, FFI chief and us. Expect you to show more confidence in us. Bye bye."

"To Hugh. Many thanks for explanations your No. 13. Position now clear and very satisfactory."

The set up period ended on June 11th. The three Jeds had not slept more than six hours since they had arrived.

Two days later Jedburgh team Hamish [18] arrived just at the right time to help them out. The drop took place near Belâbre, on a DZ prepared by Hugh. But the plane gave the green light too low and the contact with the ground was a little rough. The radio operator ended up with a double sprain and would limp until the end of the mission. Since Surcouf was still operating around Le Blanc, Hugh decided to send the new team to the La Châtre-Aigurande sector where elements couldn be armed.

As seen by Anstett, the situation at the middle of June was the following:

"In the enthusiasm created by the opening up of a second front, the members of the Resistance increased by almost 3,000 men, of which only half have weapons. But they are not united because the FFI and the FTP are irreconcilably separated."

According to him this duality was encouraged by certain Section F agents who were arming only the FTP, as in Saint-Benoît or Valençay.

18. Team No. 1 composed of two Americans and a Frenchman: Lieutenant Robert N. Anstett (Bobby or Alabama) from the Coast Artillery Corps, Aspirant then Lieutenant L. Schmitt alias Blachère (Lucien or Lousiana) of the BCRAL and Sergeant I.J. Watters (Lee or Kansas) of the Signal Corps.

In the Le Blanc sector things were better because the DMD supervised the distribution service.

"The AS, he continued, have about 800 men and the FTP about 1,000. The ORA is implanted in Brenne and Châteauroux, and its leader, Colonel Martel (Chomel) alias Commandant Charles [19], has decided it is time to send his men into the maquis."

Jeds and regional and départemental military delegates agreed on one thing: the lack of training and self-confidence of the troops, made worse by the lack of officers. They agreed that guerilla actions would have to be tightly controlled. A German attack could easily compromise all future progress, as happened in the Luant forest with the FTP or near Valençay with the AS.

Hamish left for their sector on June 15th and arrived safely. Even though they didn't find as many trained men as expected they were pleased that there were plenty of recruits and that a system of command was being set up. The different maquis groups practically controlled the zone and it was possible to drive in the open, taking care nevertheless to avoid German patrols sent out after the preceding days' skirmishes. Lieutenant Anstett decided to limit operations to cutting communications and to avoid any showdown that would result in destruction of the armed underground groups.

On June 17, rumors of complaints arrived from the neighboring département of Creuse. Anstett immediately asked to meet the FFI and FTP leaders in Aigurande and an agreement was reached, but, as it turned out, would not be respected. Then, on the request of the Creuse départemental FFI chief, the team left for its headquarters forty miles further south, where they were well received. The Jeds thought they had found the perfect place for a new team until they learned that an Allied mission was already on the way [20].

On the 20th, on their way back to camp, they passed two German armored cars on patrol. Arriving at camp, 10 mi north of Aigurande, they learned that the Germans had searched the area with vehicles

19. Actually Colonel Raymond Chomel, alias Charles Martel.
20. It was the interallied mission Bergamotte which would be parachuted on June 26th to operate in Region R.5.

specially outtlitted with direction-finding equipment, and intercepted a maquis car.

That same day, Croc, [21] Martel, Surcouf and Hugh met in Mézières-en-Brenne to try to settle problems of command. Finally Martel gave up the idea of leading the Indre Resistance groups, and took military command under Surcouf's authority, with the title, Chief of staff and military advisor to the FFI commander. This avoided a showdown. The mobile units of the maquis, organized in battalions and companies, were placed under his direct authority. The sector chiefs continued to command the static elements and each of their own small maquis.

Since the Creuse was considered safer, it was decided that, in case of a massive attack in the Indre, the mobile groups would take refuge in the Creuse in good order.

"Experience will show, reported Hugh, that this idea was false. Thanks to the caution shown by the Indre maquis, the département will not suffer, as do its neighbors, from the actions of German repression columns. Moreover, the enemy was poorly informed as to the true size of our maquis groups and considered them too far away from the vital Bordeaux-Poitiers-Châtellerault route to do any serious harm."

On June 25 and 26, the same men met at Hugh's headquarters with Ellipse, DMR of Region R.5, and Rolland, FTP départemental chief [22]: the decisions reached five days before were confirmed and officers' training was dealt with. The DMR insisted on launching immediate action in hopes of instilling an offensive spirit in the troops. Not all the participants agreed with this approach.

"We did not consider that the time was ripe for this, Hugh later said, a view that was confirmed by London. It will be seen that it took us three weeks to a month to obtain a really firm grip on the situation."

In the sector entrusted to Hamish, Anstett received a visit from the two military delegates on June 21. They all agreed on the future plan

21. Georges Lhéritier, départemental military delegate for the Indre.
22. Respectively "Colonel" Eugène Deschelette and "Colonel" Despains.

of operations and talked about keeping small groups of armed men scattered around the countryside, even though the extension of the maquis seemed to encourage concentrating forces. Two days later the Jed team set up camp near Saint-Sévère-sur-Indre.

The organization finally was beginning to take shape. Companies of 160 men, composed of four self-sufficient platoons including a heavy weapons platoon, were constituted. Certain weapons had to be used in place of others, lacking: Stens in place of Thompsons, Garand rifles in place of M1 carbines, Brens in place of bazookas ... The two officers easily shared duties: the American would stay at headquarters to manage of support, the Frenchman would take charge of training the cadres in the different maquis.

"We insisted, Anstett related, on discipline and security measures. There were a lot of accidents, so we required weapons to be left unloaded except on guard duty and during operations. An Arab soldier, guilty of rape, was judged and sentenced to death. Two traitors within our ranks were also shot, one as a member of the Militia, the other for having given our position away to the Jerries in Guéret."

In La Châtre there was an enemy garrison of 700 soldiers, mostly Austrians. But that didn't bother the Jeds. Enemy patrols or planes regularly came close to the maquis, but they avoided any major actions.

"Our presence, and particularly that of two Americans, was widely known by now. More importantly, the fact that we were there with the specific purpose of working with the FFI, gave our organization all the military respectability it needed."

Air operations remained crucial, both for equiping the rapidly growing maquis and for the credibility of the Jed team vis-à-vis the guerilla fighters. Several DZs had been reconnoitered and accredited but, as time went by, Anstett came to the conclusion that there was no spot in the sector suitable for landing a Dakota: the best he could do was a small field for a Lysander.

The team's day was busy. Starting at 08:00, Schmitt began officers' training for the FFI leaders, while Anstett answered the telegrams and checked the containers received the previous night. At 13:30, the BBC messages announcing parachute drops came on the air. If one of them concerned Hugh, orders were given to the corresponding company and to the motor-vehicle park. In the afternoon, Schmitt went to Aigurande and Anstett inspected the depots. Watters, still limping, took care of coding at the Jeds headquarters, set up in a cottage less than a mile from the regimental headquarters. The day usually ended with an exercise supervised by one of the two officers. Dinner was normally served at 19:30, after listening to the BBC messages.

At the end of this intermediate phase, the Jeds were satisfied with the results. Thanks to the numerous parachute drops, the Resistance movements in the Indre had at their disposal five excellent mobile battalions along with the maquis groups organized in the different sectors.

On July 8, Team Hamish settled near Vijon. The area was up in arms and the Germans didn't take long to react this time. From the eye of the storm, Team Hugh reported to London of the tragedy that took place in the neighboring département:

"Have learnt following bad news. German forces of at least one battalion with armoured cars attacked SAS July 1 in Verrières Forest. Approximate losses SAS 11 killed including one officer, 35 captured as well as two jeeps. We are trying to contact remaining SAS. Following day Boche [23] attacked maquis groups operating in the area but they managed to escape. Some maquis have arrived in Indre. Others probably with Samuel have gone towards Charente. Terribly sorry about SAS but not surprised. They were too close to Poitiers and their jeeps talked about north of Orléans."

South-east of Poitiers on July 3rd, the SAS did in fact suffer a bloody defeat, proof that operations in France were not exactly morning constitutionals, and that members of the Special Forces had to be extremely careful on security regulations, and not let themselves get carried away by the enthusiasm and the irresponsability of the patriots.

At the same time another tragedy was taking place, this time north of the Loire. On June 13, six SAS, the advance party for Operation Gain, were dropped into the gap between the forest of Fontainebleau

23. French slang word for Germans. TN.

and the Loire valley. Five days later they were joined by a group near Pithiviers. The jeeps were dropped and the base was established in the Orléans forest. Then on July 4, a reinforcement team of twelve SAS landed on the DZ, controlled by the Germans. Nine of them were immediately taken prisoner, with only three able to escape.

Still with the idea of isolating the battlefields of Normandy, other SAS members were parachuted into Brittany. This time it was not a question, as for Operation Bulbasket or Gain, of interrupting the enemy's logistics flow, but of preventing the Normandy front from receiving reinforcements. This time, SAS parties and Jed teams jumped right into the enemy forces ranged in battle order.

Frederick, George and the SAS in Brittany

The story of the Bataillon du Ciel is well known. What is less well known is that two Jedburgh teams operated with the SAS at that time.

According to the May 21st SAS brigade operations order, Brittany was defended at that time by six static infantry divisions deployed along the coast. Inland the enemy maintained two parachute divisions and an armored division [24]. Four territorial or security battalions were stationed in Dinan, Vannes and Rennes.

Large inland areas, far from important cities and highways, had no troops whatsoever. Two of these areas, the hills south-west of Guingamp and the Lanvaux moor north of Vannes, were chosen because they were quiet and provided easy contacts with the elements of the Resistance.

For the French paratroopers, the mission was clear: cut off, as much as possible, communications between Brittany and the rest of France. Concerning the Jedburghs, Brigadier McLeod later told the commander of the 4th SAS:

"SHAEF has decided to make maximum use of the Resistance groups in Brittany from now on, and to furnish them with as many weapons and supplies as possible. Creating these groups is the work of the Jedburgh teams under your orders. They have their own equipment

24. The 155th Reserve Panzer Division, stationed in the area around Rennes since the end of 1943, had just left for the Carcassonne region.

communications material to make direct requests for arms and supplies.

Commandant Bourgoin, chief of the 4th SAS, was to take charge of them when they arrived in Fairford on May 30.

"These two teams, pointed out the British liaison officer, are each composed of three men with particular knowledge of the Resistance movements in the zones where your men will be engaged. They are to operate with the SAS reconnaissance teams. In the meantime, while they're in camp, the Jeds will give lectures about the nature and the organization of the French Resistance, and the help that maquis groups and sédentaires can offer [25]."

The first problem arose was the chain of command. When the teams arrived in Fairford, SFHQ had not obtained official agreeement that they be formally and in all things attached to the 4th Battalion chief.

There were also problems with the teams designated by SFHQ. After a short stay in Fairford, they would be replaced by two other teams that had received Bourgoin's blessing [26].

"I'm very sorry, McLeod wrote to Bourgoin at the time, that SFHQ has been stupid enough to send you unacceptable officers ... I think that the latest decisions about the command of the Jedburgh teams and the dates of their employment — the drop has been postponed for three or four days — will solve most of the problems."

SFHQ's point of view, and later that of the FFI Headquarters, appeared however somewhat different: in their documents Samwest and Dingson [27] were still associated with the Jedburgh teams.

After spending two days in the SAS camp to get acquainted with Capitaine Leblond's group, Team Frederick [28] was dropped on June 9th at O3:00 on a DZ that had been prepared on the edge of the

---

25. Residents sympathetic to the resistants' cause. TN.

26. Considering the origin of the three French officers members of the two teams that were finally chosen, it would appear that the military capacities of the first officers was not the problem, but rather their origin or their political ideas.

27. The two SAS bases in Brittany. See below. TN.

28. Team No. 48 - Major A.W. Wise (Kinross), Royal Warwickshire Regiment, Capitaine Bloch alias Paul Aguirec (Vire) of the BCRA and Sergeant Rogert R. Kehoe (Peseta), Signal Corps.

Duault forest, where the Samwest base was to be installed. Along with the Jeds, about forty SAS jumped from two Stirlings. The planes also dropped containers full of weapons that were quickly hidden away in safe places with the help of the neighborhood peasants.

"The first maquis group we met, recalled Major Wise, was named Tito. It was made up mostly of FTPs, very brave but with no discipline whatsoever. Two days after we had arrived the whole region knew where our base was and all the local Resistance chiefs came knocking to ask for weapons."

In the morning of June 12, a skirmish between a maquis group and a German patrol turned into a pitched battle, and soon the Germans called in more troops. Then they retreated with their dead and wounded. But Leblond was afraid they would come back in force, and gave the order to evacuate towards Dingson base, near Malestroit.

The Jeds first headed for Trémargat with Squadron Leader Smith, liaison officer for the SAS brigade. Then on June 14, thanks to information from the resistants, they were able to find and look after Lieutenant Botella who had escaped from Samwest. He gave them precious information about the SAS remaining in the sector. Arrangements would be made for these twenty men, including two officers and seven NCOs, to be sent into the maquis to be used as instructors.

During the first week of their stay at Peumerit de Quintin, where their command post was set up under a large tree, the Jeds tried to contact all the local chiefs to see about the possibility of uniting the different political tendancies of the Resistance. Each day they traveled 15 or 20 miles in German-controlled territory to establish contact and plead the cause of uniting all the groups under the single organization of the FFI.

"We were fully agreed, said Wise, to provide weapons to those men who had been fighting for months unarmed. Our initial reception was cordial and the men and their leaders gained confidence. Under these circumstances, Marceau, the FTP head, was designated leader of the FFI for the département Côtes-du-Nord. For us this was a major success."

From then on, Marceau and a command squad remained with the Jeds, who took charge of operations. A BRAL agent, in charge of intelligence, completed the départemental staff. Seventeen sectors were created. Their boundaries were defined in relation to the German forces: it would thus be easier to follow their movements and act accordingly. Orders were transmitted by a team of five girls who lived at the headquarters.

After three weeks of hard work, the Jeds were rewarded by seeing their organization take shape. Sabotage activities were also carried out — the Brest-Berlin telegraph cable, telephone lines, the railroad — and they were able to avoid any direct skirmishes with the Germans.

When Capitaine Leblond passed through the region on his way to England where he had been sent by Commandant Bourgoin to explain the situation in Brittany, he was able to note that the efforts of Frederick to unify the resistants were beginning to produce results. Nevertheless the ORA complained about having been asked to take sides for the FTP, and not having received enough arms.

During the new moon, the maquis received regular drops of equipment. Then on July 8, the Jeds and the départemental headquarters left for Canihuel.

Team George was parachuted during the night from 8 to 9 June, for Commandant Bourgoin. But Dingson base was attacked by the Germans on June 18, just as Leblond was arriving from Samwest. After fierce fighting, both sides scattered to wait for better days and the SAS lost all contact with the Jed team. The Jeds were relocated at the end of June in the Loire-Inférieure, working hand-in-hand with the local DMD to try to smooth over differences between the various Resistance groups.

For the SAS and the Special Forces, the phase concerned with isolating the battlefield in Normandy thus came to an end one month after the beginning of the invasion. For the Jedburghs it had been mostly a period of getting familiarized with their surroundings and building up steam while waiting for the break-through by Allied conventional forces, and its follow-up.

29. Team No. 47 - Captain then Major Paul Cyr (Wigton) from the American infantry, Capitaine Ragueneau alias P Erard (Save) from the 1re DFL and Sous-Lieutenant Gay alias C Le Jeune (Rupee) from the BCRA.

Chapter V

Chouan warfare in Brittany

On July 25, 1944, after fifty-five days of heavy fighting in the Normandy bocage [1], the U.S. First Army launched an assault against the German defenses in the sector of Saint-Lô.

Three days later, the tanks leapfrogged past the infantry and broke through into open country. They switched into high gear and rolled towards the south.

After they reached Avranches on August 1st, General Patton's Third Army exploited the breach in the German defenses. He was operating on the right flank of the Allied forces with four corps and the French Forces of the Interior under his command. His job was to isolate Brittany and secure its strategic ports.

Taking advantage of the help of the FFI, supported by the SAS and the Special Forces, VIII Corps headed west on a forced march, and assaulted Brest, Lorient and Saint-Nazaire.

To the east, the pursuit was hot: Angers was liberated on August 10, Chartres and Orléans on the 17th. The pocket around Falaise was closed off on the 20th.

The race was now on against the German columns who were trying to retreat from the jaws of the Allied trap as quickly as possible to

---

1. TN. Landscape of small fields separated by lanes and surrounded by hedges.

within the borders of the Reich. They were chased by Allied tanks and aviation, and harassed by the partisans who were suddenly appearing everywhere.

On August 25 when French and American troops entered Paris, the advanced guard of the Allied tanks was already in Troyes.

Giles and Felix in the Finistere and the Côtes-du-Nord

On July 4, Colonel Eon of the BCRAL was summoned to the French Forces of the Interior headquarters in London:

"I have decided, announced General Koenig, to put you in command of the FFI in the five départements of Brittany."

Eon then received from Colonel Vernon the plan for structuring the Breton FFIs:

"This plan, noted Vernon, includes sending in nine extra Jedburgh teams, so as to complete equiping the drop zones as soon as possible. Then it provides for a program of arms drops to bring the number of armed fighters in Brittany up to 30,000 by the beginning of the month of August."

A command structure of about twenty officers will also be established.

Next the designated French and Allied officers met at the FFI headquarters.

"I prefer to personally select the teams sent to each department from among those available at the Jedburgh training center," requested Eon.

As soon as the suggestion was accepted, a list of the teams was drawn up.

"I would also like, he continued, to be authorized to brief these teams personally about the tactical aspects of the mission."

This was carried out between July 8 and 10. Taking as an example the Chouan fighter, he insisted upon the choice of targets, the need for absolute secrecy and the danger of building up large forces at a single base in an area that enemy motorized elements could easily penetrate.

Team Felix [2] , put on alert at Milton Hall on July 7, was briefed in London the following afternoon:

"Your mission, said Major Horton, is to organize and arm the Resistance lighters in the eastern part of the Côtes-du-Nord. After you land, your first job is to look for airstrips and beaches suitable for sea landings along the coast. You will also need to establish contact with Frederick and the Grog base, where Commandant Bourgoin can be found."

Actually the briefing was quite superficial and the only available document was a Michelin road map. They had no information about the Resistance forces that they were to meet, and in particular knew nothing about their different political ideas.

"Moreover, related Felix, our target area was revealed to us by the navigator just five minutes before take-off."

The team was dropped on July 9 at 00:45, two miles north-east of Jugon. The reception committee was well organized by Frederick, but their only DZ option, imposed on them, was poorly situated between two main roads. Worse, the dispatcher asked for only one run and sent everything out in a single stick, in order: the twelve containers, the French officer, the radioman, the British officer, two bicycles and five boxes. The Jeds thus wasted two hours looking for their radio set.

On the ground they were met by François, FFI départemental chief, and the two leaders, civilian and military, of the sector. The resistants, surprised by the Jeds arrival, were amazed and enthusiastic. While they were gathering up the containers and piling them into ox-carts, their chiefs led the paratroopers to a neighboring house.

Nearby they also found Squadron Leader P.H. Smith, liaison officer with the SAS brigade assigned to Mission Wash. He had left to take part in the parachute reception with the Jugon Resistance leader, but had gotten lost in the woods and wandered around for four hours before running across the carts full of containers.

2. Team No. 89 - Capitaine Souquet alias Kernevel (Carnavon) of the Colonial Infantry, Captain John Marchant (Somerset) of the Wiltshire Regiment, Serjeant P.M. Colvin (Middlesex) from the Sherwood Foresters, who were to operate in the north-east of the Côtes-du-Nord from July 9 to August 23, 1944.

The next morning a meeting was organized. Also taking part would be a delegate from regional headquarters and Team Frederick.

"After we informed the resistants about the aims of our mission, recalled Felix, they drew us a picture of the situation in their region. We learned that the FFI weren't organized yet and that the different groups — FN, FTP, Libération, AS, ORAF (sic) — each had their own structure and couldn't agree on much of anything."

Consequently, Felix decided to meet with the leaders of the different organizations.

"The leaders who participated in the meeting supported us totally, Felix went on. They were all either from the FN or the FTP. They agreed to forget about political questions and just concentrate on military aspects."

When Bourgoin was mentioned, no one had even heard of him.

" The only known SAS team member was a certain Lieutenant Fouquet [3] . We were never able to meet him, but his actions, especially around Lamballe, constantly annoyed us."

The Jeds blamed the SAS for having ordered the Resistance fighters to move out into the maquis too early. They then started carrying out sabotage actions which produced nothing other than attracting the Feldgendarmerie and the Gestapo. This resulted in the maquis being forced to move on before it was even set up.

Felix' first round of visits, from July 10 to 15, gave him a good idea of the situation in the region concerning available strength, weapons, morale, problems to be overcome before the different groups could be united, potential air drops and what military actions to prepare.

They went around in uniform in broad daylight, which had a considerable positive effect on the morale of the population and the resistants. The Jeds spent the night at farms and were never at a loss for food and lodging. But they were cautious, never staying more than two days in the same place:

"We carried nothing but the radio set and what was strictly necessary, but that was darn heavy. The rest of the equipment was

---

3. Actually, Sous-Lieutenant Fauquet, part of Mission Wash.

hidden in Jugon. In each new sector we went through, we were accompanied by the chief of that sector. A guide with perfect knowledge of the region helped us cross major highways and find our way around villages."

The day before Felix arrived, Team Frederick left Peumérit for Canihuel. After three weeks of work, the maquis were beginning to take shape, and the team took advantage of this to deal with sabotaging enemy telephone lines.

On the morning of July 12, while the radio operator was sending messages through to London, a warning came in about Germans and Russians sweeping the woods. The Jeds were used to this kind of alert and didn't pay much attention, other than posting a lookout. A few minutes later shots broke out and riders straddling small horses appeared [4]. By miracle the five men of the command post were able to escape carrying with them the quartz crystals and the code. Howerver all the gear and the radio set were lost.

During the three weeks that followed, Frederick had to entrust its messages to Felix, Giles or the SAS. Enemy pressure was such that the team had to move around constantly, first toward Plésidy, then Kerien on July 28.

Team Giles [5], the counterpart of Felix in the Finistère, was put on alert and briefed by Major Horton starting on June 16.

"It is very important, General Koenig reminded them during his visit, for you to send us information about the FFI in the département, because we know very little about them."

Just before leaving, Capitaine Lebel, the Frenchman on the team, got a message from London asking his advice about the choice of a BBC code sentence that would give the signal for widespread guerilla warfare.

He suggested Napoleon's hat still in Perros-Guirrec and his suggestion was adopted.

4. Probably from the Ost-Reiter-Abteilung 281, actually made up of Ukrainians.
5. Team No. 3 - Capitaine Grall alias Paul Lebel (Loire) from the BCRA, Captain Bernard M.W. Knox (Kentucky) from the American infantry, Serjeant Gordon H. Tack (Tickle) from the Royal Armoured Corps.

After a false alarm on July 4, the team left from Harrington [6] at 23:00 on the 8th. Two hours later, the pilot announced lights in view and the Joe-hole was opened. Then the B-24 circled for twenty minutes. This didn't particularly bother the paratroopers who had decided to jump blind anyway.

The Jeds finally jumped in a single run. As soon as they hit the ground they were surrounded by a group of very excited young people.

"A lot of FFI leaders have been arrested, the reception committee chief announced, including Commandant Poussin [7] who was supposed to be your contact. So I'm sending you to a maquis in Châteauneuf-du-Faou where there's a very organized leader."

While the committee collected parcels and containers, the paratroopers got ready to march, grumbling about the weight of their knapsacks, weapons and radio set. Around 04:00 the convoy started out for Châteauneuf with nozzles of German guns sticking out of all the open windows.

"Even though we were travelling on side roads, Knox recalled, we were pretty nervous because that truck made as much clatter as a Sherman tank!"

When they arrived at Briec, the convoy stopped in the center of town for a quarter of an hour to wait for a straggler. By now, the sun was up so the trip continued on in broad daylight.

The maquis was installed in a small wood west of Laz. It was made up of about fifty men, commanded by a regular NCO in the absence of his superior who had left for the Côtes-du-Nord to get weapons. Lebel and Knox lost no time in setting up a command post and training the partisans in the use of the new weapons they were bringing with them.

In the afternoon the BBC broadcasted the message, 'The moon shines over the dolmen', announcing a parachute drop for the following night.

6. Base of the 801st Bombardment Group (Heavy) (Provisional) from March 28, 1944 on.
7. Mathieu Donnard, alias Poussin, départemental FFI chief since June.

"We were rather worried, Knox related, at the prospect of going back to the same DZ, but decided to risk it."

This time there were even more supplies than before, and the men were so tired that, when day broke there were still some containers left to be picked up. Nevertheless the return trip to camp went smoothly.

During the morning they learned that German paratroopers had entered in Laz five minutes after the last Resistance vehicles had left. They had searched all the surrounding farms without any luck. This information was immediately sent to London by carrier pigeon to avoid betraying their position by using the radio.

On July 11, the maquis leader arrived back and introduced himself as the FTP military deputy for the center of the département [8]. The Jeds told him of their mission and the need for available DZs and reception committees all over the département. Two sites were reconnoitered for the teams intended for Brest and Morlaix.

Judging that they had established sufficient contacts, Lebel and Knox decided to remain at Châteauneuf. Then they learned that the teams designated for the south of the département had just arrived.

Gilbert and Francis in South Finistère

Four teams had been briefed on July 8th and 9th, and their respective zones of activity in the Finistere agreed on: Francis in the south-east, Gilbert in the south-west, Hilary in the north-west, Horace in the north-east. But Giles, who had left earlier, hadn't been informed about these decisions.

As for Francis and Gilbert [9] , even before the briefing was over, they received orders to report to Harrington immediately ... Fortunately

8. He was actually Capitaine Yves Legall alias Lagardère, commander of the FTP Compagnie Cartouche, then the Normandie Battalion established in central Finistère.
9. Team No. 45 - Major C. Ogden-Smith (Dorset) of the Royal Artillery, Capitaine Guy Le Borgne alias Le Zachmeur (Durance), Colonial Infantry, Sergeant A.J. Dallow (Groat), Royal Armoured Corps ; Team No. 76 - Captain Christopher G.W. Blathwayt (Surrey) of the 60th Rifles, Capitaine Paul Carron de la Carrière alias Charron (Ardèche) of the Infanterie, Sergeant N. Wood (Doubloon) of the Royal Armoured Corps.

their welcome at the Carpetbaggers' base was warm and efficient, and they took off as scheduled at 23:00.

Two hours later, Team Gilbert arrived over the DZ, indicated during the briefing as being situated south-west of Coray. The plane was flying too fast and too low, so that the packages — except the container with the Eureka set — broke open as they hit the ground: the radio set was in poor shape and the rifles were broken.

The DZ, which was later revealed to be the Guide zone near Coadry, was swarming with more than 200 men, led by SAS. They were at ease and sure of themselves, talked, smoked, horsed around with the lights ...

While they were picking up the parcels, two German trucks went by on a nearby road and stopped at an intersection not 500 meters away. But the occupants seemed not to have heard or seen anything out of the ordinary.

As soon as the Jeds alit, they called a meeting of all the officers present on the site:

"Let's make it clear, explained the Jeds. No attacks must be launched without direct orders from London !"

So, in spite of the fact that the Resistance fighters outnumbered the Germans at the crossroads, they left them alone [10].

Then the team melted away into the night, along with the partisans carrying their baggage. After marching several miles, the group stopped in a ditch to rest. They had the impression that, all along the way, German patrols seemed to be posted at every road junction, setting off green flares at regular intervals. In the morning a guide led the Jeds to a farm where, all day long, local leaders came to meet them. Each one was informed of General Koenig's orders and the importance of not creating large units groups.

A coded message asking for a new radio set and rifles was sent to Team Giles so they could relay it to London. For security, a copy was entrusted to Team Francis. The telegram was written on July 10th: it was relayed by Giles on the 11th and by Francis on the 12th. The

10. The team would later learn that the Germans knew of the site and the BBC sentence because to documents found on Commandant Poussin.

grapevine worked so well that SFHQ, realizing that the teams were all three based in the same area, sent back an urgent message ordering them to disperse.

Gilbert realized that Quimper was at the heart of the Resistance organization, and decided to settle south-west of that city, in a château belonging to Monsieur Joncours, a contractor who spoke perfect German and passed himself off as a collaborator.

The property was full of nooks and crannies, with trails to retreat safely beyond the Odet River towards Gouesnach if necessary. More importantly, the place was teeming with people so comings and goings wouldn't attract attention.

On July 10, the Resistance fighters furnished the Jeds with a car and three suits of civilian clothes so that they could cross Quimper in broad daylight. Much to Charron's bewilderment, the British categorically refused to do. But an hour later, when they learned that the car had been stopped at a German checkpoint, they all congratulated each other on being so cautious.

After a night spent in a ditch protected by twenty FFI personnel, the Jeds — now rested after 36 sleepless hours — climbed into a personnel truck full of bags of coal, sent to them by the contractor, and managed to get safely to the château.

That was where Colonel Berthaud [11], the new départemental chief, contacted them. Relations of mutual trust were established right away. The choice of the château turned out to be a sound one, since liaisons were perfect both with the resistants and with the two other teams: even when they were in the field they could be reached through the police network.

Team Francis jumped an hour after Gilbert. Because of a mistake in determining the drift, the three paratroopers landed in a wooded area and Major Ogden-Smith got lost looking for the reception committee. Finally, after contacting the chief of the Quimperlé sector who had organized the committee, Capitaine Le Zachmeur decided to set up camp in a cave three miles from the city. Then, during the afternoon

11. Lieutenant-colonel Roger Bourrières, alias Berthaud or Lemarchand.

they tried to get a message through to London and orders were given to locate Ogden-Smith.

On July 11, Francis finally established a liaison with London and two arms depots were created for the sédentaires. To fulfill their assigned missions — inspecting the inland maquis, preparing to arm the coastal groups, briefing the leaders and training troops — a mobile unit was created with the Jeds, plus André de Neuville, the owner of the cave that had been transformed into command post, an FFI radio operator and a SAS who had become separated from his unit.

On the 14th, the partisans finally found Ogden-Smith: he had been hiding from German patrols. He almost hadn't made it:

"During the briefing in England, Le Zachmeur said later, we had agreed that, if we got separated, we would meet in Saint-Fiacre, near Le Faouët. But once on the ground, we realized that Le Faouët was swarming with Germans. We couldn't have chosen a worse place for a rendez-vous!"

The situation in the back country was indeed considered serious enough for the Germans to beef up the XXV. AK by assigning them three security battalions. One of these, the 1221st [12], assigned to Quimperlé to fight the Resistance fighters had installed its headquarters in Le Faouët.

Francis met Giles on July 16 near Châteauneuf. Sensing danger, the mission was then camping on a plateau above Saint-Thois.

The mission began well: they had established contact with the different maquis, reception committees had been formed and the local chiefs were able to insure pick up of drops on the eight approved sites, each with the code name of a different kind of fruit.

However, on July 12, during a visit from Berthaud, an incident occurred: a Gestapo agent was noticed in his car and immediately executed. The next day, the mayor of Laz came in person to warn of the arrival of large German forces. As soon as night fell, the Jeds broke

12. According to XXV. AK official journals, the 1221st was made up of Russians. According to Tessin, *Verbände und Truppen der deutschen Wehrmacht und Waffen-SS*, it was the *Sicherungs-Btl.*(O) 1221, made up of soldiers with hearing problems (O = *Ohrenkranken*).

camp and reached Kernour in staggered intervals. Along the way they lost the radio receiver — it would be found the next day — and transmitted their message of arrival on the air, with no way of receiving a reply.

In Kernour, Giles received a visit from two FTP départemental chiefs, one of whom was hardly more than 24 years old.

"They naturally wanted to use their weapons right away, Captain Knox recalled, but, after hours of persuasion, they finally declared solemnly that they were in agreement with the plans of the Supreme Allied Command !"

After meeting Team Giles in Châteauneuf-du-Faou, Major Ogden-Smith and the rest of Team Francis travelled by night to Guiscriff. They had just arrived when pulled up in German trucks in front of the house where they had been taken in. On the run again, they had to find their way back to Châteauneuf in the dark.

On the 18th, the maquis camp in Saint-Thois was discovered abandoned during the night, with the exception of a rear guard detachment left behind to keep track of the Germans. The following day was spent on the lookout in the woods and meeting with Giles who informed them that more Jeds were on their way.

Two evenings before, the BBC had aired the pre-arranged messages announcing the arrival of nine parachutists on the Pénity site. Given the time and the distance, it was decided that Capitaine Lebel would drive to the DZ by car. When he arrived he found three new training officers for the maquis and six more Jeds.

These two new Jedburgh teams had been called up on July 2nd to operate in the Ile-et-Vilaine region. But, the day before they left London, their area of operations was suddenly changed: once they made contact with Giles south of Huelgoat, they were to head immediately for their new zones in north Finistère and organize the Resistance groups that they found there.

Hilary and Horace between Brest and Morlaix

A drop scheduled for July 9th, was postponed several times because of bad weather and a series of unforeseen problems. Finally

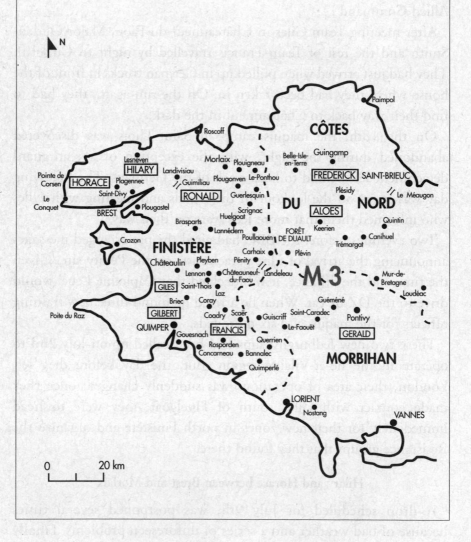

AREA OF OPERATIONS
IN THE FINISTERE,
COTES-DU-NORD AND MORBIHAN

N

CÔTES

Paimpol

Roscoff

Belle-Isle-
en-Terre   Guingamp

Morlaix   Plouigneau
Lesneven   FREDERICK   SAINT-BRIEUC
HILARY   Landivisiau   Plougonven   Le-Ponthou
Pointe de   Plésidy
Corsen   Plagennec   Guimiliau   DU   ALOES   NORD   Le Méaugon
HORACE   RONALD   Guerlesquin   Keerien
Saint-Divy   Scrignac   Quintin
Le   Huelgoat
Conquet   Plougastel   Brasparts   FORÊT   Canihuel
BREST   Lannédern   Poullaouen   DE DUAULT   Trémargat
Crozon   Carhaix   Plévin
FINISTÈRE   Pleyben   Pénity   M 3
Châteaulin   Châteauneuf-   Mur-de-
Lennon   du-Faou   Landeleau   Bretagne
GILES   Saint-Thois   Laz   Loudéac
Briec   Coray   Guéméné
GILBERT   Coadry   Scaër   Guiscriff   Saint-Caradec   Pontivy
Poite du Raz   QUIMPER   Gouesnach   Le-Faouët   GERALD
FRANCIS   Querrien
Rosporden   MORBIHAN
Concarneau   Bannalec
Quimperlé

LORIENT
Nostang   VANNES

0   20 km

on the 17th, the six team members climbed into a Canadian Halifax crew. Their personal equipment was fixed onto the sides of the packages. They had neither S-Phone nor Eureka. The Americans were wearing the regulation Parachute Jump Suit, even though they would have preferred the new green combat suit M-43, darker and more practical. Major Summers and Sergeant Zielske had exchanged their carbine for M-1 Garand rifles.

The flight over water was disturbed not by enemy flak but by lightning striking the tail of the aircraft. The drop was successful in spite of the fact that the Pénity DZ was not intended for jumpers: Major Summers and seven other parachutists landed safely. Only Capitaine Marchant landed in a tree, fell on his head and was unconcious for twenty minutes. However the packages were scattered and one team wasn't be able to find its radio and two bags until the 19th: Lieutenand Chadbourne's rucksack disappeared along with the three rifles.

The problem now was to get to the action zones. For this, Lebel intended to come back to Pénity the next day with a convoy of vehicles. He would drive the Jeds to Lannédern, to the closest known maquis in the Brest sector.

Team Hilary, [13] after assembling its equipment and establishing a liaison with London, took off immediately for Plougonven.

"A doctor from Poullaouen, said Lieutenant Chadbourne, drove us in his car, just a metal frame without any doors or windows. We had to stop twice because the car was on the verge of breaking down, then cross the Morlaix to Carhaix road ... Fortunately we didn't meet anyone and finally arrived at a farm occupied by sédentaires belonging to the Libération movement."

After four days contacts were made and information about the location of glider landing grounds and dropping zones [14] sent to

13. Team No. 6 - Capitaine Edgar Mautaint alias Marchant (Charente) from the Infanterie, Lieutenant Philip E. Chadbourne (Nevada) of the Infantry, Lieutenant R. Hervouet alias Pariselle (Kopek) from the BCRA.

14. Were they thinking at that time about an airborne operation on Brest?

London. It became more and more evident that the farm was not safe. The news of Hilary's presence had spread like wildfire, and it seemed almost certain that the Germans had been notified. So, after a long nighttime detour towards the east to avoid Scrignac, the team, and their two guides, moved out to an FTP maquis south of Guerlesquin. Along the way the group came across many enemy patrols but was not spotted. This was surprising since the guides hadn't stopped talking all night long. Day was breaking when the journey finally ended at the maquis, to which a reception committee had just returned.

Four days later a group of twenty partisans arrived at the camp with the Germans on their heels. The enemy troops — almost 300 men — attacked from the south and forced the Jeds to move out towards the north-west. As they were progressing along a canyon, they heard gunfire in the woods. They were sure that they were surrounded so the American and the two Frenchmen decided to turn back and strike out towards the east, to try to break out of the trap. But nothing happened, and after walking all night in the pouring rain, they arrived in a maquis just being formed, well hidden in the woods north of Ponthou.

In his report, Lieutenant Chadbourne gave his impressions of the two major movements in the region — Libération and FTP — after a few days in the field:

"The general picture in Finistère, to say the least, was confused upon our arrival. The exact number of maquis, their location, and their strength was not known. The FTP Resistance Groups were the best organized, if one can apply the word 'organize' here. The Resistance fighters belonging to Libération preferred to remain sédentaires and hide their weapons."

He noted that this attitude, along with differing political views — the FTPs were Communists or Socialists while the others weren't interested in politics — made for quarrels between the two groups that sometimes broke out into violence.

The FTPs were often very young, inexperienced, while the second group were older and more cautious, often former military men.

148

Once they were organized and armed, the latter group were easier to control.

"The extent of training everywhere was deplorable. Men carried pistols and Sten guns, armed and cocked, in their belts, grenades were lossed about carelessly, and so forth. All had an intense hatred for the Germans. Their loyalty and faith could not be doubted for a moment. We were received everywhere as heroes: the uniform we wore had a great effect on their morale."

Capitaine Marchant added:

"The FTP complained that the FFI had secret arms dumps, and the FFI accused the FTP of having, by their actions, alerted the Germans and put all the maquis in the region in danger. Political and personal rivalries were in part responsible for this lack of unity: before our arrival no leader had been able to obtain any kind of agreement between the two parties. Our first job was to unite them.

Consequently, orders were given to the FFI:

"Set up groups of 30 to 40 fighters who can be joined, when the time comes, by the armed sédentaires. Show the FTP that they aren't the only Resistance fighters and that you all have to get along together."

Finally the leaders of the most important groups, gathered together by Hilary for a conference, recognized the need for an agreement. Callac, of the FTP north-east Morlaix battalion, Robert from the FTP north Plouigneau maquis, Noël from Libération, Gil, assistant to Doctor Lejanne, head of the Morlaix clinic, and Georgelin, director of navy conscription and FFI commander, accepted Hilary's authority.

The other important task was the organization of a medical service prepared for the fighting to come. Mobile teams ready to join the maquis were thus created among the medical personnel of the region. First aid stations were also prepared in Landivisiau and Plouigneau, and the surgical facilities at the Guerenvan sanatorium were made available by Doctor Thomson.

All this work of organizing and supporting the maquis was made all the more difficult by the Germans, who patrolled night and day, and also by London, who extended the action zone from Landivisiau to

Belle-Isle-en-Terre, and refused to answer requests for parachute drops.

Hilary was pressured by the enemy and thus had to move again and settle on the coast, six kilometers north-east of Plouigneau, where four maquis were operating: two FFIs and two FTPs. But all the good intentions of union and mutual assistance were frayed by the lack of arms. And yet requests had been made and dropping sites indicated.

An unfortunate incident then occurred concerning an urgent request for a parachute drop on a DZ code-named Dakar. London's answer came back: Drop refused because of enemy flak. The request was renewed, insisting on the fact that the German anti-aircraft battery had left a month ago: no answer! Hilary, desperate, suggested other sites, but the team would never know whether they were accepted or not.

Elsewhere Team Horace was still waiting to be picked up by Giles. A girl, sent to ask Captain Knox to organize transportation to the Brest region, came back in the evening of July 18 without having been able to deliver her message and Giles didn't show up.

The team gave up waiting and tried to find another contact and get the advice of people who knew the area: they all confirmed how difficult it was to get to Brest and to operate there. Moreover the whole population now knew that paratroopers had arrived and, of course, the Germans had posted a 1,000,000 Francs reward for information leading to their capture dead or alive.

Around midnight Knox finally arrived by car and told what had happened:

"Last night, as I was coming to meet you, the militiaman that we were interrogating escaped. So we had to break camp immediately, cross the Aulne Canal and settle in a valley near Lennon."

As arranged, Knox led Team Horace further north, to a maquis which, it turned out, had also moved out under enemy pressure. There was nothing to do but to go to Giles' HQ, where people who had had to leave Brest confirmed the discouraging news:

"Since the Allied invasion, the Gestapo and the Militiamen have destroyed every maquis created in the sector. It would be foolish to operate in the region, especially in uniform."

Most of them advised trying to carry out the mission while

remaining outside the zone. This was, of course, impossible.

Summers and Levalois then decided to go to Brest anyway and they scheduled a meeting with the maquis leader for the evening of the 21st.

Along the way, the team, and Lebel with them, happened across a patrol of German paratroopers on the road from Châteaulin to Châteauneuf, and had to turn back. It was the maquis leader who, managing to evade the enemy checkpoints, picked up the Jeds in his car. The night was so dark that he was even driving with his headlights on.

Three days went by ... In the meantime and without Horace's knowledge, Giles had notified Berthaud, who had asked the chief of the Brest arrondissement to take care of the team. On the afternoon of July 25th, therefore, two Frenchmen arrived. Neither the Jeds nor the members of the maquis knew who they were, nor did they recognize the name of the person who had sent them:

"We are to take you in our truck. It is full of wine for the Germans. But we have to hurry because our pass expires at 21:30 and it will take us two hours by road to get to the retreat!"

Summers was so eager to get to his action zone that he didn't hesitate a minute about going with them. The three men jumped into an empty wine barrel and the truck jounced off for a 40-mile journey which would last two and a half hours. In their barrel the Jeds were extremely uncomfortable, and as the hours went by they wondered about the outcome of this expedition. If these unknown men were not collaborators, then surely an enemy patrol would end up finding them. And if that didn't happen then they would all suffocate to death!

"After what seemed to be years, recalled Summers, we came to some woods five miles north-west of Brest. We spent the night in a hole. When we peeked out at dawn, we discovered that we were in the middle of the German positions and not far from a mirador! Well, we had arrived."

Early in the morning of the 26th, the leader of the greater Brest arrondissement joined them and told them that a briefcase containing reports and information about the DZs would be brought. The radioman, Zielske, doubted that he would be able to transmit and receive because he was too close to a power line. So they decided to settle in a safe house three miles north-east of Lesneven.

The journey again took place in the truck full of wine barrels. This time, they got a flat tire right in the middle of the town of St. Divy which was filled with Germans. A German patrol even helped the driver change the tire.

The next day, the Jeds heard that the briefcase carrier had been arrested by the Gestapo. But he was released and was able to turn the precious documents over to them. London was immediately informed about the presence of two 14,000-ton tankers in the port, and the possibility of sinking them to block navigation: the mission would be carried out by bombers, but unfortunately outside the navigation channel. Messages were also sent to indicate dropping zones.

But the area was getting dangerous and the Jeds again had to move on after SFHQ let them know that the drop sites had been refused because of the presence of flak batteries nearby.

Gavin and Guy in the Mayenne and Ille-et-Vilaine

It was then — August 1st — that Horace got word of an impending Allied advance. The American 6th Armored Division had just crossed the Sélune River at Pontaubault and turned west toward Brest, while the 4th continued toward the south to cut off the Brittany peninsula.

Two Jedburgh teams sent out from England on July 11 should also have been operating in this future zone of action for the American tanks. Like the the other teams, their mission was to check out drop sites, organize and equip Resistance groups, and only enter into action when ordered. Their designated area of operations was the département of Ile-et-Vilaine: Gavin in the north and Guy in the south [16].

16. Team No. 82 - Commandant Jean Carbuccia alias Jeanclaude (Shilling) of the Infanterie, Captain William B. Creux (Sixpence) of the Infantry, Sous-Lieutenant Paul Valentini alias Masson (Halfpenny) of the BCRA; Team No. 75 - Capitaine André Duron alias Dhomas (Dronne) from the Infanterie, Captain A.A. Trofimov (Gironde), Royal Artillery, Sous-Lieutenant Groult alias Deschamps (Dordogne) from transmissions.

The two teams were put on alert at Milton Hall on July 7, and showed up with the others in London for the briefing. But the news wasn't very good: SFHQ had lost contact since March and had no information about the Resistance groups or working conditions in the département. The Jeds would just have to manage as best they could.

Guy took off from Harrington at 22:40 on July 11, followed five minutes later by Gavin in another B-24. The two planes had no trouble crossing the English Channel and arrived over the designated jump zone around 01:30. The first team was dropped 800 meters beyond the lights and the second just a bit closer. Nevertheless all the paratroopers landed safely except for some bruises. But Guy's radio set and rifles were shattered and the radio operator's knapsack couldn't be found.

The DZ was situated in the Mayenne, 80 miles east of the designated action zone. The reception committee, furnished by the BOA of the département, took charge of the two teams and led them first to a farm and then right into the village of Courcité.

On the 13th, when it became apparent that they would not get any contacts through the BOA, Commandant Jeanclaude decided to dress as much like a civilian as possible, and go out on reconnaissance, leaving his ID papers behind. He pedaled around on his bike more than a week without establishing any liaison. On the 15th, at Rouez, south of the Sillé forest, he met Colonel Michelin, chief of staff for Region M, then General Rodolphe, chief of the M.4 sector. They promised to try to locate the Ile-et-Vilaine leaders.

On the appointed day, Michelin did not show up. On the next day, Jeanclaude was tempted to accept Colonel Laboureur's [17] offer to stay in the Mayenne. He met Laboureur again in Epineux, near Sablé. The latter had some good news and some bad:

"We have been able to contact the north sector of Ile-et-Vilaine, but not the south."

They all agreed that Gavin would stay in the Mayenne and Guy would proceed to the south sector of the neighboring département.

17. Lieutenant-Colonel De Rollin, FFI départemental chief.

The next day, July 24, at the Saint-Mars-du-Désert maquis — made up of about thirty men — they made contact with Dennis, an English agent, and Tanguy, the FTP leader in charge of the five départements of north-western France. They were surprised when they heard from these two that two landing sites in the Ile-et-Vilaine had already been used for drops.

"The problem of establishing contact and then moving into the action zone with all our equipment, recalled Commandant Jeanclaude, including weapons, bags, radio sets and the two Eurekas, was a thorn in the side of the operation. SFHQ had, or could have had, a liaison in Ile-et-Vilaine, since the FTP were active there and had received supplies by parachute. Instead of being dropped more than 60 miles away from our sector, we could have landed on one of the zones that Dennis knew about or had already used. If they couldn't do that, then they could have at least dropped us in the Côtes-du-Nord, where another team had been sent, a lot nearer to the Ile-et-Vilaine than Courcité."

It seems that the two Jed teams abandoned the idea of working in both départements and decided to head for the north of the Ile-et-Vilaine, 120 km away. It was unthinkable and dangerous to expect to carry all the supplies on their backs — to say nothing of the requirement to remain in uniform. They decided to use a vehicle to transport their baggage and left it under the guard of the three young partisans that the BOA had assigned to protect them since they had arrived.

They left during the night of July 25, in uniform, with a guide furnished by Tanguy. The Jeds' first stop was in Hardanges, the second in Niort where their bags were waiting. At daybreak, Commandant Jeanclaude and Capitaine Dhomas exchanged their uniforms for civilian clothing and left on bicycles to contact some people named by Tanguy. The rest of the group followed on foot after nightfall.

They stopped next time near Gorron, where they were supposed to meet the guide to take them to Fougerolles-du-Plessis. But he wasn't there and the day went by while they waited, hiding out in the countryside. One of the young guards got hold of a bike and rode back to Niort to find out what the problem was. Then a partisan appeared: the guide couldn't come back because the Gestapo was in Fougerolles. And he led the men to a safe house where they could sleep for the night. The next day, as the Jeds were wondering how they were going to be able to go on, two gendarmes appeared and took charge of the group. Next, a guide sent by Tanguy notified them that Tanguy was waiting for them at the next stop, Ferré, north of Fougères.

They began to think they would never get to the Ile-et-Vilaine by walking at night, so they bought a used car from an inhabitant of Gorron for 10,000 Francs. The vehicle was to be delivered on the road beyond the village.

At 22:30 the Jeds left to get the car. The seller was there, with two other civilians. The deal was settled and the car pushed out into the road, when suddenly a German troop carrier vehicle appeared and screeched to a halt in front of them.

Eight German soldiers jumped down and surrounded the car that was blocking the road.

"The others saw them in time and hid in the hedges, said Capitaine Dreux. But Masson and I were in uniform and couldn't get out of the car in time before we were surrounded. We drew our pistols and were ready to fire when I suddenly realized that the Germans were quite confused and didn't grasp the situation very well."

A strange dialogue took place then between the patrol leader asking them questions in German and the Jed answering with OK and other less flattering American expletives. Finally the German gave up trying to understand, and not really anxious to fight, had his men push the car aside, climb back into the truck, and they all disappeared into the night.

Once things had calmed down, everybody gathered round except Captain Trofimov and a young man named Louis who had been the first to hide. After looking for them for a half-hour, the Jeds decided to leave in the car that they had carefully camouflaged with branches in the German fashion. In this way they crossed the town of Colombiers under the nose of the enemy sentinels.

"The rest of the trip was fine, according to Dreux, because the car ran perfectly whenever we came into sight of Germans. It was well worth the price because it enabled us to cover the last 60 miles of our journey in one night whereas had we been walking it would have taken at least four nights!"

Early in the morning of July 31, the group arrived in Ferré where Jeanclaude and Dhomas were waiting for them, still in plain clothes. After managing to escape from the Gestapo and the Militia who were surrounding Fougerolles, they had recontacted Tanguy in Landivy before meeting the Ile-et-Vilaine leaders at Tinténiac, south of Combourg. On the 30th they had seen the FTP chiefs, then contacted Team Felix at Jugon, south-east of Lamballe. Felix had seen François, FFI leader for the Côtes-du-Nord, the day before, and received a liaison agent from Colonel Marceau [18]. In agreement with Guy and Gavin, the Dinard region was included in Felix's sector.

On Tuesday August 1st, the whole group, except for Trofimov, who had made his way back to Gorron, and Louis, who had been sent to Ferré as they would learn later, arrived in St.- Christophe-des-Bois, where the pro-Resistance priest of the village church put them up.

The next day they made their way to Combourg which had already been liberated by American armor. The arrival of the Americans was no surprise because the Jeds had been notified about the advance towards Avranches. They were nonetheless amazed to see how quickly the tanks covered ground. They hadn't thought they would be overtaken so soon by the regular troops.

Meanwhile, some gendarmes found civilian clothes and a false ID for Captain Trofimov, and he soon found himself in the middle of the retreating German troops. However, in Gorron the enemy seemed to want to organize a defensive position. A gendarme was sent to Landivy to warn the Americans who were progressing towards the Mayenne.

The next day, August 5, Trofimov also started out for Landivy with a guide. On the way he passed an American patrol and gave them all the

18. Colonel Le Hezaret, FFI départemental military chief.

156

information he had. As he turned around and started back, he ran into elements of the 106th Cavalry Reconnaissance Squadron, in advance of the 90th Infantry Division. Along with them, Trofimov entered Gorron and found that the Germans had left without firing a single shot. Trofimov served as interpreter for the liberators and helped the gendarmerie to cooperate with them, then on August 6, he linked up, first with the headquarters of the First Infantry Division, then with the SF Detachment of the Third Army [19]. The next day he found Team Guy again at Combourg.

While the two teams, Gavin and Guy, were settling in Combourg, Capitaine Dhomas was invited by Major Broussard, from the SF Detachment of the Army, to meet the 6th Armored Division in Loudéac.

The latter, whose headquarters were in Merdrignac, had just been ordered to stop and clean up the pockets of Resistance that had been left behind. Thus the partisans arrived just at the right time: they could sweep the countryside and round up isolated enemy soldiers, allowing the tanks to keep rolling without worrying about what was going on in their rear.

Thus we see a beginning of cooperation on the continent between FFI, Special Forces and invading troops under the control of SF Detachments created by SFHQ for the most important Allied units.

During this time, in England, Colonel Eon, the designated commander of the French forces in Brittany, was preparing to go into action. The program had been put together on July 3rd by SHAEF.

The following day it would become that of Mission Aloes, and it was to be particularly difficult:

- insure that air-dropped weapons were distributed over all of Brittany, organize and train groups of guerilla fighters using these weapons;

- prepare a plan for guerilla operations in liaison with the Supreme Allied Command;

- insure command of these operations and their coordination with the general Allied offensive breaking out of Normandy.

19. Captain Trofimov was actually on the border between the First Army area, to which the 1st ID belonged, and that of the Third Army, to which belonged the 90th ID and the 106th Group.

From July 16 to 20, Colonel Eon received some of the Allied officers in Duke Street, then, on the 21st, he went with General Koenig to the headquarters of the 21st Army Group, where, after lunch, General Montgomery's chief of staff briefed them on the main objectives of the coming operation:

"The forces heading out from the Normandy beachhead will turn west and go into Brittany via two main routes: Dinan-Brest and Rennes-Redon. They will concentrate on both thorough cleansing and maximum speed, and as they advance generalized guerilla warfare will break out."

And Major General De Guingand continued:

" The most important condition is absolute secrecy, so we will wait until the moment of launching the operation before creating the command apparatus of the FFI in Brittany."

Gerald in the Morbihan

A week later the same officers met again with the head of the SHAEF G-3 and Brigadier McLeod of the SAS. This time it was decided that all the French forces operating in Brittany, including the SAS 4th Battalion, would be placed under Eon's orders.

The area of operations designated by General Koenig covered the five Breton départements: Finistère, Côtes-du-Nord, Morbihan, Ile-et-Vilaine and Loire-Inférieure. Maine-et-Loire and Mayenne could be included later. Colonel Eon would have at his disposal a staff made up of personnel who were presently in Great Britain. A certain number of officers would be kept in reserve, to be sent as reinforcements wherever the need was the greatest.

On the 29th, Colonels Vernon, Eon and Passy went to SAS headquarters to organize the system of command. Finally it was General Bradley's 12th Army Group which took command of the Brittany FFI, via the Third Army and the operations section of the FFI staff.

That same day, Colonel Eon presented a report about the situation in Brittany, inasmuch as it was known by the London staff.

In the Côtes-du-Nord, the Frederick Jeds, settled near Plévin, reported five organized FFI battalions south-west of Saint-Brieuc. Frederick was working with the SAS Wash which controlled 3,000 armed men and complained of not receiving enough weapons. Felix, near Lamballe, was trying to organize the sédentaires and small maquis groups.

In the Finistère, there was no real SAS group to speak of, but five Jed teams. Gilbert informed that 20,000 men were available in the département: the number appeared high and it was hard for SFHQ to know what to think. And Horace repeated that the FFI chief in Brest believed that he could take over the city and keep the port from being destroyed if he could obtain weapons. This must have seemed slightly presumptuous to SHAEF planners!

In Ile-et-Vilaine, Gavin and Guy had arrived at their destination after their six-day adventure. However they had doubts about one of the Loire-Inférieure FFI chiefs and had postponed operations for about ten days. Coming from the Morbihan, Jed team George arrived on June 30 in the Loire-Inférieure, along with the two military delegates for Region M.

"After they sent out distress signals, said Colonel Eon, we had no news from them until July 17. At that time George gave no explanation for their silence, simply indicating that they were based near Ancenis and were commanding the Loire-Inférieure in agreement with local leaders. Four days later we were informed that the team was now in the Ile-et-Vilaine, still with the delegates. Their arrest was announced and they were immediately placed under suspicion. George was submitted to the usual security controls after a two-week radio silence."

Finally, in the Morbihan, the number of men was estimated at 4,000 divided into battalions of 500 to 700. Nevertheless the situation was critical because of the lack of weapons and ammunition. The Germans had destroyed the SAS Samwest base and discovered numerous stashes of equipment.

Team Gerald [20], intended for the Morbihan, was to have left Fairford on July 13. Its departure had been postponed until the 17th after a trip

20. Team No. 73 - Captain Stephen J. Knerly (Suffolk), Field Artillery, Lieutenant Claude L'Herbette alias Beaumont (Norfolk) of the Infanterie, First Sergeant Berent E. Friele (Selkirk) U.S. Army Reserve.

to Harvell. But just as the pilot had taxied to the end of the runway and was waiting for the signal to take off, he received instead the order to unload the passengers: the designated DZ was considered unsuitable for jumpers.

The following night a Stirling with three Jeds, twenty-four containers and four baskets on board, took off at 22:30. The over-water flight was accomplished without incident and, as usual, the parachutists started getting ready ten minutes before the green light went on.

"On the command Action Station, the mission report states, Lieutenant Beaumont, first jumper of the stick, decided that his leg-bag was too heavy at 70 lbs and was afraid to jump with so much weight. Nevertheless, he jumped clear as did the radio operator. But Captain Knerly, the last jumper, got caught on the dispatcher's safety strap, then tangled up in his static lines and his parachute rigging got twisted. After spinning to undo the twists, he swayed in the wind until his hip suddenly crashed against a road."

Fifteen minutes later the team was grouped around the reception committee, but without the baskets that had come down with them. Three of these, containing the radio set and other equipment, were found during the morning. But the fourth, with the Eureka in it, could not be found in spite of a day-long with almost 200 men, that worked around a German company camped less than a mile from the site. When they got back to England the Jeds would learn that the fourth basket never cleared the plane and the pilot had to ditch it over the English Channel.

With their equipment they also carried their own money plus three million francs in three packets of a million each, and three million more in checks, in a sealed envelope to be given to the SAS operating in the Morbihan. An hour after landing the envelope was already on its way to Commandant Bourgoin.

On July 19, the team was entrusted to a group of fifteen young men commanded by a regular army sergeant who had participated in the 1940 campaign. Guided and protected by this group, the team made its way to a refuge beyond the limits of the département, 7 miles towards the north.

The next day and the four following, appointments were made with the various leaders and the ORA battalions in the area [21].

During the next three weeks contact was also established with Maurice, the right-hand man of the commander of a battalion based near Guéméné [22]. Gerald then had at its disposal two battalions ready to enter into action within two hours, and a third within a half-day.

Since London's orders were to establish contact with the commander of the 4th SAS, an appointment was made. And on July 25, Lieutenant Beaumont left, dressed in civilian clothes, with false papers, for a 40-mile trip through the city of Pontivy, occupied at that time by the Germans. He arrived a half-hour early for his appointment, and waited another two hours before Bourgoin appeared.

"We were furious, Beaumont recalled. All the stories that we had heard about the SAS made us think that their actions were more of a hindrance than a help to the resistants. They seemed to want to direct all the operations in the region, even though our role was simply to advise and only take command in case of necessity."

In spite of this, relations with Capitaine Déplante, chief of the SAS Grog base, were excellent. They met him at the end of July and he approved the work of the Jeds and their request to operate independently. The Jeds turned over a sum of 6 million francs to him and kept the rest for their personnel expenses.

"Before leaving London, Gerald remembered, Colonel Eon told us that the Bretons were used to paying for everything they got. Every soldier received a monthly salary of 100 francs, plus a subsidy of 1000 francs for his wife and 600 francs for each child. And we tried to pay for their food while they were in the maquis."

The 750,000 francs remaining after the last SAS payment were dwindling fast and they sent a message asking for an extra two-million franc subsidy. No answer came back and Gerald was soon unable to pay all the battalions. This didn't seem to create any real problems however.

21. 1st (Vannes), 2nd (Auray) and 3rd (Pontivy) FFI Battalions of the Morbihan.
22. Capitaine Potvin alias Maurice, adjutant to the chief of the 3rd FTP Battalion.

"We were surprised and delighted, Gerald continued, to discover that, in spite of four years of German domination, the morale of the guerilla fighters was as good as it was. When we asked for volunteers, every hand went up. And when we asked what effect the bombing of the cities had on the population, a subject that particularly interested us, they were all convinced the bombings were necessary and blamed the Germans."

The battalions were as independent as possible. The Jeds participated little in their day-to-day organization, limiting themselves to noting their basic necessities. The weapons came from the BOA or the SAS. Even though several of the men had been in the maquis for more than a year, most had joined up since the Allied invasion. Their ages varied from 17 to 60, the average being about 26.

In the area there existed a group of former sappers, commanded by a reserve NCO, specializing in sabotage of communications lines and with particularly satisfactory results.

"On leaving England, Gerald recalled, we were given a code sentence that was to be the signal to start a general uprising in our area. That communication came 24 hours late. We had heard a rumor that American forces were advancing into Brittany, so we gave restricted orders to start attacking convoys, and generally harassing the Germans."

On August 3rd after nightfall, the whole team left camp with an FFI group. When they arrived at the road from St. Caradec to Pontivy, the twelve-man unit divided into two elements, with a Bren, four Stens and a rifle for each one, so as to cover both possible directions by which an enemy convoy might arrive.

The two Americans, who had brought along explosives more out of habit than out of necessity, decided to cut down the northernmost tree, to strap the explosives to the trunk and attach one end to a Bickford detonator.

They were in luck. A column of three German vehicles was arriving from St. Caradec and the tree fell just in front of it, killing several Germans and disabling the first truck. When they heard the explosion, the guerillas peppered the second truck and the Volkswagen following it with automatic fire. Then they heard a long whistle, the signal to withdraw: the action has lasted only four minutes.

A peasant, summoned the next day by the Germans to clear away the debris, was able to report on the results of the ambush: two vehicles destroyed, 30 killed including one officer, 15 wounded.

That same night, from August 3rd to 4th, at the other end of Brittany, Capitaine Charron of Team Gilbert and Capitaine Mercier, FFI commander in Rosporden, heard the long-awaited radio message: Is Napoleon's hat still in Perros-Guirrec? Mercier called his group together.

"I have just one thing to say to you. We were the rabbits, now we are the hunters !"

During the night, the order went out to attack Rosporden. But a trainload of Germans stranded at the railroad station reacted. Then Russian reinforcements were called in from Briec. They launched a counter-attack and retaliated against the civilian population. The skirmishes lasted all day. In the evening, following orders, the detachment withdrew to the maquis.

At the same time, the entire staff of Mission Aloes was preparing to jump south of Guingamp, on the Bonaparte site near Kerien [23].

Arrival of mission Aloes

The tripartite operational headquarters staff that was to command the Allied forces in Brittany apparently had some trouble getting organized, as Major John E. Rees, U.S. Army, stated in his report:

"Around July 16, Colonel Van der Stricht requested me, with Lieutenant — future Captain — Charles T. Barnes of the Air Corps, to report to Colonel Eono (sic), commander of Mission Aloes. After being received in Duke Street, we were shown to a charming office where we did absolutely nothing until the arrival of Colonel Stevens, designated chief of staff for the mission."

23. According to the JMO of the FFI command in Brittany. The Allied report however situates the DZ prepared by Team Frederick — which doesn't even mention the arrival of Aloes in its report — "just south-west of Bourbriac, in the Côtes-du-Nord", and another report "near the city of Plésidy 10-15 km south of Bourbriac."

According to Rees, Stevens was working at that time day and night to try to organize and plan the different aspects of the transfer to France.

"It was all rather difficult, because Colonel Eono had many more ideas than what he could possibly carry out with the organization that he had at his disposal. While we were waiting, it was decided that the members of the mission, about fifty men at the time, would go to ME 65 for a training program to prepare them for their future role, even though this future role was never clearly defined"

Around July 24, then, the men arrived at the Jedburgh training center at Milton Hall. This was the first time that they had been united as a group, and they began training in maquis life, then tried out the radio gear and the weapons and equipment. In spite of difficulties of all sorts they were finally equiped and reasonably busy. During this time, Stevens and Rees were trying to assemble the rest of the men, and to discover how and when they would be leaving for France. The make-up of the staff was finally decided with the assignment of the last Allied officers.

The chief of staff was Colonel Passy, assisted by Colonel Stevens. G-1 was directed by Capitaine Raynal, G-2 by Major Drinkwater of the SIS, assisted by Capitaine Mansion and Lieutenant Barnes, G-3 by Commandant Dupérier, and the 4th bureau by Major Rees with Capitaine Raymond. Captain Schoofs, British Army, was in charge of the headquarters communications center. Liaison officers were also designated, from the SAS, or to the Third Army or COMAC. A war correspondent, Capitaine Maurice Schumann, was also expected.

The move to France was to be carried out by stages. Capitaine Dampierre, chief of headquarters, would leave first to look for shelters and create security teams. Then Colonel Eon would make command contacts with Commandant Bourgoin and the FFI départemental chiefs, while a larger group of men, directed by Colonel Passy, would install headquarters and transmissions, and organize the intelligence and security networks. Finally the rest of the staff would arrive.

Each member of the personnel normally received a personal weapon, a camp kit, civilian clothes and false identity papers. Squad weapons were provided for about one hundred men, and the office equipment weighed around 500 lbs. A total sum of 30 million francs was to be divided among the different echelons.

On July 31, General Koenig decided that four Jedburgh teams would be dispatched to the FFI départemental chiefs to insure liaisons. And an advance team would prepare several possible sites for establishing headquarters in the area around Loudéac, as well as a landing strip for non airborne qualified officers, including Colonel Eon.

Echelon A was ready to jump as the advance team. Echelon B could arrive either by plane or by parachute, as soon as transmissions were ready and liaison problems resolved with the SAS, the 12th Army Group and the Third Army. Echelon C, organized around the operations section, was already capable of reaching the DZ, which hadn't been designated yet but would be proposed by a Jedburgh in the Côtes-du-Nord. The last echelon would be transferred under the same conditions.

But, as Colonel Eon noticed when he came to visit the four Jed teams before their departure, the personnel was taking too long to get to Milton Hall: eight officers out of 18 were missing from the staff and eleven out of 17 from the command reserve.

However the pace of events soon accelerated. On August 2, during a meeting held in the Operation Room with the FFI staff, Brittany section, the latest information about the American offensive was given. And on the 3rd, at late morning, the Allied leaders confirmed the information concerning the American advance via Rennes and Dinan.

"I don't believe, General Koenig intervened, that our plans need to be changed. But the speed of the Allied advance could lead us to abandon part of them. This is the case, particularly, concerning the idea of sending Allied officers with the Eon mission."

As far as the SAS and the Special Forces were concerned, it was decided to send four parties into Brittany during the night of August 4th. An SAS squadron whose advance echelon had already arrived would be sent into the Loire-Inférieure to block all enemy movement from the valley of the Loire River towards Redon. Another would be dropped in Finistère, on a site prepared by Jed team Horace, with special orders to preserve the viaducts of Morlaix and Plougastel from destruction. Horace was also in charge of receiving an Operational Group of four officers and thirty men, whose job would be to take control of the Guimiliau railroad viaduct. Another OG, set up in the region around Saint-Brieuc by Jed team Frederick, would have the same job at the Méaugon viaduct.

Another important point was raised during the meeting: relations between the American troops and the FFI, particularly in Brittany and in the Laval-Orléans region. The Third Army was afraid that mishaps might occur when the GIs, trigger-happy from fear of snipers, met up with armed civilians. Orders should therefore be given by the Jedburghs to local leaders to send out an unarmed team, to make contact and inform the advanced units of the exact position of Resistance troops.

Along the same idea, the delegate from the U.S. 12th Army Group requested that instructions be given to the civilians to turn in their arms as soon as the Allied troops had passed through:

"General Bradley's request is simply to protect the Resistance fighters themselves. His troops will open fire on anyone bearing arms without a uniform."

"Resistance fighters, General Koenig answered, are not civilians but soldiers. An essential part of Colonel Eon's mission was in fact to group them into organized and disciplined units."

But finally the rapidity of the American progression meant that generalized guerilla warfare would be launched in the five Breton départements before the program of arms drops had been completed [24]. Consequently it was decided that the BBC would air the code sentence at 18:00 on August 3rd.

The next day, during the daily briefing at the FFI Headquarters, it was learned that the Americans had passed through Rennes and Dinan. When the meeting was over, General Koenig spoke to Colonel Eon in private:

"The situation is changing rapidly. It's important that the FFI command in Brittany be unified right away. We haven't heard from

24. Actually armed FFI troops in Brittany didn't appear to be greater than around 20,000 men, far from the intended 30,000.

Capitaine Dampierre, the advance scout. In spite of that, I want all the personnel, whether they are airborne qualified or not, to jump together in the center of the region.

Eon agreed immediately and all the other non-parachutists followed his example including, Dupérier, Schoofs and several other officers and men. To be on the safe side, the British command requested a written statement from Colonel Eon stating that he accepted full responsibility for allowing untrained men to jump.

The Allies were irritated by the way things were going, as Major Rees indicated:

"The members of the mission were confused: we weren't entirely ready and the mission order which we had been working on was completely changed."

The mission explained during the final briefing, judged by Rees to be entirely inadapted, was basically one of coordination: insuring internal liaisons with the Jedburgh teams to be dropped in the four Breton départements, keeping in touch with London and the Third Army and making contact with Commandant Bourgoin of the SAS. Collecting and transmitting military intelligence was also important. But the final goal was, as Colonel Eon insisted, to exert direct control over all Resistance action in Brittany.

How did London see the enemy positions as the Americans were preparing to enter the Côtes-du-Nord?

"Its strength, said G-2, is estimated at 80,000 men. The back country is infested with Germans and Russians who, as far as we know, avoid the known maquis hideouts. Parachute drops can be made quite safely, since no enemy element is situated within three miles of a DZ."

The personnel and material for Mission Aloes were finally dropped during the night of August 3, with no major problems. There were a number of parachutes that did not open, resulting in the loss of a dozen weapons containers, and a certain number of boxes could not be located on the ground [25].

25. In particular a packet containing 9 million francs, which would later be found 2 miles from the DZ, with only 8 million ...

"Six members of the mission, recalled the G-4 chief, had never jumped before. But that didn't stop them: they wanted to seize the opportunity, which is to their credit. One of them however, Capitaine Schumann, who had joined us at the airbase, didn't jump. I don't know why."

The jump was a success, but the arrival of thirty parachutists instead of the six expected created havoc among the reception committee.

"Colonel Passy, Rees continued, took charge of operations and soon the men and equipment were assembled and the staff headed off for a farm nearby that had been prepared to receive us."

After conferring with the local FFI and FTP leaders and the départemental staff, Colonels Eon, Passy and Stevens decided to install their headquarters in the village school in Kerien. This was accomplished by the end of the following afternoon, after a safety net had been prepared in case of surprise intrusions.

The liberation of Brittany

During the night of August 4, while Major Rees was making the rounds, he was stopped by a familiar sound of engines. Out of the darkness hurtled two Jeeps: riding in one of them was Major Broussard, of the U.S. First Army staff. Rees then realized that the Army was already ahead of them and that their situation had completely changed.

"When we arrived in Brittany the day before, he recalled, the Germans controlled the main roads and were careful not to enter the woods or isolated villages. Now we were going to find the Americans on the roads and the Germans in the woods. Even though the invading forces had caught up to us, there were still all sorts of enemies, including some organized in large groups, remaining around us."

During the day the news of the liberation of Saint-Brieuc reached headquarters. Three hundred white Russians were supposed to be dug in at the east end of the city, around the airfield. According to Commandant Dupérier, sent out to negociate, they were ready to surrender, but only to the Americans. The four American officers present — three majors and a lieutenant — left immediately for the airfield, hoping that their appearance along with other superior Allied officers, would convince the Russians. They went behind the Russian lines waving a white flag. But after heated discussions, the Russians refused to surrender their weapons.

Then all of a sudden from the south appeared the first vehicles of Task Force A, including reconnaissance and tank-destroyer units, supported by a battalion of combat engineers. As no infantry was available, they were counting on the FFI they ran into to insure communications and headquarters security.

Colonel Fuller, commanding the 15th Cavalry Group, left with Commandant Dupérier to request the surrender of the Russians. But the latter opened fire, severely wounding the two officers. While all this was going on, Colonel Eon had quietly taken over the city and officially established the new prefect of the Côtes-du-Nord.

Once the officers had returned to headquarters, a company of German paratroopers from the 2nd Division managed to creep behind the lines to the edge of Kerien. All the armed men and the FFI present hurried to defend the town and, after a violent firefight that lasted half an hour, the enemy retreated at nightfall, setting fire to about thirty horse-drawn wagons carrying their equipment.

All over Brittany the order launching guerilla warfare and the arrival of American tanks had changed the situation: the enemy was scattered in small groups, under attack everywhere.

On August 7th Aloes headquarters were transferred to Mur-de-Bretagne. Most of the activity at that time was involved with intelligence collecting, in constant liaison with the Jedburghs or the resistants. Each mission was adapted to the new situation. Thus Colonel Stevens had joined the Third Army to insure liaisons, while Major Broussard remained with Colonel Passy. The latter was busy destroying the last pockets of enemy resistance, especially in the region around Paimpol. By staying in the field, he managed to steer clear of the quarrel between Colonel Eon and General Deligne, the territorial commander appointed to Rennes.

The messages sent to the FFI Headquarters by Eon give an idea of his concerns. They were centered on operations in his sector and the necessity of informing the French about what was going on. Little by little, a dual approach had taken hold: London dealt with the special forces teams in the field and Aloes gave the information it gathered directly to the Americans, then each reported to the other. Eon also had to handle conflicts between persons and organizations — FFI and FTP, VIII Corps and SAS, etc. — that he tried but failed to solve. He could do nothing better than to turn the problem over to the future territorial chief in Rennes:

"It will be necessary, he indicated in a message sent on August 11, for the staff of the 10th Region to take control of the situation as soon as the Jerries are wiped out."

On August 19, even though three départements — Finistère, Morbihan and Loire-Inférieure — were still under his responsibility, Eon decided to put all the personnel of his mission at the commander's disposal. His headquarters were installed at that time in the château of Kerriou, near Pleyben, right next door to the troops surrounding the enemy defenses in Brest. In these new headquarters, Capitaine Lebel, from Jed team Giles, was in charge of G-2 and G-3.

The teams in the field also experienced the confusion of the first days of Liberation, achieved either by the arrival of the first American tanks or spontaneously by the departure of the Wehrmacht troops. They also lived through revenge motivated atrocities carried out by the retreating German columns, and what the new Gaullist civil servant in Vannes discretely called exaggerations by the liberated populations. They were basically independent until they met up with Aloes. The team members or the maquis they were living with decided what, if any, action to take, depending on whether or not there were any Germans left around.

Teams Gavin and Guy, who had been working east of Saint-Malo in cooperation with the 83rd Infantry Division, left the zone on August 23 and went to Normandy where they caught an LCI for the trip back to England.

The same day Team Felix also moved north, after having helped their FFI clear out the pockets of resistance between Dinan and Saint-Brieuc. Further west Frederick, who went home five days later, had been doing the same thing with Task Force A in Paimpol.

In the Côtes-du-Nord an extra Jedburgh team had been dropped shortly after the arrival of Mission Aloes, but on a different DZ. The plane had been confused by fires lighted as it passed overhead by a group of maquis fighters trying to obtain arms: this was common practice in Brittany and elsewhere. The mission of Team Daniel [26] — insure liaisons between Colonel Eon and the FFI départemental military chief — was both impossible and useless, since the authorities in question were constantly moving around and often very close to each other. So it tried to find something else to do until it left on August 21, and participated, among other things, in the fighting in Saint-Brieuc and Guingamp.

In the Morbihan, guided by the FFI who had just occupied the Meucon field, a combat command from the 4th Armored Division entered Vannes at the end of the afternoon on August 5th, thus cutting off the last exit road towards the east for the Germans. The next morning another armored group was approaching the outskirts of Lorient.

Gerald, in the region around Pontivy, was taken by surprise by the arrival of the tanks of the 6th Armored Division — they thought the Americans were still in Avranches — and relieved to be out of reach of the Germans who had been chasing them. After having helped Civil Affairs units deal with various local problems, the mission took over, under U.S. orders and in spite of the reluctance of the SAS, control of all the maquis in the region and participated in the fighting at their side.

On August 18th, they met with a delegate from Aloes before going to Rennes where the SF Detachment sent the mission to the advance headquarters of the army group. After they had briefed the staff on the situation in the Morbihan and received a bottle of Cognac in return, the Jeds left for Coutances where a plane was waiting to carry them back to England.

26. Team No. 10 - Captain Kem D. Bennett (Apotre) and Sergeant R. Brierley (Florin) of the Royal Armoured Corps, Lieutenant Albert de Schonen (Argentier) of the Cavalerie.

Jed team Douglas [27], intended as reinforcements in the département, was dropped during the night of August 5. During the briefing at Fairford, it was joined by an extra radioman in charge of internal communications with Aloes. Then it learned that its parcels were in transit and it would either have to postpone departure or leave without its equipment. The second solution was adopted with the promise that the equipment would be dropped the following night.

At 22:00 the plane took off: it wasn't until then that the Jeds were informed of the exact point where they would be dropped. Then the pilot, unable to see any lights on the DZ, decided to return to his base, where the team spent the rest of the night stretched out on the floor of the officers' mess hall.

The next day the Jeds traveled to the Keevil airstrip and took off in a Sterling along with about fifteen SAS sent to Dingson as reinforcements.

A second Sterling followed them with nine boxes on board: three for the Jeds and six for the Aloes radio operator. The drop zone indicated by the pilot was fifteen miles south of the spot where the reception committee was waiting. So the plane had to circle before finding the right DZ.

"For fifty minutes, Captain Rubinstein related, the plane had to undertake evasive actions to avoid the extremely accurate anti-aircraft. We were ready to jump with the Joe-hole open ... The violent maneuvering by the pilot had created chaos inside the Sterling and all the static lines had become entangled.On the DZ, waiting for them, they found Capitaine Leblond of the SAS and nearly 150 men and women of all ages. Only eight boxes were found and the Jeds were sorry that they couldn't jump like the SAS, with their rucksacks as leg-bags. Then they climbed into a truck to be driven to Nostang where a boat met them. They continued alone to the départemental headquarters."

27. Team No. 8 - Captain R.A. Rubinstein (Augure) of the Royal Artillery, Lieutenant Roblot alias Ranglou (Anachorete) of the Colonial Infantry and Sergeant J.D. Raven (Halfcrown) of the Royal Armoured Corps, plus Sous-Lieutenant J. Poignet.

Finally, after changing shelters several times, Rubinstein managed to contact Lieutenant-Colonels Bourgoin and Maurice. He had money for them and gave Bourgoin five million francs and 500,000 to Maurice.

"These two leaders, well organized and disinclined to work with Colonel Eon, were not pleased with our arrival. Above all, they confirmed my first impression that it was too late to undertake large guerilla operations because the Germans had left."

After losing radio contact with Aloes, they decided to go to Mur-de-Bretagne, the last known Aloes command post. They had nothing left to do and since the food they had asked for was delivered via Dingson to Meucon, they took advantage of an empty plane to fly back to England on August 24.

The mission of liaison with Aloes was carried out in the Finistère by Team Ronald [28]. In addition, the team could also furnish information about the enemy to the units and help organize the maquis, if necessary. They jumped on August 5 around 03:00. On the ground the Jeds discovered that the reception committee was not expecting them and that they had landed on the wrong zone, designated for a different Jed team.

After spending the night in the woods, they contacted Colonel Berthaud near Quimper, who informed them that the FFI were surrounding the city where 400 Germans were holed up. They would surrender only to Americans, so Lieutenant Trumps had a message carried to them by a local police officer. He said he was the leader of an advance armored guard ready to attack the city. When the Germans received this ultimatum, they sent out patrols and soon discovered that it was only a bluff. The combats resumed, therefore, and continued until the enemy executed a sortie towards Brest, harassed all along the way.

Trumps and Capitaine Charron of Team Gilbert then made their way to Rosporden, where a skirmish was underway on the outskirts of

28. Team No. 19 - Lieutenant Shirley R. Trumps (Bouvier) and Sergeant Elmer B. Esch (Pound) of the OSS, Lieutenant Desseilligny alias Dartigues (Bouton) of the Artillerie.

the liberated city. Then they participated with Blathwayt, the FFI and the American tanks in the fighting near Concarneau. Trumps was wounded by a mortar shell during this battle, but that didn't keep him from insuring liaisons between Aloes and Task Force A operating on the Crozon peninsula.

While Ronald left the zone on September 6 or 7 [29], Gilbert stayed around for about ten days longer. Until September 20 its role would be to obtain money and equipment for the FFI, support them during combat and cooperate with the different Allied units passing through: armor, infantry, psychological operations, intelligence, etc.

Team Francis also participated in the fighting around Quimper and made a triumphal entrance into the liberated city on August 8 with Gilbert and Ronald.

It was based at Quimperlé and devoted its energies to equiping 1,500 partisans from Scaër to Carhaix, an arduous task. On July 25, weapons dropped too late in the early morning, and poorly camouflaged at Bannalec, were found by the Germans. Another drop was cancelled at the last minute because German patrols were lurking near the site. The next day the Quimperlé headquarters was surrounded by a German force of 600 men.

It then became clear that parachute drops could no longer take place near the coast and that the command post would have to be abandoned. After the Germans discovered ten empty containers, they attacked a nearby maquis, and the radio set — received on a Giles DZ and entrusted the day before to the guard of the fifty guerilla fighters of that maquis — was lost.

In the evening of the 28th, André de Neuville, owner of the cave where the command post was installed, fell into a trap as he was trying to salvage some stored equipment. Francis then decided to set out on foot for Carhaix, and stopped at daybreak at an isolated farm near Querrien.

The next day, towards evening, a hundred feldgendarmes (German military police) surrounded the farm, and after a few minutes of

29. The two Americans didn't get back to London until the 16th.

fighting, Major Ogden-Smith was wounded and captured, along with the SAS Moydon who had been following the team since its arrival. The second radioman, even though seriously wounded, managed to hide. Le Zachmeur and Dallow disappeared into the night after shooting the German captain who had led the attack. They arrived in Guiscriff on the 31st in the midst of a parachute drop.

Le Zachmeur learned then that Odgen-Smith and the SAS had been killed by the Germans:

"The Major was wounded in the stomach and deliberately killed by the feldgendarmes. As for Moydon, his leg had been fractured by a grenade and he had run out of ammunition; he was shot down with a burst from a sub-machine gun. Both of them were in uniform and wearing the badges of their rank."

The farm was burned, the animals slaughtered and the farmer killed. Because the Major had a briefcase containing secret documents and a map of the different approved DZs, Gilbert was asked to send a report to London about the incident [30].

When the Napoleon code signalling general insurrection was given, 500 armed Resistance fighters were assembled in the town of Scaër which had been evacuated by the Germans, and a field hospital was installed. Thanks to the requisitioning of some trucks, a mobile reserve unit of 200 men was created. This element participated in an August 5 action to free partisans in Rosporden and drove back a column of Russians who were threatening the city.

After the liberation of Quimper, Team Francis tried to contact Colonel Eon's headquarters at Mur-de-Bretagne, but ended up meeting Colonel Passy instead. He requested them to gather information in their sector and transmit it to Ronald who would relay it. Furthermore, Capitaine Le Zachmeur was authorized eight days later to assemble the 500 sailors in Quimperlé into a flotilla

30. A report would be written up later and entrusted to Mission Aloes so that the American forces laying siege to Lorient could be informed that the two Feldwebel from Quimperlé who had orderd the execution had taken refuge in that fortress.

with orders to keep Germans in Crozon from escaping towards the Pointe du Raz.

"On August 28, recalled Le Zachmeur, Colonel Eon named a Navy officer to manage land-sea liaisons. Our mission was over and we insisted on being sent back to England. We left on September 9 for Great Britain."

Giles was also in the sector, waiting impatiently for the Napoleon's hat message, to set their guerilla fighters on the heels of the German 2nd Parachute Division. Since August 2, the latter had effectively left Châteaulin and taken the road toward the east on foot, by bicycle or in carts.

As soon as they received the message, the seven companies posted along the road to Carhaix attacked. They harassed the enemy columns, laid ambushes and blew up the Landeleau bridge. Finally they forced the Germans to turn back and abandon their advanced guard in Carhaix.

"During these fights, recalled Captain Knox, we took a lot of prisoners, mostly very young. We found jewelry, money, civilian ID cards in their pockets. They refused to tell us where these things came from, but they did admit to having participated in extorsions. They were later shot by the FFI."

On August 4, an FFI group was sent out to meet the Americans and to serve as their guide. They came back proudly honking the horn of a Jeep. Behind the wheel an officer of the Royal Navy, and with him a colleague from the Royal Marines, seemed surprised to find the Jeds there, and explained straight-faced that they were headed for Brest.

The next day brought two more Jeeps from the 86th Cavalry Squadron, the reconnaissance element of the 6th Armored Division, who had become separated from their unit during a skirmish with some paratroopers on the road between Pleyben and Châteauneuf. Seeing Americans, the population of Châteauneuf began to celebrate merry and hang out Allied flags, a bit prematurely, it would turn out. During the night a group of Germans retreating from Carhaix entered the city and massacred at least fifty inhabitants.

The next day, these same Germans surprised an American column coming from Scaër, destroyed the vehicles and killed almost all of the men.

"If the commander of that column had known about us, regretted Knox, he could have contacted us and avoided that ambush. In all of my future discussions with American officers, I never met one who had the least idea that there were Allied paratroopers in the Finistère."

During the following days the team worked near Crozon with the 17th Cavalry Squadron, then went to Brasparts and Plabennec where they met Horace. They finally got back to their base on September 10.

At daybreak that Major Summers' Team Horace heard the roar of the first Allied tanks rolling along the road just 400 yards from the woods where they were hiding. Summers and his radio operator then escorted the 6th Division G-2, while Levalois stayed behind to continue the mission.

Lieutenant Walsh, part of the SF staff, then suggested that the team go home to London. Summers refused, considering that his mission was far from over.

Finally on September 10, after organizing the desertion of a Russian company, undertaking a reconnaissance by Jeep behind the enemy lines and participating in the surrender at Corsen Point with the 2nd Rangers Battalion, the team left Le Conquet and joined up with the Ninth Army before taking a plane to England.

Further East, Team Hilary had remained in the region around Morlaix after meeting up with the American Cavalry.

"The Colonel commanding the cavalry, explained Capitaine Marchant, named me military governor of the arrondissement. You can't imagine how hard it was for me just to take over my job. The city was going wild: in the streets many men who never set eyes on a maquis were wearing arm bands and sticking hand grenades under their belts. The Americans wanted the city, the viaduct, the prison and the German hospital to be guarded by Frenchmen, so that their troops could sweep the countryside and neutralize of any isolated enemy groups."

The Guimiliau viaduct was guarded at that time by OG Donald. The OGs had jumped during the night of August 5 to join Hilary and help them protect the bridges, roads and railroads around Landivisiau. When Task Force A met the group, and since he could not take orders from SFHQ, Lieutenant R.D. Hirtz put himself at the disposal of the Task Force to protect the population of Landivisiau. Then the OG fought for a while around Roscoff.

The Cavalry has been relieved, so Hilary said good-by to Colonel Eon and traveled by requisitioned car to the Third Army and then SF Detachment No. 12.

"In Versailles, Marchant regretted bitterly, we were rather poorly received. There was nobody there but a group of officers and soldiers who seemed not to know how to put us up. After living off the land for two months, they found nothing better than to offer us a tent in the suburbs!"

Needless to say the Jeds took off immediately for Paris and only went back to Versailles the following day, in time to continue their journey to Bayeux and back to England by plane on September 6.

Chapter VI

Supporting the 12th Army Group

When the Allies were preparing their break-through out of the Normandy bocage, they imagined the German retreat, which would determine the outcome of the Battle of France, being carried out in one of the following ways:

- a relatively orderly withdrawal, from position to temporary position, abandoned at the last minute under enemy pressure;

- a rapid retreat towards the boundaries of the Reich, leaving behind a skeleton force designed to delay the Allied advance and give the bulk of the army the time to withdraw.

Actually the agressivity and dynamism of Lieutenant General George S. Patton's Third Army left the Germans no room for choice. Their advance was so rapid that the Seine was crossed at Melun on August 24 and Nancy was freed by the tanks of the advanced guard on September 5.

In this phase of the Battle of France, the FFI and the special forces which shared their lot, played an important role. The American generals were impressed by the help that the underground fighters had given them in Brittany, acting as guides and scouts. They praised the groups and gave added support in favor of the use of the Special Forces. Thus, SFHQ — who, up until August 15, had sent only two Jedburgh teams into operation north of the Loire — decided to send nine extra teams in ahead of the motorized columns of the 12th Army Group.

Alfred, Augustus and Audrey beyond Paris

Team Alfred [1], hastily summoned to the English capital during the morning of August 9, was to jump near Beauvais, on the left wing of the American forces. But its departure was delayed until August 23. Meanwhile, the advanced armored guard was rolling towards the Seine and Elbeuf, squeezed between the British and the U.S. First Army.

Their initial mission — assist in the organization of the FFI in the Oise, then provide an additional link between London and numerous FFI — was enlarged during the last hasty briefing: when the mission found that it was within forty miles of the combat zone, the Jeds were to recruit a few volunteers and break their way through to the battle lines, picking up as much information as they could along the way.

The team finally took off from England on the 23rd just before midnight. Two hours later the weather was so bad over the Granvillers-aux-Bois DZ that the plane had trouble dropping the containers and packages. Then, as the pilot was gaining altitude to drop the paratroopers, the lights disappeared and the wind reached hurricane level. They had to return to their base.

The next night, the plane circled almost an hour before finding the site. But the drop took place right on target in the middle of the reception committee, and the material which had been dropped the night before and hidden in a nearby quarry, would be recovered later. Only the radio set and personal kits were missing. The team had foreseen a spare Jed radio set just in case.

After spending the rest of the night with the leader of the resistants in La Neuville, Lieutenant De Wavrant went to Clermont to contact Commandant Monturat (Dupont), départemental FFI chief for the Oise.

---

1. Team No. 93 - Captain L.D. MacDougall (Argyll) from the General List, Lieutenant Herenguel alias De Wavrant (Aude), detached from the Infanterie to the BCRA, and Serjeant Albert W. Key (Wampum) of the Royal Armoured Corps.

"The situation in the département, explained the latter, is simple: we have volunteers but no organization and no weapons. Four hundred men in all have arms, old shotguns or hunting rifles, while five thousand could be called up. Besides that, the Germans, who occupy every village, have requisitioned all the vehicles."

A message was sent immediately to SFHQ:

"Contact established with départemental FFI chief. 500 to 600 maquisards in zone, poorly organized but very motivated and requesting weapons and more weapons."

400 armed men in all in Compiègne-Clermont region. No weapons in the Beauvais region.

Then the Jeds settled in the woods near Cressonsacq and shared the equipment that had been dropped by parachute among the different sectors. And the following night they waited in vain for a drop on the DZ, although the operation had been announced for the 27th by the BBC [2].

The morning after, a liaison agent brought information about the presence of parachutists at Francières, seven miles to the east. Captain MacDougall went to meet them, and discovered five SAS who had jumped blind after their plane had given up searching for lights. Everyone was surprised to learn that the pilot had not dropped the twenty containers he had on board, at least not that time around.

The next night, the reception committee returned to the DZ again, in response to another message via the BBC. Around 02:30 a storm broke out. The containers, dropped around ten miles away, were recovered by the FTP, who were careful not to return them to their rightful owners.

"On August 28, recalled MacDougall, we were forced to change our CP. We settled in an underground shelter dug in the woods by an artillery team during the last war. That same night, London sent their first message requesting information on DZs that had already been

2. Concerning parachute drops, the men were told during briefing that there would be a week's delay before they could expect anything. This was true for all of the teams.

approved. This caused a four-day delay and hindered our prospects of accomplishing anything useful."

Time went by and still no parachute drop! While waiting, they sent information about the situation in Creil, Senlis and the valley of the Oise River, blocked by convoys, with forty enemy tanks south of Compiègne. They also reported on the enemy's preparations for blowing up bridges over the Oise, and they suggested that an SAS group act to prevent their destruction.

The liberation of Beauvais and Clermont was then announced, prematurely, by the BBC. The Jeds thus received orders to try to protect the bridges of the Somme River around Amiens:

Try to keep bridges intact for about four days. This objective is extremely important. Can drop arms to you from Typhoons if you need them.

As arrangements had already been made to lay two ambushes during the night, Wavrant stayed put and MacDougall left with the radioman for Amiens to meet with the chiefs of the local Resistance groups. Travelling in a horse-drawn wagon, they actually didn't get any further than Ferrières, where they ran into American tanks that had got there before them. The British were already at the gates of Amiens anyway.

Their first ambush blocked an important convoy at Francières and resulted in several enemy losses for only one killed maquisard. The second ambush group wasn't as lucky: the men were returning in the morning empty-handed, when they came upon a group of thirty GIs captured by the Germans. They freed them and escorted them to the American lines.

"But in spite of the massive arrival of American troops, recalled MacDougall, there were still plenty of isolated enemy groups left. They were well-armed and determined to avoid capture. Often the members of these groups refused to surrender to the FFI and fought to the last man."

Wireless contact with London was reestablished, and the team's job was done, so they went to Paris for three days. And on September 28, fresh from their landing the day before on Hendon Field, they reported back to the London FFI headquarters.

In next-door Aisne, Team Augustus [3] was parachuted during the night of August 15 to 16 onto a field equiped by the BOA near Colonfay, south of Guise. The team operated for a while around Nouvion, then, following a suggestion by the resistants, they settled in Rugny, south of Soissons.

On August 28, noting the rapid advance of the Allied tanks, the Jeds decided to take a truck ride further north. Along the road they passed armored columns moving toward the Aisne River. In Soissons they contacted staff officers of the U.S. 3rd Armored Division and briefed them about German defenses on the right bank and about Margival Camp, which were of to particular interest to the Americans.

On the 30th, SFHQ sent a message similar to that sent to Alfred, directing them to take up positions on the bridges over the Somme. It seems that Augustus received the message, because, that same day, the team headed for Besny-Loisy, just outside of Laon, where Allied tanks had already arrived. There they asked a maquisard contact if he could get them a car to cross the lines. The rest of the story is told by the deputy zone chief who was later put in charge of the investigation concerning the incident:

"Around 21:00 the Jeds left in a horse-drawn cart the Germans had abandoned that very morning. The maquisard farmer went with them, as they wanted to avoid the main roads."

Half an hour later, the farmer left them and they continued along the road in the dark towards Barenton-sur-Serre, where they had a contact. Around a quarter past ten it began to rain, a downpour that made it impossible to see even a few feet in front of them, and impossible to hear any suspicious noises.

What happened then? The chairman of the investigation continues:

"When they got to the main road to Barenton, they were probably unable to see the two Jerry tanks in time and so were stopped. The cart was searched: once the Germans saw weapons and radio equipment,

3. Team No. 39 - Major John H. Bonsall (Arizona) of the Field Artillery, Capitaine Jean Delwiche alias Decheville (Hérault) of the Artillerie and native of the Laon region, Sergeant Robert S. Cote (Indiana) of the Signal Corps.

there was no doubt about their fate. At 22:45 the inhabitants heard seven shots: first two, then five others shortly after."

The German tanks departed thirty minutes later, leaving the bodies of the two dead officers with their hands raised and the radioman shot down a few yards away as he was trying to escape.

In the neighboring département of the Seine-et-Marne, West of Paris, more Jedburghs were also busy preparing for the arrival of the American forces. Team Aubrey [4] left London on August 11 around 17:00 and arrived at the Harrington airfield after a comfortable trip by car with a FANY who stayed with them until they took off.

After an excellent meal, the Jeds watched a film in the mess hall while waiting for departure. Everybody was very helpful. Since they were the first Jeds to jump in plain clothes, each stage of their preparation was photographed. They shook hands with the pilot, the navigator showed them the route and at exactly 00:15 the Liberator lifted into the air.

"The efficiency of that American crew was unbelievable, recalled Captain Marchant. We knew exactly where we were all along the way and we had complete confidence in the dispatcher who gave us the order to jump at 01:55. Our descent went well, but it seemed shorter than usual. On the DZ near Plessis-Belleville Major Armand [5] himself was waiting for us."

The four men walked to Saint-Pathus while the committee was recovering the containers dropped from two other planes. The night ended talking and drinking champagne with the leader of the Resistance group in the town whose residents made up the reception committee. According to Armand, there were no Germans in the sector.

The following night, after the 21:30 curfew, the team biked to Forfry where a safe refuge had been arranged at the home of the village garage mechanic. This was all the more welcome since Serjeant

4. Team No. 25 - Captain Godfrey Marchant (Rutland) of the Intelligence Corps, Capitaine Chaigneau alias J. Telmon (Kildare) of the BCRA and Serjeant Ivor Hooker (Thaler) of the Royal Armoured Corps.
5. René Dumont-Guillemet (Armand), organizer in February 1944 of the SOE Section F Spiritualist circuit operating north-east of Paris.

Hooker was suffering from a wild attack of mumps. Fortunately the radio antenna could be hung in a pear tree and he could use it from his bed. On August 14, after they received the go-ahead from London, the two officers decided to proceed to the eastern suburbs of Paris where Armand had supposedly recruited 1,500 volunteers who were ready to fight.

You must remember, said Marchant, that the densely built-over area of the Paris suburbs was far better suited to guerilla tactics than the sparsely wooded and gently undulating countryside of the Seine-et-Marne ... Nevertheless we cabled London that the 1500 men could, if necessary, be moved to the Meaux area.

The British officer, who had ID papers proving that he was of Spanish origin, to explain his strong accent, stayed in the capital with Armand. Every day, in a garage, he taught sabotage courses to resistants, including several gendarmes in uniform. At night his students derailed trains by placing time-pencil initiated charges of dynamite on the ties.

"What can we say about the general state of affairs in Paris between August 14 and 21? continued Marchant. No electricity, the curfew, street fighting at night, contradictory rumors, executions in the Bois de Boulogne ... Many people who defied the curfew order were shot dead in the streets. In the restaurants there was no lack of food or wine. And you could get better meals than anywhere in London, although they were extremely expensive. Lunch for three persons with a hors-d'oeuvre, châteaubriand steak, camembert cheese and peaches, for about 4,000 francs. And still the restaurants were all crowded!"

Capitaine Telmon, who had obtained ID papers and passes, cruised around the suburbs on a motorcycle visiting the various Resistance units. He also made several trips to Forfry.

By August 21 it was getting hard to travel because the Germans were beginning to withdraw. So Marchant started back to Saint-Pathus by bicycle with Armand's radioman, arriving only after numerous detours.

The next day a number of SS with *Schutzpolizei* (security police) settled in the village and 150 soldiers of the Wehrmacht set up camp in Forfry, where Marchant had found his radioman. The Germans were able to capture their radio emissions without being able to locate them exactly, so the operator had to use the emergency frequency.

On the 24th, the enemy left both towns as quickly as they had come. A message could finally be sent to London confirming the possibility of carrying out a parachute drop, and the batteries of the Eureka and the two S-Phones were charged up in preparation for the next interlunar reception.

"We had some three hundred armed men available at that time, continued Marchant. But if equipment was provided we could place another 700 in the field. The Germans were retreating fast through our area and we feared that by the time extra arms and/or SAS troops arrived there would be no Germans left to fight. London seemed curiously reluctant to send us extra arms during the interlune period although we had repeated in several messages that we had Eureka and S-phones in good order."

On the 25th the roads coming out of Paris were empty of Germans and the time seemed ripe to head for the maquis. Armand decided this on his own. But hardly had he finished giving out orders when a message arrived from London forbidding any action until the green light was given. Marchant was consulted about issuing a counter-order, but decided not to as that would only lead to greater confusion.

So on the 26th the Jeds put on their uniforms and waited for Capitaine Telmon's men to arrive from Paris. These men had received orders to travel by night, using different routes, and to avoid any offensive action against the Germans.

The Jeds spent the day and the following night hidden in the woods. On the 27th around 09:00 they get news of an FFI convoy of some twenty vehicles arriving in Saint-Pathus. Along the way a fight had broken out with an enemy column: three officers and about forty soldiers were captured with one FFI killed and three others wounded.

A half hour later, the convoy stopped along a sunken road bordering a lake in the Rougemont woods, between Oissery and Forfry. They had weapons on the trucks, greased and boxed as if they had just come new from the factory. But only the Brens were in working order, along with the four Piats and their 12 bombs, that the three Jeds knew how to use.

Before any defense could be organized, two maquis trucks coming through Oissery were attacked by a German armored car. At the same time a light tank intervened on the north side against the FFI trucks that had already arrived. This first skirmish lasted about an hour and cost the FFI two killed and five wounded, including one who had his jaw broken by a Piat. During the following lull, the wounded were carried to a shelter where nurses looked after them. But two more tanks in position on the other side of the lake opened fire. And then it became clear that the assailants were SS [6]. The only thing to do in this case was to disperse.

At 12:30 when a third column of tanks could be seen progressing along the road from the west, the men heard the order "Every man for himself" and fled eastward into the woods.

"But towards the woods, Marchant recalled, the path was barred by three enemy soldiers. I turn around, dive under a truck, then into the lake where I stay for nine hours while the Germans are machine-gunning the lake at water level from both sides."

Around 22:30 he got out of the water and, in spite of a full moon and the newly-mowed fields offering no shelter whatsoever, managed to crawl his way out of the net and followed his compass to the village of Nanteuil about ten miles away.

The following night he came back to Forfry looking for news. 45 Germans had been killed during the fighting, 86 Resistance fighters. Any prisoners and wounded had been executed and their bodies burned. Among the killed was Capitaine Telmon, hit by a tank shell as he was helping a nurse to escape along the river.

On August 30, American patrols moved into Forfry, then Serjeant Hooker arrived from Paris where he had been hiding. When they had fled, he had had time to ditch the codes and escape with Armand, who had heard of Telmon's death from the nurse.

6. Part of the SS Panzerbrigade 49, which had arrived in Sézanne on the 21st of August 1944, and was traveling by road toward Meaux.

"We were guided by a young girl we had met by chance, he told Marchant. In Puisieux we stopped to buy civilian clothes and burn our uniforms. Next morning we were awakened by a machine-gun battle: when we ventured out of our hideout we discovered an American column advancing along the road to Soissons by devious routes. We hitched a ride to Meaux and then an American officer of the Counter Intelligence Corps drove us to Paris to Les Invalides HQ where I got a change of clothes."

The team had been overtaken by the Allied forces so the British officer and NCO made their way to Normandy where they could catch a plane to England.

Arnold and Cecile in Champagne

On August 31, when advance units of the Third Army arrived at the Meuse, nine Jedburgh teams were operating in the eastern part of the Paris basin: two in Champagne and seven in Lorraine.

In the Marne, Team Arnold [7] was parachuted during the night of August 24. The three Jeds, dressed in civilian clothing, with their equipment and thirty containers, took off from the Tarrant Mushton Airdrome at 22:30 in two Halifaxes belonging to the RAF Group 38. Two hours later they jumped over Igny, west of Epernay. Everything went smoothly.

They were met by Major Bodington [8] who left them with two guides. Then they were led to a hunting lodge in the forest where the owner and his family put them up. During the morning, the containers were opened and equipment distributed.

But the three leg-bags, with the officers' personal weapons, maps, uniforms and quartz crystals for the radio could not be found.

7. Team No. 21 - Capitaine Michel de Carville alias Coudray (Sussex) of the colonial Infantry, Captain J.H.F. Monahan (Londonderry) of the Royal Fusiliers assigned to the Commandos, and Serjeant Alan DeVille (Millième), Royal Armoured Corps.

8. Nicholas R. Bodington, former Reuter's correspondant in Paris and Buckmaster's adjutant, was on his third mission to France: August 1942, July 1943 and July 1944, during which he rebuilt the Pedlar circuit in the Marne.

Bodington promised to send a message to London asking for their replacement, along with some money.

Then the officers got together:

"Do you want to take charge of the area between Epernay and Dormans? Bodington asked."

"OK, answered Coudray. But I'm also supposed to send on any information you may have."

"Good. I'll give you four agents to take the information to the American lines. We have an arms drop scheduled, which will bring our maquis up to 400 men. Can you take care of that?"

In Try, where they spent the night, the Jeds could watch the enemy crossing the Marne in horse-drawn vehicles. Since the Americans were approaching, order was given to the maquis to assemble there. But when an advance unit of the 7th Armored Division came into view, the bridge over the Marne had already been blown and on the opposite bank the enemy successfully warded off American attempts to cross.

So they pulled back and the Jeds followed them to Condé-en-Brie to give their G-2 information about the region. This would be useless because — and the Jeds didn't know it — the bridges in Château-Thierry had been captured intact. Collecting up the weapons dropped by parachute took up the next four days.

"Some of the arms were deposited at Montier-en-Der, near Saint-Dizier, Captain Monahan recalled, and the rest would be entrusted to the FFI of Epernay. They had volunteered to serve in the regular army".

The Jeds also tried, during this time, to keep certain zealous patriots from launching a collaborator hunt. But as Monahan said:

"There weren't very many collaborators, so the Liberation in that part of the country went remarkably smoothly."

At Chêne-la-Reine, the village Resistance group informed the Jeds that they had been ordered to go to Reims as reinforcements for the Americans [9].

9. This order corresponds to General Patton's new role for the FFI: some of them, chosen to serve as guides and lookout patrols, were allowed to keep their weapons and receive gas for their vehicles.

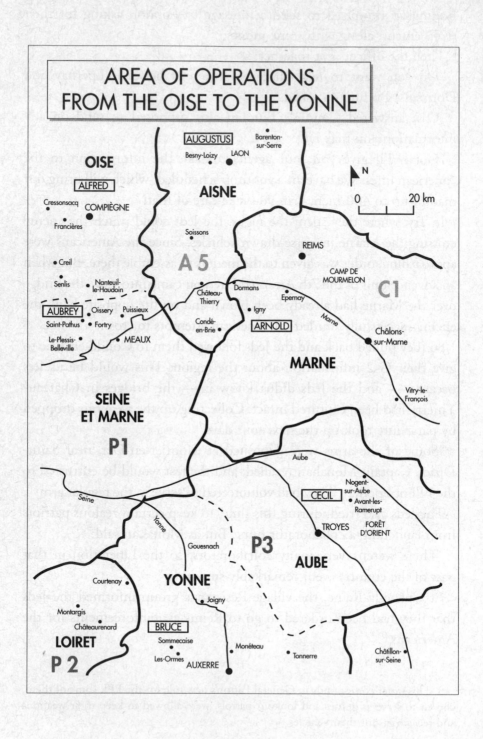

AREA OF OPERATIONS
FROM THE OISE TO THE YONNE

AUGUSTUS

Barenton-
sur-Serre

Besny-Loizy   LAON

OISE

ALFRED

AISNE

Cressonsacq   COMPIÈGNE

Francières

Soissons

REIMS

Creil

CAMP DE
MOURMELON

Senlis   Nanteuil-
le-Haudoin

C1

A 5

Château-
Thierry   Dormans

Epernay

AUBREY   Oissery   Puissieux

Igny

Saint-Pathus   Fortry

Condé-
en-Brie   ARNOLD

Châlons-
sur-Marne

Le-Plessis-
Belleville   MEAUX

MARNE

Vitry-le-
François

**SEINE
ET MARNE**

P1

Aube

Nogent-
sur-Aube

Seine   CECIL   Avant-les-
Ramerupt

Yonne   TROYES   FORÊT
D'ORIENT

Gouesnach   **P3**   **AUBE**

Courtenay   **YONNE**

Joigny

Montargis

Châteaurenard

LOIRET   BRUCE

Sommecaise

P 2   Les-Ormes

Monéteau   Châtillon-
sur-Seine

AUXERRE   Tonnerre

N

0   20 km

"This order appeared to be frivolous rather than serious and we insisted that the group would be much better employed in protecting their own village. Nevertheless they departed for Reims and that same night some Germans came from the local woods into Chêne-la-Reine looking for food. The task of protecting the village had to be given to a group from Igny."

Since their mission was over in the region, Bodington and the Jeds decided to go to Montier-en-Der on September 2. Then they continued on to Saint-Dizier where they thought they might come in handy. Actually the situation in that sector was clear: two companies, one formed by the FFI, the other by the National Front, had been getting along fairly well with each other. Contact was soon established with Colonel De Grouchy, FFI commander in the Haute-Marne, whose CP was situated in Aubrieve.

On September 8, the FFI in Saint-Dizier were warned by the DMR of Region D: the enemy might try to break through towards the North-East in the direction of Chaumont and Châtillon-sur-Seine, and threaten the Third Army communications. The Jeds went to see the Special Forces Detachment of Patton's Army [10] to get precise orders and, if possible, weapons. In exchange for a maximum number of fighters mobilized in Chaumont, Arnold was promised a drop of arms, quartz and personal equipment.

Back at Saint-Dizier they found Bodington waiting for them. One of his companies, in liaison with a squadron of Moroccan spahis from the French 2nd Armored Division (2nd DB), had been sent South and had had contact with the enemy in Bologne, north of Chaumont. On the 11th, Team Arnold, and another unit made up of FFI from Joinville and Saint-Dizier, followed the 2nd DB.

On September 13, they heard from the priest of Brethenay that the road was clear, and the Jeds offered to reconnoiter the route for the 2nd DB combat command. The road was indeed free and Chaumont

10. The SF Detachment No. 11 (EM FFI), code-named Underfoot, was made up of sixty operations, intelligence and signal specialists assigned to Army headquarters, among them 20 to 25 officers. Two thirds of the latter were generally assigned to Army corps and divisions.

had just been liberated by other elements of the Leclerc Division arriving from the South-West. This event was somewhat overblown, however. Witness the report of SF Detachment No. 11:

7-12 September. 1,500 Forces Française de l'Intérieur, an American Operational Group of 50 men (sic), and a platoon of Cavalry were dispatched to take Chatillon. The enemy was attacked 6 miles east. 200 prisoners were taken and 100 enemy killed. FFI companies from St Dizier and Joinville marched toward St Blin to reinforce troops attempting to cut the line of the enemy retreat toward Neufchateau on 12 Sept. This operation was coordinated by a Special Force Detachment. 10 September. The Corps commander ordered FFI to preserve bridges to the north of the 79th Infantry Division and the Second French Armored Division, and to contain enemy pockets at Chaumont and Neufchateau. 270 FFI from Reims to Chaumont for this mission. Chaumont was evacuated in the face of this threat. The enemy moved southward.

On the next day the FFI returned to their sector of origin and on the 15th, the scheduled parachute drop took place. But the weapons received were no longer of any use: the SF Detachment had them gathered and placed under guard in Saint-Dizier.

After writing up a report about the exactions of the German troops [11] in the villages along the edges of the Trois-Fontaines forest, the Jeds went to Paris and then to visit Capitaine Coudray's family in Normandy. They returned on the 24th and took off for London four days later.

In the neighboring département of Aube, Team Cecil [12] was parachuted two days after Arnold. Its mission was to help Diplomat, an F Section circuit, organize the FFI of the département.

Like most of the other teams at the time, Cecil was put on alert on August 9th and took delivery of its equipment at Milton Hall. Four days later, it headed for London for briefing at Devonshire Place.

11. This time it was undoubtedly the SS of the Panzerbrigade 51.
12. Team No. 17 - Major David J. Nielson (Delaware), Royal Engineers, Capitaine Alfred Keser alias Frayan (Lys) of the colonial Infantry and Serjeant R. Wilde (Centavo), Royal Armoured Corps.

"In the building, said Major Nielson, the teams to be briefed followed one behind the other without so much as a minute's break. The few British officers available were overworked, and to make things worse there weren't enough maps!"

After an aborted take-off on August 18 because of foul weather, the team returned to Harrington a week later. When the men arrived, around 19:30, they were immediately met by the dispatcher. The base was particularly busy that night: three Liberators had already left for the DZ and four others would follow for a different site. The Jeds were driven out to the plane by car and took off as scheduled at 21:10, with twelve containers and eight boxes, plus three additional crew members undergoing flight training. The flight was quite comfortable except for some flak fire over Cherbourg. The dispatcher took care of everything. At 01:30 the static lines were hooked up.

"Running in !" yelled the dispatcher.

Capitaine Frayan was already on the edge of the hole, sitting with his feet dangling out. But the plane continued to circle for a quarter of an hour.

"Go !"

Number 1 jumped, followed by the containers whose straps slapped against the fuselage with a frightening shriek. Serjeant Wilde was bothered by the static lines and jumped late, then the Major, last man out, closed the door.

A crash of snapping branches shivered through the trees: the two officers managed to slide to the ground, but the serjeant put his hip out of joint when he landed, causing him pain for the next two weeks. The pilot had faithfully followed instructions, but the Eureka was unfortunately placed on the edge of the woods instead of in the center of the clearing, which was too small to receive the parachutists anyway.

Abelard [13] and the local Resistance chief were on the DZ with about fifty men and wagons. Frayan was the first to be located. He was chided

13. Maurice Dupont alias Yvan. Parachuted into the Aube during October of 1943, he had "hibernated" until spring when the Diplomat circuit was activated for the purpose of sabotaging the railway lines in the region around Troyes for D-Day.

because the committee was persuaded that the British officers hadn't jumped after all the material had been dropped from the first three planes. Three hours later the two other Jeds came out of the woods and the atmosphere eased up. The whole team was offered a meal. The Jeds' personal equipment had disappeared and a few containers, whose parachutes hadn't opened, were damaged. One of them, with a white cross chalked on it, contained a million francs in bills for Abelard.

"When we arrived at the aerodrome, Frayan related, the containers were already on board and we were unable to change anything. We cannot imagine why this money was not handed to one of us. It was a perfect chance to give more luster to our arrival in France. Too bad.

All the material was correctly loaded into cars or wagons and headed for the depots by noontime. In the South-West gunfire could be heard: in Troyes the tanks of the 4th Armored Division were fighting it out with the SS Panzerbrigade 51."

Cecil set up its headquarters in Avant-les-Ramerupt, north-west of the Orient forest. And requests for parachute operations to equip 2,000 men were sent through to London. But after waiting a few days, the team learned on August 31 that no drops would be coming: the region was now considered as overtaken by the Allied forces.

The command post and Abelard next moved to Nogent-sur-Aube where new requests were sent to London, along with information about possible dropping zones. Then, after contacting Commandant Montcalm, the FFI départemental chief [14], in Troyes, the team made the rounds in the south of the département where there was still some scattered fighting.

"Montcalm seemed to be keeping large troop reserves in Troyes, recalled Frayan. It is true that even though the city was liberated, the enemy hadn't by any means been cleared out."

Liaison was established in Châlons-sur-Marne with Lieutenant-Colonel Robert L. Powell of the SF Det No. 11. He confirmed the FFI mission: hunt out the Germans remaining in the woods and keep

14. Commandant Alagiraude, whose authority over the entire département had only been recognized by the FTP a few days before.

them from committing atrocities against the civilian population. When they got back to Troyes, the Jeds learned that fighting in the south had increased, and that most of the Resistance units had been engaged in Auxerre, Tonnerre, Châtillon, as reinforcements for the Yonne units.

In the city, in-fighting was in style. Abelard, Montcalm and the FTP couldn't agree on anything. The head of Mission Verveine in the Morvan had just been named by General Koenig FFI chief for the six départements in the region, so the Jeds went to his headquarters in Auxerre to try to clarify the situation.

"We suggested to Diagramme, said Frayan, that the different elements be split up and that an unknown FFI chief from outside the département be designated. For us, it was clear that Montcalm's orders would never be followed."

So Diagramme decided to keep a single battalion in Troyes and to send another to Châlons with Montcalm. As for Abelard's unit and the FTP, they would be sent into the Yonne where Commandant Zaigue of the FTP would act as tactical commander [15].

These orders were carried back to Troyes. But things didn't happen exactly as planned. Abelard considered his task of organization over, and, as a British subject, decided not to follow his battalion.

Finally it was the AS Nicolas and Marceau battalions who went south, whereas the FTP Vel battalion stayed in Troyes.

The Jeds tried to collect as much as possible of the material abandoned by the enemy to equip their men.

Then they contacted Commandant Millet of the EM FFI, and went to look for the SF Det No. 11, which they found near Etain, east of Verdun.

From there the team traveled to Paris in the hope of being parachuted into Germany — as Colonel Powell had suggested — or elsewhere in France, without returning to England. But in between

15. Actually Commandant Deglane, FTP départemental chief, was acting as political director. Zaigue had just arrived in the Aube, sent by the Parisian staff of the Communist Party.

times a message had arrived ordering them to report to Hôtel Cecil immediately for travel to London. Three days later, on the morning of September 25,

Serjeant Wilde boarded a plane at Orly, followed in the afternoon by the two officers. After a flight to Hendon lasting one and a half hours and a routine security check, a car took them back to London headquarters.

Nearby in the Meuse, two teams were dropped during the night of August 20. And in the Meurthe-et-Moselle, two other teams had been operating south of Nancy since the beginning of September.

Benjamin, Bernard, Archibald and Philip in Lorraine

Teams Benjamin [16] and Bernard [17] were briefed on the 17th for departure two days later: information about the Resistance proved sketchy, there was no detailed map available. Finally the two teams took off from Fairford Air Base on August 20th, each in a different bomber.

Above the Argonne, the planes only spotted the lights once they were directly over the DZ, a tiny field surrounded by trees, south of Clermont. So the jumpers and parcels crashed through tree branches. The inexperienced reception committee was made up of only about fifteen men and they took two days and three nights to recover the forty-odd containers and the chutes.

The two teams were escorted to a camp set up on the edge of the Beaulieu forest, where contact with London was made at 06:30 via Bernard's radio. Since the other radio set had been destroyed when it hit the ground, the Jeds decided to stay together until a new set could be dropped by parachute.

16. Team No. 81 - Major A.J. Forrest (Stirling), Royal Artillery, Lieutenant Paul Moniez alias Marchand (Ulster) of the Infanterie, and Sous-Lieutenant Kaminski alias Camouin (Serre) of the BCRA.

17. Team No. 43 - Capitaine Etienne Nasica alias Prato (Argens) of the Infanterie, Captain J. De Waller (Tiperary) from the Rifle Brigade, and Serjeant Cyril M. Bassett (Lancashire), Royal Armoured Corps.

On August 23 two officers arrived: the Jeds took them to be the DMR Planète's assistants, come to inform them about the local situation:

"Planète is in Nancy where he is preparing an important operation in the Vosges, said Lieutenant-Colonel Aubusson [18]. He wants the Germans to be harassed on both banks of the Meuse River."

Available forces were limited to 600 FFI in the countryside and 300 in Saint-Mihiel, plus 300 FTP in Stenay, Spincourt and Souilly.

"And to add spice to the confusion, Captain Waller would confide later, Aubusson told us that there were almost three thousand Soviet POWs working in the mines in the Bassin-de-Briey."

The two team leaders decided to separate — Bernard was to take the west of the Meuse and Benjamin the east — and return to their initial plans. Six parachute drops were urgently requested at the beginning of the new moon to arm a nucleus of two hundred men in each sector. Contact was established with the FTP to try to organize cooperation with the FFI, and Benjamin prepared to cross the river.

But in the morning of the 24th, the Gestapo and the Militia arrested several local resistants at Islettes. The Jeds were warned a few hours later and moved out, taking with them as much material as they could carry. It was a good thing they did, because in the afternoon a hundred and fifty Germans broke into the camp that had just been evacuated.

The Jeds gave up their plans and during the night moved west toward the forest of Chatrices. After a three-day walk, they arrived, only to learn that one of the FFI chiefs had been captured, and with him a map showing the DZs scheduled for parachute drops.

The next day the Jeds met Major Rooney, chief of the SAS party Rupert, which had been operating in the area for four days. SFHQ informed Benjamin that the Americans would soon be arriving and that they would be needing guides sent to them across the lines.

On August 30, therefore, guerilla fighters were sent to meet the 3rd Cavalry Group of the XX Corps, and three large patrols reconnoitered Sainte-Menehould and Les Islettes with Commandant Dulac's FFI [19].

18. DMR chief of staff, with Commandant Agnelet, FFI départemental head.
19. Colonel Laure (Dulac), ORA Commander in the Argonne and the Verdun sector.

To the south, in the valley of the Biesme, Capitaine Prato was wounded during a skirmish with a German patrol in Futeau.

The next day at daybreak, Sainte-Menehould was occupied by the Cavalry, followed by Combat Command A of the 7th Armored Division heading for Verdun.

The Jeds turned over command of the maquis to Dulac, and headed for Verdun looking for the headquarters of the Third Army.

"As we were coming back, close to Clermont [20], explained Waller, a German outpost fired at our truck, hitting everybody except yours truly and Lieutenant Marchand. All we could do was take to the woods, leaving our radio set and equipment behind."

The Jedburghs, together again finally at Epernay on September 2, reported to Lieutenant-Colonel Powell in Châlons the next day. After a week of R&R with Prato and Bassett evacuated to England, they were directed to the Chaumont region on the 11th, to support the Pedlar circuit which was working in association with Team Arnold.

The group participated in a daytime parachute drop on the 13th in Gargonville, then, after the liberation of Chaumont, helped Major Bodington demobilize his guerilla fighters.

From the 18th to the 22nd, they helped assemblate excess weapons and store them in Nancy.

On October 2, the four Jeds arrived back in England. They were bitter: parachuted two months too late, they regretted that SFHQ showed so little interest in the region where they were engaged!

The first team operating in the Meurthe-et-Moselle — code-named Archibald [21] — had received the standard mission: help organize the FFI, furnish them with weapons and insure liaisons with London by contacting the DMR of Region C.

---

20. During the preceding night an element of the 15th Panzergrenadier Division had ousted Dulac's FFI and settled in Clermont.

21. Team No. 74 - Major Arthur du P. Denning (Cumberland) of the Hampshire Regiment; Lieutenant François Coste alias Montlac (Montgomery), BCRAL, and Sergeant Roger E. Pierre (Sen), U.S. Cavalry.

A mustachioed British Major, a French Lieutenant graduate of Saint-Cyr [22], and a nineteen-year-old New York radio operator, had met in the hospital after each was hurt during training, and decided to get together to form an Interallied team when they got back to Milton Hall.

After spending two weeks in a tepid August London waiting for planes and good weather, the Jeds finally received their departure order: they would jump in uniform instead of in plain clothes as had been programmed initially. They went to Harrington on August 26, just in time to don their parachutes and take off at 20:45.

"Briefing was very sketchy, recalled Major Denning. Most information was based on experience of six months previously. This was not really necessary as Mission Pedagogue, Colonel Buckmaster's Section, was already in the area [23]. A fact which was not given us in our briefing. Neither were we told that we would take a large sum of money for Planete. Pedagogue was not informed that we would be dropped into the area, nor did he know what the Jeds were to do."

The flight was smooth. Around 01:00 three bright lights appeared, forming a triangle, which seemed to confuse the pilot, who flew over twice going the wrong way. Denning jumped first, got carried away by the wind and ended up in the trees. On the ground, two groups were waiting for the team on the Chandernagor site. One of them was from the maquis in the Charmes forest and was made up of sixty men with arms, two trucks and a car, under Capitaine Noël's orders. The other, under Capitaine Dudo, was made up of about sixty sédentaires from the sector. After the usual congratulations, the discussion between the two officers as to the sharing of the equipment turned bitter.

"Dudo, Denning explained humorously, wanted the arms for his men to hide under their pillows or some such good hiding place but didn't want the parachutists."

Captain Noël willingly accepted the responsability of conducting us some 40 km. to his maquis, but rather naturally wanted some arms for his troops.

22. Elite French military academy. TN.
23. This F section circuit had recently been established in Lorraine.

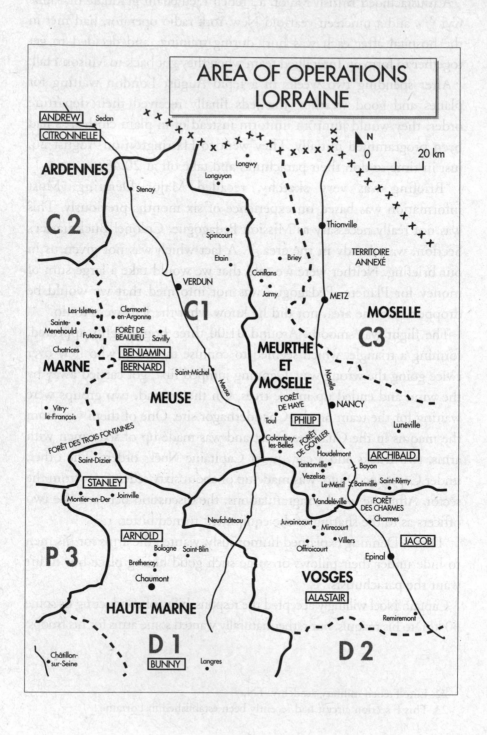

AREA OF OPERATIONS
LORRAINE

N

0   20 km

ANDREW   Sedan
CITRONNELLE

ARDENNES

C 2

Stenay

Longuyon   Longwy

Spincourt

Etain   Briey

Thionville

TERRITOIRE
ANNEXÉE

VERDUN

Conflans

Jarny

METZ

Les-Islettes   Clermont-
en-Argonne

Sainte-
Menehould   Futeau

FORÊT DE
BEAULIEU   Savilly

C1

MOSELLE

C3

Chatrices

MARNE

BENJAMIN

BERNARD

MEURTHE
ET
MOSELLE

Saint-Michel

Vitry-
le-François

FORÊT
DE HAYE

NANCY

Toul   PHILIP

Lunéville

FORÊT DES TROIS FONTAINES

Colombey-
les-Belles

FORÊT
DE GOVILLER

Houdelmont

ARCHIBALD

Saint-Dizier

Tantonville   Bayon

Vezelise

Le-Ménil   Bainville   Saint-Rémy

STANLEY

Montier-en-Der   Joinville

Vandeléville

FORÊT
DES CHARMES

Neufchâteau

Juvaincourt

Charmes

P 3

ARNOLD

Bologne   Saint-Blin

Brethenay

Chaumont

Mirecourt

Offroicourt   Villers

JACOB

Epinal

VOSGES

ALASTAIR

HAUTE MARNE

Remiremont

Châtillon-
sur-Seine

D 1

BUNNY   Langres

D 2

Denning played Salomon and decided how the spoils would be divided.

"Unfortunately, he continued, Noël's choice of containers gave him nine rifles, fifteen Stens and two Brens which had been damaged, mostly because their parachutes weren't attached correctly."

Denning, with the help of a particularly handy Yugoslav captain, immediately started trying to repair the total of eighty non operational firearms on the site. Meanwhile runners were sent all over the region to organize meetings with various leaders.

The presence of sixty Germans within a mile of the DZ hindered the search for the package containing the Jed set and Denning's rucksack. It would be found two days later, but the equipment was useless, so a message requesting a new radio, rifles and medical supplies would be sent to London via the Pedagogue network.

On August 27 Major Power's 2nd SAS team arrived for Mission Loyton which had been operating since the beginning of the month about 25 miles from there, and Team Alastair, also intended for the Vosges.

"We took advantage of the SAS presence, recalled Denning, to establish contact with London. Presumably this direct contact was responsible for London omitting to replace our original sets."

Planète came to Charmes to make contact and recover the 35 million francs that had been entrusted to the Jeds. But he refused to give 500,000 francs to Noël and he gave responsibility for the contacts necessary for recruiting guerilla fighters to his representative in the département. Since this arrangement didn't seem to bring any concrete results, Montlac and Denning decided to concentrate their efforts on the Noël maquis. As more and more weapons arrived, the maquis zone of action was gradually enlarged.

They were warned by an informant that the Germans intended to launch a division against the maquis, which they had estimated at 20 Allied officers and 2,000 well-armed men, although there were only three Jeds and 300 fighters. So the team moved to Leménil-Mitry leaving behind a skeleton group of 150 men to deal with the scheduled parachute drops.

The Germans attacked, as expected, on September 3, but they came back empty-handed. They were furious and burned houses in Saint-Rémy. The SAS Major considered his mission of support to the Jeds as having been fulfilled, now that the Americans were said to be in Toul, so he left for Saint-Dié. Since Capitaine Noël threatened, kidding, not to let him go unless he got them some weapons, he sent a message to London on the spot and made an appointment with the FFI for one o'clock in the morning on the DZ.

"Right on time, recalled Denning, two planes flew over, without any BBC warning. All the SAS had to do was give ten hours' notice for two planes, whereas we, the Jeds, hadn't been able to get anything in ten days! Our reputation was seriously damaged."

Denning wanted above all to solve the weapons problem, so he decided to go see a member of Pedagogue. During the trip, the civilian car in which they were riding was followed by at least thirty bicycles and an armored car, then the road was blocked by the feldgendarmes. But the contact finally took place, and things seemed to start looking better for the maquis.

On September 2, Capitaine Montlac tried to prevent a depot in Tantonville from being destroyed by fire. But the maquisards arrived too late: 80 Germans were killed and 19 prisoners taken, including the commander of the depot who had ordered his men to fire on the civilian population and the firemen [24]. The maquis lost ten killed and several wounded, Montlac among them. While this was going on, Denning, 20 miles away, made contact with the 42nd Squadron which was scouting for the XII Corps marching toward the Moselle. The American recon units didn't know about passwords and safe-conduct passes the Jeds were supposed to use to identify themselves, but they certainly appreciated the quality of the information they got. Denning heard of Montlac's mishap and so, with the help of the Americans, organized the evacuation of the men who had been wounded at Tantonville. But when he got back to Noël's maquis, he learned that

24. The prisoners, sent by convoy to the Americans, would be killed trying to escape.

they had been transported to the Lunéville hospital along with the civilians.

Since the American cavalry wanted a safe bridge to cross the Moselle and reach Lunéville the following evening, the FFI occupied Charmes after a brief skirmish. Unfortunately the Americans were blocked far from there and, after four days of fighting, the FFI were forced to leave the city, abandoning their wounded who would be shot by the Germans.

For about ten days the region between the Madon and the Moselle was a no man's land where any armored patrol was suspect: Germans and Americans sometimes traited each other by just a few minutes.

"It was during this time, recalled Denning, that Team Philip passed through the region and stopped at the maquis headquarters in Leménil-Mitry."

The two team leaders agreed on their respective zones of activity: Philip would take the north of the département and Archibald would remain in the south.

"I informed Capitaine Derouen, Denning continued, that it was impossible to pass through the Haye forest. It was common knowledge that the Jerries were occupying it. They left one afternoon and apparently were ambushed. We were unable to maintain contact with them even though London had requested us to do so."

And he added:

"That team was very keen to get on with the job, but appeared to me to be too impetuous, tending to subject the FFI to unnecessary risks."

The other team's point of view differed of course, and its report, very well-documented, sheds a separate light on events.

Philip's main mission was to equip the maquis that it would find in the Meurthe-et-Moselle, and to provide information to the advancing Allied ground forces. But the team was also requested, during a special briefing by a young Frenchman in civilian clothes, to prevent the Germans from destroying electric and telephone lines, main communications routes and the mining installations between Nancy and Verdun.

203

The team, code-named Rupert [25] at first, took off from Harrington on Thursday August 31 at 21:25, and was dropped at 02:00 on the Restaurant site near Mirecourt in the Vosges. A half-hour later their baggage arrived, with two French officers who were dropped from another B-24 and were to work in the Vosges.

In the beginning the Americans were supposed to jump with a leg-bag containing their equipment. But at the last minute it was decided to drop the equipment separately by parachute: both parcels — containing civilian clothes, two rifles, and two bags with coding documents — would never be found.

"We were received by two different maquis, said Capitaine Derouen. They were well-organized. There was nevertheless a certain confusion on the DZ: too many people and too much noise. Since no one from Planète's office was on the site, we decided to follow the Offroicourt maquis, made up of about one hundred men."

Around 03:00 three trucks left the DZ with weapons and packages. On the main road from Mirecourt to Neufchâteau, they ran into a German patrol. The first two German soldiers were immediately shot and the others scattered into the night.

After meeting twice with the Resistance delegate in Mirecourt, the team — whose code name had become Philip since September 1st — made its way to Viviers-les-Offroicourt where a car was to drive them to the leader of the Saint-Jean maquis who could take them to Nancy. They waited for the car all night and part of the next morning, then finally around noon contacted an American reconnaissance detachment in Juvaincourt. They then returned to the DZ to look for their two leg-bags.

In the afternoon a message was sent through to London, announcing their arrival in Villers and confirming the absence of liaison with Planète. The team then made its way to Nancy via Vandeléville, where they again met up with the American reconnaissance detachment. At

25. Team No. 95 - Capitaine Lberos alias Derouen (Kintyre) from the Infanterie, Lieutenant Robert A. Lucas (Caithness) of the Infantry and Specialist 3rd Class Joseph M. Grgat (Leinster) of the U.S. Navy.

Vézelise, a Gendarmerie sergeant indicated that the Germans had launched an attack against the maquis around Tantonville. A little further on, in Forcelles-Saint Gorgon, they met a Resistance fighter who offered to lead them to the Ménil maquis.

So early in the morning on Sunday September 3, Team Philip arrived at Leménil-Mitry where no one was expecting them: Major Denning had left to make contact with the Americans and Capitaine Montlac, seriously wounded, had just been transported to the German military hospital in Lunéville where he had been operated on soon after arrival.

This maquis, contrary to the others that they had seen in the Vosges, was made up of a large number of men, 300 armed and 400 without arms, led by Commandant Noël, and was living in precarious and risky conditions. For example, after the Jeds arrived two hundred guerilla fighters were engaged in Bayon against Germans armed with tanks and mortars: they would lose a number of men including their captain who was killed.

A message was then sent to London mentioning Philip's presence with Archibald and requesting a parachute drop for 500 men on a DZ two miles south of Bayon.

At the request of the 'centaine' [26] leaders, Capitaine Derouen took command of the maquis and decided to momentarily suspend the mission of protecting the Bayon and Bainville bridges, and to prepare raids on river crossings, after a thorough study of the occupation of the bridges: guards and disposition of instruments of destruction.

Around 20:00 Major Denning returned with Commandant Noël who approved the measures that had been taken.

"The Archibald radio operator was with them. He had lost his equipment when he jumped and he was a better operator than Grgat, so we asked the Major to loan him to us, since our missions were similar. But Denning refused."

The following day, September 4, the 'centaines' were reorganized after the losses sustained and teams went out to reconnoiter the

26. Unit composed of one hundred men. TN.

bridges. Then early in the evening, Team Philip left for Nancy in a truck with three maquisards.

The Philip Jeds passed through Lebeuville, Vézelise and Houdreville and were approaching Houdelmont when they realized they were being chased by a platoon of motor machine-guns. They managed to hide in a clump of trees two hundred yards from the road, then noticed that the cars following them had the American white star painted on them. They were actually a reconnaissance platoon of the 25th Cavalry Squadron. Once the commanding officer recognized his error, he explained that the inhabitants of Houdreville had told him that a German vehicle had just gone through. Before going back to the village, where they would spend the night in nearby woods, Jeds and Americans searched for sergeant Grgat. But in vain; he had lost his nerve and disappeared into the dark when things were getting tense.

The two officers gave up the idea of trying to get to Nancy from the south. They entrusted the search for their radioman to the mayor and the gendarmerie of Vézelise, and tried to get through to the capital of Lorraine via Toul.

"On the 6th at 20:00, recalled Derouen, we contacted the Colonel commanding a regiment of American tanks [27] whose headquarters were located south of the Goviller forest. He told us that he was all alone as advanced-guard and that the Germans counter-attacked in force at Bayon. He advised us to spend the night in the forest."

The organization of Patton's Army was at that time being completely overhauled. The preceding day the XV Corps, with only his staff and Corps troops, had received orders to protect the south flank of the Army. And at the moment only the 2nd Cavalry Group was fighting its way toward the Madon River.

Philip arrived in Toul by way of Colombey-les-Belles, and contacted the captain of the gendarmerie, the FFI chief and Lieutenant Ripley representing the Special Forces. The team hoped that the latter would be able to get their orders from London and establish a liaison with Planète.

27. Colonel Charles H. Reed, commander of the 2nd Cavalry Group.

But no help was available from that quarter, so on the afternoon of the 9th they reported to headquarters of the SF Det No. 11 where they ran into Lieutenant-Colonel Powell and Team Arnold, then Denning, who informed them that the radioman Grgat had been sent back to London via Paris.

On the advice of Lieutenant Walsh, detached to the XX Corps in Jarny, Powell entrusted Team Philip with a new mission:

"In liaison with Battalion Chiefs Joly and Duval [28], you will arm 3,000 FFI volunteers in Verdun and Conflans. Once these men are armed and regrouped in the north, you will protect our left flank. A radioman will be at your disposal either at Sainte-Menehould or at Verdun."

On the 10th, the team moved into the Hotel Vauban in Verdun with two operators: one on loan from Lieutenant Couten, FFI commander for the city, the other from the local intelligence squad. They made the rounds of the different groups in Briey, Longuyon, Longwy, and sent the first requests for airborne supplies. But since London didn't answer, Philip returned to the SF Detachment headquarters where the Jeds learned on September 17, that they were going to be sent back to London and then parachuted into Alsace or Germany for a new mission. Their instructions were to report to SF Det No. 12 at the Hôtel Cecil in Paris.

Via Châlons, Montmirail and Meaux, the team reached Paris, where it took them four days to get their mission orders. That was fine with the two Jeds who were free to visit the capital. On Saturday September 23, Lieutenant Lucas left France, followed by Capitaine Derouen the next day.

We left Team Archibald operating in the no man's land between the Madon and Moselle rivers, as the Germans were massing reinforcements on the right bank. Soon after Philip's visit, a gendarme on a motorcycle brought a message from the Americans to the Ménil

28. Commandant Pierre Joly, FFI départemental chief of staff for the Meuse, and Commandant Duval alias Cosson, chief of the Mangiennes maquis, north of Verdun.

maquis, requesting assistance at the Haroue bridge. One hundred and sixty maquisards took up positions around the bridge, but at the first cannon round, the American light tanks and armored cars retreated, and the FFI had to pull back.

Commandant Noël now had a mobile group protecting communications lines and intercepting German columns that had been overtaken by the Allied advance. On September 16, when a combat command of the 4th Armored Division entered the city, 300 FFI from the Noël group came to provide security.

Denning then suggested that the 79th Infantry Division integrate the Noël battalion into its own forces. But the project had to be abandoned because it had been decided that the FFI formations would be incorporated into the regular French Army. Then Denning was arrested by the American CIC for using false ID papers and taken to Paris.

When he returned to Lorraine, Planète, the DMR, who was about to leave for London, asked him to stay in the region and help him integrate the Noël battalion with the FFI formations in the region around Blainville and Lunéville. Then the Third Army G-2 suggested organizing a mission behind enemy lines to collect information. Finally, Major Denning returned to England on November 21, followed three days later by his radio operator.

Having the FFI cover the south flank of Patton's army in Lorraine was not a new idea. As soon as the army had broken through at Avranches, the protection of the right bank of the Loire had been assigned to the SF Detachment and a parachute drop of arms for 3,000 FFI fighters authorized by the Army. Thus during the night of August 12, twenty-eight planes dropped arms over Châteaubriant, and two weeks later, 3,400 men controlled the north bank of the river from Nantes to Angers.

Then the protective curtain was stretched to Tours and Briare, with FFI forces reaching almost 10,000 at the end of the month, plus 7,000 others indirectly involved on the left bank, covering the south flank. A total of 25,000 FFI were thus engaged from Nantes to Châtillon.

Opposite:
Lieutenant-Colonel George Richard Musgrave, Royal Artillery, was the third commanding officer of the Jedburgh training center at Milton Hall. Note in front of him the planning board for the coming sessions and the two mailbaskets, vitally important: IN, full, and OUT, empty. (National Archives)

Below:
July 14, 1944 at Milton Hall. The Allies celebrate Bastille Day, the French national holiday, in appropriate fashion. The French soldiers in their national uniforms, surround an American infantry parachute regiment captain and lieutenant. The captain is wearing the British parachute wing on the lower part of his sleeve. (National Archives)

Above:
The French soldiers share the radio instruction room with easy-going Americans and two impeccably-dressed British NCOs. One of them is from the Royal Corps of Signals, which provided most of the English radio operators.
(National Archives)

Opposite:
At the SOE ME 65 center at Milton Hall. Training in reception of radio messages. One of the students is a French captain, another an English corporal.
(National Archives)

Above:
"At Milton Hall, a Jed team receives its radio gear" says the caption of the era.
The American Master Sergeant, signing for his material in presence of the
English captain, is credible, but the two French lieutenants are less so.
This is typical of the Hollywood syndrome. (National Archives)

Opposite:
The transmitter-receiver set type B
MK II, the "suitcase set", is the
favorite model used by the network
agents and the Special Forces
teams in the field.
Its characteristics were:
weight 30 lbs, range 500 miles,
dimensions 18 1/2" x 13 1/2" by 6".
(Frederic Lautier)

Opposite:
The transmitter-receiver
type A MK III has the same range
(500 mi) as the MK II model, but
it has a considerable advantage
over its predecessor: it weighed
only 18 lbs and thus is much
more worthy of its nickname,
the 'suitcase set'.
(Frederic Lautier)

Opposite:
Milton Hall, spring of 1944. Jeds on the obstacle course. This type of installation was to be copied at Aldershot, for the Parachute Regiment, on a type of combat course known very appropriately as the 'confidence course'. (National Archives)

Below:
At the SOE ME 65 center at Milton Hall. Two Jeds climb a brick wall during a training course. (National Archives)

Opposite: *Milton Hall, spring of 1944. The British officer in charge of the sabotage course talking to his students. Note that on his right sleeve he is wearing the parachute wing of the British Airborne troops rather than that of the Special Forces. (National Archives)*

Below:
Milton Hall, spring of 1944. Sabotage course. Among the men can be seen members of Jed teams Jacob (Sjt Seymour - 1st row), Desmond (Cne Maunoury alias Bourriot - 2nd row), Aubrey (Capt Marchant - 3rd row), and Arnold (Sjt Alan de Ville - 4th row). (National Archives)

Opposite:
*Milton Hall,
Spring of
1944. Jeds on
the pistol-firing
range.
(National
Archives)*

Below:
*A sampling of
gear used by
the Special
Forces:
cortex, limpet
(magnetic
mine),
mortar shells,
receiver set,
'time-pencil'
detonation.
(National
Archives)*

Above:
At Special Forces Headquarters in London, the British briefing officer gives their mission orders to three members of a Jedburgh team, probably Jed team Francis, dropped over Corrèze on August 10, 1944.
(National Archives)

Above:
At Harrington Air Base, where the three Carpetbagger squadrons of the 801st Bombardment Group (Heavy) were installed on March 28, 1944, the runway crew fills the tank of a black-painted B-24 Liberator.
(National Archives)

Above:
*In one of the prefabs (Quonset Hut) with rounded corrugated iron roofs,
an American Technical Sergeant stores the carefully-folded dorsal
parachutes. Other parachutes can be seen on the shelves,
along with loose leg-bags and various types of cases and nets.
(National Archives)*

Above:
*At Harrington Air Base ground crews remove containers from the open-air depot
and load them onto bomb wagons to carry them to the planes.
(National Archives)*

Above:
At Harrington Air Base, containers being loaded onto a Carpetbagger B -24. (National Archives)

Below: *The caption of the time reads "Jeds getting ready in the locker room before takeoff." The French captain who is not a parachutist, in black beret and battle-dress, looks a lot like Capitaine Schuman who was to jump into Brittany with Interallied Mission Aloes.* (National Archives)

Above :
The caption says Jeds, but these are actually French officers being sent by the EM FFI to a network or maquis group. Note the package with personal gear attached to it, a method that the Jeds hated. The scene takes place at Tempsford, the first Carpetbagger base. (National Archives)

Opposite :
In the "locker room' before takeoff, can be seen all sorts of people being sent by SFHQ into France. Here "agents finish dressing for their night mission", says the caption.

On the right :
Harrington Base, Zone T. Before night takeoff on 12nd of August 1944, a Jedburgh team poses in front of the B-24 that will carry them over France. These people are from Acenis mission. Young woman is Cécile Pichard and beside her, Maurice Roschbach. (National Archives)

Above:
A B-24 Liberator crew waiting for the jumpers they will be dropping over France that night. In preparation for the Normandy invasion, the 492nd Bombardment Group had four squadrons of B-24s operating out of Harrington Air Base. (National Archives)

Above:
Under the watchful eyes of the Liberator crew, the Jeds don their equipment before going aboard. Two American parachutists do a final check. Note that the men are wearing only the English dorsal parachute, without any ventral back-up chute. (National Archives)

Below:
In zone T at Harrington, members of several Jed teams finish getting ready beside the runway. This scene probably takes place around the middle of August, at a time when many teams were parachuted into occupied France on certain days. (National Archives)

Opposite and below:
Different views of
a Jedburgh with his
equipment, ready to leave
for the field. Most of his gear
is English: helmet,
miscellaneous equipment
gear, revolver, camouflage
jacket and pants, rucksack.
Only the M1-Carbine
parachute stock is American.
(National Archives)

Above:
*"Lieutenant-Colonel Obolensky is one of the men in the prefab locker room",
says the OSS caption. Serge Obolensky was to accompany Operational Group
Patrick, parachuted into the Massif Central on August 15, 1944.
(National Archives)*

Above:
Lieutenant-Colonel Obolensky, who was to jump into France in August of 1944, helps an OG finish getting ready. On his sleeve he is wearing the British emblem and that of the OSS para wings. Note the nationality arm band on his left sleeve and the ammunition bag attached to his belt. (National Archives)

Above:
A combat group from OG Donald posing in front of the B-24 that will carry them to France. The men are wearing combat uniforms with the Special Forces emblem on their right sleeve. Instead of a ventral parachute they are carrying, after the English fashion, a combat haversack. (National Archives)

Opposite:
The transmitter-receiver set known as the Tellerphone or S-Phone or Sugar Phone, used for voice guidance of planes during parachute drops, is being shown here in Italy by a pathfinder from the British 2nd Parachute Brigade.
(IWM)

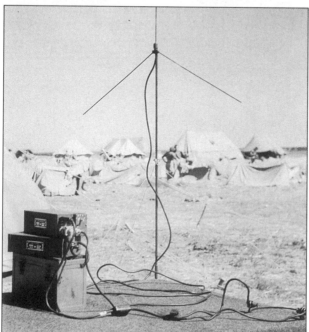

Opposite:
The PPNIA Eureka beacon with its trident antenna that could be raised nine feet high. The gear also includes a battery, wirebox and transmitter-receiver set. It is being shown here in Italy by the Pathfinder section of the British 2nd Parachute Brigade.
(IWM)

Above:
The members of a Jedburgh team get ready before leaving for a mission. The team is made up of a British leader in battle-dress, a French officer and an American NCO radioman wearing a 1942 model jumpsuit that was used on the Mediterranean front. (National Archives)

*Opposite:
An American member of OG Donald, parachuted into North Finistère on August 5, 1944, "struggles with his gear in the locker room", as indicated by the caption of the time. He is wearing the emblem of the OSS on his right sleeve. (National Archives)*

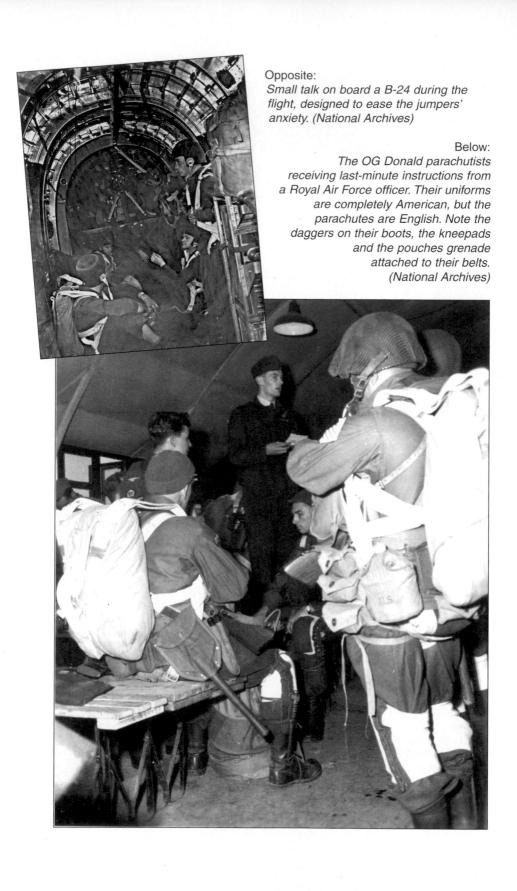

Opposite:
Small talk on board a B-24 during the
flight, designed to ease the jumpers'
anxiety. (National Archives)

Below:
The OG Donald parachutists
receiving last-minute instructions from
a Royal Air Force officer. Their uniforms
are completely American, but the
parachutes are English. Note the
daggers on their boots, the kneepads
and the pouches grenade
attached to their belts.
(National Archives)

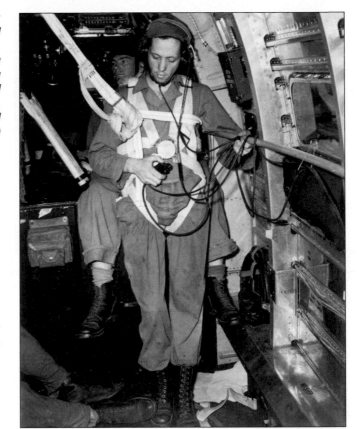

*Opposite:
On board
the B-24,
the dispatching
sergeant getting
ready to send
out the jumpers.
(National
Archives)*

Below:
*One of the
parachutists
has just jumped
through the trap
door, known as
the 'Joe hole',
of a B-24.
(National
Archives)*

Above:
A Jedburgh landing in France by night. After gathering in the sail of his chute, he is getting ready to pick up his backpack and head for the reception committee. (National Archives)

Opposite:
U.S. Cavalry Major J.W. Summers, who jumped into the Finistère on July 17, 1944 as leader of Jed team Horace. (National Archives)

Below:
In the maquis somewhere in southwestern France, a Jedburgh is showing some réfractaires how to use the Stens that were dropped by the Allied planes. (BDIC)

Opposite:
A maquisard cleaning his machine gun during a lull in the fighting. (Private collection)

Opposite:
It almost looks like a Boy Scout camp, but the boys are men, and their faces wear the marks of tough maquis life and the constant threat of attack by the German occupational troops. (Private collection)

Opposite:
Young maquisards rest after a training exercise, while a medic looks at the foot of one of the recruits. These are the maquis groups that were given priority for arms drops from London or Algiers. Note how young the guerilla fighters are, and how their uniforms seem more suitable for Boy Scouts than for soldiers. (Private collection)

Opposite:
*A typical maquis scene : instruction in the use of the FM 24-29. The senior officer is teaching the young recruits how to serve this piece of artillery. Here n° 2 is learning how to insert the charger.
(Private collection)*

Opposite:
*Limoges, August 1944. The Allied officers who liberated the city are being decorated : Major Staunton, Captain Brown from Jed team Lee and his teammate Lieutenant Angoulvent.
(Private collection)*

Above:
Somewhere in the south of Brittany, probably after liaison was made with the American forces, two American and British Jedburghs are hamming it up for the photographer. The invading troops have reached them and time has come for a little fun. (Private collection)

Opposite:
*A small group of resistance fighters near Poitiers in civilian clothing, bare-headed or wearing an Adrian helmet or a Basque beret, with FFI arm bands. Their weapons are completely ill-assorted : Mausers, French blunderbusses, Stens, German hand grenades ...
(BDIC)*

Above:
Meetings between the invading troops and the FFI with their Special Forces leaders are always a good time for a toast to the Allies. The radiant faces are still marked by the hard fighting against the retreating Germans that they all participated in. (BDIC)

Opposite:
Left, RTO Joseph Litalien and right, Captain Lionel Guy d'Artois, SOE. These Special Forces Leaders were dropped on Saône-et-Loire 23rd May 1944. (National Archives)

Above:
Elements from the Pommies Corps Franc (CFP) entering Tarbes after the liberation of the city in August 1944. The CFP, part of the Organisation de Resistance de l'Armee, was at that time made up of almost 8000 men. They received many weapons through several Jed teams operating with them in the area. (Private collection)

Opposite: During the liberation of Tarbes, the new city officials assemble on the Allées Nationales. In the picture can be seen in particular Marine Corps Lieutenant-Colonel Fuller, leader of Jed team Bugatti, parachuted over the Pyrenees Mountains on June 28, 1944. (BDIC)

*Opposite:
An ex-Jedburgh, Christian Longetti, now part of the Special Allied Airborne Reconnaissance Force, whose insignia can be seen embroidered on the right sleeve of his jacket. He is also wearing the metal pin of the Forces Francaises Libres on his right pocket as well as the cloth emblem of the parachutists of Free France (France Libre).
(Private collection)*

In the Loire valley, the SF Det No. 11 played an important role by integrating the FFI action into operational plans and controlling airborne supplies. But no Special Forces team was sent north of the river. To the south, two Jedburgh teams — Harold and Tony [29] — were parachuted into the Vendée region. Those working in the Morvan or Berry, would mainly participate in the destruction of German troops retreating from soutwestern France.

The Morvan command

In Bourgogne, we left the special forces just as the Frenchmen participating in Mission Verveine scheduled to operate in the Morvan had finally arrived in the field.

On July 7, Lieutenants Lemaître and Michon with Miss Heim arrived in France, but far from the intended DZ and with no reception committee. They were greeted by a makeshift group of local residents who were expecting equipment, while a serious battle between the FFI and the Germans was taking place near the site.

When they took inventory of the equipment dropped, the team was dismayed to discover that there was no radio set, so they had no contact with London.

They took refuge in a safe house, but had to leave on the 8th because the Germans had been informed of the parachute drop and had launched an all-out search.

"When we left London, said one of the two officers, we had agreed to report to the headquarters of Colonel Lemniscate, delegate for the northern zone. We were to wait there for the BBC personal message letting us know that we could meet our chief, Colonel Diagramme, at Charolles, in Saône-et-Loire."

29. Team No. 76 - Major V.E. Whitty (Ross), Royal Armoured Corps, Lieutenant Pierre Jolliet alias Rimbaut (Tyrone) of the Colonial Artillery and Serjeant H. Verlander (Sligo), KIng's Royal Rifle Corps, parachuted during the night of July 15, 1944 to work with the SAS Mission Dickens. Team No. 5 - Major Robert K. Montgomery (Dollar), U.S. Infantry, Lieutenant Paris alias Devailly (Ecu) of the Colonial Infantry and Sergent John E. McGowan (Quarter), USAAF, parachuted during the night of August 17, 1944.

But the agents could find neither Lemniscate or Pair, his BOA. Through local Resistance fighters they were lucky enough to meet a radioman at Cosne-sur-Loire who loaned them an emitter with which they were able to establish contact with London. Then, little by little, from sector chiefs to the départemental FFI leader, they made their way to the command post where they learned that their Colonel was in the region around Charolles.

Diagramme arrived during the night of the 6th and contacted Commandant Romans-Petit, FFI leader for the Ain, and Colonel Bayard, chief of staff for Region R.1. Through them, he signaled his arrival to London. Then he went on into the Saône-et-Loire.

His movements were considerably hindered by the German police, who detected his presence first at Lons-le-Saunier, then followed him west, twice searching houses that he had just left. He arrived at his destination on July 15 and made contact with Capitaine Ferent, départemental FFI leader, and also with the sector chief.

He learned from the latter that the intended contact with his adjutants Lemaître and Michon would be extremely dangerous, so he warned the BCRAL not to air the designated sentence and decided to continue on to Lieutenant-Colonel Hastings' headquarters. Hastings being his predecessor with Mission Isaac, he supposed that he should be somewhere near the Nièvre départemental chief.

So Diagramme headed for Colonel Moreau's CP and met him at the Ouroux maquis on July 22. Guess who was also there: all the départemental FFI authorities, with Télémètre, Lemniscate and Pair. But no one had any news about the rest of his team.

Since Hastings (Télémètre) had received threatening orders from London, he had been doing nothing except carrying out his military obligations.

He had received information that the enemy was considering using tanks against the maquis, so he had been urging the guerilla fighters to use the anti-tank weapons that they had at their disposal: bazookas, PIATs and mines.

"Through our captured Russians, Hastings indicated, I also laid down the foundation for desertions by them to the maquis, and obtained through the SAS a promise that the Allies would not hand them over to the Russian Government after the war if they surrendered to us."

On July 21, he examined the different actions taken by the enemy against the maquis.

"The attacks followed the same pattern i.e. attempts by the enemy to penetrate the maquis by informers who subsequently escaped and indicated to the enemy the maquis whereabouts."

The next day Diagramme and Hastings, who had barely met in London, got together in the middle of the Morvan. The Englishman gave the following report of their meeting:

22 July. I was glad to report the arrival of Diagramme. With his energetic character, things started to improve rapidly. He approved everything I had been doing and informed London by telegram accordingly. He seconded my request to Lemniscate, Defoe and Grandjean that they act on the regional level and forget their old tendency to consider themselves attached to a specific maquis group. He insisted that the hierarchal chain of command not be by-passed and that a proper intelligence-collecting system be created.

The report of Verveine's leader was more explicit:

"I had noticed the existence of numerous clans setting Colonel Moreau against the FTP and the Nièvre départemental chief of the maquis, so I tried to reestablish some kind of order and suggested conciliatory gestures that everyone seemed to accept. I had the feeling that, from the beginning, much of the anarchy was brought about by the arrival of Colonel Dupin, who had falsely claimed the right to command in the Morvan, who was contested by many and who London finally and wisely disowned."

In the maquis, rumor had it that Dupin was surrounded by a team of monarchist officers. It was normal that the men who traditionnally favored democracy should react forcefully.

"When I met Télémètre, continued Diagramme, I got the impression that he was uneasy. He had received orders from his services to stop all activity until the arrival of his French teammate, and had been disowned by numerous members of the maquis. This was probably part of the reason why he was ill at ease. It is also true that a few weeks before, he had openly sided with Dupin's team, and had even incorporated into his own staff some of that colonel's officers."

Diagramme finally managed to make peace among the different factions surrounding the départemental chief. He was careful not to live with any special maquis group and kept Hastings under his wing to prevent any mishaps.

"Wherever we went, Hastings recalled, Diagramme regarded and treated me as his equal. I always referred to him as a Frenchman and senior to me. His attitude and his understanding facilitated our cooperation and increased the prestige of the mission. There was no jealousy, sectarianism or narrow-mindedness in his attitude."

After a quick visit to the maquis in the Nièvre, Diagramme moved on to the Côte-d'Or, where he contacted the DMR's adjutant in region D, Capitaine Davout d'Auerstaedt (Ovale). They both agreed to establish closer ties between the Côte-d'Or, the Nièvre and the Saône-et-Loire. But Diagramme never got an answer to his request for a meeting with Ovale's chief, Colonel Hanneton (Ligne).

Back at the Nièvre départemental headquarters, and still without news from his command team, he returned to the Saône-et-Loire to handle a few urgent matters.

Hardly had he left when the command team arrived in Ouroux and immediately got down to work. The first problem they tackled was the organization of parachute operations, which were taking place at that time in total confusion. Teams specializing in stealing material dropped by parachute diverted weapons, money and various objects from their true destination. Since both Lemniscate and Diagramme were absent, Lieutenants Michon and Lemaître dealt directly with the BOAs of the département to insure that each drop was carefully guarded and that the material and money received be reserved for the regional chief. In this they managed to obtain the consent of the FTP and the cooperation of their leader, Commandant Roland, to work alongside the FFI.

During the first days of August, Diagramme, learning that his team had arrived, decided to leave Michon at Télémètre's headquarters and to entrust Lemaître, assisted by Miss Heim, with the job of directing the mission personnel installed in the Saône-et-Loire, near the headquarters of the FFI départemental chief [30].

Meanwhile the Germans were far from inactive. Every ambush or parachute drop was answered by an attack on a maquis. On July 1st in the area around Donzy a large German column surrounded a maquis of 200 men: after four hours of fighting, the enemy withdrew abandoning twelve dead [31]. On the 5th, at Balleray, they chose the FTP Melnick maquis, which had just received five tons of equipment the day before. Jedburgh team Harry continued to follow the Libé-Nord-ORA maquis, while the SAS set up in the nearby valley of Chalaux, not far from the Peinture drop zone.

"On one of our parachute operations on Peinture, said Captain Guthrie, an American and a RAF plane collided in mid-air. It appears that the American plane was looking for another ground and came to Peinture, where the Eureka was operating, as he could not find his own ground. All the crews of both planes were killed. I was exceedingly anxious that the Germans should not realize that Peinture was a DZ and I hoped to keep the accident a secret."

However, the news spreads like wildfire.

"If the Germans find out that there has been an air accident, said the mayor of the town who had come to see the Jeds, the population will be in great danger."

"Give me a day, answered Guthrie, to get the crew of the first plane buried. The plane itself has crashed in the woods and can't be seen except from the air."

"OK. Then I can report to the authorities the other plane that fell out in the open. The Germans most certainly will not realize that it went down during a parachute drop."

---

30. Reading the documents written at the time is difficult because the participants can be designated by their code name or their pseudonym. Thus Viat is Diagramme, but Lemaître can be either Quartier or François, Michon can be Physique or Pommier, Miss Heim is also Danubien, and Lieutenant Coli alias Catari or Elevation or Prunier.

31. Some documents refect to 176 Germans killed during this attack on the FTP Félix Tonton maquis.

A week later it was learned that part of the money intended to defray the expenses of the maquis — in order to avoid having to requisition food, a system which was not at all appreciated by the civilians — had been aboard one of the aircraft that collided on July 18. Once a detailed cargo manifest arrived by radio message, the disappearance of 30 million francs out of a total of 60 million loaded on board in unmarked containers, was confirmed. Several days went by, and then they learned that the missing money had been sent to the SAS, and that the inconspicuous box containing it was stowed away in a cellar along side boxes of weapons.

A massive daylight drop was scheduled about this time, and the Jeds were ordered to organize the reception committee. But the maquis in the area had been subject to numerous attacks recently and Camille had lost a lot of vehicles when they had had to evacuate Vermot, so the team asked that the drop be postponed. When conditions were more favorable and the time was ripe for an operation, they got no answer from London.

Mission Verveine and the Jeds feared for the safety of the wounded and thus orders were given for the field hospitals to be located as far as possible from the camps, or grouped together near Montsauche, where they could be protected.

Around the same time, Guthrie suggested organizing training sessions for the maquis chiefs directed by Colonel Dubois, Moreau's adjutant, and himself. A dozen maquisards were thus introduced to basic instruction at the company level in arms, tactics, topography and living off the land.

SAS Mission Houndsworth was now made up of eighteen officers and 126 troopers with nine armed Jeeps.

"Things began to get serious, indicated the author of the mission report, when the first Jeeps arrived. Then two 6-pound anti-tank guns were dropped."

One of the 6-pounders was put in position at the SAS camp, the other at the Bernard maquis — where Camille had taken back command after recovering from his wound — with Guthrie's approval. The two guns came in handy several days later when the maquis were attacked.

214

"On August 3rd at 09:00, recalled survey engineer Tual in his report, 560 enemy troops from the air infantry surrounded Saint-Martin-du-Puy, then Chalaux, and attacked the camp of the Goths."

This camp was set up around a dried-up pond where old springs still seep out of the ground, located in the Saint-Martin woods near the farm of the Goths.

It was protected by a well-organized defensive ring located a mile from the center of camp, with lookouts on the high points and mine fields and booby traps in between.

The enemy, in spite of all their zealous maneuvering, couldn't manage to penetrate inside this defensive line around the camp of the Goths.

The maquisards inside used twenty-five Brens and the anti-tank cannon to break the assault by firing back at the machine guns and mortars supporting the German attack. At daybreak on the 4th, the Germans withdrew after suffering heavy losses: 45 dead and more that 35 seriously wounded were counted by the inhabitants of the neighboring villages and hamlets.

Of course the Germans couldn't allow this continue, and the Château-Chinon security battalion went into action several times, with occasional air support, for example on August 11 at Larochemillay after the Luzy ambush by the Louis maquis, part of Libé-Nord. It even appeared that elements from outside the region were engaged, such as aviators at the camp of the Goths or an SS battalion at Lormes, which was said to have lost 80 killed during that one day [32].

On August 3rd, another ambush was laid by the Bernard maquis to intercept the mail sent from Paris to the Feldkommandanturen in Nevers, Dijon, Lyon, Epinal and Grenoble. Three bags containing interesting information were taken. Hastings requested that a light plane be flown in from London to pick them up. Once again, he got no answer.

32. According to FFI headquarters in London. If this is true, they could have been elements of the *SS-Panzer-Grenadier-Ausbildung-Btl 18*, stationed in Thiers at that time.

On that same day, the Morvan learned of the arrest of Lemniscate. The DMR had left for Paris with Pair and was seized on July 20 by the German police.

It was suggested that Diagramme leave Mission Verveine and replace Lemniscate. But no one was available to take over Pair's job of air operations officer. So Guthrie suggested to London that he take over the BOA himself, assisted by Ratissoire, Pair's assistant.

Diagramme returned during the discussion and took over military direction of P.3, while at the same time keeping an eye on the neighboring départements of the Côte-d'Or and Saône-et-Loire, normally part of Region D.

At Settons Lake, Diagramme, along with Hastings, set up the mission command post and entrusted command to Physique who was to replace him during his absences. Then he tried to assign an officer to each FFI leader in the other départements.

" We don't need two officers for the BOA, he told Guthrie."

" OK, Guthrie agreed. Ratissoire is quite capable of handling it himself."

"Are you still interested in the liaison mission between the Resistance and the SAS?"

" No, the SAS are perfectly capable of getting along by themselves as far as liaison are concerned."

" In that case, I suggest that Gapeau, your assistant, be sent into the Yonne"

Even though Guthrie could theoretically take orders only from London, he agreed because of Diagramme's position at the FFI headquarters.

" It didn't bother me a bit to get rid of my assistant, recalled Guthrie" He hadn't cooperated with me in the least and hadn't managed to make himself very popular with the French either."

The Jed then asked Diagramme about his own job Several days later Diagramme told him that he and Colonel Moreau had decided that Guthrie should organize mobile shock columns in the various maquis."

" We're going to need a lot of vehicles, Guthrie remarked, plus a car for me to travel from one maquis to the other."

216

"No problem, answered Moreau. You can have whatever you need."

But, as Guthrie feared, no vehicles appeared. So he had to stay at the Montsauche maquis and couldn't travel at all

In the Saône-et-Loire, Quartier had already succeeded in establishing cordial relations between the turbulent FTP and SOE elements, and reinforce the authority of the FFI départemental chief. In the Côte-d'Or it was Lieutenant Corrida, recently arrived from London, who got the job. Reserve Capitaine Varennes (Carpentier), recruited nearby, was also sent to the Aube and the Haute-Marne.

From his contacts with the different départemental leaders, Diagramme became convinced that the Morvan, which he conceived as including the Saône-et-Loire, Côte-d'Or, Nièvre, Yonne and Aube départements, could be considered a tactical entity which could be consolidated by a few general measures. He gave orders to create, for the five départements, a hierarchy permitting rapid establishment of a tactical command structure in the Morvan at the appropriate time. Then it was simply a question of coordinating the operations of the different maquis groups to obtain better results.

Another of Diagramme's problems was to give focus to the maquis activities, to get rid of the anarchy resulting from individual initiatives. To do this, he suggested creating a counter-espionage service and military courts, each one provided with at least one qualified judge, and centralizing requisitions in the office of the départemental chief. He also recommended creating a commissariat for food supplies, so as to put an end to requisitioning of food. Looting of post offices, banks, tax collector's offices, tobacco shops had to be stopped.

Hundreds of ambushes were carried out against German columns by small detachments, with remarkable results. On August 23, when London gave the order for generalized guerilla action, ambushes and the placing of obstacles occured everywhere along the roads of the five départements of the Morvan.

Finally on September 6, General Koenig, at the request of the Commissary of the Republic for Bourgogne and Franche-Comté, created the FFI region of the Morvan and named as commander

Colonel Dubac (Diagramme). An advanced CP was set up near Settons Lake and a staff, with telephone connections to Ouroux, Avallon-Saulieu-Charolles and Clamecy-Nevers, was set up in Auxerre.

Bruce and the FFI in the Yonne

As soon as he got back to the Morvan, Diagramme reinforced his previous contact with the American Third Army and established a daily liaison with the SF Det No. 11 [33].

To organize his staff he was assisted by Chef de Bataillon Millet, assigned to him by General Koenig. His diplomatic instinct, coupled with the authority he represented, were a precious aid to Diagramme.

"As could be expected, recalled the latter, it wasn't easy for me to take command. Actually the five départements making up the FFI region of the Morvan were part of three different FFI sectors: P.3, D.1 and R.1."

On September 7, he obtained the support of Lieutenant-Colonel Laurent, P.3 FFI chief, who accepted the job of Chief of Staff for the Morvan. Colonel Fayel, in charge of P.2 and P.3, was contacted a few days later and agreed, not without misgivings, to the new organization: he declared that he had received instructions from the National Resistance Committee (CNR) not to relinquish his command.

"As for the leaders of sub-region D.1, continued Diagramme, Colonel Claude [34] and Capitaine Ovale, even though they had been informed of General Koenig's decision, they continued to act independently and pretended to ignore the new order delineating the Morvan region."

Even though Diagramme had been recruited on the site, which was not the case of Colonel Eon who had been parachuted directly from London to take command in Brittany, he had just as much trouble making himself respected by the local leaders. To further complicate

33. A liaison was also established with the Army B headquarters.
34. Perhaps Colonel Claude Monod (Moret), regional FFI chief for Region D. In his report, Diagramme confuses Region D and the sub-region D.1.

218

things, the Morvan region was soon situated on the boundary between the operational zones — and the respective influences — of the Allied invasion forces from the North and from the South.

Thus on September 9, Colonel Drumont, sent into the Yonne by the COMAC to take command of sectors P.2 and P.3, tried to convince a major part of the FFI operating in the Yonne and Aube départements to move north-east to join the Americans. At the same time, Diagramme was more worried about the coming liaison with the French forces arriving from Lyon and the need to cover their right flank by blocking the Germans retreating from the South-West.

Since the middle of August, a Jedburgh team sent from England had been operating in the département. The team, code-named Bruce [35], had orders to make contact with the Donkeyman, a circuit of the SOE F Section.

"We left Harrington base on board a plane baptized Slick Chick, recalled Lieutenant Favel. Around 00:45, the pilot announced that he was looking for the target. A few minutes later we caught the gleam of lights from the reception committee, but the identification letter wasn't clear."

The plane flew over again for a second check, and on the third run, at an altitude of 1500 feet, the men jumped in good order.

"While in the air, Favel continued, the lights were seen to be one continuous flame in a straight line, obviously not separate bonfires. I thought it was a village burned by the Germans."

The jumpers landed in gardens surrounded by houses near a main street. No one was hurt, so they assembled rapidly and were met by civilians who were awakened by the thuds of the containers falling nearby. Actually the Jeds were in Montargis, twenty miles from the intended DZ and right next door to a German garrison.

The civilians advised the Jeds to get moving immediately.

35. Team No. 89 - Major William E. Colby (Berkshire) of the Field Artillery, Lieutenant Lelong alias Favel (Galway) of the Infanterie and Sous-Lieutenant Villebois alias Giry (Piastre) from the BCRA.

"It was obvious from the scattered positions of the containers that we could not locate the radio nor our equipment without spending at least an hour or two searching, in which time a large crowd would be gathered and the Germans alerted. So we proceeded off to the south-east through the fields."

As the first rays of dawn appeared, the Jeds hid in a ditch at the edge of a wood, 150 feet from the main road. All day long they watched the Germans going by toward Montargis to search the city and the surrounding towns, as the team would learn later.

As soon as night fell, they stared out again, using their compasses to guide them in the general direction of a safe house that they knew of. A storm broke out and, so as not to get lost, the three men roped themselves together with their pistol straps. After walking in the mud for several hours, they heard voices in front of them. Then the beam of a flashlight revealed an isolated house.

Having decided to make contact with anyone who could possibly help them, two Jeds took up protective positions and Lieutenant Favel knocked on the door.

"We were invited in and there we found a radio set with an operator who had come from London a week before."

From this country house situated north of Châteaurenard, a message was sent to London, and the following day, some Resistance fighters came to drive the Jeds by car to the refuge that the team had requested at the last minute before leaving England. From there, men from a Donkeyman company helped them make their way through several enemy convoys to Sommecaise, where they found Roger [36].

From discussions with the latter, it seemed that there was no unified command structure among the Resistance movements and that small armed groups were spread out all over the département. Their numbers were however constantly increasing since the mobilization

36. Roger Bardet alias Chaillan, implicated in the Dericourt affair with the SD and hiding out in the Yonne where a radioman and a secretary were sent to him on May 6 by the Buckmaster section.

220

announced three days earlier. An order received from London, corresponding to what the Jeds had been told during their briefing, requested that attacks be stopped and the FFI of the area assembled while waiting for the order for mass action. Roger himself had 500 armed men at his orders. There were about the same number of Germans who were quartered in the two or three main cities in the département. They rarely dared venture out, and when they did, they generally travelled in convoys.

A while later, the team made contact with Commandant Chevrier, new départemental FFI chief named in June. Chevrier and Roger were not getting along together: each one wanted to command. Roger had received his orders from general headquarters in Switzerland giving him authority over the Yonne, while Chevrier had been dispatched from Paris.

Team Bruce suggested that they act as liaison agents between the rivals and asked London to bring an end to the confusion by determining who exactly was in command. In the meantime, since Chevrier maintained excellent liaisons with all the elements in the département and had thus a political advantage over Roger, the Jeds cultivated their relationship with him.

For radio liaisons, the team depended on Roger. They strongly felt the need for a radio set of their own, and one whose batteries didn't needed recharging every hour or two.

"Lieutenant Giry, recalled Major Colby, was working on Roger's set in co-operation and conflict with the operators under Roger. We had our own crystals which had been on our persons for the jump so he made his own skeds. The traffic of all operators was tremendous but he managed to keep our contact of the highest order."

The two other team members helped train the men in using the new weapons dropped by parachute and helped organize new companies. They also took part, as observers, in various guerilla actions against the Germans.

On August 21, the Jeds met Commissaire Lefèvre from the organization Honneur de la Police, who had come down from Paris to request a parachute drop for the resistants fighters at the Paris City

Hall. After discussions with him, and judging that it was possible, the team asked London to drop light arms and anti-tank weapons over the Ile de la Cité, either during the day or at night, and without broadcasting any warning message.

"Of course we realized, Colby said, that this was an unprecedented idea, but considered the publicity and morale effect extremely large and worth the risk of the operation."

The next day, August 22, armored vehicles were reported in Courtenay and the Jeds decided to go meet them to see what their leader expected of the FFI [37]. But at the 4th Armored Division Command Post they had no idea: maybe information and security around the advance positions. Before leaving, the Jeds turned over to the staff Captain John Courtney, a P-38 pilot who had been shot down in the region and furnished by Roger with civilian clothing and a false ID.

Since the recon units had asked for information, teams were sent around to different cities to collect information about the enemy. Peggy Knight — Ensign in FANY and Nicole, Roger's secretary, in the Resistance — played a starring role, going through the city of Montargis swarming with German troops.

The American units seemed to be progressing east and north-east, and the Jeds thought that the FFI could be used to cover their exposed right flank, and push the Germans back south as far as possible. So the rhythm of ambushes accelerated, villages were occupied and observation posts set up to warn of any enemy movement. Cooperation with the American troops allowed the latter to intercept columns which they wouldn't have noticed if the FFI hadn't been so vigilant.

One such column, fleeing Montargis towards Auxerre, was thus stopped in broad daylight near Sommecaise and Les Ormes. But the German concentrations were too big, so Troop C of the 2nd Cavalry Squadron was called to the rescue and the FFI were requested to stay

---

37. Mission Kipling of the 1st SAS, who had been operating in the region since August 13, 1944, also made contact the same day with American units, "whose leader simply refused to believe that there were so few Germans in the area!"

222

out of sight so that the Germans could surrender to regular troops. Finally the column, consisting of 1,000 to 1,500 men with artillery and horse-drawn vehicles, was literally annihilated. Ammunition, equipment and over one hundred horses were abandoned on the roadside. The soldiers who managed to escape in small groups fled toward the east where they fell into the hands of the FFI.

Since they still had not received precise orders from London, the team tried to contact an American staff member with enough authority to dictate the mission of the FFI in the region.

At the Third Army SF Detachment, they discovered that Chevrier had been appointed official FFI chief of the département and that he had received orders signed by Lieutenant-Colonel Powell in the name of General Patton. In agreeement with General Koenig it was requested that the FFI insure protection of the right flank of the Third Army in the départements of the Loiret, Nièvre and Yonne:

"Lieutenant-Colonels Moreau for the Nièvre, Chevrier and Bardet for the Yonne, will define the limits of operational zones for each maquis in their respective départements, so that no sector is left unprotected. Liaisons are to be established with the FFI chief of the Dijon region. Every other day, a liaison agent will report the latest information and operations to SF Det No. 11, and return with orders for the EM FFI [38]."

In view of this order and considering the importance of the task entrusted to the FFI, Powell radioed London and requested priority in arms for his area.

This cooperation effort resulted in the liberation of the city of Auxerre by Chevrier's troops on August 26. That day the 4th Armored Division finally eliminated enemy resistance in Troyes while the 35th Infantry Division was patrolling on its right flank. Even though the war was moving away from the Yonne, enemy convoys continued rolling east all night long. The FFI ambushed them or forced them to

38. These orders were addressed to Colonel Marc and Lieutenant-Colonel Pierre in Orléans, Lieutenant-Colonel Moreau, commander of the département of Nièvre, and Lieutenant-Colonel Chevrier, only départemental commander of the Yonne.

take long detours by occupying and setting up defensive positions in the villages along their route.

In Monéteau, for example, the FFI took over a large fuel depot and prepared to defend it. Shortly afterwards the Germans came back to fill up their vehicles and perhaps destroy the depot. Two or three hundred white Russians, using mortars, attacked the FFI. The FFI had only a few Brens, but in spite of this they succeeded in forcing the Germans to withdraw. The gasoline that they had saved would be enough to keep all the FFI vehicles in the département running during the whole month of September.

- On about the 30th of August, recalled Colby, the commanders of units under Chevrier became sufficiently dissatisfied with his personality to commence an incipient revolt. They had the idea that at first they would run the département by a Committee. We discouraged this idea as impractical in any military organization.

Some talk was heard of Roger being the preliminary choice as intended chief. But when Chevrier was consulted, his natural political flair helped him turn the situation to his advantage: not only did he manage to get himself named as the head of the so-called committee, which effectively meant he maintained control, but by organizing daily meetings he managed to improve relations between the different units.

This was absolutely necessary, because the problem now became one of pushing Chevrier into making and especially executing a logical plan for the defense of the south flank of the regular troops. For this the towns between Briaire-sur-Loire and Tonnerre were occupied and units from various origins worked together, without assigning a specific sector to a specific group, so that no group could take effective control of any specific sector.

At that time the Third Army was particularly interested in the bridges over the Loire River. It appeared necessary to destroy them all. On August 31, at a meeting in Sens, Colonel Powell requested that as many bridges as possible be destroyed. The Yonne FFI received orders to blow up the one in La Charité, and Chevrier and Colby inspected the others to check out their condition. The bridge in Briare, slated to be destroyed, would finally be spared thanks to a last minute counter-order from the Third Army. In Sancerre the bridge was finally blown up, but only after long and stormy discussions with the French SAS who were against it.

"The area of La Charité at that time, recalled Colby, was heavily held by the Germans, and as it was far too strong for attack by the FFI, request was made for air bombardment of this bridge. Preparations were made to bring a 120-mm captured German gun near this bridge to blow it by artillery fire. The Air Corps claimed to have destroyed the bridge, the FFI of the region claimed there was no air attack on it, and the bridge still existed. The Germans remained in the vicinity of La Charité building up their force to collect a large unit before pushing east."

By then, the Yonne was practically liberated, and the line of defense on the southern flank had been pushed back to Cosne, Clamecy, Avallon and Tonnerre. The crucial question became the employment of the troops of the Yonne since, to find Germans, they had to go into neighboring départements, where they had no right to intervene. The first troops that operated outside the Yonne near Cosne were covered by the intervention of the leader of Team Bruce who managed to calm the susceptibilities of the local leaders. Colby and Favel intended to have Laurent, as P.3 commander, coordinate the use of their troops in the Nièvre.

Then Colonel Diagramme arrived in Auxerre. He had been appointed to the command of the Morvan Region by General Koenig, and it didn't take him long to settle problems of coordination. He had no qualms·about engaging the Yonne troops in other départements, often without even informing the local commanders.

On September 6, the Germans left La Charité and blew up the bridge over the Loire. The Jed team's work was then to contact local chiefs across the countryside and prepare the intervention of the Yonne FFI at their sides, following Diagramme's orders.

Each FFI element followed its own particular route, but they all generally ended up in the ranks of the First French Army.

Chapter VII

Guerilla war between the Loire and Garonne rivers

During the battle of France, the region roughly bordered by the Atlantic Ocean, the Loire River, the Rhône River and the Pyrenees, was in a unique situation: it was the only part of France where no engagement of the Allied forces was planned.

This area was called the Greater South-West in documents from the FFI Headquarters in London, and was situated beyond the route of the Allied forces invading through Normandy and through Provence. Thus, from the beginning, the liberation of this region was entrusted to the French Forces of the Interior and the Allied Special Forces that supported them.

But FFI and FTP were often at odds, and political rivalries for control of the liberated territories often took precedence over the military operations designed to accelerate the departure of the German forces and, later on, to cut their lines of retreat.

Algiers had foreseen this type of problem and prepared a plan to install an acting government in Toulouse or in the Massif Central. Then the French proposed creating an airhead from which regular troops arriving from North Africa could fan out and cover the flanks of the invading forces.

But the Allied command hesitated to get involved in this type of adventure and limited its objectives to destroying a maximum number of enemy units. The help given to the FFI would thus be allotted with this policy in mind.

Alec, Ivor and Hamish below the Loire river

In July 1944, the possibility of a break-through beyond the Normandy fields led SHAEF to classify as of extreme importance the valley of the Loire River between Orléans and Nevers. It was also decided to establish an SAS base between Nevers and Gien, from which enemy communications could be cut and convoys attacked.

However this operation was postponed, because the SOE considered that the presence of uniformed troops in an area where its underground agents were already working might result in severe retaliatory actions.

An SAS team, code-named Haggard, was finally parachuted during the night of August 9, along with Jedburgh team Alec [1] whose job it would be to liaise with between the SAS and the Resistance groups by contacting the SOE F Section Ventriloquist circuit. Even though they were to operate in the Loir-et-Cher, the two teams were dropped in the north of the Cher, 50 miles east of the intended site.

"We were received by the local resistants, Alec said, but we had to wait until the 12th to meet our contact, Antoine [2]. We all agreed to stay where we were and help the FFI in the sector."

From August 14 on, enemy columns coming from the south or south-west began arriving in Vierzon and Bourges heading for the Loire. They were poorly armed and had an exotic collection of vehicles, including bicycles and horse-drawn wagons.

The estimated 16,000 German soldiers had been harassed along the way and they began to realize that they would not be able to continue

1. Team No. 27 - Lieutenant George C. Thomson (Cromarty), U.S. Army, Lieutenant Bordes alias Allette (Oxford), of the Colonial Artillery, and Technical Specialist 3 John A. White (Colorado), Signal Corps.
2. Philippe de Vomécourt, head of the Ventriloquist circuit, set up in April 1944.

to use the northern route. So they gradually adopted a more southerly route allowing them to cross the Loire at La Charité and Nevers.

"During the night of the 19th, according to Alec, the situation was so tempting that we decided to send the maquis into open combat. The enemy was beginning to blow up important military installations in Bourges, and Commandant Colomb, chief of the FFI, decided to go over there, even though we advised him against it."

When he arrived around noon on the 21st, he found the situation completely transformed: the city was occupied by five thousand Germans. The FFI took some prisoners and by questioning them learned that Bourges was situated in the center of the corridor which the enemy hoped to use to escape back to the Reich.

The maquisards took up positions along the roads leading to Bourges and made contact with Colonel Benoît, commander of the FFI 1er Régiment d'Infanterie [3] (1er RI) in the southern part of the département, where a new Jedburgh team had just been parachuted, whose mission was to block the routes leading toward the south-east and Nevers.

Further south, during the week of July 8 to 15, Hamish was continuing work on establishing three battalions — two near Vijon and one at Aigurande — each one composed of two companies of 150 trained men each, plus a third company in training. A parachute drop, scheduled for the 14th with ten planes but cancelled at the last minute because of bad weather, was carried out on the 15th with only seven aircraft.

All this activity attracted the attention of the Germans who entered the area the following day, July 16. The maquis trucks, full of equipment and heading back to the former command post, found themselves face to face with the lead German armored car. Shots were fired on both sides, then the Germans moved away. A truck sent out to pull one of the damaged vehicles was attacked. While the enemy was maneuvering, two

---

3. Incorrectly termed "1er Régiment de France" in Team Alec's report. After commanding the 1er RI of the Armistice Army in Saint-Armand, Colonel Bertrand (alias Benoît, Dupin or Bordure), took over command of the ORA Centre Group.

sections of maquis fighters were engaged. In the end more than 500 FFI participated in the combat which only broke off at twilight, when the Germans withdrew toward Châteauroux.

"During this time, recalled Lieutenant Anstett, our camp had been moving to a new site five miles to the north-west. We had lost 15 dead and three wounded. All Châteauroux heard the German declare that they would do whatever it took to exterminate us and avenge the death of the commander of the column."

Then news came in from the Creuse: German forces might be intending to launch a full-scale operation on July 21. London had no information about it, so Lieutenant Blachère went down to get more details. But neither the interallied mission, nor the départemental FFI chief had got wind of the operation.

To be on the safe side, the Jeds moved north to Beddes, four miles north of Châteaumeillant, and the armed groups scattered and disappeared in the countryside.

"Shortly after we arrived, recalled Anstett, we began to suspect that priorities had changed as far as weapons were concerned. In spite of numerous requests, we had to wait until the end of July to get a straight answer: mortars and heavy machine guns were simply not available."

The team kept busy training the FFI, collecting information and attacking convoys. Information about an aircraft production facility and V-1 and V-2 sites in the Bourges region was sent to London. The team got a tip about three trucks travelling from Châteauroux to Saint-Armand. An ambush was laid and 22 militiamen who refused to surrender were killed. Four days later another ambush cost the Germans almost twenty men and women.

On August 5, Ellipse, the DMR of Region 5, asked for a meeting. But no precise date and place could be decided on.

About that time the Jeds came across a small group of about 150 FTP, poorly equiped. Their leader, Lieutenant Hubert, agreed to lend his group to the Jeds, but refused to integrate his men into the FFI group commanded by Lieutenant-Colonel Robert [4]. In spite of this,

4. Lieutenant-Colonel Robert Vollet, commander of the FFI group Indre-Est.

the Jeds decided to furnish the FTP with weapons. This soon resulted in all kinds of départemental chiefs lining up at the command post to ask for arms and money.

"From what we could see, Anstett continued, the situation in the Cher seemed quite complicated and we alone couldn't do much about it. We thought that a Jed team might be the solution, so we sent a message to London about it."

Team Ivor [5] arrived during the night of August 6, dropped near Beddes. As planned, Hamish, arriving from Vijon, was waiting for them when they landed.

The Jeds were incorrectly dispatched and fell outside the DZ in an abandoned gravel pit. The American radio operator's leg-bag had remained attached to his leg and he was killed landing. All his equipment, including the radio set, was useless. The Frenchman fell into a hole and a bullet from his loaded revolver went through his leg just above the knee. As for the Briton, he sprained an ankle on the edge of another hole. The two injured men were treated by the group doctor and Sergeant Goddard was buried that same day with military honors in the Beddes cemetery.

Cox and Dantec made contact with Colonel Benoît, with whom they were to work, through Hamish, who had managed to find him recently.

"Colonel Benoît had succeeded in setting up a group of 1,200 men, said Anstett. For us it was clear that if anyone were to take command in southern Cher, he was the man. That's why we sent him Team Ivor as soon as they arrived."

Benoît drew a detailed picture of the situation in the south of the département for the newcomers, and described the three existing organizations which actually had few ties between them, the 1er RI, Combat and the FTP:

5. Team No. 9 - Captain John H. Cox (Monmouth), of the 188th Field Regiment, Royal Artillery, Lieutenant Colin alias Dantec (Selune), French Foreign Legion, detached to the BCRA, and First Sergeant Lewis Goddard (Oregon) of the Signal Corps.

"The 1er RI is made up of career officers who have kept in contact and remained in the region under cover. They have been joined by soldiers who became réfractaires and hid in farms. We have put them through a tough selection process and only retained the surest men."

Benoît had been fingered by the Gestapo and forced to leave the region. On June 10, 1944, he had been sent by the COMAC to organize the Morvan group.

"I ran into problems with the DMR Diagramme (sic), Benoît continued, so I came back secretly on July 20."

Only to learn that the Gestapo had arrested his successor, Commandant Rochère, and discovered many of the equipment depots.

"Further south in the part of the département belonging to R.5, the organization Combat occupied Saint-Amand on June 6 and 7. But the Germans reacted immediately, sending in paratroopers from the Avord Training School, who recaptured the town, executed about forty people and burned some houses."

In the west of the département, 500 FTP had returned to the Cher in good order after a retreat into the Creuse.

"The Resistance fighters, Benoît explained, complain that the FTP didn't come to help them when the Germans retook Saint-Amand. However, at that time, they didn't have much contact with the other groups and their activity was mainly political."

As a result of these different events, the Cher FFI organization was more or less disrupted and lacking in leadership. Meanwhile neighboring groups gradually encroached on its territory. The Indre FFI, for example, which fell entirely within R.5, had practically annexed the sector west of the Cher River.

Facing them, the Germans were maintaining strong garrisons in Bourges, Vierzon and at the Avord airfield. Patrols covered all the main roads and controlled traffic, assisted by observation aircraft flying overhead. On the other hand, the militiamen, detested by the population, didn't dare set foot outside the cities. The entire population supported the Resistance and all of the gendarmes worked with the maquis.

"Two battalions of the 1er Régiment de France [6], continued Benoît, are in Saint-Amand and Dun-sur-Auron [7]. I've contacted some of the men to encourage them to desert. Most of them have no political sentiments and joined the regiment to avoid being sent to work in Germany. Others consider themselves tied by the oath they swore to Pétain. Their activity is controlled by the Germans and they have even participated in skirmishes against the maquis.

Team Ivor, in turn, informed Benoît about their mission in the area — liaison, organization, arming the maquisards — insisting on the fact that SFHQ hoped to see plenty of guerilla action.

On August 8 the two Jeds left for Frappon château, near Saulzais-le-Potier, where a command post had been prepared. They asked Hamish for help and received in return twenty Hamish Brens with ammunition, plus the containers that had arrived when they themselves had jumped, containing rifles and Stens. Nevertheless liaisons remained problematic and limited to the frequencies allowed by the quartz they had been able to save.

On August 12, Hamish announced that a radio operator had arrived at its CP, and two days later Sergeant Loosmore, the former radioman for the Andy team, parachuted into the Haute-Vienne, was picked up in Beddes.

Then a new set of quartz crystals arrived by parachute and finally on August 28, they exchanged their signals plan for Andy's, which had better frequencies and skeds.

Liaisons with the DMR were also a problem. London had considered this top priority when they left. But the two Jeds were handicapped by their wounds and couldn't get around easily, so they sent London the address of a mail drop to try to set up a meeting. It was never used. Benoît, who had been trying to contact Ellipse for several weeks, would be just as unsuccessful.

6. Force loyal to Pétain and the Vichy government, not to be confused with the FFI 1er Régiment d'Infanterie. TN.

7. These are in fact the 2nd and 3rd battalions, commanded by Battalion Chief Ardisson and Squadron Chief Aublet. The headquarters and the 1st battalion are in Le Blanc.

The maquis rounds began on August 13 with the FTP who, after lengthy negotiating, accepted to cooperate militarily with Colonel Benoît. Then the chiefs of the FFI Surcouf-Blanchard company put themselves under his authority. On the way there, the Jeds met Lieutenant Daoudal who handed them a message signed by Lieutenant-Colonel François, FFI commander for the Creuse, telling them that southern Cher was now affiliated with his département.

"Jed team Bergamot [8] was working in the Creuse, noted Cox, and we thought it extraordinary that no one had said anything about that when we were briefed in London. So we answered saying that until we had more information we could not evoluate this message."

Around the same time the team, along with Colonel Benoît, met the leaders of the two battalions of the 1er Régiment de France. They agreed to join the Resistance when the number of Germans had been reduced and when the militiamen had disappeared. In return, Benoît requested that any pro-Nazi soldiers in their ranks be arrested. The two officers finally agreed and promised to maintain strict neutrality as far as the maquis groups were concerned. For the moment, they loaned four of their armored cars to the FFI.

But on August 8, General Berlon [9], commander of the regiment, was arrested near Aigurande.

"That made things more complicated, the Hamish leader recognized. I don't know the real reason that he was arrested, but I was sure that the problem could only be solved by the French, and the French alone. Unfortunately opinions about using the Régiment de France differed."

The first parachute drop for Ivor finally arrived during the night of August 14. Then Lieutenant Dantec, dressed as a civilian, made the rounds of the 1st RI units with Colonel Benoît. It was at that time that Benoît suddenly received a message from COMAC ordering him to leave immediately for the Morvan. They asked London to intervene,

8. Interallied mission Bergamotte, parachuted into the Creuse at the end of June 1944. See below.

9. See below Team Hugh's version of this episode. TN.

but London could only suggest that they be sent them to the DMR Ellipse!

After inspecting the 3rd battalion and the elements from the Chantiers de Jeunesse that had joined them, the two officers came back to the command post. There they learned from Cox that an incident had occured at Dun:

"Certain elements coming from East Indre under the orders of a certain Commandant Robert, surrounded the battalion of the Régiment de France, intending to disarm the men and take them back into the Indre. Colonel Aublet refused, saying that he already had an agreement with us."

Cox and Dantec first contacted Hamish to discuss the problem, then went to meet Robert at Crevant. Robert declared that he was just acting under orders, so they decided to go see Surcouf and Hugh near Le Blanc. During the meeting held on August 17, it was agreed that the Indre FFI would not interfere in business concerning the two battalions of the Régiment de France. And a border line between Indre and Cher territories was agreed upon.

When they returned to the CP, Ivor discovered a message from Commandant Rewez of Mission Bergamotte: Ellipse was passing through the Creuse and suggested that one of the Jeds come to see him. So Dantec left on the morning of the 19th with Daoudal to meet Rewez and Ellipse.

Ellipse agreed with the decisions made. But, concerning the 1er Régiment de France, he requested that the units be dissolved and integrated into the maquis groups once any pro-German suspects had been eliminated. As for the south Cher being affiliated with the Creuse, he didn't want to interfere with the arrangements that had been made.

"Then Colonel François, FFI Creuse, spoke up, explained Cox. He didn't want Benoît making military decisions."

Ellipse allowed Dantec to decide that problem, and Benoît was finally retained as commander. When Ellipse was questioned as to Benoît's return to the Morvan, he answered that he was too far away to make an informed decision, and let Dantec choose the solution that best suited him.

On August 20, the Germans began evacuating Bourges and Châteauroux, and it looked like their convoys were taking the road to La Châtre and Nevers.

Hugh, Julian and Patrick in the Departement of Indre

In the southern part of the Indre, the FFI was feeling the consequences of the dramatic events in the département of the Vienne.

On July 10, nearly 2,000 German soldiers and several hundred militiamen coming from Poitiers, Châtellerault and Châteauroux converged on Belâbre via Le Blanc, Montmorillon and Saint-Gaultier. The units of the Marceau battalion managed to escape to Dunet during the night. Two companies from the Vienne who had taken refuge in the Luzeraize forest lost almost twenty dead before they finally decided to move south, taking with them as they left the command post of Jed team Hugh.

The enemy occupied Belâbre for a while, then left, promising to come back and shoot 150 hostages if there was any more terrorist activity in the area.

Two days later, the Clermont-Ferrand staff reported the operation to the German military command in France, noting that it was carried out in the region around Belâbre by the LXXX. AK from Poitiers in collaboration with the 960th Flak Battalion from Châteauroux [10]. Hugh then moved north and settled in the Brenne region with Martel [11] and Surcouf.

"After the attack on Belâbre, we decided to reduce guerilla activity. The decision was influenced by the fact that at least one German division was present in the Creuse, moving north toward the Indre with the intention of finding and destroying the maquis in the area."

10. The results were reported as follows: 50 killed, 4 automatic rifles, 6 Tommy guns, 16 carbines, 2 emitters, 7 cars, 8 trucks captured. Hugh estimated losses at 30 partisans and 44 Germans killed.
11. Colonel Chomel, FFI départemental leader in the Indre. See Chapter X. TN.

Nevertheless a message was sent to London on July 12, asking for a bombing raid on the CP of the colonel commanding the columns that had intervened in the Indre, Vienne and Creuse. The Resistance had discovered his command post in the Bonneuil-Matours château, south of Châtellerault.

More than ever Hugh and his liaison officers had to keep moving, to avoid from falling into the hands of German patrols. On July 20, for example, Lieutenant Prince Joachim Murat was shot down by automatic fire as he was leaving a café in Mézières. The Jeds at the same time were leaving through a back door.

But thanks to the measures taken by the Jeds — dispersion, security, intense training, command units — six thousand men could be assembled into a coherent working squad. For the Jeds, this was a success they could be proud of.

During this time, a build-up of German troops was noticed in the south and west of the département, the first signs of a probable retreat. Then, during the last days of July, traffic was very busy in the north and north-east, so orders were sent out to curtail guerilla activities.

Actually at that time the Germans were more afraid of Allied aviation than of the maquis groups, and they tended to travel in isolated vehicles. But with the increase in ambushes, they would soon be obliged to travel in convoys.

"At the beginning of August, recalled Captain Crawshay, Hugh was named military delegate for the Indre and Indre-et-Loire. We were now operating on a larger scale, and even made contact with a maquis in the Maine-et-Loire, north of Tours. Teams Julian and Ivor promised us their help in the north-east Indre and Cher."

The Germans had got the jitters and their convoys leaving from Bordeaux, La Rochelle or Nantes avoided going through the Indre.

On August 10, the number of maquis fighters had reached 8,000 to 10,000 men. That was the maximum number that could be reasonably deployed considering conditions in the surrounding rural area. Unfortunately, few weapons were dropped because priority at that time was being given to drops over Brittany.

This is when Team Julian [12] arrived in the zone.

"You will be placed under the orders of Hugh, acting military delegate in the Indre, the briefing officer had told them on August 8. He will help you make contact with Resistance groups. Your job will be to organize and train them."

During the night of August 10, the team was parachuted onto the Mascara landing site in Frédille, seven miles west of Levroux. The committee was well organized and all the containers dropped by the three planes used for the mission were picked up in good condition.

Crown from Team Hugh and Surcouf were on the site, of course, to greet the newcomers and fill them in about the situation in the region. They all agreed that Julian should take charge of the maquis groups located north of an imaginary line going from Loches to Châteauroux to Issoudun.

The Jeds lost no time beginning training of the three companies located in the north Indre sector: every other day a new group of Resistance fighters would arrive in the Landres woods to learn about explosives, grenades, Brens, Piats and bazookas.

The Allied paratroopers also made the rounds of the various maquis, establishing contact with Commandant Francis, sector chief, and Marie of the SOE Wrestler circuit, which had been operating in the sector since June [13].

At the beginning of the month of June intelligence reports reaching the Indre indicated that two hundred SS [14] troops had left Poitiers intending to blow up the dam and the electric plant near Argenton-sur-Creuse.

12. Team No. 7 - Major A.H. Clutton (Stafford) of the Union Defence Force, Lieutenant Joseph Vermot alias Brouillard (Vermont) of the Spahis, and Company Quarter-Master-Serjeant T.H. Menzies (Essex), Royal Corps of Signals.

13. Pearl Witherington, former Stationer messenger, took over directing the circuit and a two-hundred-man maquis after their chief was arrested by the Gestapo.

14. Perhaps from the 19th Regiment of Police whose companies were scattered around southern France. No operation is mentioned by the HVS 588 in Clermont-Ferrand.

"The dam was immediately surrounded by a thousand men from the FTP, explained Hugh, and we asked London to send paratroopers."

The dam, which furnished electricity for the south of the city of Paris and its region as well as the Paris-Toulouse railway line, was occupied by 300 soldiers from the Wehrmacht.

"In answer to our message, Hugh continued, London sent over thirty American paratroopers commanded by Captain Cook. Lieutenant Colonel Prince Obolensky came with them: his rank and his imposing stature would give credibility to the American presence during the celebrations and ceremonies that went along with the Liberation."

Operational Group Patrick actually included four officers and twenty-one NCOs. This was not Serge Obolensky's (Butch) first adventure: he had been parachuted into Sardinia in order to deliver the message of Badoglio's surrender to the Italian forces fighting there. After that he had commanded the OG in Brindisi before returning to England. This Russian prince who had emigrated to the U.S. now found himself surrounded by partisans saluting with a clenched fist!

"The dam garrison was well armed, Hugh pointed out, but they finally left, so the maquisards could occupy the electric plant, intact, without firing a shot. The best thing to be done with these insignificant forces sent by London, was to parade them around the countryside to give the impression that a brigade of Allied paratroopers had arrived!"

The American version of this episode is slightly different, of course. The OG was dropped during the night of August 14, to take the dam and the Eguzon electric plant and prevent the Germans from destroying them. The team headed toward the site with two hundred maquisards. There, contact was made with the commander of the French unit sent by the Vichy government to help the Germans protect the installations.

"My orders are to defend Eguzon against any assaillant, the French officer insisted."

"Mine, delivered by General Koenig of the French Forces of the Interior, replied the OG leader, are to take Eguzon and keep it intact for France."

Implying that he had a large number of forces at his disposal, he added that he was ready to attack. The French officer then realized

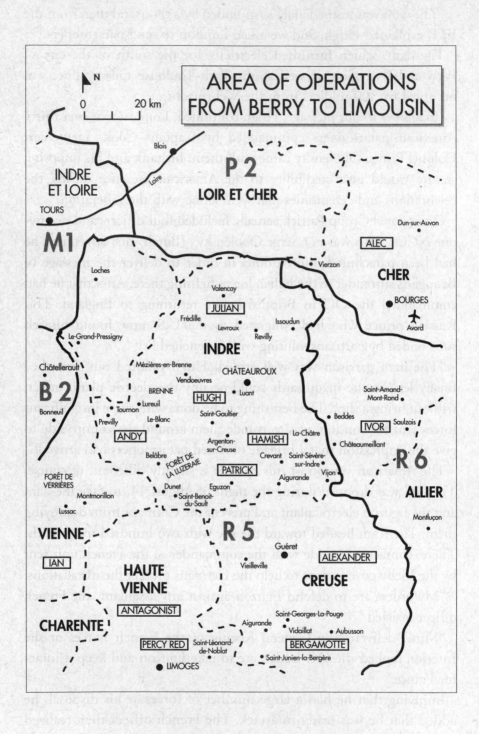

AREA OF OPERATIONS
FROM BERRY TO LIMOUSIN

N

0   20 km

P 2

INDRE
ET LOIRE

LOIR ET CHER

Blois

Loire

TOURS

M 1

ALEC

Dun-sur-Auvon

Vierzon

CHER

Loches

BOURGES

Valencay

Avord

JULIAN

Frédille

Levroux

Issoudun

Le-Grand-Pressigny

Revilly

INDRE

Châtellerault

Mézières-en-Brenne

CHÂTEAUROUX

Vendoeuvres

Saint-Amand-
Mont-Rond

B 2

BRENNE

HUGH

Luant

Bonneuil

Tournon

Lureuil

Saint-Gaultier

Beddes

Saulzais

Previlly

Le-Blanc

IVOR

ANDY

Argenton-
sur-Creuse

HAMISH

La-Châtre

Châteaumeillant

Belâbre

Crevant

Saint-Sévère-
sur-Indre

R 6

FORÊT DE
LA LUZERAIE

PATRICK

FORÊT DE
VERRIÈRES

Dunet

Eguzon

Aigurande

Vijon

ALLIER

Montmorillon

Saint-Benoit-
du-Sault

Lussac

Montluçon

VIENNE

R 5

Guéret

IAN

Vieilleville

ALEXANDER

HAUTE
VIENNE

CREUSE

CHARENTE

ANTAGONIST

Aigurande

Saint-Georges-La-Pouge

Vidaillat

Aubusson

PERCY RED

Saint-Léonard-
de-Noblat

BERGAMOTTE

Saint-Junien-la-Bergère

LIMOGES

that they both had the same objective, that was, to preserve the plant, and he agreed to inform the Germans that they would not be attacked if they left without destroying the installations. And that was how, the next day, the dam was occupied without a shot being fired.

Hugh explained: "Strict orders were sent out by General Koenig concerning the 1er Régiment de France. As military delegate, I was not in any way to flirt with them."

At one time, around the middle of August, it seemed that three-quarters of the regiment were ready to join the Resistance, and bring along their weapons, but General Berlon hesitated.

"We managed to work out an agreement with the maquis controlled by Team Hamish, Hugh confessed, to have the general arrested. In our position as military delegate it would have brought General Koenig under fire if we had made this decision ourselves."

Once Berlon was arrested the regiment joined the Allied camp: certain elements were used around Eguzon and other companies were sent to reinforce the mobile battalions.

"I must say, Hugh admitted, that they proved their courage and military capability in all the actions they took part in afterwards."

Bergamotte and Alexander in the Creuse

South of Berry, from D-Day on, there were major military operations taking place in an atmosphere of civil war. The Resistance in that area was tough and repression action by the Militia just as fierce.

The Germans had a very appropriate nickname for the Limousin, Little Russia!

At the end of the month of June Mission Bergamotte arrived in the Creuse. Its members included Commandant Rewez (Robert), Major John Blomfield of the British Army, Major Jack T. Shannon from the U.S. Infantry, an English doctor — Major Forrester — and two radio operators: French Sergent Blong and Corporal Langmaid.

This was the first interallied mission sent into France for the EM FFI, and its mission order, signed by General Koenig, would become a model for the other teams sent from England afterwards.

The team left London in the afternoon of June 26 arriving at its departure base at 21:00, and took off an hour and a quarter later. At 02:00 one of the planes was flying over the Pension drop site, located five miles east of Bourganeuf, in the Creuse [15].

"Colonel Ellipse, military delegate for region R.5, was directing the reception committee, Shannon recalled. After we had had something to eat, we all drove to the CP of Lieutenant-Colonel François, military chief of the Creuse [16]. Then we made the rounds of inspections, dinners and appearances so that the Resistance fighters in the whole département could see that an American officer had arrived from London to fight with them."

When the rest of the mission finally arrived, a separate command post was organized near Vidaillat.

"We wanted to be as far as possible from Colonel François' CP, Shannon continued. It was chaos over there, mostly due to the fact that they were looking after a lot of female suspects that had been arrested, along with numerous other prisoners, including four officers and sailors of the Kriegsmarine. Their submarine had returned to Bordeaux after cruising to Japan, and the sailors were driving to Paris with the intention of returning to Germany when they happened to run into the FFI. Until July 17 the mission continued its inspections and worked closely with the DMR, recommending improvements which were mostly adopted, but only after long discussions."

Shannon and Blomfield worked together, while Rewez spent most of his time on intelligence work for the départemental service [17].

After three weeks in the maquis, the mission had an idea of the situation in the département. François had about 1,600 men at his

15. The British members of the mission would not arrive until a few days later: their plane had mechanical problems.

16. Georges Fossey, AS départemental chief since November 1943. See Team Ivor above.

17. The short report written up by Major Shannon gives only a vague idea of the activities of the mission and the role they played vis-à-vis the AS-ORA in the Creuse. For example, it doesn't mention the huge parachute drops (a total of 60 aircraft) that took place on July 4, 1944 at Thalamy and July 15, 1944 at Peyrelevade, which Bergamotte must have participated in.

disposal — members of the Garde, FTP and maquisards — organized into four battalions and two separate companies. In the north-east sector, according to Shannon, Commandant Jacques [18] had assembled two battalions of 400 men each, made up of GMR who had joined the FFI on D-Day, maquisards and members of the AS, including career officers who were often uncomfortable in this kind of warfare.

Sometimes the mission participated in actions around Guéret. For example on July 14, a convoy of about ten vehicles was seen moving toward Bourganeuf. An assault group immediately laid an ambush and an estimated fifty Germans were killed. The convoy leader then abandoned his vehicles and fled into the woods. But when he saw that he was not being followed, he turned around, and after a wide detour, came back to his trucks. There was no one guarding them so he ordered his men in and they all started off down the road again.

"That blunder, Shannon realized, could be blamed on the ill-adapted means of liaison that we were using: telephone wires or bicycles. Operating in such difficult conditions and trying to coordinate our actions was an impossible task."

Moreover at that time there was no communication possible between neighboring départements.

"Around July 17, he continued, enemy reinforcements for Normandy started moving without notice across the département, and we couldn't relay the information: our whole intelligence and liaison circuit was broken."

These reinforcements were Generalmajor Jesser's troops, who had been fighting against the maquis in the Cantal and were regrouping to enter into action in the Creuse and Corrèze [19].

Six days before, while Jesser was fruitlessly sweeping the north of the Corrèze, the Guéret prefect had informed the German authorities:

18. Probably William Brodhurst, fugitive from the unfortunate SIS circuit Alliance, who had become Commandant Jack at the end of 1943.
19. A reconnaissance group and a motorized regiment of two battalions specializing in "terrorist" warfare, which had arrived at the LXVI. AK in June coming from Montargis.

"An American general, four high-ranking English officers and a Force of one thousand English and Americans have arrived in the Bourganeuf region with heavy artillery and tanks."

A company was sent out from Limoges to reconnoiter around Bourganeuf. It arrived two days later in Saint-Léonard-de-Noblat and then went on to Saint-Junien-la-Brégère without meeting up with any opposition. And a plane flying over the region reported no suspectious activity.

But on the morning of the 16th, the reconnaissance battalion of the Kampfgruppe reported by radio that they had just had contact with the enemy in the Creuse. At 14:30 a dozen light tanks and troop transport trucks were intercepted near Saint-Georges-la-Pouge. Oberst Coqui, from his headquarters in Merlines, gave orders to his entire group to march north-west and search the zone between Route 89 and the Aubusson-Bourganeuf line.

Around 16:00, a German squad entered Vidaillat. An FFI company surprised them in the village: the Resistance Force forgot orders and attacked, destroying a tank. In revenge, the Germans burned the town hall and the school and confiscated all the wine ...

During the night, at 02:30, SS in about forty trucks preceded by a car with a blue, white and red flag on it, penetrated the Cosnat FFI company by giving the correct password to the sentry on duty. The company was surrounded, but managed to break out, killing more than 50 Germans and losing twelve dead and three wounded. The CP was invaded as well, but after a short battle, the staff also managed to withdraw toward the south. This type of nighttime activity was not the Jesser column's style. Even though a report by the LXVI. AK took credit for it — it mentions the death of 40 terrorists and omits the fact that half the village went up in smoke — it was more likely an action of the German police in Limoges coming to rescue the submarine sailors that were being kept prisoner at Cosnat.

"During the attack, Shannon recalled, the German submarine crew members tried to escape: the two sailors were shot but Commander Ludden and his officer managed to escape. They were apparently caught later and hanged."

244

The conclusion of this episode was reported twelve days later to the *Hauptverbindungsstab* 788 in Clermont-Ferrand:

A navy officer and two sailors were able to escape from the terrorists. When the Jesser group raided the region, these sailors were caught between the terrorists and the Germans without being able to make themselves known to the latter.

They survived on beets and raw vegetables and were finally able to reach Limoges.

Sunday July 17, 1944 was a particularly beautiful day, sunny and warm. At the Bergamotte CP, a certain distance from the François CP, the men were taken completely by surprise when a messenger arrived panting:

"François has been attacked. The Germans will be here any minute now!"

While Shannon was grabbing his gear, a burst of gunfire went off from a nearby Bren and was answered by a round from a German armored car! Two cars were quickly loaded and the team managed to escape by a back road and proceed to a substitute command post.

"At 04:30 Shannon continued, the Germans, guided by militiamen, invaded our new CP. They captured the two cars containing all our equipment — radio set, first aid kits, etc. — and the 500,000 francs belonging to the mission. And before leaving they set fire to the château that had been our refuge."

Around noon the départemental CP was attacked again: here also, the enemy seemed to be well informed. Orders were given to all the FFI to make themselves invisible and wait for orders.

After a few skirmishes with the German troops, the units, disorganized, scattered into the woods. They had lost part of their equipment. Team Bergamotte also settled in the woods where it would stay for two weeks.

German columns patrolled up and down the roads, and it became difficult for the maquisards to get food because many of the farms were occupied by the Germans. But Jesser's men couldn't be everywhere, and the numerous Polish and Russians of the territorial forces weren't really interested in picking a fight.

From July 26 on, by the way, the German group was split in two: the territorials went one way and a rapid assault column the other.

As soon as the back roads were free, the maquis groups could get reorganized. Six battalions were created, quite well armed and equipped despite shortages of light mortars, fuel and radio sets.

And after the merging session held in Vieilleville on July 27, all the maquis groups agreed to let Colonel Fossey (François) take command.

A staff made up of officers from the Garde, the FFI and the FTP started working the next day. In the G-3, Shannon was in charge of operations and Blomfield of training. On August 10, Commandant Rewez finally joined them.

Two days later, the Jesser Kampfgruppe had left the region and maquis activities were in full swing, when the twenty-ninth Jedburgh team sent into France from bases in England arrived in the Creuse after various adventures.

At the beginning, Team Alexander [20] was supposed to accompany thirty French SAS paratroopers to Mission Bergamotte in the Creuse. Then, under the orders of Bergamotte, it was to participate in the organization and equipment of the Resistance formations, with the specific goal of attacking roads and railways from Perigueux and Toulouse to Limoges and then on to Châteauroux.

"We arrived at an SAS airfield on August 12 with two other Jed teams [21], reported Captain Alsop. It soon became apparent that no one had the faintest notion who we were or what to do with us, and that furthermore no one was particularly interested."

The team finally discovered the Lancaster, and had just enough time to clamber aboard before they took off at 22:00. In the plane there were already fifteen French SAS paratroopers for Mission Snelgrove, which was to operate south-west of Aubusson. After the Jeds had shouldered their equipment, they decided that Alsop would jump first, then Franklin and Thouville.

20. Team No. 57 - Lieutenant Stewart J. Alsop (Rona), U.S. Army, Lieutenant René de la Touche alias Thouville (Leix), from the Infanterie, and First Sergeant Norman R. Franklin (Cork), of the Signal Corps.
21. The two teams were Anthony and Alan, assigned to the Saône-et-Loire.

As they crossed the coastline the plane came under fire by flak and had to swerve violently. In the process it lost the other two planes. Around 02:30 the navigator announced that they were approaching: the trap door was opened ... Then the plane circled for a while seemed an eternity. This was when the dispatcher decided that he would not use the ordinary procedure — Running in, Number One, Go, etc. — but that Alsop could jump as soon as he saw the lights.

Someone in the plane jerked a flashlight: Alsop disappeared into the night immediately. Franklin, who was about to follow him, was held back by the dispatcher. The rest of the stick finally jumped a few minutes later.

Thouville ended up hanging from a high tension wire but managed to disentangle himself. Franklin landed in a cemetery. No one was hurt, and that was lucky because the site, intended for dropping only equipment, was particularly dangerous for jumpers. Actually the site was in the Saint-Giles forest, in Haute-Vienne, almost forty miles from the DZ where the SAS were dropped.

"Considering the fact that the reception committee was expecting gasoline, explained Alsop, of which they were badly in need, and not totally uperfluous parachutists, they were extremely hospitable and helpful."

Using one of the cars, Thouville left to look for Alsop who, in the meantime, had climbed down out of his tree several miles away. After wandering around for several hours, the American ran into a gasogene car and hitched a ride back to the CP, set up in an isolated château, where a meal worthy of Gargantua was waiting, the first among many others.

The Haute-Vienne was at that time almost completely liberated. The German forces were holding only the city of Limoges — which was beginning to be infiltrated — and the main roads through the département.

At the maquis command post, the Jeds were surprised to find more Englishmen and Americans than Frenchmen:

"There was a Jed team with Captain Charles Brown, an Operational Group and Hamlet, a British Major who was the main Allied representative in the département."

Thanks to Hamlet [22], a liaison was established right away with Bergamotte through a doctor who was heading for the Creuse. Along with the SAS, the Jeds reached the Creuse during the night of August 15 after travelling in an old gasogene truck, driving with the lights on all the way except when going through intersections and certain villages.

"We had been given to understand in London that Mission Bergamotte might conceivably turn out to be the Gestapo in sheep clothing. Also, it had been officially stated that the Creuse Maquis was kaput."

Actually at its CP, fifteen miles east of Bourganeuf, the Jeds found the mission in good shape: it had complete control of the situation and was busy laying ambushes on roads linking German strongholds.

"What the FFI needed most at that time, added Alsop, was gasoline. But London hesitated to send any. Most of the deskmen on the other side of the Channel failed to realize to what extent its organization was dependent on gas. The maquis was visualized creeping about in the woods. Of course, in certain limited areas, and under certain circumstances, there was some creeping in the woods to be done, but by and large the FFI was motorized."

In Shannon's view, Bergamotte was the only mission, among the numerous Allied missions that he came in contact with in occupied territory, to exercise total control over operations [23]. In other words, the mission, rather than the local maquis chiefs, made final decisions about operational policy.

The Creuse, probably for this reason, was the only département he knew where AS, FTP and FFI accepted a unified command structure.

Team Alexander had received orders during their briefing to make contact with Ellipse or his adjutant, so they travelled to his command

22. Philippe Liewer, "organizer" of the F section Salesman circuit, parachuted with Violette Szabo into France for the second time on June 7, 1944 by SFHQ.
23. Curiously, in its official report, the OSS placed Mission Bergamotte under the control of SPOC in Algiers.

post on August 18. There they received a new mission: locate the two rival maquis leaders in north Dordogne — Rac of the AS at Thiviers and Louis of the FTP at Excideuil — and coordinate their efforts.

It was impossible to get there directly because of German troops concentrated along the roads, so they were advised to take a detour through the Corrèze. A Bergamotte gasogene truck gave the Alexander Jeds a lift as far as south of Egletons, where violent fighting was taking place.

They spent the night in woods close to a stalled German convoy. The next day, in answer to a written order from the DMR, the Corrèze FFI furnished a car which took the Jeds to Thiviers, the heart of their area of operations.

Tilleul and James in Correze

In Corrèze, where Alexander had just passed through, Jed team James [24] had been operating for about ten days already.

The team had been briefed on August 9 and 10 by Lieutenant Wastin:

"Your mission is double. First, help the FFI get organized, trained and equiped. Then liaise with SFHQ and an SAS party until the party is able to get along on its own."

These SAS were part of a group of missions from the French 3rd Battalion, parachuted between the Vendée and the Franche-Comté to protect the southern flank of the Allied forces advancing out of Normandy. Their communications were normally handled by the Jedburghs.

Jeds and SAS belonging to Mission Marshall took off from Fairford on the 10th at 23:00, on board a Sterling full to overflowing. Three hours later the plane was flying over the DZ. The signal fires were huge, showing that the region was completely safe. The Jeds jumped first and landed easily about a thousand yards from the last blaze.

---

24. Team No. 26 - Lieutenant John K. Singlaub (Mississippi) of the Infantry, Lieutenant Jacques Le Bel alias Pinguilly alias Leb (Michigan), from the BCRA and Sergeant Anthony J. Denneau (Massachusetts), Signal Corps.

On the site, located north of Egletons near Bonnefond and prepared by Flight Lieutenant Simon of the RAF, Mission Tilleul with at least two hundred FFI greeted the newcomers warmly.

Interallied Mission Tilleul, commanded by Major de Guélis, was parachuted on July 7. It was made up of seven persons in all, including Squadron Chief Thomas, Captain Bissette (who had taken part in the Dieppe operations), Captain Simon (American) and MacKenzy, a doctor who had lived in a Yugoslavian maquis [25].

In a note written after the war, a former officer of the FFI staff expressed a mediocre opinion of this mission. This reflected the BCRA's attitude of hostility toward the Buckmaster agents:

"Mission Tilleul was sent into Corrèze shortly after the departure of Mission Benjoin. Its French representative was Commandant Thomas and its English representatives Major De Guélis and Captain André Simon. The members of this mission had quite different personalities which led them to undertake diverging actions without significant results [26]."

Jacques Vaillant de Guélis was a publicity agent with a French father and an English mother. He had served as a liaison officer for the British Expeditionary Force in 1940. Captured in Boulogne, he escaped and joined the SOE F section as a briefing officer. He was parachuted into France in August 1941. There he reconnoitered sites suitable for clandestine coastal landings along the Mediterranean, collected interesting documents — ration cards, passes, etc. — necessary for future agents, and recruited men of quality whom he happened to run across, including Philippe Liewer, the future Hamlet. He then took the first return pick-up flight by Lysander organized by the SOE in Châteauroux.

When Massingham base was created in Algiers, Maurice Buckmaster entrusted him with the F section branch, which was participating actively at that time in preparations for the Corsican operations. He left that job in October 1943: the branch had had a reputation as giraudists; they then became outwardly gaullists and flew the RF flag.

26. Commandant Lejeune's note on tripartite missions. February 9, 1946.

F/L André Simon had a dual nationality. Like his friend Guélis, he had participated in his share of F section drama. He had been dropped in France in 1942 to try to bring Daladier back to England, but was arrested in Châteauroux by the French police who thought he was a German agent.

He was freed with the help of his former captain who was now a general at Vichy. In return the general asked him to transmit a message to London from the Army staff headquarters, asking what they could do to get rid of the Germans. But Simon's return trip to England took longer than expected. He had to take a felucca [27] in Perpignan and finally arrived in London at the end of August. By then the message was completely outdated, because in the meantime, the SOE had established better contact.

According to Louis Le Moigne there was ill feeling between the Haute-Corrèze AS, the R.5, its staff and Mission Tilleul: "Duret appears sceptical about the military qualities of the men assigned to the mission. Jean-Jacques is reticent about Rivier, the R.5 colonel. The interallied mission and the R.5 leader live permanently with FTP units, and the Haute-Corrèze AS has not received a single parachute drop through them [28]."

Among the tasks that the mission dealt with was the preparation of the Ussel-Thalamy airfield, requested around July 20 by the COPA [29]. The arrival of Jesser's brigade delayed the project, but, on August 2, Simon also requested that the airfield be prepared: he was expecting the arrival of several dignitaries and thought that a landing strip 2400' by 1800' would be necessary.

Work began to fill in the trenches and ditches on the morning of the 6th. The workers were protected by guards placed in ambush

27. Small Mediterranean vessel, long, narrow and lightweight, with sails and oars. TN.

28. L'Armée Secrète en Haute-Corrèze. Le Moigne, from the AS, commanded the Jean-Jacques battalion of the Haute-Corrèze demi-brigade under the orders of Commandant Jean Craplet (Duret), of the ORA. Colonel Rousselier (Rivier) was the regional FFI chief.

29. Even though SAP was the official term, COPA continued to be generally used.

positions. The work was finished by the 10th, in record time. During the evening, Polygone, delegate for the southern zone, listened to the BBC along with the members of the mission. A message was aired, but, to everyone's disappointment, it announced that the expected dignitaries would not be coming after all. The mission would never know who was supposed to come or why the visit was cancelled. Some thought it was because of dignitaries involved with Plan C?

Jeds like Capitaine Wauthier of the 3rd SAS, set up a command post in nearby Chadebec, well hidden in the woods and far from the main roads. They attempted an initial contact with London on the morning of August 12th, but their brief report of arrival was to pass only after the second try. James recalled:

"During the next skeds we found it impossible to make contact with the Jed set. The operator used Mission Tilleul's radio (a B.II). On this radio we asked for a B.II set to be sent to us in a SHS parachute drop. We also asked for two carbines to replace two that had been broken. The parachutage for the SAS arrived, but we received absolutely nothing."

"That was, continued James, our first introduction to the negligence of the London section. Fortunately, within a few days we were able to get a B.II radio set from the AS chief Hubert [30]."

A month after their arrival, the Jeds noticed that the Germans occupied only the four largest cities in the département, just to keep the Bordeaux-Clermont road open. Their strongholds were completely isolated and the garrisons, practically surrounded, only dared venture out on Route 89.

"The FTP, under the orders of Antoine [31] who had just liberated the département of the Lot, were fanatically brave but only moderately reliable. They could line up 4,000 to 5,000 men, completely equiped with weapons furnished either by Tilleul or captured from the enemy."

30. Léonard Hounneau, commander of the Tulle Corps Franc.
31. Roger Lecherbonnier.

In Brive, Patrick [32], AS chief, had 2,000 men at his disposal, well-armed thanks to the mission: charity begins at home! Around Tulle and Egletons, only a third of Hubert's 3,000 FFI had weapons, either German or furnished by Baron[33].

"Hubert's group was a very effective unit, even though they didn't have enough weapons, James explained. Rifles were requested for them several times from London, but nothing ever came through."

And finally, around Ussel, the Duret group could line up 1,000 men with 370 rifles, 500 Stens and 72 Brens. All they got from Mission Tilleul were twenty-five automatics.

"Under these conditions, added James, considering that the maquis was quite well organized and that Mission Tilleul was furnishing the weapons, we concluded that the best way to help the troops fighting in the field was to advise them and lead them into battle."

On August 3, an enemy column left Tulle heading for Clermont. It was made up of four tanks and about fifty vehicles, most of them gasogene, with twenty French drivers who had been requisitioned for the occasion.

This column was all that remained of the 4th battalion of the *Sicherungs-Regiment* 194, coming back to its base in the Allier after a journey that had taken it as far as the city of Sète and the Quercy. The column was harassed all along Route 89, and finally took refuge in Egletons. The city was immediately invaded by FTP groups and three companies of the Tulle Corps Franc. Patrols from both sides spent twelve days skirmishing on the outskirts of the town.

On August 13, SAS Capitaine Wauthier, after contacting Commandant Thomas of Mission Tilleul, met with Antoine and Duret. The latter had informed him that he intended to attack the Egletons garrison. Wauthier was reticent since the attackers had no artillery or mortars.

---

32. Probably Colonel René Vaujour (Hervé), AS départemental chief, who controled four battalions from the Brigade of the Aces.
33. Baron was the SAP chief in Region R.5.

But early in the morning of the 14th, the Jeds learned that the FTP had attacked Egletons without even informing the Hubert companies who had been helping them lay siege to the city.

The Germans had abandoned the center of town and taken refuge in a trade school which they had fortified to resist the enemy.

"Nevertheless, James pointed out, during the day the BBC aired General Koenig's order to attack all the German garrisons between the Loire and the Garonne, however large they may be."

Thus the Egletons attack, launched at dawn, became legitimate at 13:30 hours.

The Jed team, with Tilleul's approval, decided to help the FTP, who seemed to lack training and good leadership. When the team got to the city in the evening, it was already dark and they had to postpone reconnoitering until the next day.

The following day it became evident that the German defenses were entrenched in the school and that it would be impossible to beat them with the weapons that the FTP had at its disposal. The only hope of succeeding would be either a well prepared attack or a long siege. The Germans' attention was attracted by movements of partisans around a house whose attic was being used as an observation post. They let go a few rounds from a machine gun and wounded Lieutenant Singlaub in the face.

Around 9:00, three low-flying Heinkel 111s dropped several bombs. They were followed four hours later by three FW 190s which strafed the FFI or FTP positions [34]. Immediately after the first attack, Leb and Singlaub each installed an anti-aircraft battery with three or four Brens placed under the command of an experienced officer.

At 15:00, Captain Bisset and Lieutenant Leb left looking for Antoine, the FTP leader, to find out what he intended to do. They finally met his chief of staff and gave him their opinion:

34. The HVS 588 noted that on August 15 at 16:00 planes dropped bombs weighing from 100 to 1000 lbs. L'Armée Secrète en Haute-Corrèze is a day off in its chronology. For sake of coherence it is the Jed team's version that is used here.

"If the Germans are sending so many planes, it must mean that they attach a certain importance to the garrison and that they may send troops from Clermont-Ferrand to liberate it. We need to attack promptly."

Meanwhile Singlaub was waiting at the advanced post where the SAS of Mission Marshall arrived during the afternoon. The presence of these well-trained troops, bringing along a few 60-mm mortars with them, encouraged the maquisards who had been unsettled by the air raids.

Night fell and Mission Tilleul decided to spend the night at Hôtel Fonfreyde, on the road to Bonnefond where an major parachute drop was to take place.

"Capitaine Wauthier, after asking the RAF for a bombing raid on the trade school at 17:00 the next day, assembled the FTP company leaders in Antoine's absence and had them adopt his plan of attack. In our opinion he was acting too hastily, since he hadn't received an answer yet to his request for aerial support."

His plan was simple. Starting at 14:00, all the elements in close contact with the enemy would move back 200 yards. At 16:45 the SAS would open fire with the mortars and Piats [35]. Immediately after the shelling, two companies led by Lieutenants Singlaub and Leb would attack. But instead of the Royal Air Force, it was the Luftwaffe that attached and, of course, the planned assault was cancelled.

In the evening, the Ussel garrison was attacked by Commandant Duret's troops, who set fire to the elementary school where the elements of the *Sicherungs-Regiment* 95 had taken refuge. Surrounded by flames, a hundred Germans surrendered.

At Brive and Tulle negociations with the German garrisons were also under way, so Singlaub left Egletons about 22:00 to represent the US Army there. The garrison in Brive had actually laid down its weapons earlier in the evening, and the official surrender of the 800 men from Tulle would take place the next morning.

35. This anti-tank weapon could also be used against stone walls up to 300 meters away.

Leb and his radioman who had stayed in Egletons again tried to get a bombing mission from London. Suddenly a message arrived indicating that a column of 2,000 Germans travelling in 150 vehicles had just left Clermont for Ussel. As soon as they relayed that information to London, the Jeds headed for Antoine's CP where the atmosphere was total chaos: the Tulle garrison had managed to escape and was heading north to attack the Egletons besiegers from the rear!

"For us this rumor was unfounded. But it was impossible to make this clear to Antoine's staff. Instead of immediately raising the siege of Egletons School and preparing strong ambushes between Ussel and Egletons, which is the prime role of maquis troops with their particular type of guerilla arms, the siege was lightly lift to send three companies to guard the road from Tulle to Egletons against the mythical Germans escaped from Tulle."

The truth was that on the evening of August 16, Jesser's Kampfgruppe did indeed receive orders to intervene to liberate the Ussel, Egletons and Tulle garrisons. So the Ist Battalion, SR 1000 moved out of Clermont with artillery and Flak batteries, including 295 vehicles, 4 tanks and two radio cars in all.

Just before Bourg-Lastic, the advance guard rode into an ambush laid by an AS company from the Puy-de-Dôme. From then on the column inched along carefully, with the tanks leading and the artillery positioned in battery at every difficult passage. Flying over their heads, an observation plane reconnoitered the surroundings and warned of any suspect movements.

In front of the approaching column, the Haute-Corrèze AS prepared to block the Ussel road. They had run out of certain types of ammunition and the men were tired. Mission Tilleul had promised a parachute drop in the evening on the Thalamy site, so a reserve company was sent out to greet the four planes expected. But not a single plane showed up. [36] Consequently nothing stopped the advance

36. Finally on the evening of the 19th, the demi-brigade (equivalent of a regiment but made up of independent battalions) would obtain ammunition from a former drop.

guard of the enemy column from going through Ussel late at night. The garrison was empty so they went on to Egletons where they arrived the next day, August 18.

Once Egletons evacuated by the Germans, Team James assembled at Saint-Yrieix-le-Biotot at the end of the morning. Then, seeing that the enemy was continuing toward the south-west, they decided to settle closer to Tulle, at Saint-Pardoux-la-Croisille.

"At 18:00, James recalled, the BBC announced triumphantly that the FFI of the Corrèze had attacked the garrison at Egletons which had fallen."

Then, an hour later, some RAF Mosquitos carried out a violent bombing raid on the trade school. James was philosophical and noted in its report:

"This bombardment, so long awaited, arrived about ten hours after the Germans had left and at least one day too late."

Once beyond Egletons, part of the German column, now reinforced with the 2nd battalion of the SR 1000, continued to make its way toward Tulle on back roads north of Route 89. Hubert's AS companies were now harassing the detachment. It would take them eight hours to cover the twenty miles between their position and Tulle [37].

When they got to Tulle and found that the garrison had left, they turned around and headed back to Egletons. At dawn on the 21st, the Jesser Kampfgruppe started back to Clermont. Their progress was slow because of the blockades and ambushes laid by the Haute-Corrèze demi-brigade.

Andy, Percy Red and Lee in the Haute-Vienne

Their car broke down, so the Jeds of Team James spent five days in Saint-Pardoux. They took advantage of this free time to make contact with Antoine, who asked them to train his FTPs in the use of the 20-mm German gun. On August 23, they tried to meet Ellipse, but he had unfortunately just left for the Haute-Vienne.

37. "Motorized I/SR 1000 has delivered IV/SR 194 at Egletons. Ussel garrison apparently taken prisoners. No news from Brive and Tulle." (HVS 588 daily record).

In this latter département, the first designated Special Forces team was Jed team Andy [38]. Its mission was to help Ellipse organize the maquis and to cut the four railroad lines converging in Limoges.

"With regard to the first point, remarked Major Parkinson, I would have appreciated more information on the general policy for our area. However, 48 hours after our arrival in France, we received a 10-point plan of operation for the area, which was excellent. It gave the policy to follow enthusiastically, leaving the details to be done by us. This was enthusiastically agreed to by Ellipse when we eventually met him and talked it over with him."

In his report, Parkinson complained about the length of the briefing, which he found too cumbersome. In his view, detailed descriptions of possible targets could have been avoided, since the maquisards were well informed. Likewise he considered it unfortunate that the stick and the plane crew were not able to talk together before the jump.

The plane carrying Andy had left on the evening of July 11. It had been decided with the pilot that the Jeds would jump first, before dropping the packages. However, when No. 1 approached the hole, the containers' static lines were tangled over the exit: Parkinson barely had time to thrust his leg out to brace himself as the dispatcher grabbed his shoulder to pull him back.

On the second run, the pilot signaled that everything was OK and Capitaine Vermeulen jumped when the dispatcher yelled Go, followed by Parkinson. The descent seemed extremely short: barely ten seconds. On landing, the Frenchman's foot was seriously injured and the Briton's left leg broken in two different places.

"As I was about to jump, Sergeant Loosmore recalled later, the static lines were all tangled up and I almost went out head first! The dispatcher held me back and sent me out on the third run."

Parkinson realized that his leg was broken. He called two partisans who carried him to a nearby farm and installed him comfortably on the kitchen table. The house was full of workers. There were also four agents dropped a half-hour before the Jeds.

"Somebody introduced an American officer to me, Parkie remembered. He was Second Lieutenant Carl Bundgaard, of the 505th Squadron, 339th Fighter Group [39], who had bailed out of his fighter plane two weeks before. He would stay with us until we returned to England. For him, nothing was a problem: he assisted Lundy with the coding and decoding of our messages, worked the generator on all skeds, once for an hour and a half without relief."

Fifteen minutes later Vermeulen arrived; his foot was hurting him terribly. Less than an hour after, a doctor came to examine the injured officers and Parkinson's leg was strapped between two sticks used as splints.

Then the Jeds were driven by car to a château ten miles away. It must have been around 05:00 when the arrival message went through on the first try.

"The DMR's deputy was notified of our arrival by the head of the reception committee, recalled Parkinson, and he came to see us around noon."

We had a long talk. Croc [40] was surprised to see us in the Indre, since we were supposed to be in the Haute-Vienne! So he sent a message to Ellipse who came to visit us a week later [41].

At the beginning of the afternoon, the doctor came back with a surgeon who put Parkinson's fractured leg into a plaster cast. After two days and nights of rest, the team was led to a maquis situated in the woods near Preuilly-la-Ville, north of Le Blanc.

"We stayed there two days, Parkinson added, well fed and well guarded. The battalion was attacked by the Boche after we left, but they managed to get away with only a few casualties."

It is true that on July 23, a large German unit — 800 men and 32 trucks according to the official report — surrounded certain

39. Normally the 339th Group escorted the bombers of the 8th Air Force. After the break-through at Saint-Lô, its P-51 Mustangs participated in attacks against retreating enemy columns.
40. Georges Hérand (Croc ou Henri).
41. In this way we learn that the team was not where it had planned to be. In the mission report, the only towns mentioned are Preuilly and Le Blanc.

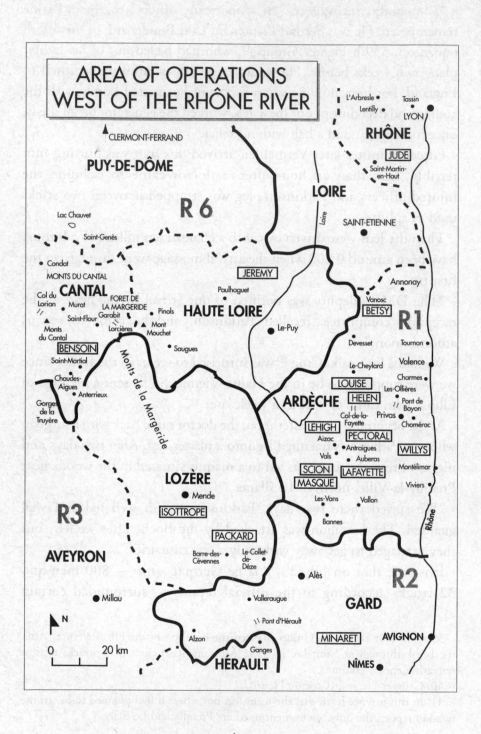

AREA OF OPERATIONS
WEST OF THE RHÔNE RIVER

CLERMONT-FERRAND

PUY-DE-DÔME

R 6

Lac Chauvet

Saint-Genès

Condat

MONTS DU CANTAL

CANTAL

Col du
Lorian
Murat
Saint-Flour
Monts
du Cantal

FORET DE
LA MARGERIDE
Garabit
Lorcières

Pinols

Mont
Mouchet

Sauges

BENSOIN

Saint-Martial

Chaudes-
Aigues

Anterrieux

Gorges
de la
Truyère

Monts de la Margeride

L'Arbresle
Lentilly

Tassin

LYON

RHÔNE

JUDE

Saint-Martin-
en-Haut

LOIRE

Loire

SAINT-ETIENNE

JEREMY

Paulhaguet

HAUTE LOIRE

Le-Puy

Annonay

Vanosc

BETSY

R1

Devesset

Tournon

Le-Cheylard

Valence

Charmes

LOUISE

Les-Ollières

HELEN

Pont de
Boyon

ARDÈCHE

Col-de-la-
Fayette

Privas

Chomérac

LEHIGH

Aizac

Vals

PECTORAL

Antraigues

Auberas

WILLYS

Montélimar

SCION

LAFAYETTE

Viviers

MASQUE

LOZÈRE

Mende

Les-Vans

Vallon

ISOTTROPE

R3

PACKARD

Barre-des-
Cévennes

Le-Collet-
de-Dèze

Bannes

Rhône

AVEYRON

Alès

R2

Millau

Valleraugue

GARD

N

Pont d'Hérault

0   20 km

Alzon

Ganges

MINARET

AVIGNON

NÎMES

HÉRAULT

elements of the Carol battalion of the Charles-Martel Brigade in Preuilly.

The partisans managed to withdraw with minimum losses (two killed and one wounded), for at least fifteen enemy killed.

The Jeds thus left the woods in three cars with weapons poking out of all the windows. The vehicles used back roads and dirt tracks, and took care when approaching a village or a curve: distances were measured and the second car advanced only after getting an all-clear signal from the first.

They finally arrived at a farm twelve miles from Preuilly. The two officers were put into bed on the ground floor, and Carl and Loosmore climbed the stairs to the attic with the radio gear.

"While we stayed in this hideout, Parkinson said, we had a variety of visitors: Crawshay, Legrand, Croc, Ellipse ... It was decided that Carlow and I would go back to England and that Lundy would stay with Ellipse as radio operator."

Normally someone came in every morning with the local news. But that day, they waited until noon and no one had appeared. No one had called either, and the Jeds were wondering what could have happened, when suddenly they heard a burst of machine-gun fire coming from the direction of the village, a mile away. The farmer sent his sons out for information and the Jeds got their gear together and thrust it into their knapsacks.

Suddenly the farmer's wife appeared in the doorway. Her face was livid:

"Gentlemen, the Germans are here!"

Vermeulen jumped out of bed, over the window sill and limped towards the woods as fast as he could.

Parkinson, in nothing but a pair of white shorts, followed. He fell and crawled several yards before suddenly feeling himself lifted up by a pair of powerful arms; Carl had come down from the attic and was carrying him to safety in an old drained swamp. Bullets were whistling past them and suddenly Carl stumbled! For a minute they thought he had been hit, but he had just lost his balance under the weight of his load.

Loosmore showed up then, with part of the equipment, which they concealed in the bushes near where the Major was hiding. Then the two non-cripples made several trips back and forth to the farmhouse to recover and hide the rest of the equipment. Sporadic fire could still be heard around the village.

Parkinson, who had by this time exchanged his shorts for battle-dress, organized guard duty and waited for the Germans. But it was the farmer who appeared.

"What's going on?" the Major asked.

"There's been fighting in the village. The Jerries are on the road now, three hundred yards from here. I have to get back to the farm. Good luck!"

The enemy trucks were in fact very close. They stopped for a long time, then finally started up again.

A short while later the farmer returned to see the Jeds: the Germans had left for sure after searching the woods on the other side of the road.

But, during the fighting in town, Prince Murat and his chauffeur had been killed [42].

"His death was a great blow to us all. The Prince had at all times done his utmost to help us. He commanded all the convoys in which we were carried around the countryside."

When night fell, the Jeds made their way back to the farmhouse with their weapons and washing kits, but left the rest of the equipment hidden in the bushes.

A week later the excitement had died down and a plane leaving for England was announced.

The Jeds were teary-eyed when they said good-by to the farm family, then headed for the Le Blanc airstrip where they arrived after a three-hour ride through the night.

"An hour after midnight we heard the engines, then after exchanging signals the plane touched down and we were carried

42. The town is probably Mézières-en-Brenne, where Team Hugh was also located that same day. Curiously M.R.D. Foot, in SOE in France indicates that the prince was killed near Team Andy, but in the vicinity of his house in Dordogne.

aboard. We were airborne at 01:35, the plane having spent seven minutes on the ground [43]."

The journey home was uneventful and on July 28 at 04:45 Team Andy — plus the American fighter pilot and minus the radioman claimed by Ellipse [44] — landed in England.

Three weeks after the Andy team left for what they thought was the Haute-Vienne, another special forces team took off from England towards Limoges: OG Percy Red commanded by Captain William F. Larson, code-named Leander. This was one of the two Norwegian teams assigned to operations in France, since no better use could be found for them.

Thirty American paratroopers took off in the evening of July 31. But over the Limousin region they ran into trouble. This didn't surprise the more superstitious members of the group, because this was their thirteenth jump.

Only one of the four planes was able to find the DZ that night. The three others came back the following night, but the last plane only managed to find its target south of Limoges on August 5 [45].

Once contact had been established with the local maquis directed by Hamlet, the group headed for the CP of interallied mission Bergamotte.

There they met a Jedburgh team and some French SAS parachuted together, who had just arrived.

On August 14, when the attack on Limoges was over, Doctor Fred Agee (Antagonist), an Operational Group surgeon, was dropped by parachute to take care of the wounded maquisards.

From then on, Jeds, OGs and SAS operated together, organizing and arming 5,000 guerilla fighters who would play an important role during the surrender of the Limoges garrison.

43 . M.R.D. Foot describes the pick-up zone as being in Limoges, which seems highly unlikely.

44. Actually Loosmore joined Jed team Hamish.

45. Note that the report on the activity of the FFI in the Haute-Vienne mentions for the date of August 3, 1944, a "U.S. commando dropped by parachute at Eymoutiers."

On August 9 at 22:45, two Sterlings took off from the Keevil airfield carrying twenty-three French SAS for Mission Samson and Jedburgh team Lee [46]. At 01:15 the Jeds jumped from 800 feet up, the leaders of the second stick.

"The jump was satisfactory, Brown noted, although it seemed to me we were dropped from too high up. I had never jumped with a leg bag attached to one leg only, and its twenty-foot long strap, got wrapped around my neck. My harness wasn't tight enough and so I slipped forward and could not properly pull down on my front lift webs."

Actually the stick landed a mile and a half from the lanterns on DZ Françoise. Brown was lost in a field for about twenty minutes until he managed to find a young boy who showed him the way to the reception committee.

"The transmittor in my leg-bag was completely smashed, continued Brown. As was the one wrapped in one of the packages. On the other hand, the knapsacks and radio for Captain Montgomery's team [47] that were dropped along with ours landed in good shape. Following our orders, we made contact with Major Charles Staunton, of the British Army, whose code-name was Hamlet [48]."

The team installed its base near Hamlet, on the outskirts of a village called La Croisille-sur-Briance, twenty miles south-east of Limoges. The first day was spent trying to make contact with London ; they finally got through during the second sked with a B.II radio set. Afterwards this set would continue to be used, with only a few transmissions disturbed by jamming or poor atmospheric conditions.

On August 11, the Jeds, who were absent when the action started, missed the ambush laid for an armored train below Salon-la-Tour.

46. Team No. 16 - Captain Charles E. Brown (Rice), U.S. Cavalry, Lieutenant Angoulvent alias Viguier (Sous), of the BCRA and Lieutenant Maurice Pirat alias Chevalier (Reis), from the 45th Signals battalion.

47. The Tony Jed team which would be dropped on August 17, 1944 in the Vendée.

48. Staunton is actually the "nom de guerre" of Liewer, from the Salesman circuit.

Actually the operation was a disaster, resulting in the death of two SAS personnel and Captain Larson, the Percy Red commander. Another SAS member was captured, but would be freed later from the Limoges prison.

The ambush had been laid during the night, but was spotted by the train crew who peppered the bushes along the sides of the sabotaged tracks with machine-gun fire. The partisans scattered in panic: the OG captain's body was abandoned on the site and found in the afternoon by Captain Brown when he came to inspect the battlefield. He was buried the following day with military honors.

"Hamlet filled us in on the Resistance movements in Haute-Vienne, explained Brown, their organization, state of armament, morale, record of operations, etc. It became clear that if we sent in new fields and asked for parachutages, we would merely hinder rather than help the existing program."

The Jeds decided to use the approved DZs:

"At that time the need for gasoline was much more important than arms, and nearly every message we sent for the first two weeks mentioned this fact, as we were helpless without vehicular transportation for liaison and transport purposes."

When the team arrived in the Limousin, the Haute-Vienne Resistance movement was relatively strong. German garrisons occupied Limoges and Saint-Léonard-de-Noblat, but the maquis more or less controlled the rest of the département: they could not, however, stop large troop concentrations from making sorties or large well-protected convoys from travelling.

On the other hand, the railway network was almost completely paralyzed by sabotages, and information about any trains coming or going was immediately relayed to the resistants by the railroad personnel who worked hand-in-hand with them.

"Major Staunton, recalled Brown, took the view that he should arm all those that really wanted to fight, and concentrated hs efforts on arming the FTPF, disregarding the communist leaning of their organisation and the possible dangers to postwar security."

Responding to questions and criticisms expressed by certain Frenchmen, Brown continued:

"I was and am in agreement with this policy, because these were the men who really wanted to fight and who did the work."

He added:

"I met their leader, Georges Guingouin, on August 12. I must say that, in his relations with us, he never allowed any political considerations to interfere with the military plans which we made in common with Major Staunton and Captain Viguier."

On August 13, the team received a message informing them that the German garrisons in the south intended to proceed to Limoges where — once again — a sortie was being prepared. With Guingouin, we decided to alert all the Resistance groups and cover all the roads leading to Limoges.

The next day, OGs, SAS, Jeds and Staunton blew up the Saint-Léonard steel railroad trestle on the Limoges-Ussel line, the only possible target on the route of an possible enemy withdrawal. The operation was conducted quietly without arousing the suspicion of the Germans who were staying around the village: Viguier and Brown, with two guides from the maquis, handled reconnaissance, and the OG did the demolition. The bridge wasn't guarded.

From August 15 to 17, the team was kept busy working on a deep anti-tank ditch being dug on Route 20, 500 yards north of Fombelaux. Mines were placed, trees chopped down and the Saint-Germain-les-Belles bridge destroyed. Guingouin was named head of the FFI in the département by Ellipse on August 17, and with his help, the job was successfully completed. This mission took on considerable importance when, on the 16th, London sent a message saying that the 159th Infantry Division was in the area, moving north [49].

In preparation for the expected sortie by the Limoges garrison, a request for a Mosquito bombing raid over the German barracks was sent to London on August 18, using the emergency frequency.

49. The 159th was a Reserve Division in charge of guarding the Aquitaine coast.

"We wanted to persuade the units of the Mobile Guard and the Reserve Mobile Guard — twenty-six squadrons with a total of 3,000 men — to come over to the Resistance. Although outwardly they seemed determined to side with Vichy, and hence to defend the blockhouses on the outside perimeter of Limoges, we had information that certain officers were willing to negotiate."

At dusk on the 18th, a meeting was organized near one of the roadblocks with a Lieutenant-Colonel from the Guard. The officer seemed hesitant to take the final step so Guingouin gave him a twenty-four hour ultimatum. As they were negociating, a camouflaged car suddenly came speeding out of the night towards the city.

"The Jerries!" someone screamed.

Everyone ran as if the devil were on their tails.

"Actually the car belonged to a maquis group on its way into the city to shoot it up, in true Chicago gangster fashion. The car had been painted to look like a German vehicle."

Once they realized their mistake they looked around for the lieutenant-colonel. He had disappeared. It didn't really matter anyway, because in the end all of the Guard units left Limoges the night before the Germans surrendered.

Since the month of June, seventeen squadrons belonging to the 3rd, 5th and 6th regiments of the Guard, had been grouped in and around Limoges. But what Charles Brown didn't say — or rather, what he didn't know — was that contact with the Resistance had already made quite a bit of headway. Liaisons between Lieutenant-Colonel Besson — the commander of the Limoges Guard group — and the DMR were taken care of by the DMR's deputy, along with the regional and départemental leaders of the ORA.

On August 10, during a meeting held in Séreilhac, the commander of the Guard regiments was advised to keep his units where they were for the moment.

The order to leave the city would not be given until six days later by Guingouin himself in Linards.

On the 21st, through the Swiss consul, talks were arranged with Generalmajor Walter Gleiniger, commander of the Limoges

Feldkommandantur 586. The officials had received passes to meet at the consul's residence.

"Major Staunton led the Allied delegation, explained Brown. Viguier represented the Free French, Capitaine Guerry the FFI and I represented the U.S. Army. Three Germans sat across the table from us: General Gleiniger, Lieutenant-Colonel von Liebich and Captain Noll."

At 18:15 an agreement was reached and the plenipotentiaries decided to come back two hours later to sign the act of capitulation. But the SD refused to give up: they kidnapped the general and made for Saint-Léonard [50].

At 20:30 the soldiers of the French Forces of the Interior enter the city with their weapons slung over their shoulders. They had liberated the maquis capital with a minimum of losses [51].

50. There are two different versions of Walter Gleininger's death: either he was executed after his arrest or he committed suicide when the SD came to arrest him.

51. G. Guingouin, *Quatre ans de lutte sur le sol limousin* (Four Years of Struggle on Limousin Soil).

Chapter VIII

Retreats and guerilla warfare in the mountains.

In preparation for the invasion of Provence, scheduled for the summer of 1944, the southern part of France was put under the control of the Allied command in the Mediterranean, in charge of Operation Anvil.

The line separating the zone controlled by SHAEF and the one controlled by AFHQ was drawn up by taking into account geographical and operational considerations, but also technical problems such as the range of the planes involved.

For the FFI, and the Special Forces that were supporting them, the former free zone — except R.5 and the northern parts of R.1 and R.6 — was not under the responsibility of SFHQ, but of SPOC, which coordinated special operations from Algiers.

The zone controlled by AFHQ was far from homogenous. In Region R.4, encompassing the valley of the Garonne River and thus prolonging the Greater South-West, operations undertaken by the maquis followed the same pattern as those in R.5. and Region R.6, located in the heart of the Massif Central, was greatly influenced by neighboring regions to the North.

In spite of this, the zone assigned to the Special Project Operations Center was well adapted to the mission entrusted to it: to coordinate the activities of the Resistance in the South of France with reference to preparation and execution of Operation Anvil.

Mission Benjoin and retreats in Auvergne

At the beginning of May, 1944, the RF section of the BCRA sent into Auvergne a team organized along the lines of Citronelle. It was code-named Benjoin, and included an officer from each army and a French radio operator [1].

"Your mission, the leader was told as he left London, is to make contact with the maquis group that has been reported in the Auvergne mountains, directed by a fellow named Gaspard [2], who is very anxious to remain independent. You will have to determine his political alliances and convince him to allow his men to fight alongside the Allies."

The paratroopers jumped onto the Plongeon site, in the Margeride forest, during the night of May 8. The radioman injured his foot and was hobbled until the end of the mission. The reception committee, ten members of the FTP, was directed by the leader of the COPA.

The situation in this area was no more complicated than anywhere else. The AS was the largest organization and a military delegate had just been named. Various Allied missions, most of whom didn't know the others existed, were crisscrossing the mountains looking for landing sites and contacts. But because of its geographical situation, its maquis and the coming invasion, the area had been chosen to serve as a retreat: in London the BCRA was studying the Force C project, while in Auvergne the regional AS was likewise preparing a plan for a retreat on Mount Mouchet.

Gaspard knew nothing about what London was planning as he tried to establish liaisons with the exterior. On April 15, he managed to

1. Major Frederick Cardozo (Vecteur), South Lancashire Regiment, Capitaine Gouy alias Chouan (Mediane), First Lieutenant Jacques Le Baigue (Spirale) from the Coast Artillery Corps and Sous-Lieutenant Jean Trollet (Somali).
2. Emile Coulaudon, a Medical Corps NCO, who became the leader of a "corps franc" and eventually rose to the rank of colonel.

meet Major Philippe [3] , who had organized the Stationer circuit, in Montluçon. Gaspard told him about his own projects for creating retreats and asked for weapons, ammo and officers.

Philippe relayed the request to the SOE F section. He got a quick answer: two weeks later, three English officers, including John Farmer, was dropped in the Allier. And on May 10, once it had established its Freelance circuit, it received a major arms drop near La Truyère, which would be followed by many others.

Consequently, south of the Benjoin mission, a Buckmaster circuit was already at work with the same mission.

"This apparent overlap is not really as superfluous as it seems, they thought in London. Gaspard's zone is wide and two teams with their radio operators will be hardly enough to secure supplies and look for adequate DZs in the mountains!"

Benjoin's first days in the field were naturally spent meeting the different regional authorities. Relations became very cordial with the COPA leader, once he realized that the mission wasn't there to take his place. He included the mission operations in his own program for parachute drops during the moon periods and between.

Pyramide, the DMR [4] , came to spend two days with the maquis. The mission took his advice and decided to procure weapons for Gaspard's troops. Everything was not that easy in Auvergne, however.

"The R.6 military leader, whose real name was Couledon, Lieutenant Lebaigue explained, was not easy to get along with. The fact that another mission was operating in the same area with the same mission as ours wasn't much of a help. The other mission was directed by Captain Farmer, and Couledon took no interest in anyone except them."

At the end of Gaspard's first meeting with Benjoin, the discussion turned short:

3. Major Maurice Southgate (Hector for the SOE), parachuted into France in October 1943, arrested on May 1, 1944.

4. Capitaine de Courson de Villeneuve had arrived in March of 1944 and was arrested on July 2 of the same year.

"OK, let's see what you can do. I need three thousand blankets, boots, weapons, etc.!"

Relations with Farmer were polite. Major Cardozo met with him on May 17, and they agreed that Mission Benjoin would continue to work with Gaspard.

Cardozo, like many of the Allied officers in the Special Forces, was fond of France. He got along well from the start, and made friends easily.

Henri Ingrand, named Commissary of the Republic in Auvergne in May 1944, had this to say about him:

"I really appreciate his personality. He is both terribly British in his behavior, his calm, his way of appearing easy-going in the face of danger, and also very un-British when he talks about himself, his life after the war, his tastes and his ambitions."

When Benjoin arrived, two thousand men were living in the Margeride and around Chaudes-Aigues. Most of them had been there for a long time. They had taken refuge in the Cantal after various operations in Corrèze and the Puy-de-Dôme with Gaspard and his military adjutant Prince [5]. Their weapons, mostly Stens, were pitifully inadequate.

Lebaigue also learned that a new maquis was being formed near Condat and that the men had no weapons. The mission decided to designate a DZ for them and submit it to London for approval.

On May 15, near Paulhaguet in the Haute-Loire, Henri Ingrand (Rouvres), regional director of the MUR, presided over a meeting of the various leaders of movements in Auvergne. But neither the Allied paratroopers, the ORA nor the DMR took part.

Gaspard obtained approval for his plans for a retreat on Mount Mouchet, a large moor-covered plateau encompassing parts of three départements, and another near Chaudes-Aigues, protected by the canyons of La Truyère. He confirmed that career officers would be in charge of training the men.

---

5. Lieutenant-Colonel Robert Huguet, future head of the 1st bureau at regional FFI headquarters.

On May 20, the regional headquarters ordered the mobilization of all able-bodied volunteers. Some départemental leaders even posted notices telling the men where to report.

On foot, by car, bus or train, the volunteers arrived in the Margeride: in two weeks 2,700 men had joined up at Mount Mouchet, 1,500 at La Truyère. The two retreats were full and a third had to be established at Saint-Genès, near the border between the Puy-de-Dôme and the Cantal. It signed up 6,000 men almost immediately.

At Gaspard's base in the Mount Mouchet forester's cabin, headquarters were installed with the usual sections, and a parking lot containing several hundred vehicles.

To be able to control the activities of the different maquis, Gouy and Lebaigue settled at the Mount Mouchet CP while Cardozo remained in Moulergue to keep in contact with Pyramide and direct the COPA, whose chief had fallen into the German police net on May 27.

Men were arriving every day from Saint-Flour and Clermont-Ferrand. According to Lebaigue, the policy decided upon was not to recruit more fighters than weapons available, but it was impossible to send the volunteers back home. To try to furnish equipment for them many parachute drops — 28 planes between May 26 and June 9 — were organized on the Plongeon site, deep in the heart of the retreat.

"Naturally, Lebaigue explained, so many men and so much activity, beyond the problems of supplies, administration and security that they raised, could not escape the notice of the Germans."

On June 1st, General Von Brodowski, chief of the Clermont-Ferrand *Haupverbindungsstab* 588 was informed by the Vichy SD that recruits were being signed up as part of an Allied plan, and equiped with weapons dropped by parachute from Anglo-American planes. He phoned his superior in Lyon:

"Send me enough troops to destroy this mobilization that is occuring, particularly in the Cantal, east of Saint-Flour, in the Margeride forest, and around Mount Mouchet."

The first attack — launched on the south flank on June 2 by the equivalent of a battalion sent up from Mende — was easily repulsed by a counter-attack. Lebaigue knew that the Germans were testing the enemy forces before undertaking major action.

The mission radioman warned London during the day:

"Maquis attacked, lack ammo for Brens and French automatic rifles, American and Hotchkiss machine-guns, torpedos (sic) for bazookas, and all types of ammunition. Send special drop even tonight. Morale excellent. We'll beat 'em."

For the moment the partisans remained assembled in the Margeride forest and defensive fortifications of the stronghold were reinforced.

On the morning of the 10th, the enemy attacked from the other three sides — Saugues to the east, Pinols to the north and Lorcières to the west — with the equivalent of a division, using mortars, artillery and armored cars.

The action was prepared by Brodowski and led by Generalmajor Jesser, loaned to him for the occasion by the Military Command in France. The task force in Saugues included the 958th Flak Battalion and three mobile companies of Tatars of the Volga, using whatever vehicles they could get their hands on. In Pinols the soldiers were from the battalion of the *SS-Polizei-Regiment* 19. The Jesser troops — SR 1000 and reconnaissance — were on the west side, while more Tatars were closing the circle on the south. All in all, almost 5,000 men.

"The maquis fighters resisted the shock, Lebaigue continued. But in the evening, it became clear that we would not be able to hold our positions. So we decided to move out towards the canyons of La Truyère by the road that had been left open to the south."

The next day the command post and the units that had not received weapons evacuated Mount Mouchet under the protection of the other companies. At 21:00 a general retreat began, covered by particularly effective diversionary activity. The fight ended on the maquis side with a toll of 70 killed and 30 wounded who were all shot later by the Germans. The enemy lost an estimated 200 killed and 600 wounded.

On the 12th, the Germans took over the spot where the former CP had been evacuated, and failed attack by burning several villages.

From June 13 to 15 the Benjoin team stayed in the La Truyère retreat. All the maquisards from Mount Mouchet gradually ended up there. The CP was installed at Saint-Martial, near Chaudes-Aigues and the units got reorganized. They were now spread out in independent mobile companies. The camp was alive with activity day and night, and the DZ Veilleuse was used to full capacity: 40 planes dropped weapons during the following nights and up until June 20th, including twenty-five during the night of June 13 alone. The only offensive activity undertaken was an attack on a large convoy on the Garabit viaduct.

On June 15, Lebaigue left Saint-Martial to visit the maquis of Lioran and Condat with Colonel Huguet. The Condat maquis had been hastily formed and hadn't any real leadership. The men had just scattered in fear of a German attack. The best fighters — about four hundred men — had assembled south of Murat under the command of Capitaine Simonet.

After four days spent at Plomb-du-Cantal, Lebaigue started back to Saint-Martial on the morning of the 20th, to give Trollet some messages to relay. All the roads were covered with single cars or convoys, signs that the Germans were planning a major operation in the region. So Lebaigue turned back and went out on a job with Simonet instead.

Actually the Germans had decided to neutralize the La Truyère retreat, which covered an area about twenty-five miles in circumference. An attack was launched by four mobile columns supported by artillery and aviation, all converging towards Anterrieux and Saint-Martial. The maquis resisted, but they couldn't hold out for long against the crushing superiority of the German forces. Gaspard gave the order to withdraw north towards Plomb-du-Cantal and Lioran.

That was the end of the retreat experiment concerning retreats in Auvergne.

A completely new organization was implemented: the zone was divided into sectors. Each sector would have its own independent company totally in charge of roads and operations. So each group made its way to the new sector assigned to it.

"Vecteur went to Corrèze, recalled Lebaigue, and I stayed in Lioran with Mediane and Somali."

Cardozo had had no news from Pyramide since June 8, so he made contact with him through the radioman Henry Koenig (Africain). On the 17th he notified London that he had left the Cantal FFI for the FFI of Corrèze who had no contact with London. On the 20th in Neuvic d'Ussel he met Colonel Fayard, ORA leader for Region R.6.

The remainder of Team Benjoin followed Gaspard to Chauvet Lake on July 1st. Since Trollet had no radio set to contact London, a request was sent to London via Cardozo and the radioman Africain, for a set and enough weapons to arm the two hundred guerilla fighters in the sector.

On July 3, Cardozo had a date with Pyramide in Mauriac. But the meeting never took place, because the DMR and Christophe, his deputy, had just been arrested by the Gestapo in Clermont-Ferrand.

Ten days later, Gouy and Lebaigue joined Cardozo [6] in Mauriac, where the representatives of the ORA, the FTP and the MUR were meeting to chose commanders and members of the FFI staff.

"Polygone and Isotherme [7] were also present, explained Lebaigue. Mission Benjoin had been invited just to be polite. After a long discussion, Gaspard was elected regional FFI chief of R.6, with Colonel Mortier of the ORA as military deputy and a staff made up of members of the different movements."

The mission members had just been spectators to one of the acts of the psychodrama pervading the southern zone at that time. The nomination of new FFI leaders — after the arrests in June and July and with a view to the self-liberation of the French people — was a scene from this play, with, in Auvergne, the Caïman plan as a backdrop.

On July 14, around 08:30, seventy-three B-17s escorted by fighter planes carried out a parachute drop on the Serrurier site controlled by the Pleaux maquis, near the Eagle Dam (Barrage de l'Aigle).

6. Mission estimates. According to the book Les FFI au combat, the numbers were 160 French dead and 100 wounded, for 220 German dead and 130 wounded.

7. Guy Vivier, from Mission Isotherme, new DMR of R.6.

276

The first drop by the 8th Air Force had been scheduled to take place during the daytime on June 25 as part of Operation Zebra, but had had to be cancelled because of the German attack. On July 11, SHAEF recommended undertaking on July 14 a massive daytime parachute operation, code-named Cadillac. The Cantal was listed as priority 2, after the Vercors, but before the Saône-et-Loire, Corrèze, Lot and Haute-Vienne.

On the afternoon of the 13th, among the cascade of coded messages, Cardozo picked out the one announcing a drop of 689 containers for the next day. At 19:30 the BBC aired the pre-arranged sentence — The cannibals are devouring the Eskimos — and repeated it two hours later for confirmation.

At the Eagle Hotel in Aynes, where last-minute problems of the reception committee were being ironed out: Major Cardozo was there, very calm.

His role was essential in this affair, since it was because of his insisting and repeating that London finally decided, after the union of all the FFI groups in Auvergne, to include them among the recipients of Operaton Cadillac [8]

Everything was ready by 05:00. At 06:00 contact was made with London. An hour later, the aircraft took off from their base: on the other side of the Channel it was just 05:00.

The weather was beautiful. The flying formation was now in permanent contact with the men on the ground. Seventy-two Flying Fortresses appeared, surrounded by a swarm of fighter planes. On the DZ flames from the huge fires licked the air. The roar was deafening. Thirty-six B-17s descended toward the zone in waves while the others turned toward the Corrèze.

Six successive waves flew over and dropped 400 containers which landed in the pasture with metallic thuds. As they flew by, the crews waved from their cockpits. The sky above the partisans' heads was full of blue, white and red parachutes. The roar lessened, then disappeared altogether. On the ground, the work of assembling and

8. Gilles Lévy, *L'opération Cadillac*.

removing the 47 tons of equipment was begun. It wouldn't be until 1.A.M.

Unfortunately that day which had begun so well finished sadly for Mission Benjoin: in the afternoon, while explaining to some partisans how to use his Colt 32, Lieutenant Lebaigue accidentally discharged a bullet through his own liver [9].

Mission Musc in the Ain and Haute Savoie

Learning from experience, the Auvergne FFI had abandoned position warfare to devote themselves exclusively to guerilla fighting and thus be able to take part in the later battles of Liberation.

In the mountains east of the Rhône River, the drama played out in the Vercors would later be a subject of controversy. And in the Ain, FFI activity was just as debatable. These events have already inspired plenty of writers, so we will give only a general outline.

The interallied mission Musc was parachuted five months after Union, arriving in Savoie, France, on June 7, 1944: actually it was the last avatar of Mission Xavier-Cantinier.

In September 1943, Richard Heslop (Xavier) [10] of the SOE F section Marksman circuit — along with Capitaine Jean Rosenthal (Cantinier) of the BCRA, under the control of the RF section — were sent into the northern part of R.1. After spending three weeks in the field, the two agents were picked up on October 16 near Mâcon and taken back to London to turn in their report on the situation in the maquis on the Swiss border. Two nights later, they were again set down in Lons-le-Saunier by another Hudson, so that they could continue their job of organizing. With them arrived a runner, Elizabeth Reynolds, and Captain Owen D. Johnson (Paul) of the U.S. Army.

"I was assigned to the Marksman circuit, explained Johnson, to be Xavier's radioman. Our mission was to arm and organize the maquis

9. He was operated on in Riom-ès-Lontagnes and treated at Collandres before going back to Clermont on October 20 and then to OSS headquarters in Paris a week later. Even though Major Cardozo wrote up his own report of the mission, our story of Benjoin's activities is based essentially on Lieutenant Lebaigue's report.

10. During his first mission in France, Heslop was imprisoned by the Vichy police, but freed before the Germans invaded the free zone.

278

in Haute-Savoie, the Ain and parts of the Jura. I believe it was one of the first, if not the first, interallied mission, with three officers: a Briton, a Frenchman and an American."

Rosenthal, in his report, gave the mission the title of 'first Interallied Maquis Mission.'

For Colonel Henri Petit (Romans), head of the AS maquis in the Ain, this mission was a godsend, for his men needed outside help to be able to fight:

"Colonel Heslop established his CP in the Ain, next door to mine, and we got along well: we shared mutual admiration and friendship through the Liberation. The mission also included a Frenchman, Jean Rosenthal, who had settled if you can call it that because he travelled around a lot in Haute-Savoie."

Until the end of 1943, Johnson lived on a farm in Haute-Savoie. But, beginning in January 1944, the operations undertaken by the Vichy forces in charge of maintaining order made liaisons with Heslop more and more difficult, so Johnson returned to the Ain. He was put in charge of organizing parachute drops and using the Eureka and S-Phone. In April, his job as radio operator, including his codes, was entrusted to a French Air Force operator who had been recruited recently.

Actually, in spite of promises, no parachute drops occurred in the Ain before the January moon period. In Haute-Savoie 220 containers were dropped experimentally through the cloud cover, into a zone supposedly controlled by Heslop: but too many of the boxes were either lost or recovered by the enemy, so this was never tried again.

Militiamen and GMR were operating in the region at that time. In the Ain, the Bernod plateau was attacked on February 6. The départemental headquarters staff, after a surprise attack by a German detachment, barricaded itself in at the Mountain Farm (ferme de la Montagne).

"Xavier kept wonderfully cool, Romans remembered. Paul, very calm during this storm, barricaded a window with an old mattress, leaving just a peep-hole, and fired away with his Winchester, as if he were in a shooting gallery at the county fair."

Partisans and paratroopers managed to get out of the farm and into the woods, but not without losing some men. Romans — who was with Elizabeth [11] in Haute-Savoie — found the survivors spread about in the different refuges in the area. German repression was visible everywhere: farms were burned and prisoners executed. At Boyeux, Johnson was playing nurse to a wounded maquisard that he had been caring for since the fight.

Romans-Petit had been named Haute-Savoie départemental chief in November 1943 with the job of reorganizing the FFI forces there. He had come back to the Ain after commanding the Haute-Savoie for two months. He subsequently planned the massing of the guerilla fighters around the Glières dropping zone.

This assembling was not to the liking of the ORA. Colonel Chambonnet (Didier), of the regional AS-MUR, was against it, too. On the site, Lieutenant Morel (Tom) also had doubts:

"The enemy has taken up position all around the plateau. Should we disperse before the drop?"

London, questioned by Rosenthal, answered Affirmative. That would seal the fate of Glières.

To the maquis, the attack by the German troops was an almost total surprise, but a catastrophe was nevertheless avoided. Now the men had to bandage their wounds and analyze the lessons of this defeat. The sector chiefs were summoned, and Romans, with Heslop as advisor, gave them new orders:

"Change your camps frequently. No groups of more than one hundred twenty men. Don't stock food, use requisitioning coupons. Start diversionary operations — ambushes and sabotages — immediately when a German assault is announced."

After the CP was installed in the Bresse plain, it became much easier to receive messages, and many parachute drops were carried

11. Romans-Petit, in Les maquis de l'Ain, describes her as an American woman participating in a sabotage mission requested by Xavier. She spoke good French but with a hard accent. On her way back to England she was arrested in Paris, imprisoned at Fresnes for three months, then finally liberated in Vittel by the advancing Allied forces.

out whether or not there was moonlight. Heslop and Romans agreed to concentrate their efforts on three or four DZs located near active groups and suitable for receiving large quantities of material. Almost a thousand containers of weapons were received between January and May.

They made a try at establishing a signal communications network between the CP and the different maquis, but it didn't work out, even though thirteen radio operators were available at one time: the necessary quartz crystlas were never sent from London. However, three walkie-talkies, dropped by parachute as an experiment, worked perfectly, although only at short range.

Twice — in March when Heslop was wounded and in July during his absence — Johnson took over command of the mission.

"Xavier, Johnson pointed out, considered his role as one of an advisor or a liaison officer. He acted accordingly and never would take command."

There was some mistrust in relations between the mission and the MUR, as Colonel Romans recalled:

"A climate of misunderstanding persisted and resulted in some sticky incidents right up until the Liberation. The day after the Germans left, Xavier was bluntly told to leave France immediately, which was inelegant to say the least. Cantinier was in contact with the harsh realities of maquis life since his arrival in Haute-Savoie and especially since the events at Glières, and his attitude toward the regional leaders had softened up a bit, even though his view had been pretty tough at the beginning. On the other hand, he and Xavier had less to do with each other as time went by."

And he added, pointing out how important a role personalities play at this level and in these circumstances:

"The two men were very different. The first, Xavier, was a respectful soldier; the second, Cantinier, was recklessly bold."

The official historian of the SOE described Rosenthal as particularly intelligent and courageous. In the team, he was the one who defined the strategy of the mission, while Heslop brought audacity and authority.

The day after D-Day, all road and train traffic had been blocked in the Ain, thus separating two-thirds of the département from the rest of France and consequently creating the problem of protecting the civilians isolated in this new free zone. At the request of Colonel Auguste Vistel (Alban), regional FFI chief, Romans had temporarily taken on the job of prefect.

"For more than a month, while we were waiting for the promised daytime parachute drop, Johnson recalled, we managed to keep the Germans on the outskirts of the liberated zone. On June 26, thirty-six aircraft dropped enough weapons to equip the armistice army, certain elements of the AS as well as two FTP companies."

Perhaps this was part of Operation Zebra, scheduled for June 22 and postponed for three days because of bad weather: a DZ in the mountainous area of the Ain had been on the list of those to be served. But other drops were also mentioned during those same days: at Etables on the 23rd for the ORA [12], on the 24th at Lescheroux where three tons of weapons were delivered to the AS Saint-Amour group and on the 26th at Moulin-des-Ponts for the Guth FTP group.

Rosenthal was parachuted into the Saône-et-Loire on June 7.

"My mission, he pointed out, was to prepare the Haute-Savoie for liberation. Xavier was more in charge of liaison between interallied headquarters and the départements of the Ain and Jura."

So Rosenthal, now code-named Apothème, had been back and forth to London to get orders from SFHQ! His arrival coincided with that of Mission Musc, directed by Heslop.

"As soon as I arrived, he continued, I tried to reach Didier and Bayard [13] at the regional level, to tell them how dangerous an uprising of the Resistance would be in R.1. The landing on the

12. According to the history of the ORA battalion in the Ain, the unit "received a parachute drop on June 24 on the Port dropping zone, consisting of 540 containers of arms and ammunition. It took all day to pick up and distribute the weapons and we were not disturbed by the Jerries." This must be the "armistice army" that Johnson is talking about.

13. Colonel Marcel Descour (Bayard-Périmètre), regional ORA leader and chief of the EM FFI for R.1. Didier, arrested in June, 1944, was replaced by Alban.

Normandy beaches didn't mean that France was liberated. Afterwards I saw Romans and Xavier; I transmitted orders from Generals De Gaulle and Koenig. They didn't seem to agree with me and I got quite a cool reception. They thought I had got wet feet, and they were heady about being Free Frenchmen."

Rosenthal went to Annecy on June 10, visited the authorities and introduced the American Lieutenant Niveau who had been parachuted with him. This officer from the Engineering Corps was sent by the OSS to work with the Special Forces detachment assigned to the Seventh Army organizing the invasion of Provence.

Fighting was heavy in the Ain at that time, and, in as much as their limited means would allow, the Haute-Savoie FFI tried to help their neighbors. Rosenthal was constantly begging for parachute drops. London didn't answer and he had no contact with Algiers. It was just as hard for him to contact the regional authorities: he missed Polygone and Carré three times in Lyon [14], and Bayard was in the Vercors at the time.

On August 1st he finally got thirty-six aircraft for a daytime drop — Operation Buick [15] — thanks to which he was able to equip his fighters and organize the defense of the DZ as well as that of the plateau where the brass were arriving.

North of the Rhône, Romans had drawn the winning ticket with Mission Musc. On July 6, a Dakota landed on the Izernore field and a flood of passengers swept down the steps, first a bit wary but soon perfectly at ease. They were British, American, Canadian and French officers, who were guided to their destination by liaison agents. The plane, piloted by Lieutenant-Colonel Heflin, was camouflaged in the woods before its scheduled departure for England 48 hours later [16].

14. Colonel Maurice Bourges-Maunoury (Polygone), DMR and acting DMZ for the South; Lieutenant-Colonel Leister-Schneider (Dragon - Carré), DMR of R.1.

15. Of the 192 B-17s involved in the total operation, 39 dropped onto the Moulin DZ for the Jura FTP, 39 with 463 containers in Savoie and 75 with 899 packages in Haute-Savoie.

16. In Les maquis de l'Ain, Romans-Petit dates the event, which he vividly relates, on July 7.

In the C-47 arrived Doctor Geoffrey Parker (Parsifal), an English surgeon who, with two equally adventurous colleagues, went about organizing a sixty-bed field hospital at Le Crêt de Chalame, before joining the CP and following it as it moved around.

"On July 9, Johnson remembered, the third German action against the maquis took place. There were elements from two divisions — the 157th and the 9th Panzer — as well as a column from Chaumont, with aviation, artillery and armor."

On the 10th, the Gemans launched an all-out attack against the FFI in the region of Nantua and Oyonnax. On the 15th, the départemental CP moved to the Echallon forest: it would remain on constant move for nine days to avoid being caught.

Then from July 20 on, the German troops, having been at least partially successful, moved south to undertake new operations. Starting the day before, the Vercors plateau, south of the Ain, had been invaded.

Mission Eucalyptus, Spoc and the Vercors

The maquis in the Vercors had the same problems as the other maquis in France. On D-Day they too received orders concerning sabotage and guerilla warfare in their region.

But since they believed that the headquarters were aware of the Montagnard plan, they thought that, as far as they were concerned, this message was the preview of a coming aerial landing and probably also a massive invasion along the Mediterranean coast [17]. After the BBC messages broadcast on the evening of June 5, the Vercors was totally mobilized and Colonel Descour installed his CP there.

But, starting on the morning of the 13th, the Germans assaulted Saint-Nizier, next door to Grenoble. They were fought back, but

17. Robert Aron, Histoire de la libération de la France (*History of the Liberation of France*). The Montagnard plan was elaborated in 1943 and consisted in organizing the Vercors plateau to receive important forces arriving by air, and launching actions, at the appropriate time, against the routes to be used by the retreating enemy.

returned two days later and, this time, forced the FFI to abandon the valleys of Lans and Villars.

For the FFI, the misunderstanding was chronic: they didn't believe that they had a defensive role to play; they expected to come out of their hideouts when they saw the victorious Allies coming through, to guide them toward the enemy rear. So they would have appreciated few; Hotchkiss machine guns and more mortars in the containers that were dropped on June 14.

Then the plateau was calm for more than a month. During this time almost four thousand volunteers arrived from all over. Orders were still to defend the plains where airplanes and gliders could land.

The Allies were more generous with advice than with mortars. However, at the end of June and beginning of July, the Vercors FFI received reinforcements by air. An interallied mission, an American commando, young French instructors coming from Algiers, dropped by parachute on June 21 and during the night of July 7, boosted their morale [18].

The interallied mission was code-named Eucalyptus. It came from London. Commandant Lejeune, director of tripartite mission operations at the EM FFI, wrote about this group:

Mission Eucalyptus was sent into the Vercors after the invasion and arrived just in time to take part in hard fighting that forced the maquis to evacuate the Vercors, but too late to play the role for which it had been prepared and which it was perfectly qualified to assume.

The mission was commanded by English Major Desmond Longe, assisted by his friend and fellow countryman, Captain John Housman, and Capitaine Adrien Conus (Volume). Three radio operators completed the team. Second Lieutenant Andrew E. Pecquet alias Paray (Bavarois), of the U.S. Army, was in charge of liaisons with London. Lieutenant Philip Saillard-Sawerby alias Pierre (Touareg) was assigned to Conus, also for liaisons with England. As for Sous-Lieutenant Yves Croix (Pingouin), he was tuned in to Algiers.

18. Histoire de la Libération de la France. op.cit.

Longe, a banker, and Houseman, a real estate agent, had known each other since they arrived at the SOE in 1941: the former had worked abroad and the latter had been an instructor. They were given false papers in London, but SFHQ didn't deem it necessary to invent an alibi for their presence in France: and they were to be parachuted in uniform and didn't speak a word of French. It was hard to understand how such a liaison mission could be entrusted to officers with no knowledge of the language: perhaps London did not fully understand the strategic importance of the Vercors.

Conus, a former elephant hunter and miner-prospector in Africa, had served in the groupe franc of the Oubangui-Chari Battalion, commanded by Lieutenant Pierre Bourgoin, who, three years later, would be jumping into Brittany with his 4th SAS. He had been at Bir Hakeim, then joined the BCRA when the BM 2 (Batallion de Marche N° 2) came back to French Equitorial Africa.

Pierre had signed up in Malta in August 1941, then left immediately for Tunisia where he carried out a three-month radio and intelligence mission. He completed his military training in the island, then returned to Tunisia where he worked until May 1943.

Paray, the radioman trained in the U.S., was fortunately bilingual. In Great Britain he had received operator's training on English Mark I and III sets and assimilated SOE procedure. The B mark II set was the one most often used. It weighed 22 lbs and could be hidden in a twenty-four inch suitcase, so it was sometimes called the suitcase set. But even under perfect conditions it couldn't go beyond 20 watts of power, its transmissions were weak and its antenna — more than sixty feet long — was sometimes hard to hide. The A mark III set wasn't as large: its dimensions were half those of the preceding model.

In May 1944, Paray finished his training and was assigned to the BCRA in London. He received ID papers created from the originals he had brought with him out of France in October 1940.

Around June 7, he contacted the RF section and was informed that he had been assigned to handle liaison between the base and an interallied team to be sent into the Vercors maquis. Then he met Majors Ortiz and Thackthwaite, but, even though they had spent some time in the Vercors, he didn't feel that they were really well informed about the current situation there [19].

From Major Longe's explanations, he realized that the team would be assigned to the French officer commanding in the Vercors:

"It's a liaison mission, he was told. Our orders are to keep London informed about the situation and the needs for supplies, and advise the Vercors groups so that their actions target our goals: to cut road and railway links."

For transportation into France, it was decided that Capitaine Conus and his radioman would land via Lysander. The others would arrive in France through North Africa, because nights were too short for a direct flight from England to the Alps.

The team wasn't formed in May after the arrest of the regional leaders of the Resistance in Lyon. But they didn't leave Algiers until the end of June. And no one paid any attention to Thackthwaite and Cammaerts' warnings [20] that the Vercors needed artillery and especially anti-tank weapons.

Eucalyptus' job as defined in the mission order, was to arm and instruct the 2,500 maquisards with light weapons, because true guerilla warfare has no need of heavy weapons. At best a few machine guns, or maybe some mortars, could be dropped later on.

"I left London on June 10, Paray recalled. Before leaving, I received instructions as to what to do if I had to escape through Spain. I was in Algiers on the 12th, and was followed three days later by Longe and Houseman bringing signals plans and four sets of quartz crystals. The team was assigned to the Special Project Operation Centre, SPOC in military jargon, which had been created on May 23, 1944. SPOC was commanded by Lieutenant Colonel John Anstey, assisted by Lieutenant Colonel William P. Davis of the OSS. It was housed in a dozen Nissen barracks, twenty-five tents and a mess-hall built out of

19. Ortiz and Thackthwaite were part of Mission Union from January 6 to May 6, 1944.

20. Major Francis C.A. Cammaerts (Roger), a former Cambridge professor and conscientious objector, had organized the Jockey circuit of the SOE F section in May of 1943. Its influence and authority covered most of Region R.1.

boards near the Villa Magnol on the west side of Algiers. The French Section was directed by Royal Navy Lieutenant Commander Brooks Richards. He had worked with the Gaullists and participated with them in missions in Tunisia: this undoubtedly helped cinch his nomination. Captain Gerard de Piolenc was his American counterpart. Lieutenant-Colonel Constans, from the BCRA Action Branch, a strictly military man, handled liaison."

The Air Operations Section had eighteen Halifaxes which were joined by eleven B-17s and B-24s plus seven twin-engine B-25s and a C-47. Sorties were made to the south of France, but the majority went to Italy and the Balkans [21]. Packing was taken care of at Major Ray Wooler's packing station in Blida. He was from the STS 51a school in Altrincham and had designed the training program at Ringway.

From March 1944 on, a second packing station, 100% American, had been opened at Staoueli, near the OSS school. But the personnel at the two stations was less competent than their colleagues in the English stations, which meant that more that 20% of the supplies dropped were damaged: either the parachutes didn't open or the containers burst open in the air or when they hit the ground.

The Jedburghs were assigned to British Major James Champion, assisted by Lieutenant Peg Todd (FANY). Coordination was difficult between the French Section and the Air Operations Section because their goals were sometimes quite different. Like SFHQ — on a smaller scale but more complicated due to the massive presence of the French in Algiers — SPOC had to handle a lot of agents in the field.

Six French OGs and twenty-one Jedburgh teams arrived from London and were placed under its operational control. Once Major Neil Marten, a leader of a Jed team (Veganin) who had returned to Algiers, was assigned to SPOC at the beginning of August, contacts improved somewhat.

The OGs were dealt with exclusively by Lieutenant Colonel Alfred G. Cox.

21. In 1944, 13,000 sorties took place over the Balkans and northern Italy, compared to 1,130 over southern France.

During the summer of 1944, 212 Americans secretly entered France. Nine were OSS/SO agents and twenty-one were Jedburghs: the others made up the fourteen combat platoons of the OGs.

Just before the invasion of Provence, SPOC was coordinating ten interallied missions, seventeen Jed teams, a British paramilitary group, three Counterscorch teams and ten Operational Groups.

"We, the OGs, were all volunteers, 28 officers and 180 NCOs, recalled one of them. Besides parachute training, we were taught during maneuvers in the mountains of North Africa to destroy targets behind enemy lines, to use enemy weapons and live like outlaws."

In the beginning the OGs trained as companies; then they were divided up into sections made up of two officers and thirteen men.

"Each team had five rifles, fifteen pistols, ten automatics, two bazookas, thirty grenades per man and six cases of combat rations. Each soldier carried an assortment of traps, mines, fuses and detonators."

The rifles and pistols were of the usual types — 30-caliber M1s and Colt 1911 A1 45s. The submachine guns, on the other hand, were experimental 9-mm Marlins [22]. A large radio station was installed in October 1943 on the Ile Rousse in Corsica, to communicate with the OGs and relay, if necessary, transmissions from the networks to the base in Algiers.

At the Club des Pins in Staoueli, a summer resort near Sidi-Ferruch, Massingham set up a 1,000-acre enclosed training camp where agents and members of the Special Forces underwent training. There were Britons, Americans, Frenchmen, Italians, Spaniards, assigned to missions of the SOE, SIS, OSS, DGSS and the Shock Battalion. In September 1943, the first OG candidates got their airborne qualifications.

It was also at the OSS Parachute School that trap doors were cut out on the Flying Fortresses, and that the twin-engine B-25 Mitchells, too fast for dropping personnel, were adapted to drop packages and containers. Dakotas were also experimentally landed at night on a rudimentary airstrip.

---

22. One thousand UD 42s — the official name — were manufactured. They were not used by the U.S. Army, but assigned to guerilla units.

At Chrea Gap, a well-known ski resort in the Atlas mountains near Blida, an exclusively OSS school was established in April 1944, where Frenchmen and Americans were trained in guerilla and sabotage techniques both as instructors and as fighters.

"While we were in Algeria, Paray explained, the SPOC officers came in handy for rounding out our gear. The radio equipment and sleeping bags were English. The Americans gave me a Marlin submachine gun."

The French Section gave the Eucalyptus team detailed information about the resistants in the region: numbers, organization, names of local authorities, sédentaires, etc.

"If the Allies invade from the South, the Vercors should play an important role because of its strategic position. In the meantime, the forces there have to be increased and they must be encouraged to remain active by harassing enemy convoys on the main roads around the plateau."

According to the Intelligence Section, the German troops that had assembled in the valley of the Rhône River were moving North.

"The infamous Brandenburg Regiment, with a reputation for committing atrocities during its operations, was spotted at Pont St. Esprit."

The Vercors was now a priority target for air drops.

"But they told us that the British had stopped furnishing mortars, because the security pins on the shells were too fragile to be dropped by parachute. They were studying the problem and hoped to have a solution within two weeks."

In the meantime, as Mission Union advised when it returned to England at the beginning of May, it was decided to create a landing strip on the plateau so that mortars and their shells could be delivered by plane. And so the Eucalyptus team, while at the holding station — last stop for the agents before leaving for the field — joined up with Aviation Capitaine Tournissa (Paquebot), who was in charge of supervising the work on the strip, including the construction of a platform for the radio range beacon he was taking with him.

The briefing officer in London was very clear about landing fields:

"The mission is to look for large areas where troops can be parachuted and landing strips with sufficient security to allow planes to land and be remain camouflaged for 24 hours."

He also explained that Eucalyptus was hierarchically under the orders of the R.1 military delegate. They were to send him a copy of the regular reports they dispatched to London about their activity.

"As soon as possible after you arrive, the briefing officer continued, you are to make contact with Colonel Hervieux, the commander of the Drôme and Isère départements, and with Mr. Clément, the civilian leader [23]. Also with Commandants Legrand and Bastide, the départemental leaders [24]."

The base in Algiers wanted a radio liaison with the mission and Paray could not communicate with both Algiers and London, so Croix, who had been trained by the OSS, and his American equipment were added to the mission. The two operators agreed on using the same codes so that, if communications with London were interrupted, messages could still get through via Algiers.

From the morning papers in Algiers the four officers learned that the Vercors Resistance forces had been forced to evacuate the city of Saint-Nizier, above Grenoble. Then, on June 22, they met an OG who was about to be dropped in the Vercors.

The four officers were then asked if they volunteered to jump on a moonless night. They responded affirmatively.

The team took off from Blida at 20:50 on the 24th. But when they got over the Baleares Islands, after an hour's flight, one of the engines went dead. The pilot couldn't manage to get the propellor into vertical position, so he decided to return to his base. To lighten the aircraft, all the tracts that had been loaded on board were thrown into the Mediterranean, along with six containers hitched under the wings.

Four days later they tried again, and this time they got across the Mediterranean safely and arrived over the Taille-Crayon drop site, in Vassieux-en-Vercors, at quarter past midnight.

23. Commandant François Huet (Hervieux) of the ORA, commander of the Plateau, and Eugène Chavant (Clément), civilian leader of the Vercors and one of the instigators of Plan Montagnard, along with Legrand.

24. ORA Capitaine Alain Le Ray (Bastide), FFI chief of the Isère; ORA Commandant de Lassus de Saint-Geniez (Legrand), AS and FFI départemental chief.

The red light, then the green went on:

"I jumped number 3, Paray recalled. As I was free-falling, I saw the four bright fires under me. My parachute opened. In the dark I felt the top of Captain Houseman's chute touching my feet and I had to lift up my legs to avoid it. When I got closer to the ground, my chute started vibrating badly. I landed on a rocky mountain road, with my feet caught in a barbed-wire fence. My right wrist hurt. We were led to a farm where a doctor bandaged by wrist. Then we spent the night in a hotel in Vassieux."

When we woke up the next morning, the 450 inhabitants of the village were in the street. They had been making American flags during the night, so the Stars and Stripes floated in the breeze beside the French tricolor among bouquets of flowers. The villagers were delighted to see so many Americans. In the Vercors they thought that these commandos in uniform — the OGs were also dropped that same night — were the advance party of an army of paratroopers.

Justine, Veganin and Dodge in the Drôme and Isere

Operational Group Justine [25], dropped soon after Mission Eucalyptus, was made up of fifteen men, commanded by First Lieutenants Vernon G. Hoppers and Chester L. Meyers. They had a few mortars with them, a weapon in great demand on the plateau.

Commandant Narcisse Geyer (Thivollet), chief of the southern sector, came to drive them to Saint-Martin-en-Vercors, where Colonel Hervieux had set up his CP. Since May — after the agreement between the authorities of the Isère and the Drôme, as the plateau covers parts of these two départements — Hervieux had taken command of all the Vercors maquis groups.

"We all agreed, Paray explained, that Eucalyptus would be assigned to the CP and would share their meals. The main job of the OGs

25. The code name of Justine in the signals plan was Magnesium/Barium. The signals call name was often used to designate the OGs, which is a source of confusion for certain authors.

would be to train the maquisards in the use of specific weapons, and especially the bazookas that they had just received."

After two days of training Lieutenant Hopper's team and eighteen maquisards tried their first sortie. A fifteen-mile forced night march took them to Route 75, on the south-east side of the plateau. They stopped for a rest at 06:00 and Hoppers left on reconnaissance with Sergeant de Trane and Corporal La Briek. An hour later, the whole group had taken up their positions along the road, three miles from Lalley. The ambush plan was typical: a bazooka covered by a BAR was set up on each side of the road, with the rest of the commando hidden on top of the steep cliff above the roadside. On each end guerillas with Brens were posted as lookouts, to stop anyone who tried to get around the trap.

They soon heard the roar of a motor. Sergeant Richmann and Corporal Paquet saw a convoy approaching — three trucks, a bus full to overflowing with soldiers, then two more trucks. They were going slow because the vehicles were heavily loaded. A machine gun was mounted on the first and last trucks.

When the first truck got to the ambush, Richmann opened fire with his bazooka: the first rocket went through the motor and killed the two men on the front seat against the rock. From the top of the bluff, La Briek, Delma, Calvert and Laglane threw Gammon grenades into the open trucks.

On the other side of the road, covered by Corporal Picard's BAR, Sergeant Harp fired a rocket at the third truck, which swerved for a second before crashing into the truck in front of it. A second rocket hit the bus driver as he was getting out on the roadside. Then the two Brens opened fire.

The last two trucks had managed to turn around and take shelter beyond a curve. The Germans tried putting a machine gun battery into position on the road, but the OGs easily managed to take it out.

"At 07:45, Hoppers recalled, there were no more signs of movement in the convoy. Way down the road the Germans who had got away had positioned two mortars and were peppering the hillside. So I gave the signal to withdraw."

Two partisans who had been serving a Bren up front, were missing. One of them had been hit by a mortar shell and captured, but the other one probably hid somewhere nearby. The column headed on through the Vercors, but Calvert and a maquisard stayed in the woods. Then they went to Lalley at nightfall looking for news.

"After the ambush, Hoppers continued, the Germans forced the townspeople to bury their dead. Then, to set an example, they coldly executed the wounded maquisard in the town square, even though he had insisted he was a soldier fighting with an American commando unit."

The young Resistance fighter was buried with military honors in the Vercors.

At Mission Eucalyptus, Paray had problems with his radio set from the moment he arrived: the three receivers hadn't been correctly packed and were damaged when they landed. It took two days to repair one so he could send a message to London requesting that the two others be replaced. He never got an answer. The base in Algiers wasn't able to keep its promise to the Vercors either, because of events beyond its control. In spite of this Paray managed to relay messages between Major Cox and the OGs, since their radio set had also been broken on landing.

Going through the contents of the containers, he couldn't find either his equipment, his civilian clothers or his ID papers.

"Algiers answered my first message, Paray recalled, and told me that my package was on board our plane and that it must have been stolen by the partisans. Then the base confirmed that the equipment was actually loaded onto a plane that had been declared missing and they were asking London to replace it."

Cammaerts, of the Jockey circuit, and Major Marten, leader of a Jedburgh team recently dropped in the Drôme, passed through the plateau at that time. Longe and Marten started arguing immediately. Cammaerts had become the senior Allied liaison officer and deputy to Colonel Zeller (Faisceau), who had been given command over all the FFI operating in south-eastern France, which gave him authority over all the missions working in that area.

Cammaerts felt that the Eucalyptus members, controlled by SPOC, were butting in on his territory.

He also learned about then that the F and RF sections of the SOE had been dissolved, and a new FFI section created instead. He felt ill at ease in this new organization, and hadn't received any instructions from his new bosses. Finally he decided, on July 11, to send Marten, the Veganin leader, to Algiers with a report about the situation.

Jed team Veganin [26] had been dropped at Pact, near Beaurepaire, during the night of June 8. The radioman's static line was not properly hooked up and he was killed during the jump. The team was in charge of coordinating guerilla activities in the northern part of the Drôme opposite Route 7, so the two remaining officers contacted an AS maquis which was covering the north-western access roads to the Vercors. They found themselves placed under Hervieux' orders.

So they made their way to La Chapelle-en-Vercors where they were joined by Dodge [27], a team that had been dropped during the night of June 25. The next day, at La Côte-Saint-André, both teams took part in a meeting between Capitaine Drouot (Hermine), the départemental FFI chief, Zeller, Hervieux and Cammaerts. Hervieux and Cammaerts defended the Vercors:

"The Vercors stronghold will assemble the most powerful forces from the surrounding areas and receive parachute drops."

But the Jeds were focused on the valley of the Rhône, so a compromise was worked out that suited everyone. During the meeting it was decided that the two teams Veganin and Dodge [28] would merge and that Major Marten would be sent to Algiers to insist on a rapid advance by the Allies along Route Napoleon towards Grenoble. This was Zeller's pet idea.

26. Major Neil Marten (Cuthbert) of the Northamptonshire Yeomanry, Capitaine C.L. Vuchot alias Noir (Derek) of the Infanterie and Serjeant D. Gardner (Ernest), Royal Armoured Corps.

27. Major C.E. Mannière (Rupert), of the Infantry, and Serjeant L.T. Durocher (Oswald), of the Royal Canadian Corps of Signals.

28. After Major Mannière's capture, Jed team Veganin-Dodge had only two teammates: Noir and the radioman Durocher.

During the night of July 6 the six men of Mission Paquebot arrived. They had come to transform the Vassieux DZ into a landing strip. As a result, Hervieux, in agreement with Clément, sent out orders for general mobilization, to bring the number of fighters in the Vercors up to 3,200, with 600 workers for Capitaine Tournissa.

"The people on the plateau, Paray explained, thought that Allied paratroopers were coming to help them. I don't know where that rumor started. Nobody at Hervieux' CP had ever mentioned to us anything about airborne troops."

We weren't expecting anyone except a French commando team and maybe another OG.

On July 13 the remaining members of Mission Eucalyptus arrived on the plateau. Six days before, Capitaine Conus, his radioman Pierre and four Mark III radio sets had landed in a C-47 on the Ain site, where Romans and his staff were waiting for them. On the 10th, as the Germans were starting to invade the region, they were driven by car — armed and in uniforms — to a maquis. All along the way they passed enemy convoys.

Then a guide took the two men toward Morestel, where a car was waiting for them, driven by partisans disguised as militiamen. They passed through Bourgoin and La Côte-Saint-André and finally arrived on the plateau.

"The members of the mission got along well right from the start, Conus explained. Assignments were made: Major Long and Captain Haussmann (sic) were in charge of ordering supplies and sending reports of operations to London. I undertook improving relations between the civilians and certain officers, and distributing arms among the various units in the Vercors. Croix sent weather reports to the RAF every day."

On July 14, the Vercors Republic celebrated Bastille Day with a parade, a gun salute, and a parachute drop carried out by seventy-two B-17s on the Vassieux air field where work was going on.

As part of Operation Cadillac, the Fortresses dropped 860 containers. Shortly afterward however, German planes from Valence-Chabeuil flew over and dropped incendiary bombs on the town and the surrounding area, then others strafed the plateau with machine-gun fire, making it impossible to pick up the supplies until nightfall.

The net was fightening around the Vercors. On July 17, German reinforcement troops were reported coming from the area around Chambéry. Columns of trucks from the Saône-et-Loire arrived in the valley. In Valence elements from of 9th Panzerdivision arrived to assist the 157th Reserve-Division.

"On July 20 after 14:00, the Vercors was surrounded. All the gaps, all the roads were blocked by troops with artillery. The bridges over the Isère were also guarded."

On July 21, Generalleutnant Pflaum and his 10,000 mountain troopers launched an assault against the stronghold. On the 23rd at the end of the day Colonel Hervieux ordered his men to disperse. By the 26th fighting was over and the enemy had occupied the plateau. Each fleeing partisan went his own way.

Major Longe and Captain Houseman managed to hide in the woods near Saint-Martin with some other Resistance fighters. Germans patrols were all around them and they were almost discovered several times.

They had to squeeze wet forest moss to get water. They had lost all their contacts and so decided to make their way to Switzerland, where they were interned a week later. Their radio operators had stayed with Hervieux and managed to maintain radio contact with the exterior from their forest hideout, where other local Resistance fighters were sent out from time to time to look for the Major or the OGs.

Capitaine Conus had been out on liaison in the Oisans at the time of the general attack. He was arrested at a German blockade in Saint-Guillaume.

On the point of being shot, he managed to escape and get to his destination. Mission Paquebot managed to get to Romans, after living in the woods and receiving food from resistants in the Drôme.

Lieutenant Meyers had undergone an urgent operation for appendicitis. He watched as the other wounded men were massacred, then was taken to Poland as a captive where he finished the war. His thirteen NCOs, under the command of Lieutenant Hoppers, fought beside the maquis fighters in Vassieux and Saint-Martin. They brought three mortars, and fired on enemy gliders with a 12,7-mm machine-gun.

Then they hid for eleven days in the woods above Saint-Marcellin. There was no way they could get across the Isère, which flows all along the edge of the plateau, because the enemy had blockaded the whole area.

"German patrols were scouring the sector, Hoppers explained. They shot randomly into the bushes to scare the partisans and force them down into the valley where they would be picked off like rabbits. All we had to eat were raw potatoes and, once in a while, a little cheese."

The men had received orders not to talk so as not to be spotted.

"In the beginning we whispered about ordinary things, said Corporal John Numsy. But after two days of raw potatoes, we didn't have enough strength left to talk about women. So conversation gradually turned to food and for the nine days left we each described in detail the meals we had at home!"

One of them spent a whole day talking about the different ways of making apple pie. Corporal Moses Levine, who was used to eating the best pastry in the Bronx, got sick on the fifth day, and the OGs diet didn't do anything to improve his health.

La Briek was an amateur gourmet chef and he sat beside the sick man, telling him about all sorts of exotic menus:

"I sat there for hours and invented all sorts of dishes. And when I couldn't think of anything, Moses shut his eyes and said: Go on, La Briek, go on, another one!"

During the night of August 6th a partisan told them that the bridge near Saint-Marcellin appearead unguarded. They headed down into the valley immediately and struck out toward the North. Three days later, after avoiding patrols and covering twenty-five miles on a forced march, they arrived in the Chartreuse mountains, North of Grenoble.

AS Commandant Albert Reynier (Vauban), commander of Isère Sector No. 6, greeted the OGs and got them food and blankets. They were in such bad shape that a doctor had to be called: Hoppers had lost thirty-two pounds, three of the men wouldn't be able to walk for two weeks, many would suffer from diarrhea for a month.

Chloroform and Storm troopers after the fall of the Vercors

Four days after Team Dodge, another Jedburgh team arrived in the Drôme. Chloroform [29] had been summoned on June 8th and was briefed about three missions before leaving Algeria in the evening of the 29th. The cause of this twenty-one-day stand-by was bad weather.

The first part of their mission was rather unusual. The Jeds were to deal with the problems that kept elements from the southern part of the département from accepting orders from the AS North sector chief.

The AS North had become the départemental FFI in September of 1943. According to reports received by SPOC, Pierre Raynaud [30], one of Cammaerts' deputies, had trouble working with the FTP, who were particularly powerful in this sector. Moreover, the FTP chiefs, in league with the départemental Liberation Committee, had requested that the FFI leader be replaced.

The rest of the mission was typical: support and organize the Resistance groups and cut the Valence-Crest-Die-Gap railroad line.

The plane carrying the team arrived over the DZ in Dieulefit around midnight. The drop took place at an altitude of 2,400 feet, and consequently men and materials were spread out over a wide area. No one was wounded however and only two containers of Enfield rifle cartridges crashed; their chutes had roman-candled.

29. Capitaine Jacques Martin alias Martino (Joshua), from the Infanterie, Lieutenant Henry D. McIntosh (Lionel), U.S. Army, and Lieutenant Jean Sassi alias Nicole (Latimer), from the BCRAL.
30. Raynaud (Alain) was a French NCO used by Cammaerts as a sabotage instructor. He had been parachuted in June 1943 when the Jockey circuit was created.

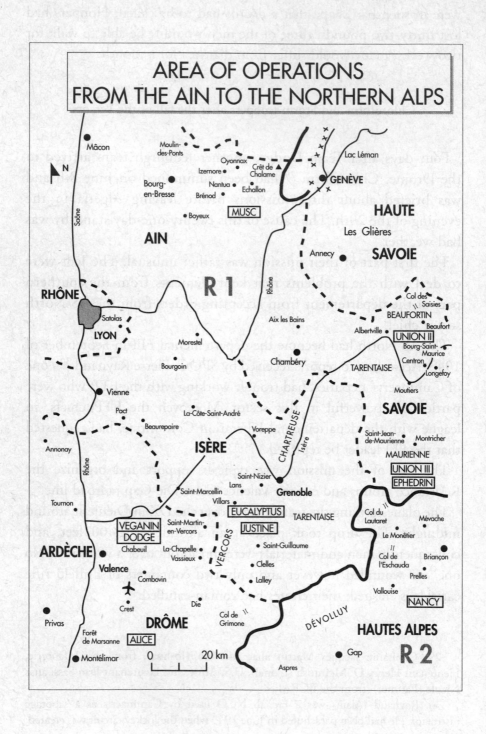

AREA OF OPERATIONS
FROM THE AIN TO THE NORTHERN ALPS

Mâcon

Moulin-des-Ponts

Oyonnax

Crêt de Chalame

Lac Léman

GENÈVE

Izernore

Bourg-en-Bresse

Nantua

Brénod

Echallon

MUSC

HAUTE

SAVOIE

Les Glières

Boyeux

AIN

Annecy

N

Saône

Rhône

R 1

RHÔNE

Col des Saisies

BEAUFORTIN

Beaufort

LYON

Satolas

Aix les Bains

Albertville

UNION II

Bourg-Saint-Maurice

Morestel

Centron

Longefoy

Bourgoin

Chambéry

TARENTAISE

Moutiers

Vienne

Pact

SAVOIE

La-Côte-Saint-André

Beaurepaire

Voreppe

Saint-Jean-de-Maurienne

Montricher

Annonay

Rhône

ISÈRE

Isère

MAURIENNE

UNION III

EPHEDRIN

Saint-Nizier

Saint-Marcellin

Lans

Grenoble

Tournon

Villars

Col du Lautaret

Mévache

EUCALYPTUS

TARENTAISE

Le Monêtier

VEGANIN

DODGE

Saint-Martin-en-Vercors

JUSTINE

Chabeuil

La-Chapelle

Saint-Guillaume

Col de l'Eschauda

Briançon

ARDÈCHE

Vassieux

Clelles

Prelles

Valence

Combovin

Lalley

Vallouise

NANCY

Crest

Die

Col de Grimone

DÉVOLLUY

Privas

DRÔME

HAUTES ALPES

Forêt de Marsanne

ALICE

R 2

Montélimar

0   20 km

Gap

Aspres

CHARTREUSE

VERCORS

"About twenty maquisards were waiting for us, explained Major McIntosh, a huge paratrooper recruited at Fort Bragg. Then we were led to the closest camp to organize contacts. This was done quickly, thanks to Capitaine René, head of the northern sector: within four days we had met Alain, Hermine, Joseph and Roger [31], as well as the FTP civilian authority."

From their discussions they learned that Alain had no problems with the men in his sector. The Valence-Gap line had been cut and was no longer being used. The same was true of the Grenoble-Sisteron line which had been cut at Aspres.

"This information was passed on to Algiers, McIntosh commented. But both lines were later bombed by Allied aircraft with high civilian losses."

Problems of command had in fact already been settled. Delcour, the regional commander, had suggested that Drouot's job be changed, so Zeller named him to the Hautes-Alpes, a département in need of an energetic leader. He was replaced by his deputy.

Drouot was thus getting ready to go to Gap when the Jeds arrived. They were immediately impressed by his leadership qualities and decided to go with him, especially since they no longer seemed to be needed in the Drôme. Zeller agreed and Algiers was informed of the change.

SPOC — even though it was preoccupied at the time by the valley of the Rhône River while Zeller was thinking of nothing except the Route Napoléon — agreed to the transfer. Cammaerts was the only one to hesitate. He finally sent a message to the Jeds on July 17, requesting them to come back to the Drôme. They should never have left without orders.

"This didn't jibe with our ideas, McIntosh stated. So we remained in the Hautes-Alpes sector."

And he added, as an excuse:

"At the time of the misunderstanding we had received no word from Algiers that Roger was the commanding officer of all Jeds, in the field."

31. That is Raynaud, Drouot, Zeller and Cammaerts.

On July 4, the team left by car and truck with Drouot and six staff members. However, once they crossed Grimone gap, they ran into Germans and had to turn back.

When the enemy finally left, three days later, the Jeds and the FFI managed to avoid the check points and get to Saint-Etienne-en-Dévoluy by nightfall.

The team then contacted Commandant Terrasson, chief of the Dévoluy sector, and they all agreed that the team would install its base in the Champoléon valley, north-east of Gap.

"On the afternoon of July 8th, McIntosh continued, we entered the Champoléon, and all along the road we were taken for Germans. Uniforms were unknown here. People ran for their houses, jumped behind cover and were vere uneasy. Arriving at Pont du Fossé we stopped at a restaurant for dinner. All the occupants at first thought we were Germans, if not Germans certainly French Militiamen. Women were crying, men begging us to leave."

After about ten minutes the door of the restaurant was kicked open and a kid appeared with a Sten in his hands:

"Hands up!"

"But we aren't Jerries, Martin exclaimed, we're Resistance!"

The team's first job was to install its CP at Les Baumes, at the top of the valley of the Drac, then to contact the officers living in the sector. But the most important thing was to get weapons. They initially tried through Algiers, but nothing but promises arrived during the first three weeks. Next they tried locally through the Champoléon priest — forty old Lebels and two automatic rifles that had been hidden in the church for more than a year — or in the numerous caches that had been created after the parachute drops of the previous year.

By July 25 the team had ready north of Gap three or four hundred men, poorly-equiped but well-trained since they had attended the week-long training sessions organized in the valley. Contact had also been made with several maquis groups in the region around Embrun and Aspres-sur-Buëch.

"Then came the attack on the Vercors, McIntosh explained. We thought that possibly we could assist the Vercors by moving to

Devoluy in strength. Also that we could possibly receive arms for resupply of the Vercors in that region. But arriving on the spot we found, due to later actions by the Germans, like the encircling of the Vercors, we could do nothing."

Weapons that were parachuted by nine planes during four drops were set aside for groups in need of them. Then on August 2, the team went back to Les Baumes. Chloroform was not the only team that couldn't help the Vercors maquisards. On June 22, summing up the situation on the plateau as Algiers saw it, Jacques Soustelle, director of the special services and secretary general of COMIDAC, declared:

"Local leaders have repeatedly requested airborne reinforcements. In token answer to these requests and as a moral gesture, the War Commissariat assigned a commando of thirty paratroopers from the Staoueli organizational center to the Special Services. The Allies intend to furnish an American commando unit with an equal number of men for the same purpose."

It is probable that the American commando unit was OG Justine which left from Blida on June 28. The day before, Soustelle had authorized the departure of Mission Paquebot, for the purpose of providing the Vercors with a landing strip where planes could unload the mortars and anti-tank guns that the Vercors defenders so desperately needed. The French commando team would come from the Bataillon de Choc training company.

Initially it was the Commandos de France in Staoueli who were assigned the mission. But they weren't operational: they needed at least forty-eight hours to get their weapons. Therefore, their inspector, Capitaine Henri d'Astier de la Vigerie, turned to the Bataillon de Choc.

The Bataillon de Choc and the Commandos de France were non-program units, that is, not included in the Franco-American organizational plans. The Choc storm troopers were created for the purpose of bringing specifically military-style assistance to the Resistance organizations inside France. Its members were recruited from among volunteers from the three armed services and men who had escaped from France through Spain. It was training in Corsica at that time, after playing a crucial role in operations on the island of Elba.

The Commandos de France — more recently formed — was the same type of organization: at first the men were supposed to form a second Shock Battalion. Airborne training was carried out by instructors of the French 1st Parachute Infantry Regiment and Americans from the Club des Pins.

On March 20, D'Astier was able to send his teams to the Chrea specialized center for training courses in weapons and explosives. At the beginning of June, the unit was renamed Groupe de Commandos de France, assigned to carry out, in liaison with the Resistance organizations, missions of destruction and harassment. These actions could be considered either as part of a specific operation, or outside the context of specific operations as part of the general insurrection. The Commandos de France had orders to parachute into France several small groups to strengthen the Resistance groups and furnish them with valuable moral support. [32]

These words were reminiscent of Plan Caïman and Force C, which had included the Commando Group, as well as the influence of SPOC looking for more OGs. The Group was commanded by Commandant Vallon and divided into three light parachute units and two heavy air mobile commando units.

But by the end of June only the 1st Commando in Sidi Ferruch and the 2nd in Moretti had finished training. In spite of an agreement worked out with Colonel Constans, the Americans from the OSS furnished weapons only very gradually.

D'Astier arrived in Sidi Ferruch with Colonel Constans and asked the Shock officer for help:

"I need a platoon right away. To be dropped in a maquis. An officer, a deputy NCO, a medical officer, and twenty-seven men. This is a BCRA [33] mission."

The chosen men got their operational equipment package

32. Note au sujet de l'emploi des Commandos de France ((Note on the use of the Commandos de (France), written by Lieutenant-Colonel Gambiez, commander of the Centre d'Organisation Spécial (Special Organization Center), created on July 25, 1944.

33. Raymond Muelle, Le 1er Bataillon de Choc, Paris, 1977. Muelle was at that time an "aspirant", i.e. officer candidate acting 2nd lieutenant, which was considered an NCO.

immediately from an OSS officer: a watch, a pistol with a silencer, an MI rifle, a survival kit and combat rations. Just to be on the safe side, a platoon of forty-five parachutists with machine-guns and two 60-mm mortars, was also created at Staoueli.

Ten days went by as the fighters suffocated in the barracks of the Zeralda holding station, transformed into an oven by the summer sun. There was an aborted departure on July 6 and a false alarm on the 12th.

Finally on the 26, it looked like a go. Maps of the Vercors were distributed. Instead of a spare parachute the men would be carrying a haversack containing twelve pounds of plastic and forty fuses. The two sticks had already embarked when a battalion officer came up to Aspirant Muelle and told him that the Vercors had fallen, so they weren't being sent to the plateau at all, but to the Drôme instead, near a village called Dieulefit.

As the two Halifaxes were approaching the DZ, the plane in which Aspirant Muelle's stick had embarked slowed down. One of its engines had broken down: they had to turn around and throw containers, weapons and ammo into the Mediterranean to lighten their lood. Sous-Lieutenant Corley's plane also turned back, unable to find the DZ.

On July 31 Corley and his unit jumped and the following day it was Muelle's turn. In the Halifax, the crew and the American dispatcher told him that his teammates had arrived safely. As he was climbing aboard, an officer from the BCRA Action service came to wish him good luck:

"Your mission give the Germans hell! You'll be jumping into the Drôme, near Dieulefit. Remember the password: The Devil undid it — The Devil did it [34]. You are expected. Bon voyage and good luck! [35]"

The plane took off at 20:30. Around midnight it started descending in circles.

The men's ears hurt. Then the wind rushed into the darkened fuselage: the trap door was open and four hundred feet under them was French soil.

34. "Le Diable le défit" — "Le Diable le fit". A pun on the name of the town: "Dieulefit" = God did it. TN.
35. Le 1er Bataillon de Choc. op.cit.

The leader of the stick remembered:

"Green light. I swung my legs over the edge. Red light. I pushed with my back and felt a tug on my wrists. My whole body seemed to hesitate. Then the wind struck me and I tumbled out horribly. I rotated first on my back, then on my stomach. Then I felt that marvellous jerk that came later and smoother than with an American chute."

The descent was short. He braced his legs.

"I swung myself forward, then doubled up into a roll ... A smell of hay, of cut grass, and men running toward me between the firelights. I hadn't finished unhitching my parachute before a civilian reached me and started helping me get untangled ..."

It was 00:25, and the stick had just arrived on the Château-Ruine DZ, near Comps. Everything went well except for one soldier who broke his leg.

Of course the reception committee didn't know the password. Its leader suggested that we disappear as quickly as possible, because the plane had already come the night before and had circled over the site for a long time before finally dropping its containers at 600 feet in runs of five at a time.

"Last night, the Resistance fighters explained, the wind was blowing hard and the drop went badly. We found Lieutenant Corley on the ground in a coma. An NCO got a badly sprained foot and another soldier broke his shoulder. We have hidden them at surrounding farms, along with some others who got bruised."

After they had rested near Vesc, the valid troops with Muelle in the lead left at 22:00 for Bourdeaux to take possession of Francillon rock which the FFI had abandoned. On August 3 at 07:00 they settled on the rock high above the Roubion valley. From there they could control the roads going to Crest and Puy-Saint-Martin.

Chapter IX
Guerillas in the South

The Allied command considered that any actions carried out in south-eastern France by the Special Forces would be part of Operation Anvil, the Allied invasion through the beaches of Provence. The Allies, and especially the Americans, had studied the battles north of the Loire River and had concluded that these SF actions were indeed important and that the regular forces could use the Resistance to help them attain their chosen targets.

The brain behind Anvil was Lieutenant General Alexander M. Patch, the commander of the Seventh Army in Naples. But Sir Maitland Wilson, Supreme Allied Commander in the Mediterranean, whose headquarters were in Algiers, along with AFHQ and SPOC, coordinated the missions in the field and most of the contacts with the Resistance in southern France. He was constantly aware of the importance to the British of the Italian theater and the Balkan peninsula.

For the French, Air Force Major General Gabriel Cochet was named military delegate of the government in the southern theater of operations, on April 22, 1944. However he would not take command of the FFI until after the invasion: in the meantime his mission was limited to liaisons, and General Koenig in London was the only French commander.

The Allies had trouble understanding the subtleties of the French command structure. The debate was never-ending: De Gaulle had his word to say and General De Lattre de Tassigny, commander of Armée B, had his own ideas. His troops were assigned the position of second echelon in the coming invasion and his headquarters were installed in Naples beside Patch's.

In Algiers, the white city

As long as the planning for Anvil took place in Algiers, there was no problem about liaison with SPOC. But when Patch and De Lattre moved to Italy, it became necessary to set up a unit control to the Resistance groups supporting Anvil. It would act as both a source of information about these groups and as an intermediary to obtain their assistance.

"What it amounts to, explained one of the members of this unit, is coordination of the activities of the diverse teams detached from the Seventh Army and the Sixth Army Group [1] to the FFI, and serving as their radio relay with the base in Algiers."

Operating under the orders of the Seventh Army G-3 in liaison with the G-2, Special Forces Unit No. 4 was commanded by American Colonel William G. Bartlett, seconded by a British deputy. The SFU-4 was created on June 29, and installed in Naples soon after, at General Patch's HQ.

It was made up of sixty French-speaking Britons and Americans, with fifty English communications personnel, twenty vehicles and its own radio gear, insuring that, once landed in France, the unit could maintain its mobility and autonomy.

A week before its creation, the SPOC planning office had presented its evaluation of the Resistance in the Anvil zone of operations.

"Once the problem of food supplies is solved, explained its spokesman, airborne forces, including troops carried by glider, could be immediately landed on the Vercors plateau, in the Drôme and Ardèche. A solid base could thus be established before entering into contact with the enemy".

---

1. Once Anvil had linked up with Overlord, the 6th Army Group would include the U.S. Seventh Army and the French Armée B.

"And what about the southern part of the zone? asked Lieutenant Colonel Edward W. Gamble, chief of the Strategic Services Section [2]."

"There we can only use paratroopers to reinforce the smaller groups in the Vaucluse, the Bouches-du-Rhône or the Basses-Alpes."

"What can we do about the points around Oraison where the Durance River can be crossed? "

"We can't expect armed groups to take them and hold them; they have neither the necessary fire power nor adequate means of defense against enemy artillery and tanks. Unless they were reinforced with airborne troops. A Jedburgh team could be sent to organize a guerilla unit and pave the way for parachutists."

"And in the zone around the future beachhead?"

"In the Var, with a long enough advance warning, one month for example, we could use Jedburgh teams to organize the FFI so that they would be ready to give tactical assistance to the airborne troops involved in the initial invasion."

SPOC received orders from the Seventh Army concerning the use of the FFI on July 4. Actually it was simply a list of roads and railway lines to be destroyed, to keep the Germans from bringing reinforcement troops into Marseilles, Toulon and the Mediterranean beaches. The valley of the Rhône River was top priority, then the Bordeaux-Narbonne corridor and the Mont Cenis pass. Next came: the Route Napoléon, the line from Clermont to Toulouse and Montpellier and the mountain passes in the Alpe. With this list, SPOC prepared to warn the Resistance groups, send out Jeds and OGs and increase parachute drops.

On July 15 it published a twenty-three page document entitled Plan for the Use of the Resistance in Support of Anvil, which would remain the basic order for the operations conducted by SPOC. In it were listed the priority regions where men and equipment were to be sent, even though they may not have been the same ones that the Anvil planners considered essential.

2. The SSS was part of General Patch's G-2, where it took part in planning, then insured contact with the OSS/SI agents in France.

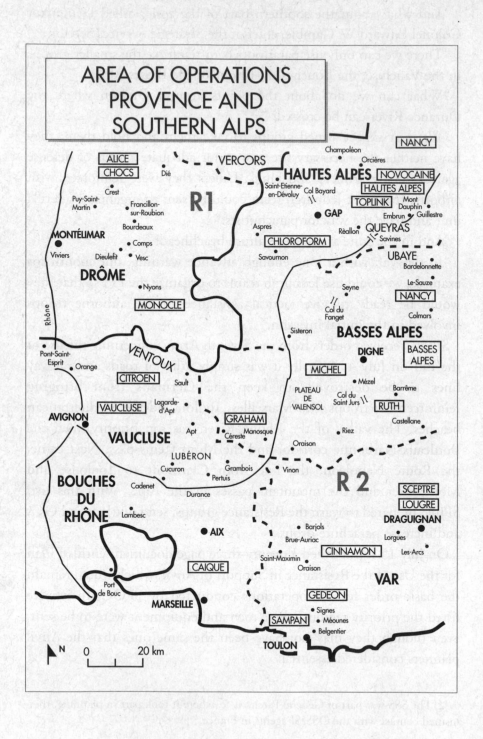

AREA OF OPERATIONS
PROVENCE AND
SOUTHERN ALPS

The Vercors region had No. 1 priority: of course when it fell, that complicated things. The Drôme and Ardèche located across the Rhône River from each other, were in second and fourth positions. Savoie was in No. 3 position, proof of the SOE's interest in that region neighboring on Switzerland. The Vaucluse came in fifth: on a plateau south-east of Mont Ventoux was a strip where Dakotas and Lysanders coming from Algiers could land. The Hautes-Alpes region — where the organizer of the SOE Jockey circuit took refuge coming out of the Vercors — was ideal for parachute drops.

At the DMOS, Colonel Cappart's section R (Résistance) dealt with FFI problems and was thus under General Cochet's orders. After some rearranging, its zone of responsibility included R.2, R.3, four départements of R.4 and the southern part of R.1 which would soon be included in R.2 [3] .

Separation between zones was entirely theoretical.

"This allowed, Cochet would state later, Resistance troops to leave the Margeride mountains and slip into Lozère and Aveyron, and troops from the Haute-Loire to lend a hand to those in the Ardèche."

On July 28 the DMOS section R was approved by the Allied command to take charge of the employment of the Resistance. The Action Section of the special services, the Staoueli Commandos and the Patrie Air Group would be placed under its orders. The Patrie Group had been set up by the French to help maquis groups in difficulty. It had about thirty old aircraft mostly assembled from the Middle East. It had initially been planned for the Vercors but would finally be assigned to Force C. But the initial Force C plan, thought up by the BCRAL, was entirely different from the ideas of the Allies who — even though they insisted on the destruction of strategic roads and railway lines, and the use of parachuted special missions —called for neither military insurrection nor the establishment of strongholds.

So Colonel Billotte — who had been appointed commander of the expeditionary Force C on July 2 by General De Gaulle — had to

3. Ariège, Haute-Garonne, Tarn, Tarn-et-Garonne for R.4; Ardèche, Drôme, Isère south of the Isère and Romanche Rivers for R.1.

update Plan Caïman and adapt it to Allied strategy. Thus, after a preparatory phase designed to support the maquis groups in the Massif Central and isolate the designated zone, landing strips controlled by the FFI and the paratroopers were prepared to receive airborne troops and supplies.

Then actions on the enemy rears could begin in the Rhône River corridor or near the Atlantic coast, even heading toward junction with the Overlord forces on the Loire River. Along the way, Force C would be reinforced by the 80,000 maquisards in Auvergne and perhaps get additional support from two Allied brigades, one English and the other American. The French would be implicated by the use of the 1st Parachute Chasseurs Regiment, stationed in Sicily at the time, the Bataillon de Choc and the African Commandos intended for Anvil.

At Staoueli and Sidi Ferruch strange rumors were circulating:

"The commando units being formed have too many officers. They will be part of Force C. They will be parachuted or landed by glider inside the Massif Central retreat that has been organized by the resistants, to lead them into battle. The commandos under Lieutenant-Colonel Gambiez [4] will make up one of the three brigades of Force C."

On July 5, discussions were started with AFHQ, which did not try to hide its misgivings: the time slot for launching operations, between August 10 and 25, was acceptable, but it couldn't agree to allow SHAEF to control its troops. And of course the operation depended entirely on the aircraft that SHAEF would agree to provide.

Actually the Allied planners found that the project had no tactical or strategic interest. Moreover, it required pulling out troops and transport planes which would compromise Anvil and weaken the fighter plane support.

They recommended a much more modest operation, consisting of dropping the French 1st Parachute Regiment in the Dauphiné Alps

---

4. Commander of the Bataillon de Choc, he had returned from Corsica to Algeria where he had taken over, on June 22, 1944, the job of director of the Organizational Center for light assault and storm units.

on D+3, to train the maquisards and operate in the enemy rear until link-up with Anvil.

After days of discussion, Wilson finally decided to postpone the action to an unspecified date, which amounted to refusing Plan Caïman. Finally in July 27, in the face of the general opposition of the Allies, the French agreed to give up the operation:

"The available forces, De Gaulle decided, will be kept in reserve to support the Resistance in southern France, when needed and depending on the Allied advance."

At the beginning of July Anvil D-Day was getting closer and the staffs different started moving into Italy: AFHQ settled in Caserte, the Seventh Army and French Armée B in Naples. On the 30th, the DMOS advanced echelon took off from Maison-Blanche: but since they had no radio gear, they had to depend on SFU-4 for liaisons.

On August 2, Cochet arrived in Italy to meet with Wilson. He came back to Algiers two days later, having declined the Allied invitation to embark with the invasion armada.

Michel, Isotrope and the Counterscorch Teams

When General Cochet left for Naples, thirteen special forces teams were operating in south-eastern France.

The first to arrive in the field was an interallied mission sent into the Basses-Alpes by Massingham. The troops arrived over a period between March and June 1944. The mission was commanded by Capitaine Henri Chanay, from the Colonial Infantry. His pseudonym Michel would be adopted to refer to the whole team. He was accompanied by a French adjutant, two Allied officers and five French agents, including a medic.

Capitaine Lécuyer (Sapin), regional ORA leader, had assigned Sous-Lieutenant Granier to Chanay as liaison agent. Together they crisscrossed the Vaucluse between March and April.

Then Chanay travelled to Lambesc, in the Bouches-du-Rhône, to coordinate actions being planned on the border between the two départements. Meanwhile, Lieutenant Marcel Lancesseur (Victor) went on inspection rounds to maquis groups in the northern Vaucluse. Chanay could not steer clear of the personal rivalries and political differences that opposed the local Resistance leaders.

Lécuyer was convinced that the FFI should limit its activities to the fight against the Germans, and that the invasion was imminent. So he intended to take control of the Ubaye valley, to be transformed into a sort of free zone.

Chanay seconded this plan, but neither Cammaerts nor SPOC were aware of what they were planning. On the other hand, Robert Rossi, regional head of the MUR and regional military delegate, upheld the FTP position: the resistants should remain in reserve to take part in the coming urban insurrection [5].

Then on June 5 they heard the message Beware of the toreador, which unleashed generalized guerilla warfare. So the troops took to the roads, and Lécuyer set up his headquarters in Barcelonnette alongside Chanay. Zeller took Chanay's side against Rossi, who asked the civilian authorities to arbitrate.

Captain Alister Hay (Edgar), of the Royal Artillery, also left Marseilles on June 6, but since his French wasn't very good, he was wrapped in bandages and pretended to have been wounded during the bombing of the city. After a skirmish in Vinon, he arrived in the Ubaye on June 10 with the other men who had escaped, and told anyone who wanted to listen that the Allies were about to invade through the South.

Cammaerts arrived about then and became confused. London aired the message ordering the maquisards to return to harassment and sabotage actions, and the Germans decided to retake Barcelonnette. The maquisards immediately set up roadblocks on all the roads leading into the city and Cammaerts had his group attack on the right flank.

During the night from June 11 to 12, thanks to Cammaerts, an urgent parachute drop took place in the valley, a few miles west of Barcelonnette involving eight planes and about a hundred containers.

5. See P. Gaujac, *La Guerre en Provence* (The War in Provence), PUL 1998.

"Beside Capitaine Lécuyer, said Sous-Lieutenant Tilly, the CP liaison officer, I heard a whistle like a bomb falling. Then a container crashed a few feet away. It was full of AT hollow-charges that fortunately didn't explode. The next morning all the able-bodied men feverishly tore open the boxes. It took a long time to clean the weapons. And the men were delighted to discover cigarettes and uniforms."

A few days earlier, during the attack on the Sauze stronghold, the group had used a Piat, with disappointing results. Some of the men pointed this out to Captain Hay. He angrily answered:

"I'll show you what you can do with English equipment if you know how to use it!"

On the morning of the 13th, a German column left Guillestre, crossed the Vars gap and arrived unmolested in Condamine [6]. Hay, and his two liaison officer henchmen, joined the maquisards settled in the Pas de Grégoire, north of Jausiers. The two Frenchmen set up the 30-cal. machine gun that they had received the previous day, while Hay lay in wait on the other side of the road with a Piat.

"Around 14:00, Granier explained, we heard the sound of an engine, then two loud explosions a few seconds apart. Edgar had hit the head tanks right in the bull's-eye. He was so excited by the fight that he came over to our side and started throwing grenades at the soldiers who had gotten out."

But the Germans were quick to react: Hay was severely wounded and Granier, behind him, also fell.

During the night the whole camp around Barcelonnette was dismantled and Lécuyer set up a new CP in Colmars, twenty miles to the south. But Mission Michel was prone to ill-luck. On July 16, the Basses-Alpes Liberation Committee was to meet in Oraison. The Marseilles SD had got wind of it, and had also identified most of the local leaders: with the help of the Militia, eight of them were arrested. The next day, Rossi, the R.2 DMR, was located and

6. It probably came from Gap where the CP of *Reserve-Grenadier-Regiment* 157 and its *Batallion* 179 were located.

arrested along with a number of other underground agents including Capitaine Chanay. Two days later they were taken to Signes and peremptorily executed.

Another member of Mission Michel, Lieutenant Muthular d'Errecalde (Lucas), had been working in the Var during the month of June organizing the FFI in the sector and preparing them to assist the airborne troops arriving as the first echelon of Anvil. As he was getting ready to embark at Saint-Tropez for Corsica to turn in his report, he was arrested along with the man who was smuggling him out. They were interrogated and shot at Signes on August 12.

A second interallied mission, code-named Isotrope, was sent into R.3 after Michel: part of the men landed in Lozère during the night from June 8 to 9. They were followed several days later by the rest of the team [7]. They worked in the south-eastern part of the Massif Central.

Less than a week after the arrival of the second echelon of Isotrope, another liaison mission arrived in southern France, this time in R.2. Commandant Gonzague Corbin de Mangoux (Amict), head of the mission, landed in a Lysander on July 12 on the Spitfire landing strip south of Sault. He was received by Camille Rayon (Archiduc), the regional SAP, in person. Seven days later, British Major John Goldsmith (Orfroi) was parachuted with Canadian Captain Paul Labelle (Nartex) and two French officers [8]. This mission had orders to get the different armed groups in the Vaucluse — FFI Ventoux maquis, FTP and groupes francs — to coordinate their action better. The French members of the team were finally incorporated into the Ventoux forces, commanded by Lieutenant-Colonel Philippe Beyne, AS départemental delegate, and Goldsmith stayed with Rayon who

7. June 9, 1944: Commandant Jean Baldensperger (Isotrope), British Major Denys Hamson (Etole), Capitaine Georges Pezant (Brochet), and Quartier-Maître radioman Louis Berthou (Pélican). June 29, 1944: New-Zealand Major William Jordan (Pintade), who broke his leg landing, and Sous-Lieutenant radioman Pierre Fournier (Perdrix). July 7, 1944: Capitaine M. Castaing (Radeau).

8. Capitaine Robert Boucart (Hors-Bord) and Lieutenant René Hébert (Corvette). Sous-Lieutenant Morand (Bécassine) had arrived in the meantime.

was very busy with air operations. Another Lysander also landed on Spitfire: it brought in from Corsica Capitaine Widmer (Colonel Cloître), who had been pulled out of the Club des Pins to become military delegate in R.2. Zeller was leaving for Algiers and took the same plane back [9]. On the Provençal coastline, two teams were already working on a project, conceived by the French but supported by SPOC, designed to protect the French ports from destruction by the Germans before they pulled out. In the beginning, in September 1943, twenty sailors from the Aéronavale were to have been parachuted into the maquis located in the zone of the invasion, to organize beach teams. Then the Navy parachute group came under the control of the DGSS and British commandos were assigned to train it.

"At the Club des Pins in Staoueli, the men got training in parachute-jumping, commando and security actions, explained Lieutenant Commander Allain, their leader. Then they undertook a thorough study of the sabotage methods used in the various European ports that had been liberated, especially Naples. Their training was completed by full-scale exercises in ports along the North-African coast from Tunis to Casablanca.

The group was then divided into five Counterscorch Teams, as they were called by SPOC ; three for Toulon, Marseilles and Sète, two more in reserve for last minute missions. Their mission: make contact with local Resistance groups, collect information and relay it on to Algiers by radio or by mail. Their mission orders were established in collaboration with the BCRA, SPOC and the Navy. It was decided on June 1st that they would be dropped during the parachute operations planned for the June-July moon period.

Sampan [10], the first team designated for Toulon, was dropped during the night of June 13 on the Armoire reserve site, near Cucuron and north of Pertuis: the assigned DZ had just been overrun by the Germans.

9. See below. TN,
10. Lieutenants Max de la Ménardière (Sampan), René Midoux (Jonque), Tony Sanguinetti (Canot), and Radio Petty Officer Guillaume Turluaire (Perroquet).

"When we arrived, explained Lieutenant De La Ménardière, we were received by the Motte-d'Aigues committee who filled us in on the local situation. Since general mobilization, the Militia and the Germans had been very active in the Lubéron: villages were searched and farms suspected of having sheltered réfractaires were burned. The house that we had been told to use as a mail-drop had been destroyed only the day before we arrived."

Travel in the area was tightly controlled: searches and ID checks were routine. Skirmishes often broke out with the FFI, who had to travel heavily armed. The local Resistance leaders had left the area and all contact with them had been cut off.

"Under those conditions, Sampan continued, I thought it would be dangerous to try to get to Toulon immediately, so I decided to leave the team hidden in the area for a while. We settled into a safe house near Grambois and organized an intelligence gathering service to keep us informed about what was going on in the region."

Actually the sailors were living hidden in the woods on a piece of property belonging to Count Carlo di Montananri du Pradello and Lord Hugh Cholmondley, who had also taken refuge there themselves. When things were quieter, a week later, the team got ready to go to Toulon, except for the radioman: his gear could not be transported without the help of the Resistance. Canot left on the 26th as advance scout.

Sampan and Jonque had learned that the Vaucluse leaders were in Aix, so they set out for that city on the 30th. There they were lucky enough to meet a liaison agent from the ORA regional command. Sampan left Aix with him on July 3rd and by the next evening they had reached Colmars, where Lécuyer had set up his CP after moving out of the Ubaye.

"From Perpendiculaire [11], Sampan continued, I was able to get some addresses in the Var and I left again by bicycle for Toulon where I arrived on the 7th. I had no trouble travelling, just one ID check by the Germans, in a village in the Haut-Var."

11. Lécuyer's (Sapin's) signals call name, used for radio liaisons with the BCRA.

318

The team finally settled in Toulon and contacts were made with Lieutenant Commander Baudoin and the friendly naval officers of the port, as well as with Capitaine Salvatori (Savary), the FFI départemental delegate. Sampan remained with Baudoin and Jonque took care of protecting radio transmissions. Canot took charge of last-minute missions and missions outside of Toulon: maquis, parachute-dropping sites. His first job was to pick up the radio operator.

The plan of action was worked out together and cabled on July 17:

"After studying enemy and FFI means of action, suggest either dropping weapons for a thousand men on D-1, to allow possible anti-sabotage of port a few hours before invasion, or parachuting an additional regiment, who could act with us and allow us to hold onto the port for 24 hours. Diversion necessary by continuous bombing alerts D-1."

The difficulty of organizing one of the three possible action plans by cable, and the volume of information to transmit, including maps and photos, forced Sampan to ask for a liaison.

The Marseilles SD had arrested the Saint-Tropez reception team, which made it impossible to send messages by boat, so Algiers suggested sending the mail through the BOA. Thus Jonque left Toulon on August 5, with a French railway company agent carrying the documents, and passed through Marseilles, then Pertuis and Grambois. The trip continued on the next day by bicycle to Archiduc's CP in Lagarde d'Apt.

On August 12 before dawn, he boarded a Dakota heading back to Cecina, north of Rome. From there he travelled to Calvi where he turned in his report.

The second Navy special mission, code-named Caïque [12], was received during the night of July 17 by Archiduc on his landing site in Apt. There Caïque learned: first that Louis Burdet, Circonférence,

12. Chief machinist engineer Parayre (Caïque), Lieutenant Granry (Cotre) and Warrant Officer Lavigne (Sloop), Radio Chief Petty Officers Coste (Emeu) and Léaud (Ara).

Rossi's successor as DMR, had had his cover blown, and then that the Resistance Movement in the Bouches-du-Rhône had been decapitated.

He met Burdet in Marseilles on the 26th. Burdet introduced him to naval and military security officers, who were able to furnish him with information about German ships and defenses. Lieutenant Commander Baudoin arrived from Toulon to say that the naval fire-fighter personnel would be ready to fight if they had weapons.

While one of the radio operators stayed in Apt, the other travelled to Marseilles on August 7. The day before, in Aix, Caïque had finally been able to make contact with the départemental SAP, who promised him a parachute drop as close as possible: any action undertaken by the sailors recruited in the ports of Marseilles and Port-de-Bouc depended on their receiving weapons and explosives.

Pectoral, Willys, Louise and Betsy in Ardeche

On the right bank of the Rhône River, in Ardèche, four special forces teams were helping the FFI. The first in the field was Mission Pectoral, which had had some trouble with their parachute landings on June 15: Commandant Paul Vaucheret (Vanel), the DMD designated by General De Gaulle, got hung up in a poplar tree and Captain Williams fell into a manure pile. Canadian Major Pierre Chassé, representing the Allied command, was the only one to land proudly on his two feet. He was greeted by the joyful shouts of a little girl.

The mission couldn't have picked a worse time. The maquisards were trying to carry out the orders for general insurrection that they had received from London on D-Day. But, just as in the Alps, the enemy didn't intend to let them take over. A German column had left Privas and been stopped on the Boyon bridge without being able to get through to Ollières-sur-Eyrieux. Ten days later, they tried again with aviation and more ground forces: the maquisards were able to hold them back until the end of the day, when they withdrew after burning a few farms.

The next day, June 29, slightly past midnight, Jed team Willys [13] landed. Things were tense from the beginning and their relations with the mission deteriorated rapidly. The problem was one of priorities: intelligence gathering or sabotage operations?

On July 5 a German column of 3,000 men left Valence in the direction of Le Cheylard via Privas. Le Cheylard was the home of the FFI départemental CP. They were stopped at the La Fayolle pass, then divided into several different elements and entered the city. The fighting was tough. The Luftwaffe was called in and bombed the surrounding villages and FFI positions. Then around noon on the 6th, the German columns turned back to Valence[14]. The region was becoming inhospitable, so the CP was moved to Antraigues, north of Vals-les-Bains.

The designated DMD was an anti-Communist career officer. He had trouble unifying the maquis groups into an organized combat corps. Contrary to the situation on the east side of the Rhône, he couldn't count on regular army officers in the different groups and the FTP were particularly powerful in this area. Moreover, to the long-standing maquisards, he looked like a late-comer.

Colonel Henri Provisor (Darcial), the official in charge of the R.1 départements west of the Rhône, finally had to intervene. Around the middle of July, in agreement with Vaucheret, he named Commandant René Calloud, an AS chief, as départemental FFI commander. The headquarters staff, made up of AS and FTP officers, settled in the mountain above Vals. Mission Pectoral — now made up of about twenty personnel — moved to Aizac. Major Chassé took charge of parachute drops and Lieutenant Bloch alias Rodot's AS 20th Company securing the Tandem site in Devesset, north of Cheylard.

13. Capitaine P.J. Marchal alias Granier (Simon) of the Infanterie, Captain J.C. Montague (Honan) and Serjeant F.A. Cormick (Chansi), both from the Royal Armoured Corps.

14 . In Toulouse the Armeegruppe G journal stated for the day of July 9, 1944: "End of major action Privas-Le Cheylard region. 135 men shot, estimated 200 others killed in combat." The FFI reported: 42 Germans killed at the pass, 400 disabled in Cheylard and 70 killed on July 6, in an ambush on the road back. Our losses include one officer and 50 FFI killed, and as many wounded.

On July 18, this DZ received the fifteen parachutists, commanded by First Lieutenants William H. McKensie and Roy K. Rickerson, of OG Louise, also known as Strontium for communications. They made contact with Pectoral and set up their base in a school near Aizac. Then Calloud assigned them to the Cheylard groupe franc, under Sous-Lieutenant Crespy's orders. With the Jeds and the twenty-five maquisards, they created a combat unit.

About this time the Allied command in Algiers ordered a bridge over the Rhône destroyed, so that navigation on the river would be blocked. Calloud and his S-1 chief Pierre Fournier, who had some good ideas about it, chose the Viviers suspension bridge below Montélimar. Fournier took charge of the operation with the OG and the groupe franc.

On the 23rd the Americans blew the bridge.

"The deck of the bridge collapsed into the river, Louise reported. Making it was impossible for the Germans to use their oil barges."

Six days later a German column was attacked at Banne, south of Aubenas, by AS and FTP elements, along with a detachment from the Garde. Not far from there, at Les Vans, the OGs laid an ambush for another convoy and destroyed a tank and six trucks with bazookas and Gammon grenades. On August 1st, at Charmes, the Americans and the FTP derailed a train transporting food supplies and fifteen tanks.

OG Louise was no longer alone in its département. On July 26 it was joined by Betsy-Oxygen, composed of fifteen French-speaking paratroopers commanded by First Lieutenants Paul E. Boudreau and Leroy E. Barner. This new group installed its base camp in the northern part of the Ardèche, at Vanosc near Annonay. Its first action was to blow up a railroad bridge south-west of Saint-Etienne in the Loire.

The next day, August 9, Vanosc was bombed by the Luftwaffe: Sergeant C.A. Barnabe was killed and three other OGs wounded. Two days later the Germans evacuated Privas and headed north towards Tournon. At that time some of the OGs were making triumphant rounds in the west of the département, while others were making preparations for the 37-mm antitank guns that were soon to be parachuted.

The guns arrived on August 15, disassembled, with some pieces damaged.

"Commandant Vaucheret wanted antitank guns, recalled Lieutenant McKensie of OG Louise. He felt that his thousands of maquisards had much greater combat potential than the handful of Americans. I didn't find his arguments very convincing, but we had to follow orders. So FFI training began with this new weapon."

The action of these Jeds and OGs was part of the program of attacks on communications lines on the west bank of the Rhône. The plan distributed in Algiers by the DMOS called for an interallied mission and three operational groups in the Ardèche and Haute-Loire.

The rhythm of parachute drops in July was rather slow, but then SPOC made up for lost time. During the first two weeks of August, thanks to the moonlight and special efforts on the part of the plane crews and the packing personnel, the four-engine planes of the RAF and the USAAF brought ten Jed teams and five OGs into southern France.

The French were busy too: a brochure was distributed on August 8, bearing the seal of the DMOS [15] , and referring to the orders given by General De Gaulle and AFHQ. The document was entitled 'Plan of Operations in the Southern Zone', and defined the mission as an excellent support tool for Anvil, with the following prioirities: help facilitate progress along Route Napoléon, try to intercept enemy movements in the valley of the Rhône and assist the men dropped near the future beachhead. The plan was ambitious: five interallied missions, eleven Jed teams, ten OGs and three antisabotage teams were to work with the FFI.

In Savoie the three assigned teams had the mission of controlling the Rhône River inlets and barring the roads leading to the Saint-Bernard gaps and Mont Cenis in the Tarentaise and the Maurienne.

---

15. The DMOS landed in France on August 21, when the battle of Provence had practically been won. "His" orders concerning the FFI got to Armée B, which was the corps most directly involved, along with the Seventh Army, on August 29, after Toulon and Marseille had been liberated and Lyon was entered.

Since Mission Union had gone home, no one was covering the two valleys, Tarentaise and Maurienne, and London had lost contact with Lieutenant-Colonel De Galbert (Mathieu), head of the Savoie FFI.

In July, the future of Anvil appeared certain, and SFHQ decided to send a team into Savoie to continue the activities of the preceding mission. It was code-named Union II, and was made up of two officers and five NCOs, all of them Americans [16].

"After a week-long wait in Knettershall with the 388th Bomber Group, explained Captain Coolidge, we took off in a B-17 on August 1st at 09:30. Each team member was in a different plane."

At 13:45 the first of the seven planes arrived over the Ebonite DZ at the Saisies gap near Beaufort. The mission got off to a bad start: Sergeant Perry's parachute never opened. His comrade La Salle was luckier: his static line was wrapped around his body, he got a blow on the head and was knocked out. When he came to, he was in the grass and his hip was aching.

At the same time 864 containers of weapons and ammo were dropped. However around Beaufort the Bulle Batallion — composed of AS, ORA and a few FTP elements — in charge of reception already had plenty of weapons, so the arms were loaded onto trucks and mules to be distributed in the Tarentaise.

During the first week, the NCOs finished training the maquisards in the two valleys, while Ortiz and Coolidge met with Colonel De Galbert, along with Capitaine Rosenthal who had just arrived from the Haute-Savoie. The seven members of the advance echelon also prepared Ebonite to receive the rest of the mission to be flown in from Algiers, but no planes arrived.

The authorities met again after the Tarentaise FFI had cut the road from Albertville to Bourg-Saint-Maurice [17] and captured the Moutier

16. Major Peter J. Ortiz (Chambellan) of the US Marine Corps, Captain Francis L. Coolidge (Aimant) of the US Army Air Corps, Sergeants Robert E. La Salle, Frederick J. Brunner, John P. Bodnar, Charles R. Perry and Jack Risler of the US Marine Corps.
17. Stationed in Bourg-Saint-Maurice was the Reserve-Gebirgsjäger-Bataillon 100, attached to Regiment 1 whose headquarters were located in Aix-les-Bains.

and Aime garrisons. At Ortiz' request, a company from Beaufort was sent to lend a hand to the maquisards, but it arrived too late — on August 13 — to keep the Germans from reoccupying the valley.

On August 14, the team made its way to Beaufort, then on to the Arèches pass where the CP was set up. In the valley, at Montgirod, the remaining members of the mission came under heavy artillery fire and had to take refuge on the mountainside with the Bulle Batallion fighters.

The Germans surrounded them rapidy and Ortiz decided to break out of the trap and head for the CP.

With his team and Jojo, Colonel Fourcaud's former chauffeur who was assigned to the Mission, they managed to reach Longefoy, in the valley, where the six men hid out until August 16. Then they started out towards Beaufort and crossed the Isère River near Centron. But they were only two hundred yards from the road and as they were leaving the village, a German officer at the head of a convoy spotted them.

Ortiz, Bodner and Risler immediately sought cover in the south-west part of the village; the others went south-east.

"The Germans started firing, Sergeant Brunner recalled, and we returned fire as best we could. I heard them shout Hände hoch! near where Major Ortiz' group was. With Captain Coolidge, I began to advance under enemy fire towards the outskirts of the village. I yelled to Jojo to follow us, but got no answer. Then the captain was wounded in the thigh, but it didn't look too bad. We got to the banks of the Isère and I jumped in and swam across."

The current was strong and the two men lost sight of each other. Once he got to the opposite bank, Brunner, who didn't speak French, went back to Longefoy: the people he met at the town hall would have preferred not to have seen him: they had heard the shooting and were afraid the Germans were after him. They took him to the priest, who was also sheltering the priest from Montgirod whose church had been burned after the Germans had discovered and killed the two wounded FFI hiding there.

"The Longefoy priest gave me civilian clothing, continued Brunner, and took me to Macot. From there the Montgirod priest showed me the way to the Ardèches pass. I left through the mountains on foot and arrived at the CP on August 17 around noontime, after walking about fifteen miles."

There he found some members of the Bulle Battalion, and Sergeant La Salle who hadn't participated in the action because the pain in his hip was excruciating and he was having trouble breathing. The two Marines decided to return to the Saisies gap where they would be more secure. They were joined there by Coolidge on August 18. He had hidden all day long in the bushes, then gone back to Centron to find out what had happened to the others. But the Germans were occupying the village.

The official inquiry carried out later would reveal that the Major had preferred giving himself up to keep the Germans from burning the village. He and his companions had been transported to Bourg-Saint-Maurice, then to Albertville. The last time he was seen he was getting into a truck in Aix-les-Bains. Coolidge thought at that time that he had been taken to Italy [18].

In the meantime two other teams had arrived from North Africa.

Jed team Ephedrin [19] left England for North Africa in May, to be parachuted into southern France. Its mission was to cooperate with the maquis groups in the Maurienne and Tarentaise, to keep the enemy from using the roads in the valleys. When the team arrived in the field it was to make contact with Colonel Cammaerts.

The team took off from Blida at 20:30 on August 12 in a Liberator. Three and a half hours later they were dropped west of Seyne, about sixty miles as the crow flies from their destination. The drop went successfully in spite of the slanting DZ and the high altitude — 2500 feet — from which the men jumped.

18. Ortiz and his companions, including Jojo who pretended he was Canadian, actually left Aix-les-Bains on August 20. Transported from one prison to another, they ended up in a prisoners' camp north-east of Bremen. They were liberated by the British on April 29, 1945.

19. Capitaine Donnart alias Rabeau (Julien), of the BCRAL, Lieutenant Lawrence E. Swank (Gantor), an American reserve officer with the Engineer Corps, and Sous-Lieutenant Desplechen alias Bourgoin (Leon), of the BCRAL.

"A few minutes later, Capitaine Rabeau explained, Mission Progression and four BCRA officers arrived. Fifty containers and numerous packages were also dropped. The SAP was expecting three men and ten containers. This resulted in a bit of confusion which wasn't helped by the fact that ten parachutes roman-candled and several containers split open in the air."

Mission Progression was in fact Union III [20], assigned to work in Switzerland. The heads of the three teams learned that Cammaerts had been arrested by the Germans near Digne, so they decided to head for the Larche pass. On the morning of the 14th, they came across Pauline [21], Cammaerts liaison agent, who convinced them to pass through the Vars and Guillestre gaps and join a group of maquisards at Vallouise, south-west of Briançon.

The group left Seyne in the afternoon in a gasogene truck, with part of the containers scheduled to follow them the next day. They crossed through Barcelonnette easily around 19:00, but with their fingers on the trigger ready to fire if necessary.

"Two hours later, Rabeau recalled, as we were approaching Saint-Paul-sur-Ubaye, we heard a shot and Gantor slumped over. We cut away his clothing and someone dressed the wound. We carried him to a hotel room in Vars: he had lost a lot of blood and was in considerable pain in spite of the morphine shots we had given him. A Barcelonnette doctor promised to come as soon as he could."

They decided to continue on around 23:00, and left Swank under the guard of a BCRA officer.

When the doctor finally arrived all he could do was give him another morphine injection. Around 02:00 Swank lost consciousness and slowly passed away.

20. British Major D.E.F. Green (Progression) and Canadian Major C.B. Hunter (Dalmatique), from the SOE, radioman Lieutenant Fournier (Autruche) of the BCRA.

21. Christine Granville, whose real name was Krystina Skarbek, member of an aristocratic Polish family, had arrived by parachute with Mission Paquebot. As soon as she had recovered from her bruises, she accompanied Cammaerts on all his rounds.

"He was buried incognito in the Saint-Paul cemetery on Sunday, August 15. I gave his personal effects and his wedding ring to Lieutenant Gennerich (Team Novocaïne), who had been his friend since leaving the U.S."

Rabeau added: "It was an accident. One of the BCRA officers was totally responsible: he had laid his Lee Enfield rifle on top of the baggage. It slid going round a turn and the shot went off."

The truck finally arrived at 10:00 on the 17th at Vallouise, where Jed team Novocaïne was located.

The next day early in the afternoon the group took off again with mules, heading for Le-Monêtier. As they were going up the mountain path toward the Eychauda gap, one of the mule's saddle strap broke and the supplies it was carrying had to be abandoned: the load disappeared during the night, including the team's 250,000 francs.

When they arrived in the valley, around 04:00, they left explosives with the local maquis chief to blow up the Lautaret road the following night and block the enemy convoys heading for Briançon.

The group continued on and crossed the Névache valley, then through the Camp des Rochilles, to arrive in Montricher around noon on the 22nd. Three training officers continued on into the Haute-Savoie and another left to train a nearby maquis. The Jeds and the Mission decided to stay at the CP set up by Capitaine Villon, the Maurienne FFI chief.

The Blos at Nancy and in the Alpes du Sud

In the southern part of Savoie — to block troop movements from Italy towards France — the August 8 plan had allotted a Jed team and an OG in the area around Briançon, and a Mission and an OG at the Larche pass. In the Durance sector, above Manosque, a Mission and an OG were put in charge of controlling Route Napoléon.

22. Capitaine Gerlotto, alias Villon, the AS Moyenne- and Haute-Maurienne group commander, whose group was made up of AS and some FTP elements. In January, 1945, his group, along with the Blanchard battalion in the Tarentaise, would form the 13th BCA FFI.

Actually the first mission dropped by parachute was part of a project conceived by the SOE in Italy to encourage cooperation between Italian and French partisans. Fifteen officers, initially intended for the Balkans and trained in Algeria in Jedburgh tactics, were sent out by SPOC, along with the Frenchmen who had been training with them. These British Liaison Officers (BLOs) were to act under Cammaerts' orders between the Durance River and the Italian border.

Thus Mission Toplink arrived on August 1 on the Savournon site, north of Sisteron. It was composed of four officers — two Britons and a Frenchman [23] — with two Italians and a radio operator. It would be working in the Queyras.

Unfortunately for the mission, the Italian partisans were having a hard time: they had been pushed across the border by the Germans and were trying laboriously to get reorganized. Major Hamilton became impatient and brought his team back into France where they settled at the Queyras maquis CP in Bramousse. From there he had material transported by mule to the Italian partisans who were in dire need of supplies.

Three days later, some BLOs belonging to a group led by Commander Christian Sorensen (Chasuble) arrived at Fanget pass, near Seyne. The team was made up of four British officers and a British radioman, plus one South-African and one French officer [24].

Sorensen actually belonged to a rich wine-making family from Algeria: he had joined Action Service after Tunisia, as had Fournier, a Saint-Cyr graduate who had fought in the French campaign. Gunn was a Scotch reservist who spoke perfect French: before the war he had lived in Saint-Tropez.

That had led him to Mission Spears, then to Syria with the FFL and finally to the Political Warfare Executive in Italy. Halsey — whose

23. Major L. Hamilton (Crosse), nom-de-guerre for Léon Blanchaert, of Belgian origin, Captain P. O'Regan (Chape), radioman Lieutenant Simon Kalifa (Paradisier), joined on August 11, 1944 by American Lieutenant M. Mospurgo (Michelange).

24. Major Havard Gunn (Bambus) of the Seaforth Highlanders, Captain John A. Halsey (Lutrin), Capitaine Jean Fournier (Calice) and Serjeant Major A. Campbell on August 4, 1944; Major Xan Fielding (Cathédrale) and Captain J. Lezzard (Eglise) on August 11.

father, the Count of Kerdrel, represented the French Railway in London — had served with the French in 1939-40, and then with the British before joining the SOE. They had all been trained at the Club des Pins.

Sorensen was injured when he landed. That didn't keep him from taking part in the meeting with Cammaerts and Georges Bonnaire (Noël), FTP head in the Basses-Alpes.

"Our mission, Sorensen explained, is to help the Resistance within the zone covered by the Basses-Alpes, Alpes-Maritimes and the Var, and coordinate its activity with that of the Allied invading forces."

"But who is the real regional FFI chief right now?" asked Bonnaire.

"I can announce, Cammaerts answered, that Colonel Saint-Sauveur has just been appointed by Algiers. We are expecting him any day now."

A discussion followed, with Sorensen concentrating on political issues and the British limiting themselves to purely military aspects of their operations.

The team knew that Toplink was getting organized in the Queyras, so they wanted to hurry and settle further south, near the Route Napoléon. So Halsey left for Barcelonnette, and Gunn and Fournier for Lécuyer's CP in Colmars.

As they travelled around with Lécuyer, Fournier with his radio-navigation beacon, and Gunn in his kilt, attracted a lot of attention. A rumor soon spread that a unit of Scottish paratroopers had landed in the area.

Halsey undertook reconnoitering the Larche gap, while Gunn and Fournier, disguised as gendarmes, travelled to Valberg where they arrived on August 8. Lécuyer, new FFI chief in the Alpes-Maritimes, installed his CP there.

Sorensen had stayed in Seyne because of his leg injury, and that is where the rest of his team arrived on August 11. South-African Captain Lezzard landed on his back. But Fielding was able to accompany Cammaerts and Sorensen to Apt and on to the Armature landing site to meet Colonel Constans. Coming back, just beyond Digne, the three men and their chauffeur were arrested by the Germans and sent to prison.

Thanks to Christine's presence of mind, money sent by SPOC, the cupidity of their prison guards, and the announcement of the Allied invasion of Provence, the prisoners were liberated on August 17.

Still with the idea of cooperating with the Italians, a third mission arrived on August 7 on the Savournon site. Its job was to operate in the Hautes-Alpes in liaison with the FFI and Mission Toplink.

On the 8th, the Pelletier team [25] left with Cammaerts to meet Commandant Héraud (Dumont), départemental FFI chief, in the forest east of Gap. At the end of the meeting, Commandant Pelletier returned to Savournon to get ready to move further east. The next day, Héraud, on his way to join them, was arrested by a patrol and executed.

On D-Day, Mission Toplink — directed by Captain O'Regan since Hamilton had had an accident and been hospitalized in Aiguilles — was still working in the Queyras with AS Capitaine Galetti, and patrolling across the border. Pelletier was with Capitaine Jean Frison, chief of an AS group, while Major Purvis stayed at the Vallouise CP. Halsey, based near Barcelonnette, was working near the Larche gap, and his teammate Gunn was in Valberg.

In the valley of the Durance, Team Chloroform set their sights on the German garrison in Gap. Blockades and ambushes were set up on Route Napoléon and the Aspres road, cutting it off from the west. To the east, the Jeds had left Champoléon valley on August 10th, and blew up the Savines bridge below Embrun on the afternoon of the 15th, under the protection of forty men from Commando Hermine [26]. The mountain trails were unfit for mules, so explosives had to be carried in knapsacks from Orcières to Réallon. Two days later, a bridge over the Durance was blown up to stop an enemy column reported heading out from Barcelonnette.

25. Commandant Jacques Pelletier (Confessional), Major R.W.B. Purvis (Manipule), Captain John C.A. Roper (Retable), American radioman Lieutenant Mario Volpe (Rossini) and two Italian liaison agents.
26. Lieutenant-Colonel Hermine or L'Hermine alias Drouot's group was made up of 200 men from the ORA divided into two commandos: Bir-Hakeim and Valmy. After the liberation of the Hautes-Alpes, the group participated in fighting in Belfort and the Vosges, where it lost two-thirds of its men.

The destruction of the Savines bridge not only isolated Gap, it also cut off one of the retreat routes towards Italy, and blocked the Guillestre garrison which was to fall prey to Team Novocaïne.

Jed team Novocaïne [27] left Blida to be dropped near Seyne at 01:30 on August 7th.

"We arrived safe and sound, reported Lieutenant Gennerich. When I went back to the site the next day, I realized it wasn't more than three hundred yards long and was situated on a plateau with steeply sloping sides, hardly the ideal spot for a DZ. When we arrived we were suprised because the mission that received us was expecting a completely different team and had never even heard of us.

Actually it was Sorensen's team waiting for Pelletier's, coming to strengthen them, and that arrived right behind Novocaïne.

The Jeds' first days were spent training the maquisards in the use of the Browning cal. 30 machine gun.

"The weapon jammed often, explained Gennerich, because the men didn't know how to use the Browning. They didn't understand either that the weapon wouldn't fire if it wasn't correctly adjusted."

Cammaerts came back from Seyne and briefed the team about its mission: travel to the Vallouise CP and cut off all the routes leading to Briançon and the Montgenèvre pass. The team took off in a gasogene truck. For lack of space, all they could take with them were the explosives, grenades and two Brens.

Their first stop was in Guillestre, at Garletti's CP, where they spent the night from the 11th to 12th, then left again for Vallouise after having travelled safely for more than sixty miles. Along the way they had contacted Mission Pelletier in the Queyras and agreed on the methods to use in executing their mission. They were joined by two South-Africans, freed by Italian partisans.

"On August 14, Gennerich explained", 'See Naples and Die' was aired by the BBC, but was not repeated. In doubt, I decided to act."

27. First Lieutenant Charles J. Gennerich (Mathieu), from the Infantry, Lieutenant Pronost alias Le Lanne (Hervy), Colonial Infantry, and First Sergeant William T. Thompson (Gille), Signal Corps.

The Jeds had a trump card in the quality of their maquisards [28] who proudly wore the beret of the Alpine chasseurs and were so fit that the Jeds had trouble keeping up with them.

During the night they isolated Guillestre from Briançon by blowing up the concrete bridge in Prelles.

"During reconnaissance, Gennerich went on, we captured two French volunteers in the German army who were observing us. The work — the bridge on the main road, along with a tunnel and two secondary roads cut at a curve — began at 23:00 and was finished by 04:00."

OG Nancy-Aluminum was also operating nearby. The team had been dropped in the wee hours on August 13th, on the Armature DZ, located five miles east of Lagarde-d'Apt. It was commanded by Captain Arnold Lorbeer, with First Lieutenant William F. Viviani, and included thirteen Italian-speaking paratroopers. Even though the site was rocky, no one was injured and the group was able to set up their tent beside a company of airmen waiting for a Dakota. But the problem was to get to Montgenèvre pass, two hundred miles away."

"We haggled with the local maquis, explained Lorbeer, to get a gasogene truck and three guides. We placed our knapsacks and sleeping bags around the sides of the truck body, with our guns ready to shoot out through the 'loop-holes', and a canvas tarpaulin over the top."

The Americans left at nightfall on the 14th, for a long uncomfortable trip, which they nevertheless found exciting.

"It started with a flat tire. Then the guides got lost. We kept going, often on the main roads under the nose of German patrols. In Sisteron our guides had to bribe the gendarmes to let us cross the Durance."

From Guillestre on, the 160-mile journey turned into a country stroll a midst wine and roses.

"It was D-Day, Lorbeer continued, and the radio was calling on southern France to rise up and drive out the Germans. The idea of

28. The AS maquis of the region around Briançon, grouped into a Hautes-Alpes batallion commanded by Commandant Terrasson, would become the 11th BCA FFI. Both Terrasson and Frison came from the ORA.

fifteen Americans travelling so far north just a few hours after the invasion was thrilling."

Instead of heading for Vallouise, where the special forces teams controlling Montgenèvre were settled, the OG went to Cervières, east of Briançon.

Then, on the advice of Major Purvis of the BLOs, the group dug in at Les Chalets de Bramousse, along with Galetti's troops, and turned its sights toward the Larche gap.

The Germans of Mont-Dauphin, isolated and without water, had finally raised the white flag. Even though they wanted to surrender to Allied officers, Captain Roper insisted they surrender to the French.

On the Vaucluse Armature DZ, Captain Lorbeer's OG was followed the next day by two Jedburgh teams.

Jed team Monocle [29] had arrived in the second wave during the night of August 13 and 14 and had taken the reception committee organized by the regional SAP completely by surprise. Its French leader and his American teammates had orders to travel to the Drôme: they would receive instructions from the départemental FFI there. So they left for Nyons and Commandant De Lassus' CP.

They arrived just at the right time, in the midst of a raging controversy about the southern invasion route — Route Napoléon favored by the French and the British, the Rhône River corridor preferred by the Americans — and FFI — German soldiers favored by the FFI, communications lines preferred by the Allies.

One day before Dragoon D-Day [30]

The fifteen members of OG Alice-Hydrogen were safely dropped on August 8 shortly after midnight on the Dieulefit landing site. The mission assigned to Lieutenants Ralph N. Barnard and Donald J. Meeks was to organize and support the resistants, reconnoiter Route 7 and destroy enemy communications.

29. Capitaine Jacques Fiardo alias Tozel (Immense),from the Artillerie, Lieutenant Ray H. Foster (Solide), from the Infantry and Master Sergeant Robert C. Anderson (Raieux), Signal Corps.
30. For security reasons, Anvil becomes Dragoon on August 1, 1944.

The OG was earmarked for Capitaine Kirsch who was commanding a company of the AS 2nd Battalion installed in Combovin. They arrived on the plateau on August 12 and wasted no time in blowing up two high-tension pylons south of the nearby Chabeuil airfield.

But Lassus, like most of the other FFI chiefs, was convinced that the OGs didn't come to the area, bringing their bazookas and heavy weapons with them, to do the jobs that the maquisards could handle with explosives. Rather than carrying out sabotage operations against enemy installations, they would have preferred to see them attack the Germans directly. In defense of Alice, it should be pointed out that SPOC had clearly indicated that destruction of communications was the most important mission [31].

So as soon as the Jeds arrived, Lassus asked Lieutenant Foster to convince the OGs to harass enemy convoys. On August 13, USAAF four-engine planes bombed the Crest bridge. They missed their target and destroyed part of the city. To appease the population Lieutenants Barnard and Meeks, with three paratroopers, visited the city.

"Morale was low, one of them explained. People were even angry. A quarter of the city had been wiped out, there were thirty-eight killed and a hundred wounded. We went to the hospital and explained to the inhabitants that the bombing was an error which wouldn't happen again."

As we have seen, Team Monocle was preceded at Lagarde by another special forces team. This one had been expected: it was Jed team Citroën [32], received by Archiduc and Colonels Widmer and Constans.

Earmarked for the Vaucluse, the team immediately contacted Commandant Beyne, chief of the Mount Ventoux maquis, and traveled to his CP in Sault where they met Canadian Major Labelle, a member of the interallied mission which had arrived the month before. Beyne gave the Jeds two companies of Corps francs and ordered them to cover

31. The plan established on August 8, 1944 provided for cutting of communications lines in the Rhône River valley by a Jed team in lower Isère and an OG in the area around Die.
32. Captain John E. Smallwood (Anne) and Serjeant F.A. Bailey (Retif), Royal Armoured Corps, Capitaine Bloch alias René Alcée (Maurent), from the Infanterie.

the right bank of the Durance between Manosque and Pertuis, on the border between the Var and the Vaucluse.

Colonels Widmer and Constans, respectively new DMR and régional FFI head named by De Gaulle, had received orders on July 29 to head for France as soon as possible. They weren't airborne qualified, so the only way to get there was to land in a plane. Their mission was to resolve quarrels among the authorities after the arrest of the principal leaders in R.2.

Widmer left for Corsica with his limited staff and took over the space in three Lysanders that had been occupied by Jed team Graham. When the planes landed on the Spitfire site in the early morning of August 2, Zeller was there waiting for them, and eager to take the plane back to Algiers.

"The pilots who carried out that mission insisted, he stated, that the strip could not take a Dakota! So the RAF stuck to its position, in spite of my objection that half of the strip — three thousand feet — was actually hidden under tufts of lavender!"

A few days later the Jeds, along with Constans and a half-dozen Gaullist authorities, flew out towards Cecina, south of Livourne, to embark in a Dakota. But on August 9 the weather was so bad that the plane had to turn back.

Finally on August 13, after circling for an hour over the site, the Dakota landed. But taking off was another story. The lavender at the end of the strip wasn't fake —it was planted in the ground. With thirty downed Allied airmen were crammed into the baggage compartment, the C-47 was too heavy to take off, so it had to leave some of its passengers behind. Rayon took the travellers to Lagarde-d'Apt where Constans, now known as Saint-Sauveur, had installed his CP. The place was crowded this August 13 morning: the passengers from Algiers, Cammaerts, eight American aviators who had disembarked from the Dakota, OGs from Nancy who had arrived by parachute in the meantime, and the Jeds of Team Graham

33. Major M.G.M. Crosby (Huge), Gordon Highlanders, Capitaine Gavet alias Gouvet (Crispin) of the Colonial Artillery and Master Sergeant William H. Adams (Desire) of the U.S. Army, who arrived later.

[33]. Capitaine Gavet raged about Constans wasting too much time in discussions with Cammaerts, while Scottish Major Bing Crosby — who had been a member of the Jedburgh selection committee in England and commanded one of the three Milton Hall companies before going to Algiers — calmly smoothed the folds of his kilt.

According to their orders received from SPOC, Graham was to operate independently in the Basses-Alpes. However Constans decided to assign it to the Spitfire landing site in the Vaucluse. So the two officers made their way to Céreste, at the foot of the Lubéron.

Normally they were to cooperate with Georges Bonnaire, the départemental leader in the Basses-Alpes, but he and Crosby didn't see eye to eye. Bonnaire wasn't interested in missions from Britain: like many other FTP officers, he was first and foremost interested in liberating the main city in the département, Digne in this case. Crosby couldn't stand watching him strut around instead of fighting. As a compromise measure, the two men decided to split the département between them: FFI in Digne and the east, Jeds in the west.

And south-east of Digne OG Ruth-Arsenic, commanded by First Lieutenants Mills C. Brandes and Carl O. Strand, Jr., had arrived ten days earlier. The fifteen paratroopers had been dropped early in the morning of August 4 — under a full moon — on Malay mountain, between Grasse and Castellane, where some FTP were hoping for containers.

Technician 5th Grade Jame E. Dyan broke his leg as he landed with one of his comrades and had to be left behind in a safe spot. After three nights of an extenuating march with heavy equipment on their shoulders, the thirteen OGs reached the Saint-Jurs maquis, in the mountains twenty miles south of Digne.

Originally the group's mission was part of Plan Vert: to paralyze railway traffic between Sisteron and Draguignan [34]. To achieve this,

34. In the plan established on August 8, 1944, the Meyrargues-Draguignan railroad was assigned to an interallied mission based in the Vaucluse and mainly in charge of controlling Route Napoléon, with the help of the FFI groups in the département, estimated at more than a thousand men.

the OGs immediately set about blowing up four bridges in the area.

"They had nothing to do, a maquisard who had lived at Saint-Jurs explained later, since anything that was worth blowing up had been destroyed long ago, so they played Boy Scout Camp in the three tents they had set up about a half mile from us."

Further south, in the eastern part of the Var, Jed team Cinnamon [35] was parachuted in the night of August 13 to 14 onto the Fantôme DZ, near Brue-Auriac between Barjols and Saint-Maximin. Its mission was to contact Colonel Joseph Lelaquet (Vernie), départemental head of the ORA, and Major Boiteux [36] of the SOE, who was coordinating the armed groups in the sector around Marseilles.But the team ran into bad luck. Captain Harcourt broke both his legs when he landed and his two French teammates were mainly worried about finding him a safe refuge and a doctor: he was carried to a farmhouse and cared for by patriots. It was impossible to locate Lelaquet: the Gestapo was on his trail, so he had made himself invisible. Capitaine Lespinasse was finally able to meet his chief of staff and Lieutenant-Colonel Joseph Gouzy, head of the north-west Var sector of the ORA. They agreed to set up small groups of guerilla fighters to harass the German reinforcement troops trying to get to Brignoles and Barjols.

Still further east, Jed team Sceptre [37] was parachuted that same night on the Prisoner site on Malay mountain, where it was greeted by the Fayence SAP. As in the case of OG Ruth's NCO, the slanted and rocky DZ proved disastrous. The French officer broke his foot and the American radio operator put his knee out of joint. The officer needed a doctor, so the Jeds settled in Mons two days later. No contact with Capitaine Lécuyer could be established, but on the other hand they were visited by Commandant Alain and Captain Jones, who had been

35. Capitaine Henri Lespinasse Fonsegrive alias Ferrandon (Orthon), from the Infanterie, Captain R. Harcourt (Louis), of the Royal Armoured Corps, and Sous-Lieutenant Jacques Morineau alias Maurin (Luc), from the BCRAL.

36. Robert Boiteux, Firmin for the Resistance and Nicholas for the SOE, organizer of the F section Gardener circuit, parachuted near Marseilles on   March 6, 1944.

37. Lieutenant Walter C. Hanna (Vaillant), Field Artillery, Lieutenant François Franceschi alias Tévenac (Intense), Colonial Infantry, and Master Sergeant Howard V. Palmer (Dévoué), Signal Corps.

parachuted two days before. These two men then left to continue their mission further south.

Two Navy teams were dropped during the night from August 11 to 12. Mission Gédéon [38] was parachuted in uniform on the Brue-Aureac DZ with a mission to assemble the Var maquis groups, organize them, participate in taking the city of Toulon with as many men as possible, and join up with Mission Sampan.

Led by Enseigne de Vaisseau Ayral, the team started off toward the south on a day-and-night forced march. On the 14th it contacted the Resistance leaders in Signes, then the next day those of Méounes and Belgentier. In the evening of the 16th they laid an ambush on the Marseilles road and captured a car. Two days later the sailors — who had been joined by the local FFI — occupied Signes.

Mission Lougre [39] had arrived the same night as Gédéon, but further east, on Malay mountain. Captain Jones had left Blida where he had been training new recruits for the SPOC Training Section. That, plus the fact that he had spent part of his youth in Fréjus, accounted for his being named to replace Errecalde in Mission Michel as soon as the weather would allow. Lieutenant Commander Allain was a member of one of the counter-sabotage groups that were to operate in Toulon.

"Before we left, Allain pointed out, we were told that we were the advance echelon of the parachute and airborne division which would be arriving on the plain of Le Muy and Les Arcs on D-Day."

SPOC therefore did its best to drop Mission Lougre before the invasion, but bad weather and administrative foul-ups prevented this.

During the night between August 9 and 10, the first attempt failed: the lack of moonlight prevented the crew from distinctly making out the fires below. The mission returned to Blida. The following night, after searching for an hour and a half in a pitch-black night, they finally recognized the DZ Prisoner.

38. Ensign 1st Class Ayral, Ensign Moore of the Royal Navy, Radio Petty Officer 1st Class Badaud, Machinists 3rd Class PO Caussin, Hécart and Félix.

39. Capitaine de Corvette (Lieutenant Commander) Léon Allain (Lougre), Captain Geoffrey M.T. Jones (York), Radio Petty Officer 2nd Class Buanic and Petty Officer 2nd Class Brezellec, liaison agent.

The two officers jumped at 00:45 behind containers filled with weapons — mortars and heavy machine guns — and radio gear. They landed in a ravine 2500 feet from their target. Result: Allain had a sprain and a cut on his right ankle, and Jones had multiple bruises.

The fires on the field had been put out as soon as the reception committee confirmed German mobile patrols in the vicinity; so the two Petty Officers were kept in the plane and taken back to Blida. They were finally dropped two days later at Brue-Auriac, and proceeded to the rendezvous destination one hundred miles from there.

On August 13, the two officers were able to hitch a ride on a mule which took them to Mons where they were warmly greeted by Joseph, the head of the local FTP. Sergeant Dyas from OG Ruth — who was being cared for in the village — joined up with them.

The Jeds had to provoke an urgent meeting of the FFI chiefs from Les Arcs to Saint-Raphaël. A runner left to summon them [40].

Around midnight, Allain said, Lieutenant de Vaisseau Sanguinetti, from Team Sampan, arrived from Toulon to make contact and obtain last minute information [41]. He had a hard time getting back to Toulon the next day.

On August 14 at 15:00 the FFI leaders — except the one from Le Muy — reported to Allain [42]. They were briefed about upcoming actions: preparing the Le Muy plain for gliders, scout teams for the parachutists upon their arrival, etc.

"At 20:14, Allain continued, while we were eating dinner together in a clearing, we were thrilled to hear code sentences announcing the invasion for within three days, then within twenty-four hours!"

The maquis went wild; ammunition was distributed while the leaders hastened back to their respective CPs. The men shouldered their weapons and ammo belts and prepared to leave for their assigned

40. According to C.C. Allain's report, the village was not Mons but Brovès, 7 miles to the east. This is not the only uncertainty surrounding this mission!

41. He was said to have left on August 12, 1944 by bicycle to meet his commander near Le Muy. He never got to see him.

42. According to another source, the leader from Les Arcs met "Captain John of the 1st American airborne division headquarters staff, in the area around Peyrusse where he had been parachuted during the night of the 13th."

targets. Allain added another target at the last minute: the radar above Fayence. It was destroyed in the early evening by the FTPs from Mons along with the AS group from Fayence and some members of SAP.

That August 14 evening, as the Allied bombers were beach-hopping along the Provençal coastline, was simply noted by the Special Forces as the date announcing the invasion and the possibility of overt action. Even though they all knew they were on the eve of adventure, no one could pinpoint the exact time or place of the invasion.

In the Alps, the message 'Vesuvius is smoking' meant temporary blocking of all the border passes within the next twenty-four hours. 'See Naples and Die' extended the time allowance for another twenty-four hours. In R.2 'Nancy has a stiff neck' gave the order for generalized guerilla warfare. At the départemental FFI CP in Valberg, the message came through loud and clear. Major Gunn immediately went looking for Capitaine Lécuyer:

"The invasion begins for tonight."

Lécuyer thought:

"Now I understand why Bamboos hung onto my shirttails and Fournier had to set up his radio beacon!"

They all hurried to the landing sites. Allain, Jones and Dyas headed down into the plain with a few gendarmes and reached Le Muy safely at dawn after coming under attack by a friendly bomber. Lécuyer and Gunn were already on their way by car to Puget-Théniers and intending to reach Draguignan during the afternoon.

Jed team Sceptre met up with us US airborne troops from the 517th Regiment, Company G who had landed far from their intended drop zones. The team took advantage of this lucky encounter to attack the defenses around the radar that the preceding night's action hadn't been able to silence. Among the men jumping out of the sky were guides and interpreters on loan to the Allies from the Storm troopers.

West of the Rhône River, the August 8 plan had stipulated the engagement of three Jedburgh teams and an OG. The problem before the FFI and the Special Forces was to break up enemy movements from the Massif Central toward the Rhône and from Toulouse toward Provence.

In the Gard and Ariege

The first team sent from Blida was Jed team Packard [43] dropped on August 1 on the Quincaille site, near Barre-des-Cévennes in Lozère. It made contact with interallied Mission Isotrope, at Collet-de-Dèze, to try to arm the FTP. Since the arrival of the FTP in the département, opinions were split. The Allies were accused of selective parachute drops; and there was some truth in the accusation.

But as time went by, Isotrope confined FTP aggressiveness. From August on, several parachute drops, late but massive, were undertaken for them. When the mission insisted that Packard turn over the weapons it had brought along to the FTP, Packard complied.

Because of this, and an underlying antagonism between some Americans and Britons, Packard remained cool towards Isotrope, with whom it was supposed to cooperate.

"There was a team of two men from the SOE, Aaron Bank, Packard's leader, explained later. But they didn't contact us very often: they went about their business and we did ours."

During the coming days the team actually worked with Commandant Michel Brugier (Audibert), CFL and FFI départemental chief for the Gard.

The second Jed team was Collodion [44] which landed in the Aveyron during the night of August 7. First it operated in that département, then as D-Day approached, it headed for Lodève in the Hérault.

That same night OG Pat-Nitrogen, with First Lieutenants C.E. La Gueux and M.A. De Marco, was parachuted into the Tarn. Its mission was to harass enemy movements toward Provence and it operated mainly on Route 113 between Toulouse and Carcassonne and further north in the direction of Castres and Albi.

---

43. Captain Aaron Bank (Chechwan) from the Infantry, Capitaine Boineau alias Denis (Fukien), Colonial Infantry. The origin of the second American, radioman Sergeant F. Montfort (Formosa), is unknown; he sometimes appears as a French Lieutenant.

44. Captain N. Hall (Augustine), Royal Armoured Corps, Lieutenant Henri Marsaudon alias Morgan (Benoît), Colonial Infantry, and Sergeant Theodore Baumgold (Ulbs), Signal Corps.

On August 12 arrived OG Peg-Platinum with First Lieutenants G.H. Weeks and Paul Swank, which was to operate in the Aude. The group was supposed to be parachuted into the Picaussel forest, near Puivert. But since August 6 the region had been overrun by elements of the 11th Panzerdivision sent out to clean up the mountain south of Carcassonne. That didn't stop five planes from dropping equipment, including Hotchkiss machine guns, that would be particularly useful for the local AS maquis.

In the afternoon of August 7, AS Capitaine Lucien Maury (Franck) had ordered his maquis to scatter. Then the BBC aired the message — 'Fifteen friends will tell you tonight that virtue shines in every eye' — announcing the arrival of fifteen parachutists. The information was immediately passed on to the Salvezines FTP maquis so that they could organize reception of the commando.

The planes started their approach. Now and again fluffy cloud formations passed beneath the fuselage, momentarily hiding the moonlit fields below. The strains of Alouette, gentille alouette, that Lieutenant Swank had been teaching the men, suddenly died away in mid-stanza as the red light went on. But no green light followed. And no one could make out any signal light or fire in the dark beneath the aircraft. The pilots hesitated, made a second run, then a third. Instead of signals, this last run was met by tracer bullets coming up from the ground. The formation immediately gained altitude and disappeared in the dark night sky.

Four days later, after the Germans had left, the OG landed on the emergency DZ at Salvezines, where they were met by Commandant Meyer (Jean-Louis), départemental FTP chief. The fifteen men of the platoon lost no time in destroying a railroad bridge between Rivesaltes and Carcassonne the next day, August 13. On the 14th they blew up a three-arched stone bridge, stopping traffic on Route 117.

On the 17th, the OGs laid an ambush in the canyons below Alet, high in the Aude valley. A mobile column protected by a screen of six hostages was coming back from Couiza where it had hoped to evacuate the supply depot of the IV. Luftwaffen-Feldkorps. When the head of the convoy got to the spot where the paratroopers were hiding, they unleashed a landslide of boulders. Lieutenant Swank had stayed beside the road to protect his men who were taken by surprise when the convoy arrived earlier than expected. He emptied his Thompson in direction of the Germans who fired back. Swank died before he could be interrogated. The Americans pulled out with their two wounded while, in the roadway, German losses were twenty-two dead or wounded.

The last Jed team sent from Blida to R.3 was code-named Minaret [45]. Its mission was two-sided. It was told at SPOC:

"Support guerilla actions in the Gard, where the FFI are having trouble because of unfavorable terrain and the lack of cover. Also you must organize subversive activity among the satellite troops gravitating around the Wehrmacht."

However, the most important aspects were not mentioned.

After three wasted [46] weeks at the Club des Pins holding station, the team was parachuted onto the Barre site during the night of August 13 to 14 [47]. On the DZ the Jeds were met by Captain Bank and two officers from Mission Isotrope: Major Hamson and Commandant Baldensperger, known as Jean in the maquis. After a short discussion it was decided to send the new team to the Aigoual maquis, thirty-five miles south.

The team left for its destination the next day, in the company of Isotrope, and settled at Valleraugue on August 18. The site had been chosen five days before by the local leaders and the English mission — as it was called in the maquis — to set up the départemental CP.

"We were well received in the maquis, Major Sharpe explained. When we arrived it had six hundred well-armed men in place

45. Major L. Hartley-Sharpe (Edmond) from the General List (Intelligence), Capitaine Cros alias Mutin (Hector), and Serjeant J.W. Ellys (Arsene), Royal Armoured Corps.
46. The translator takes full responsibility for this bilingual pun.
47. Returning home, the Halifax was probably shot down by Flak near the Spanish border.

under the orders of a military leader, Commandant Colas, and three civilians, including Rascallon who, with his wife, [48] was in charge of logistics. Their weapons came from the SAP: but they hadn't fired a shot and still had 4,000 lbs of dynamite stored away.

Maquis numbers increased dramatically with the arrival of the sédentaires and three hundred gendarmes.

"We started discussing plans with Colas to harass columns of German troops and block roads as soon as possible, especially Route 99, which had to be cut at the Alzon tunnel and at the bridge over the Hérault River north of Ganges", Sharpe continued.

Minaret didn't have much to contribute with regard to the second half of its mission, except two hundred Armenians who were convinced by a maquis agent to join up.

"A similar operation was undertaken in Mende where one thousand six hundred Turkomans and Armenians were stationed, but the city was evacuated before negotiations could be concluded [49]."

It was said that on the evening of the 17th a Mission Etoile, composed of two American officers and two radiomen from Algiers, jumped onto the DZ Pascal, near Bousquet-d'Orb. They also say that the preceding day an English sabotage mission had been dropped onto the Caracole landing site, north of Saint-Pons-de-Thomières at the foot of the Espinouse. This would be British Major Croft's Team Snow-White, parachuted into the Hérault for sabotage missions of sabotage along the German retreat routes. In its August 13th radio message, Algiers alerted Mission Schooner:

"Expect to send on 14th or 15th English team eight men with thirty containers and twenty packages. Are assigned Mérifons-Salasc region where are to form a groupe franc. Start preparations for

48. Commandant then Lieutenant-Colonel Matignon (Colas) was an aviator and the leader of the Aigoual-Cévennes maquis; Commandant René Rascalon (Alais) was départemental maquis head.

49. Mende, Feldkommandantur 989 base, was also home to the Freiwilligen-Stamm-Regiment 2 Headquarters, a training station for Volga Tatars, Armenians and Azerbaidjanis, garrisoned in Rodez, Mende and Le Puy.

transportation. Please inform Trapèze [50] and if possible send us mail drop and safe house in return message."

Yes, on the coast a counter-espionage team had been operating for more than a month, code-named Schooner [51] and assigned to the port of Sète. It was parachuted on July 12 onto the DZ Caracole, and its leader was based in Béziers. Its liaisons were carried out in two gasogene 11 and 15 hp Citroëns belonging to local residents and a Simca Five belonging to the female director of the Red Cross ambulances. In case of emergency a live mail-drop was used at the Café de la Gare du Nord in Béziers.

From the Saint-Etienne-d'Albignac chestnut plantation where the radio operator was settled, the first message for Algiers left on July 14.

"Message received. Have seen Sultan [52]. Leaving for Sète with Navarre."

To which Algiers answered the next day: Who is Navarre?

Navarre — and Algiers should have known — was the mission deputy assigned to Port-Vendres.

Collecting information on the port facilities and the ships putting in there took up the first few weeks. At the same time, Schooner made contact with some Alsatian and Polish soldiers serving in the Wehrmacht who were ready to sabotage certain coastal artillery pieces, and a unit was set up to destroy the main battery. Parachuting equipment became a major worry, especially since the counter-sabotage mission was soon extended to include the Canal du Midi.

On July 25, Algiers announced a two-plane drop on Caracole consisting of twenty containers of weapons and explosives, plus two containers with radio sets and ten special packages.

The mission answered five days later:

"If material promised is for Sète teams, who urgently need drops of weapons, ammo, explosives and armbands, better to drop it close as

50. Colonel Cambas (Trapèze), DMR of R.3.

51. Chief machinist officer Kervarec (Schooner), 1st class crew officer Flichy (Skiff), 2nd class crew officer air machinist Jean Rousteau (Vaisseau) and Radio Petty Offcer Robert Besin (Casoar).

52. Commandant Picard, deputy DMR for R.3 and DMR for the maritime départements.

possible. Speaker better than Caracole, because of transportation problems."

Thus during the night of August 2 to 3, ten containers were dropped on Caracole and ten more on Speaker, a mile and a half west of Fontès, where the AS from the Bir-Hakeim maquis in Mourèze and the FTP from Le Rocher des Deux-Vierges were ready to fight for control over the weapons. The following night seventeen more containers were dropped, this time at the Capion château, near Aniane: they were immediately picked up by the FTP and their Spanish companions. Neither Sultan nor Schooner would ever be able to get their equipment.

From August 6 on, the messages sent by the mission related to mainly German troops and services operating in the area. Information about troop movements was of particular interest to Algiers, especially about the 11th Panzerdivision which was the only mobile reserve unit in the Mediterranean sector.

Algiers cabled on August 12th to the deputy DMR in Fraisse-sur-Agout, that when the message announcing the invasion was aired, any uniformed members of the Resistance, and especially the gendarmes, should discretely leave for the maquis, after making sure that their families were safe.

On the 13th, via the same circuit, General Cochet made it be known that the main mission now was to slow down enemy movements toward the Rhône River valley and to help the Navy team in Sète.

On the 14th the order arrived, not to protect the ships in the port of Sète, but to sabotage them. This was carried out by the maritime service agents of the Ponts et Chaussées [53], the same men who would prevent the Germans from undertaking major destructions as they withdrew.

A historian has summed up Allied missions in the region realistically: These teams mainly informed the Allied headquarters about the military, and sometimes the political, situation. They asked for air support. However their presence didn't seem to have had a great deal of influence on the outcome of Allied operations [54].

53. Highway or Civil Engineering Department. TN.
54. Roger Bourderon, Libération du Languedoc Méditerranéen, Hachette.

Finally, in the Ariège, on the western fringe of the invasion zone, the August 8 plan provided for an interallied mission, an OG and a Jed team to carry out attacks against communications and to block routes through the Pyrenees.

The Operational Group was undoubtedly OG Peg, supposed to be dropped on August 7 near Puivert, five miles from the eastern border of the Ariège. Jed team Chrysler [55] arrived next on the 16th. According to General Aussaresses, he was parachuted with his radioman, wearing a British uniform, into a maquis of the Iberian Anarchist Federation, who were at odds with the Supreme Junta of National Union.

Actually there were many armed Spaniards in the département at that time, and their numbers were increasing so much that the Allied command was getting worried.

On August 8 an interallied mission — code-named Ariège by the EM FFI but better known at SPOC by the code name of the French teammate — landed near Foix. It was made up of Major Bill Probert, a member of the Intelligence Corps who had already worked in the Balkans, Commandant Bigeard (Aube) and two radio operators: the Canadian John Deller and Sergent-Chef Casanova, who was one of the family.

The reception committee was directed by Commandant Royo, from the Merviel maquis, based fifteen miles north of Foix. The 225 men belonging to this maquis were dispersed all over the département, and made up the Reconquista de Espana batallion, which says just about all there is to say about their objectives. After having made the rounds of the surrounding maquis where the men were received suspiciously by the FTP and warmly by the FFI, the team decided to begin attacking the Germans.

Before leaving Blida, Probert had warned Bigeard: Our mission is to help and advise, not to participate in the action.

55. Captain C.H. Sell (Elie), Royal Artillery, Capitaine Paul Aussaresses alias Soual (Bazin), Foreign Legion, and Serjeant R.E. Chatten (Artus), Royal Armoured Corps. General Aussaresses was interviewed for RAIDS by Eric Deroo

Chapter X

Chasing the Hun

South of the Loire River, the German troops making up Armeegruppe G had been ordered to keep the corridor between the Atlantic and the Mediterranean open, and prepare to repel an Allied invasion from either side.

But once the Allied forces had invaded through Normandy and the armed resistance movements had adopted a more agressive attitude, the German command was faced a nagging question: should top priority be given to protecting the coastline or battling the maquis?

The answer came on June 17 from General Von Blaskowitz who decided, from his HQ in Rouffiac, seven miles north-east of Toulouse, to give priority to the fight against the Resistance. As long as the enemy does not invade, the fight against the interior enemy is our main objective.

Nevertheless, two days after the invasion of Provence, and to avoid AG G being trapped, Hitler gave the order to withdraw all forces south of the Loire River — with the exception of those being used to defend ports — and to regroup on the Sens-Dijon-Switzerland line.

On August 17, the garrison in Pau began to withdraw. The following day the elements of the 159th ID south of the Gironde were advised to proceed to Toulouse, then to Dijon, via Montpellier and the Rhône valley. The remainder of the LXIV. AK, spread out all along the coast, was to head for Bourges and continue past Auxerre.

London was aware from the middle of August on that the enemy was preparing to evacuate its forces stationed south of the Loire River and west of the Orléans-Toulouse-Tarbes line.

The time had come for the FFI in south-western France to hit the enemy as hard as they could [1]. On August 17, SHAEF ordered the FFI to liberate this region, over which they shared control with AFHQ. And messages were consequently aired over the BBC, requesting the population to undertake open guerilla activity.

Seven Jedburgh teams and three OGs were operating at that time in Region R.4 and the nearby Cantal and Dordogne. The first Jead team, code-named Quinine [2], arrived from Blida by Halifax and jumped during the night of June 8 to 9 onto the Luzettes plateau, near Aurillac.

On the DZ an excited maquisard raced across the field in front of the paratroopers he had just greeted:

"We've got a French officer and he's brought his wife along!"

The officer introduced himself:

"Aspirant Bourdon of the French army. Code-named Aristide."

This pseudonym concealed the identity of Prince Michel de Bourbon-Parme, nephew of the Count of Paris, who had enlisted at the age of sixteen in the United States and trained at Fort Benning, Georgia, before joining the OSS in England. His 'wife' was Scottish Major MacPherson, who had left the Cameron Highlanders for No. 11 Commando, where he had taken part in two raids in Crete. He had been captured after the aborted attempt to destroy Rommel's CP, and taken to Italy.

He escaped and was recaptured, then he was sent to Austria, where he again managed to escape. Recaptured, he was imprisoned in Eastern Prussia. He finally escaped through Gdynia to Sweden where a Liberator picked him up and brought him back to England. There

---

1. Short History of Command, Headquarters and Operations of the French Forces of the Interior.

2. Major R. Tommy MacPherson (Anselme), from the Queen's Own Cameron Highlanders, Lieutenant Michel de Bourbon-Parme alias Bourdon (Aristide), from the Infanterie and Serjeant Oliver H. Brown (Félicien), Royal Armoured Corps.

he joined up with the SOE and the Jedburghs at Milton Hall, the Fitzwilliam manorhouse.

The team's mission was to help the Resistance fighters, undertake guerilla actions on communications between Montauban and Brive and cut off Route 20. It arrived at just about the same time as the SS *Der Führer Regiment* was entering Limoges on its way to Normandy.

"Of course we hadn't been informed, MacPherson explained. And on the DZ there were only a handful of maquisards waiting for us, poorly armed and dressed in rags. They had never heard of Droite [3] who was supposed to be our contact."

The maquis of the reception committee was part of the Cantal AS. It was directed by Bernard Cournil, garage mechanic and mayor of Le Rouget. He was delighted to see an Allied officer who he was sure would help them.

"Actually his men were neither equipped nor trained for action, the Major went on disconsolately. And we had never heard anything about problems between the AS and the FTP."

The Jeds blew up a bridge on the Aurillac-Maurs line, then attacked vehicles carrying food supplies to impress the maquisards to whom they had distributed the Brens they had brought along.

MacPherson didn't want to operate incognito. He drove around in his kilt in a front-wheel-drive car sporting a Union Jack and a French tricolor on the hood.

When passage of the convoys of the SS Das Reich Division was announced on the Figeac-Tulle road [4], MacPherson decided to lay an ambush at the Bretenoux bridge. The first half-track was destroyed, then a tank was stranded by an exploding Gammon. But the foot soldiers started coming down off the trucks as the rest of the tanks fired back. There was nothing to do but pull out.

"To slow the column down, MacPherson explained, we set up roadblocks and felled trees across their path, then defended the bridge for

3. Colonel Schlumgberger (Solvet, Droite), DMR in R.4 since January 1944.
4. The convoy was composed of the company from *Panzer-Regiment* 2 which, from Caussade on, was covering the right flank of the main part of the division going north.

six hours. Of the twenty-seven maquisards in the group, twenty were killed [5]."

The team then set its sights on the principal target mentioned during the briefing: Route 20 and the Montauban-Brive railroad line. On July 1, all railway traffic was cut off between Cahors and Souillac. But closing the road was harder to do.

The Jeds were at that time the only men who could move from one region to another, and they gained influence not only with the maquis groups but also with the other Allied missions operating in the southern part of the Massif Central. But as German pressure declined, it became evident that the time of small isolated groups was over.

"Then during the last ten days in July, MacPherson continued, the départemental and regional leaders came out of hiding. We did all we could to assist them and help them keep in contact with each other, while at the same time continuing to play an important role in coordinating intelligence-collecting."

Among these leaders was Lieutenant-Colonel Noireau (Georges), FTP départemental chief named leader of the FFI in the Lot in February:

"MacPherson seemed to have been sent into the region to collect information on what was going on and to operate when the time came. It appeared absolutely natural that superior officers know what was happening to the weapons they dropped, or rather who they were arming. They must have been informed, perhaps with a certain uneasiness, of the size of the FTP in the département [6]."

The arrival on the Causse of an Allied officer in a kilt and who spoke with the Scottish accent of the majors in films about wars in India, made a big impression. MacPherson observed these armed Communists calmly and cautiously.

5. G. Beau and L. Gaubusseau mention in Les SS en Limousin, Périgord, Quercy: "Bretenoux: a first skirmish on June 9 at 06:30 at the bridge. The AS 3rd Company prevents the Germans from crossing. The tanks force their way across at 10:30."

6. Colonel Georges. *Le temps des partisans*. Flammarion.

Even though some SOE officers were angry about it, MacPherson collaborated with Robert Noireau and the FTP. He felt they were determined above all to 'kill Jerries'. [7]

On the same night as Quinine, OG Emily-Helium also jumped. This was the first group to be sent from Algeria and was made up of twenty men including two officers and a medic. Its mission was to paralyze enemy road and rail movements in the Lot.

As soon as he arrived on the ground on the Chénier site in the Cantal, the group leader asked where he could find the maquis of Commandant Georges, part of the Lot FTPF, whom he wanted to contact immediately. This was why Captain George soon arrived in Lissac, near Sousceyrac.

"I didn't know what to think, Robert Noireau (Georges) recalled. Did he want to protect me, or watch me, or perhaps even destroy me? [8]"

And he continued:

"His men had a lot of sophisticated equipment. They lived with the natives as only Americans know how, totally independent, three hundred yards from us without getting the least bit involved with our way of life."

As would happen later on with Quinine, the two groups took to each other, however, and weapons drops were organized, but little ammunition was sent.

These weapons, along with those the Lot FFI had managed to recuperate from the Germans, the gendarmerie or the GMR, brought their total equipment to 220 tons, about equally distributed between the Jed team, the OG, the Cantal AS and George Hiller (Maxime), organizer of the SOE F section Footman circuit [9].

It was he received parachute drop carried out on July 14 as part of Operation Cadillac. More than seventy aircraft participated in

7. Max Hastings; *La division Das Reich et la Résistance*. (The Das Reich Division and the Resistance). Pygmalion.

8. Colonel Georges, who situated the arrival of the "American commando" in May.

9. Hiller jumped on January 7, 1944 near Figeac with an essentially political mission: make contact with left-wing armed groups, including the Socialist paramilitary groups of Colonel Vincent alias Veny.

dropping six hundred containers and 110 tons of weapons under the protection of 250 men from the Veny groups.

In spite of what Noireau said, the OGs did not limit their operations to furnishing arms to the maquis groups. They also carried out the mission entrusted to them in Algiers. Thus, beginning during the night of June 11, in a 5-ton gasogene truck protected by the FFI armed with Brens, they blew up the steel bridge over the Célé at Conduche, using eight 30-lb charges of dynamite.

In July, with the help of the depot overseer, the OGs sabotaged twenty-eight locomotives in Capdenac and destroyed the Madelaine road bridge, which collapsed into the Lot River, thus cutting off traffic on Route 122. They set up a firing range and trained the maquisards in the use of light arms, mortars and bazookas. In the early August, again protected by the maquisards, they blew up the steel section of the double-lane viaduct in Souillac.

Following on the heels of Quinine and Emily, Jed team Ammonia[10] arrived during the night of August 9. Its leader, Austin, was encolled in ROTC at the University of Florida before being called into active service to train parachute jumpers at Fort Benning. He had gone through the typical training course at the Congressional Country Club in Washington, then on to Milton Hall, where he was attached to Leconte, a bigor [11] from the Colonial Artillery, and Berlin, a young Brooklyn Jew.

On the morning of June 5, the team was alerted: you're leaving tonight. During the briefing the Jeds learned that they were to be dropped south of Sarlat. The reception committee would be led by Lieutenant-Colonel George Starr (Hilaire), from the F section Wheelwright circuit. For the remainder of the day, they rested and checked their equipment, as did the members of Team Quinine who were to jump with them. The other teams were given time off

10. Captain Macdonald Benton Austin (Gaspard) from the Infantry, Capitaine Raymond Leconte alias Conte (Ludovic), of the Colonial Artillery and Sergeant Jacob B. Berlin (Martial), Signal Corps.
11. A gunner in French military jargon. TN.

354

in Algiers, so that they would be absent when Ammonia and Quinine left.

Departure was delayed twenty-four hours. SHAEF's orders were strict: no Jed was to jump in uniform before D-Day, and D-Day had been postponed for twenty-four hours.

The following night, the Halifax carrying Ammonia couldn't locate the DZ, so the Jeds relaxed in Blida and then made their way back to camp. Their comrades poked fun at them:

"Did you get stuck in the Joe-hole or what?"

On the 8th their luck was no better: they found the DZ but the pilot refused to drop them because he didn't get the right signal from the ground committee. So the plane turned back, much to the disappointment of the Jeds who wouldn't have balked at jumping blind.

In Algiers the SIS/OSS chief received information from one of his agents north of Agen about the Das Reich moving north. The team was warned about this change and told to do its best to impede the division's advance.

On June 10, soon after midnight, the Jeds finally jumped. They too then experienced the silent black night, the landing on the sweet-scented grass, the excitement of the Resistance fighters, the omelet laced with truffles. They thought they were dreaming, and the Germans seemed far, far away, even though the maquisards often spoke of the atrocities committed by the occupying troops.

The Jeds tried to get the men to set up roadblocks, but that project didn't really appeal to them. Then something happened that burst the bubble of this dreamworld: the maquisards tortured to death a young man wrongly accused of treason and his parents revealed the location of the maquis to the Germans. The château which had been their refuge was burned down and the men had to move out into the woods to live.

Austin actually had many problems with these unmotivated troops. Without any liaison between maquis groups, and in view of the disagreement between the Wheelwright circuit, the FTP and the AS, anything the team tried to undertake failed. The Jeds were isolated and poorly informed: it was impossible for them to fulfill their mission.

From the Gers to the Herault

South of the Garonne River, a Jedburgh team — code-named Bugatti [12], was parachuted into the Hautes-Pyrénées on June 29. On August 12, OG Percy Pink arrived in Dordogne from England. Five nights later OG Lindsey jumped into the Cantal, along with four Jedburgh teams.

The special forces teams witnessed the German retreat and the rear-guard combat fought by retreating forces to avoid being trapped or to obtain acceptable surrender conditions.

And they also watched the fighting between Resistance groups to seize power in the South-West, a region with a reputation for being communist.

In Region R.4, Colonel Bermond de Vaulx, the ORA representative, suddenly found himself on June 4 under the orders of Ravanel, who was named regional FFI chief by the COMAC during his absence [13].

The ORA had two strong well-organized independent groups: the Pommies Corps franc (CFP), between Auch and Tarbes, and the Montagne Noire (Black Mountain) Corps franc. In the Gers and the Tarn-et-Garonne, the AS had organized its men into the Armagnac guerilla battalions. In the Ariège the FTP held the reins with the help of the Spanish Communists.

Even though Colonel Georges in the Lot managed to unify the maquis groups under the leadership of the FTP, in the Tarn there was no such cooperation: ORA, AS, Veny and FTP had preserved their independence.

12. Lieutenant Colonel Horace W. Fuller (Kansul), Marine Corps, Capitaine Guy de la Roche du Rousset alias Rocher (Hopei), 3rd Regiment of African Chasseurs, and Sous-Lieutenant M. Guillemont (Chekiang), BCRAA.

13. Jean de Bermond de Vaulx (Antoine), was at that time territorial representative of the ORA, assigned to Serge Asher alias Ravanel (Verdun), who had gone from the EMNFFI immediate action 3rd bureau to CFL commander in Toulouse.

Jed teams Martin and Miles [14] took off from Blida on August 16 at 20:45 in a Liberator headed for the Gers. At half past midnight, the plane was flying over the DZ south-east of Nogaro, and fifteen minutes later the six Jeds were safely on the ground, even though the pilot had dropped them at a 90° angle to the line formed by the lanterns. On the ground they were greeted by Colonel Hilaire and the officers of the Armagnac Battalion.

Around noon on the 19th, the two teams took a truck to the maquis located south of Auch where the six hundred men of the battalion, commanded by Capitaine Parisot (Caillou), were assembled. When they arrived an attack on Auch was being planned for the next day, so they immediately asked Algiers for a weapons drop.

As the AS battalion was approaching the city, around 15:00, the German garrison was moving out towards Toulouse, harassed along the way by elements of the CFP. At nightfall the column was stopped at the bridge over the Save, just outside L'Isle-Jourdain.

By dawn on the 20th, the Parisot battalion was in position. For ten hours it managed to keep the enemy in the valley. Then, once the CFP Le Magny Brigade had arrived, the assault was launched around 21:00 and the fighting ended with an FFI victory [15].

"We didn't stay to the end, Captain Allen explained. We had got word that the Germans were destroying installations in Mont-de-Marsan and so we left with Captain Mellows. When we arrived at 18:00, we contacted Colonel Carnot [16] so that the city would be occupied the next day whether or not the Germans had left."

The latter — after blowing up their ammunition depots and destroying their guns and part of the airstrip — evacuated the city

14. Jed team Martin: Captain T.A. Mellows (Blase), Royal Armoured Corps, Capitaine Redonnet alias Rémond (Substantif), Colonial Infantry, and Serjeant N.E.S. Carey (Placide), Royal Armoured Corps. Jed team Miles: Captain Everett T. Allen (Libre), Field Artillery, Lieutenant René Estève alias Fourcade (Lumineux), BCRAL, and Technical Sergeant Arthur Gruen (Fidèle), Signal Corps.

15. Actually only part of the 400-man column was involved in the fighting. The remainder would be destroyed in Pujaudran on August 21, 1944.

16. Jean de Milleret, chief of the CFP western group from April 18, 1944 on.

during the night. On their heels the maquisards took possession of the town. As Carnot was dining at the Prefecture, he was warned that a fifty-truck convoy was on its way from Bayonne and Dax.

Early in the afternoon of the 21st, the Jeds decided to take command of the city, when they realized that no defensive protection had been organized. Around 17:30, as they were inspecting one of the tree-trunk roadblocks on the Dax road, the promised column appeared and the enemy immediately started raking the road with cannon and machine gun fire. The vehicle carrying our gear was quickly captured, Allen continued. Mellows' hip had been bothering him since he jumped and he couldn't get into the woods fast enough. The first rounds of enemy fire hit him in the breast and stomach, and his body was found by the FFI the next day, riddeed with four Colt-45 ??? .

The battle lasted for five hours, until finally around 22:30, both sides withdrew, each one persuaded that it had been beaten. But during the fighting the FFI had captured seventeen trucks, destroyed six or seven others with mortars, and killed or wounded forty Germans. They suffered three killed and fifteen wounded.

During the night the three Jeds made their way back to Nogaro. Then, from Auch, they notified Algiers of the death of the leader of Team Martin, and received in return a message from Hilaire requesting their presence in Toulouse.

When they arrived on August 23, they found an excited city that had just been taken over by the FFI. During the night the Niel barracks — where the Armagnac guerilla battalions had taken up residence since the night before — were attacked by the Militia. In the morning the Armagnac Brigade and the Jeds moved out toward Villefranche-de-Lauragais, on the heels of the retreating enemy, heading for Montpellier and the valley of the Rhône.

"The Germans had gone through there, Allen recalled, but four days before and in a big hurry. We pushed on to Castelnaudary and Revel, then to Narbonne. 4,000 Germans had passed through that city two days before. With Fourcade we then travelled to Port-Vendres and Perpignan, in order to report to London about the situation in the port and on the Spanish border."

On August 30, the Jeds went back to Toulouse, still with the Armagnac Brigade. On the Francazal drop site, during the night of September 5, Commandant Parisot was killed by one of the Hudsons landing to deliver arms at Hilaire's request.

"When we arrived in Toulouse, Allen commented, Hilaire had started to play a dangerous political game. Unfortunately he didn't know the rules and really had no right to get involved in it at all. This resulted in the status of the Jed teams being jeopardized to the point where General De Gaulle [17] ordered all the allied missions to leave the city."

Jed team Miles thus left on September 24 and reported to SFU-4 in Avignon. After a car ride across France and a few days' leave in the capital, the team arrived in England on October 3 [18].

On August 25, four teams had met in Toulouse at Hilaire's headquarters: Martin and Miles from the Gers, Mark [19] and John parachuted into the Tarn-et-Garonne.

When it left Algeria, Team John [20] had received a mission to work in the Tarn-et-Garonne with Alphonse [21], from the SOE F section Pimento circuit, participating in the organization of the FFI and evaluating their capabilities.

However it came to light during the briefing that the team was in fact the answer to a request sent by Alphonse — more than a year before — asking for instructors who could work disguised as civilians. Moreover Algiers had no address of a safe house or even a mail drop: the team was asked whether they preferred to wait in Algiers until Massingham had been able to obtain these details, or to leave without them. The Jeds chose the second solution, and they were joined by a radio operator being sent to Team Ammonia north-west of Cahors.

17. De Gaulle is in Toulouse 15th and 16th.

18. George Starr (Hilaire) arrived in London on the 27th, followed by Sergeant Carey, from Team Martin, the next day. The French Jeds went their own way.

19. Capitaine Thévenet (Sympathique), BRAL, Captain Lucien E. Conein (Intrépide), Infantry, and Sergeant James J. Carpenter (Lester), Signal Corps.

20. Captain D.E. Stern (Beau), Lancashire Fusiliers, Lieutenant De Galbert alias Le Rocher (Lucine) from the Cavalerie detached to the BCRA, and Serjeant D. Gibbs (Silence), Royal Armoured Corps.

21. Tony Brooks, blind-dropped in July 1942 and organizer of a sabotage network whose activities had gradually spread to encompass all of southern France.

"The Fortress took off from Blida without our even being able to speak to the pilot, Captain Stern recalled. After about an hour flight, he said there were storms ahead and asked if we wanted to go on, and to which we answered, yes."

Then the plane circled around the three fires on the drop site for what seemed like an eternity:

"We can't make out the identification letter, said the dispatcher. Do you want to jump anyway?"

The Jeds decided they would only jump if the pre-arranged signal letter was visible, so the pilot descended to three hundred feet and triumphantly announced that he had seen the letter. But the packages, which were supposed to be dropped first, were blocking the trap door and a second run was necessary to get the three parachutists positioned correctly.

"This method, said Stern, forces the people to jump aslant the slipstream. I suggested that this might cause a twist but was re-assured by the dispatcher."

The three men went out quickly, and, as expected, Stern's suspension lines got all tangled up. Nonetheless the jumpers and the material landed near the lamps and free of the trees that lined both sides of the DZ.

"The container containing our personal kits was dropped without a parachute after problems in the plane, Stern continued. Some of the objects in it, especially our carbines, couldn't take the shock and changed shape rather drastically."

Since Major Probert's arrival ten days before, receptions were being organized by the Spaniards instead of the local SAP. Probert's wife had heard the message on the BBC, and, since he was away, had prepared for the arrival on a different DZ that was considered safer because it was further from the main road.

As a result, the farmers and peasants who made up the committee, in addition to being without a leader, had no experience in reception work at all. The man who had to send the signal had a very poor battery and a rather shaky knowledge of the Morse code, which probably accounts for his J being read as a P.

Worse still, the Jeds were surprised to discover that they had been dropped in the Ariège, at Trémoulet near Pamiers, a hundred miles from the Tarn-et-Garonne. Nevertheless the equipment was picked up promptly and the group spent the rest of the night in a nearby farmhouse. In the morning the Jeds were awakened by Major Probert and Commandant Bigeard. They were looking for Team Chrysler's radioman who had been dropped that same night on the nearby DZ controlled by the Spaniards.

"We were very uneasy, Stern explained, when Probert told us it was pretty hard to travel north. While we were waiting for him to get more information, he advised us to lie low on one of the farms."

Mission Aube was busy at that time in Foix, which had been besieged on August 19 and whose garrison capitulated early that same evening. And an enemy column was reported the next day coming from Ax-les-Thermes, so a hundred guerilleros laid an ambush at Prayols and hit the convoy: the Germans lost a total of 300 men.

On August 21, a battalion of Mongols [22] left Saint-Girons apparently intending to reoccupy Foix. Spaniards, FTP and FFI assembled to block its path and a fight broke out at Rimont, then another at Castelnau. Finally the next day the Germans decided to surrender after having destroyed part of their equipment.

Team John had had no news from Probert for two days, so decided to contact Richard, the local SAP representative, who introduced them to Jean-Pierre, a messenger from Pacha, his regional chief. The Jeds then learned that relations between the maquis and the Spaniards were tense, Probert having taken sides with the Spaniards, so the SAP had been ordered to stay clear of the whole matter.

"Jean-Pierre was rather reluctant to deal with us at first, but soon became quite helpful. Since the railway had been rashly destroyed we decided to travel by car and in uniform to Fleurance in the Gers, where we hoped to find Pacha. Throughout the trip we only met one Jerry, a Teutonic type wearing shorts."

22. Probably elements of an intervention group organized around July 15, 1944 by the HVS 564 from the Ost-Btl 100 or *Ost-Stamm-Bataillon*.

The SAP leader was about to leave, but nevertheless organized the radioman's trip to join up with Team Chrysler. However he had no ties with Alphonse and suggested the Jeds see Capitaine Brunel (Boursier), commander of the CFL 10th Company in southern Tarn-et-Garonne.

The Jeds thus travelled to Beaumont-de-Lomagne on August 21, just after the maquis company had scuffled near Montauban, at Saint-Porquier, with a large German and Georgian contingent arriving from Agen. Even though the company lacked weapons, they had a large number of vehicles spirited away from German requisitions, and plenty of gasoline.

"Even though Boursier knew nothing of Alphonse, Stern explained, his energy and his troops' vigor impressed us. So we decided to stay with them and try to provide them with adequate armament. We made a sensation everywhere we went and were greeted as representatives of the British and the FFI, submerged under embracings, hand shakings and laying of numerous wreaths."

The trip to Montauban in search of Alphonse was fruitless so the Jeds went on to Toulouse, after leaving their address in Beaumont in case he tried to contact them. There they joined up with the Armagnac battalion — quite impressive with its fifteen hundred trained and well-armed men. With the battalion they set out in search of the Castelnaudary Germans, in Pézenas.

The information on the Hun was badly out of date, Stern admitted. Civilians were so frightened because of the pillaging by the Mongols that it was almost impossible to collect any information without visiting each village personally. This resulted in our being continually a day or so behind the Germans, and apart from a few stray prisoners, we found nothing but wildly enthousistic Frenchmen.

From Pézenas, the team was sent by Algiers to contact Mission Schooner in Sète. Then back to Toulouse, where, thanks to Alphonse's operator, a meeting was finally organized with the Pimento circuit deputy: but the project of creating a battalion fell through.

Following orders from London, the Jeds then turned their attention toward Hilaire, who was trying to create an allied HQ in Toulouse with the different teams present in the city. Their first job was to recover of a Heinkel 177 by Wing Commander Falk from the RAF base in Farnborough.

Then they had to evacuate the Allied sick and wounded back to England. Next Lieutenant Le Rocher was sent on mission to Paris by Hilaire, while Captain Stern sent 50 tons of ammunition he had received to the FFI columns which had moved north.

When Le Rocher got back, he decided to return to London. He was joined there twelve days later, on October 16, by the two British members of Team John. That was when they learned why they never met Alphonse: he had been in the Lyon region for several months!

From the Pyrenees to Angoulême

In the effervescent Greater South-West, cities were falling one after the other, either evacuated by the enemy or liberated by the FFI: Brive on August 17, Montauban on the 19th, Limoges and Toulouse on the 20th, Auch and Le Puy on the 21st.

The withdrawal of the German territorial forces took place rapidly, if not easily: the HVS 564th left Toulouse on the 20th and was in Avignon three days later, while the 788th left Clermont-Ferrand on the 25th and took the same amount of time to reach Dijon.

Along the coastline, the order to evacuate was relayed to the LXIV. AK in Poitiers. But, once the Germans had abandoned the main routes linking the Atlantic to the Mediterranean, the units on the Aquitaine coast were virtually isolated. They thus had to force their way north, avoiding the Massif Central, known to be overrun with gangs.

On August 25, the Armeegruppe G was surprised to learn that withdrawal operations had not even started yet.

"Get going immediately, it ordered, insisting on the importance of extreme speed."

Around 13:30 an order, carried by a messenger with an impressive escort, was transmitted to the liaison officer in Poitiers:

"In view of general situation, AG G insists on urgent necessity of starting movement as rapidly as possible. If enemy action is encountered against northern wing, take southern route, Dijon. Dead line for crossing Sens-Dijon line: 10 September."

In the afternoon, the Armeegruppe continued:

It is not a retreat of Italians, Indians, etc., but of the divisions. The Corps commander is responsible for the withdrawal.

In his defense, *General der Pioniere* Sachs insisted he had never been warned to act quickly, and argued that it was impossible to include the aviators, sailors and civilians within the columns of the 16th and 159th divisions.

On August 27, he confirmed that retreat had started, involving nearly 81,000 men and women, and noted that the movements of the northern elements had to be coordinated with those of the elements coming from Bayonne and Pau.

From then on, the evacuation gathered momentum: its success depended on speed. The *Marschgruppen* advanced during the night to avoid attacks by the Allied air forces, and covered an average twenty miles per day.

They passed through Angoulême on August 31, then Poitiers on September 5 and finally Châteauroux on the 10th.

At the same time as the last Germans were getting ready to leave Bordeaux, the first maquisards were entering Angoulême: the FTP to the east of the city under Commandant Parouty (Louis); the FFI from the south and south-east sides under Lieutenant Colonel Rodolphe Cézard (Rac).

The garage mechanic couldn't tolerate the career officer, and the feeling was mutual. As a matter of fact, Alexander had been sent from the Creuse into Dordogne by the DMR specifically to try to smooth things over and coordinate their efforts.

"It wasn't easy, Captain Alsop admitted. Louis was always friendly, but remained secretive and suspicious of us: Thouville (Alsop's Alexander teammate) was from Saint-Cyr and therefore an enemy in the class struggle, and I, myself, an American, would never be anything but a dirty capitalist. However the arrival in the region of maquis groups chased out of the Vienne départements resulted in the local maquis banding together against those outsiders."

On the 30th the FFI and FTP entered the suburb of La Couronne and prepared an attack for the next day. It started at dawn, with plenty of noise, like a Hollywood movie.

"After a few skirmishes, Alsop explained, we got to City Hall about midnight, and, by the beams of our car headlights, hoisted the French flag. Then the party started! The whole population of Angoulême came out into the streets, celebrating Liberation. Some Allied aviators and paratroopers — twelve Americans and ten Britons — who had been abandoned by the fleeing enemy, were freed from their jails and treated like heroes. As in many of the larger cities, the FFI only ventured in once the Germans had left.

During the battle for Angoulême, the Jeds' radioman, who had remained alone at the CP, got a cable proving that London had completely misunderstood the messages relayed by the team, which was still thought to be in the Creuse. Thanks to Thouville, who sent back a long message in French, the situation was clarified. Then Louis and Rac separated, and the Alexander team followed Rac until November towards Cognac, Saintes and Royan.

Team Lee was also located close nearby. The team members were impatient to finally take part in the fighting that they had avoided for so long. Once the liberation of Limoges was secured, the Jeds, following the suggestion of the R.5 DMR, left for the neighborhood of Angoulême. In the evening of August 27, they were in Chazelles with Major Staunton from OG Percy Red, and the Mission Samson SAS.

"We got the very distinct impression, confided Captain Brown, that the various groups were jealous of one another, and none too keen on fighting, except the Saint-Junien FTP directed by Commandant Bernard [23] , under Guingouin's authority. We were also surprised to see Spanish Republican and Russian flags mounted on vehicles of several maquis groups along with the French flag.

After much argument it was decided to establish a joint headquarters in La Rochefoucauld. During the night, the men heard explosions

23. Probably Capitaine Bernard alias Lévêque, leader of the "autonomous sabotage group" from the Chabanais maquis.

365

coming from around Angoulême and they knew that the Germans were preparing to leave the city once their last columns had passed through.

The Jeds asked London for a bombardment on the Braconne forest, then on Route 10 towards Ruffec, before finally deciding to lay their own ambushes with the help of the SAS and the OGs.

On August 29, a reconnaissance was undertaken north of Angoulême but no adequate spot for an ambush could be found, especially since Tourriers was occupied by several thousand German troops.

Two days later the paratroopers separated and Capitaine Viguier left with the SAS to lay his own ambush. Brown and the OGs took up positions south of La Chignolle after leaving their trucks in Brie under the guard of the maquis.

Before nightfall, Brown and Corporals Hirsted and Cuy reconnoitered the area. The Germans were close by: they could be heard talking and vehicles could be seen travelling along Route 10. Hirsted went to fetch Captain Grunseth, who came back with one squad after placing the other in position.

"We had one bad moment, Brown said, when a truck broke down directly in front of us and unloaded its cargo of Germans. We waited in position for about four hours, during which time many single vehicles passed by, including Germans on bicycles and on foot, and a convoy of German ambulances. The party of Germans remained in the woods to our left front all this time, firing rifles occasionally, but never, it seemed, in our direction."

Around 21:00 a convoy finally arrived. The paratroopers opened fire with everything they had. But the Germans reacted quickly and in less than a minute had three machine guns in battery shooting tracer bullets after the Americans who headed for cover.

"When we reached the line of houses of Les Coussauds, Brown continued, we were still under fire, both automatic and small arms, and some Germans, trying to outflank us on the right, fired up the road with what sounded like machine pistols. We moved out cross country to Brie and entrucked for La Rochefoucauld. The next day Angoulême was liberated. The convoy that we had attacked was probably the last."

When they got back to Limoges, Major Staunton, who had been ordered to head north with the SAS, suggested that the Jeds and OGs do likewise. As soon as they got gas, and without waiting for a written order, which they had given up expecting anyway, the Jeds and OGs left for Le Blanc.

On the morning of September 3 they learned that the Angoulême column, which had been joined by other elements in Poitiers, was now located near Mézières-en-Brenne. They made their way to the village of Saint-Michel and heard from the local maquis that there were still a few Germans left in a nearby château. With the SAS they planned a raid that permitted them to recover quite a lot of material. But a company arrived from Mézières, alerted by the sound of gunfire, and the paratroopers had to scatter. The next day the Americans and Frenchmen discovered that all of the sector suitable for ambushes was occupied. During the afternoon the Americans met Lieutenant Colonel Obolensky, who had arrived from Eguzon where he had been guarding the dam with a unit from the 1er Régiment de France, via Guéret. They agreed to cooperate with OG Patrick who had laid a night ambush and would be relieved in the morning. On the morning of September 6 they drove to Le Blanc and then on to the the Verneuil château in Lancosne forest, with the SAS and the OGs trailing. Right beside the château they came face to face with a German bicycle patrol. In fact, the area was swarming with Germans and Obolensky had to abandon his refuge at the Le Blanc maquis. The Jeds were obliged to return to Limoges for gasoline. When they got back to the Indre, the German column had just left Mézières, and OG Percy Red [24] had been ordered to report to Obolensky. During the night of September 8, the Germans evacuated Châteauroux. The liberation of the city was celebrated the usual with speeches, memorial bouquets and parades. Lieutenant-Colonel Obolensky, the former tsarist who had emigrated to the U.S., reviewed the FTP who saluted him with clenched fists.

24. The OG would get back to London on September 10, 1944 after travelling via Toulouse, Naples and Casablanca.

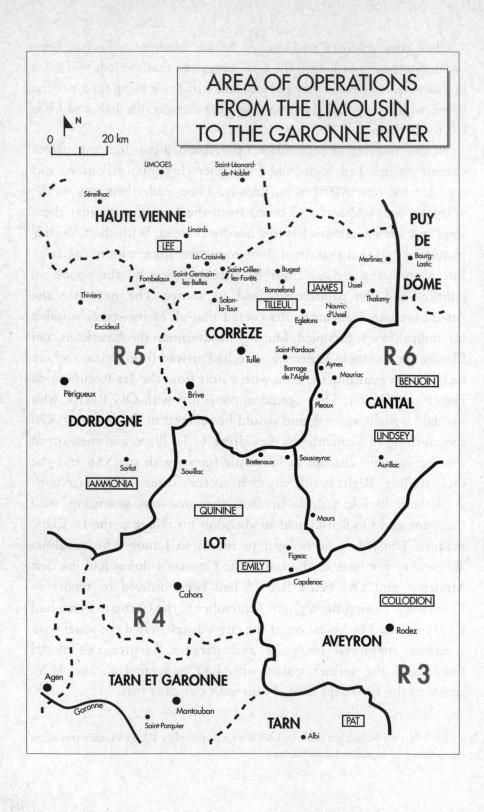

AREA OF OPERATIONS
FROM THE LIMOUSIN
TO THE GARONNE RIVER

0   20 km

LIMOGES
Saint-Léonard-de-Noblet

Séreilhac

HAUTE VIENNE

Linards

LEE

La-Croisvle

PUY
DE
DÔME

Merlines   Bourg-Lastic

Fombelaux   Saint-Germain-les-Belles   Saint-Gilles-les-Forêts   Bugest

Thiviers   Bonnefond   JAMES   Ussel

Excideuil   Salon-la-Tour   TILLEUL   Nouvic-d'Ussel   Thalamy

CORRÈZE   Egletons

R 5   Périgueux   Tulle   Saint-Pardoux   Aynes   R 6

Brive   Barrage de l'Aigle   Mauriac   BENJOIN

DORDOGNE   Pleaux   CANTAL

LINDSEY

Sarlat   Souillac   Bretenoux   Sousceyrac   Aurillac

AMMONIA

QUININE

Maurs

LOT

Figeac

EMILY

Capdenac

Cahors   COLLODION

R 4   Rodez

AVEYRON   R 3

Agen

TARN ET GARONNE

Garonne

Montauban

Saint-Porquier   TARN   PAT

Albi

The BBC later aired a message announcing the arrival in Limoges of Mission Germinal with instructions. Team Lee returned to the Limousin to meet Germinal and consult with the DMR. It was agreed that the two French teammates would stay in France under Ellipse's authority, and that Brown would return to England.

While the Haute-Vienne paratroopers fought in the Indre, Châteauroux — evacuated by the Germans and prematurely liberated by the FFI — had just been reoccupied by elements of the German 16th Infantry Division who were withdrawing east from La Rochelle, usually covering twenty miles per night. Each marching column has a vanguard equiped with 20-mm guns. An artillery group was placed at the head of the retreating forces. The rear guard was mobile in that it had been allotted trucks and bicycles.

However, from August 30 on, since the retreat was two days behind schedule, movement generally took place during the day rather than at night.

Pockets of Resistance along the Atlantic coast

The first team directly implicated in the German retreat from Bordeaux and La Rochelle across the Poitou was Jed team Ian [25], which had been sent into the Vienne at the end of June.

The Jeds took off for the first time from Harrington on the 16th. But since the pilot couldn't find the DZ and didn't even know where he was, they returned to England after the crew refused to blind drop them.

"Four days later, Major Gildee explained, we landed on a rocky stretch of ground surrounded by trees and gullies. We were all safe and sound, even Sergeant Bourgoin whose parachute did not open as quickly as it should have. But the two radio sets were damaged."

On the DZ to greet them was one of Commandant Maingard's lieutenants from the Shipwright circuit. He showed the Jeds the way back to the farm being used as a CP and asked London to replace the two radio sets. The team waited five days for them to be dropped: only

25. Major John J. Gildee (Oklahoma), from the Field Artillery, Capitaine Alexander Desfarges alias Delorme (Maine), BCRA, and First Sergeant Lucien Bourgoin (Mayo), U.S. Army.

one set arrived and it was smashed on landing ... Fortunately, using parts from the three broken sets, Bourgoin managed to rebuild one that worked.

Originally the mission was to help Commandant Maingard sabotage the Bordeaux-Tours and Bordeaux-Saumur railroad lines. But the sabotages were already organized, so it was decided to assign the team to organizing, arming and training the maquis operating in south-western Vienne, in Region B.2.

On June 21, contact was established in the Charroux woods with the AS maquis headed by René Bonnet (Bibaud). A message was sent to London asking for the necessary weapons and explosives to continue sabotage operations, especially against the Paris-Bordeaux line.

"Gildee didn't speak French very well, Capitaine Delorme explained. So we decided that he would handle of requests for parachute drops, messages and coding. He was nevertheless careful that our work remain within the framework of our mission and at our level. He called me to order once or twice, when I started acting like a saboteur or gang leader to get the maquis moving."

Before July 20, the team kept busy meeting with the leaders of the different maquis groups in the region, and obtaining weapons drops on the two available sites. They also requested a Jedburgh team for the Charente where one was greatly needed. The team travelled around a lot, in a car armed with two automatic rifles. On Bastille Day, Capitaine Delorme visited several villages with a protective escort of forty maquisards and spoke to the population.

At that time the zone bordered by Charroux, Confolens, Chasseneuil and Champagne-Mouton — where the two DZs were located — was transformed into a kind of stronghold, with tree trunks felled across the roads and bridges mined. Two field hospitals were set up. Liaisons were carried out over the telephone wires. Certain groups had requisitioned vehicles to react rapidly when necessary.

" The different units, about six thousand men in all, Gildee said, were separated into four battalions, each one assigned a specific sector. Each battalion was assigned a regular army officer as operations officer, and the remaining regular and reserve officers and NCOs who had joined up recently were equally divided among the groups."

The AS Bonnet Battalion was assigned to the Vienne, the FTP Bernard Battalion to Limoges. The two others, Garnier [26] and Chabanne [27], had no money; after a special envoy returned from Paris, twelve million francs were set aside in Angoulême.

"Actually our team commanded the equivalent of a regiment, explained Gildee. It directed operations, and the battalion chiefs were responsible for food, requisitioning and discipline."

The enemy soon reacted to Resistance activity.

In response to the increase in sabotages of railway lines between Angoulême and Civray or Saintes along with derailments and locomotives destroyed by explosives or bazookas, the Germans decided to clean out the terrorists in the region.

On July 20 Champagne-Mouton was occupied, and two columns set out from La Rochefoucauld and Montbron. On the 26th the Garnier Battalion was attacked at Ambernac, and had to withdraw. Then with the help of reinforcement troops arriving from Angoulême and Ruffec, the enemy attacked the Pressac FTP: the troops heading south to Chabanais were unable to cross the Vienne River because all the bridges were destroyed.

The diversionary column sent toward La Rochefoucauld met up with the Bir-Hakeim maquis which blocked them. But the south-western part of the sector was isolated.

So the Jed team decided to go there and reestablish liaison with the Garnier and Chabanne maquis. They left on August 2nd with a chauffeur, a guide, documents, codes and money. The most dangerous spots on their route were to be guarded by volunteers.

"As we were entering Pleuville, Gildee recalled, we fell into an ambush laid by the Germans from Champagne-Mouton. We started firing with our automatics but the car was hit by a round of gunfire

26. Made up of former members of the Bernard maquis who"didn't agree with his thinking".
27. André Chabannes (Blanqui), chief of the AS Bir-Hakeim maquis.

and the engine stopped. We jumped out and raced off through the deserted alleys of the town, with bullets whistling around us. Delorme was wounded, but the guide and I managed to get him to a farm occupied by a group of maquisards with a Bren."

The Jeds came back into town with the FFI to try and save their equipment, but they were forced to turn back and hide in the woods until nightfall. Around 22:30 under the cover of darkness, they sneaked undetected between two guard posts. At dawn the Germans set fire to several houses in Pleuville and then left for Confolens.

The next day the guide returned to the village and learned that Sergeant Bourgoin's body had been found in a field with three bullets through it, and that the chauffeur had been wounded in the stomach and then shot dead where he was lying.

The Germans were still harassed from all sides, so they finally returned to Ruffec and Angoulême, taking their dead and wounded with them, and destroying all the telephone lines before they left.

"We managed to recover another radio set, Delorme recalled, that had been hidden for a long while in a farmhouse. And luckily we were able to recruit Renault, a former radio officer of the merchant marine, who was able to reestablish contact with London."

During the following weeks hardly a day went by without an ambush being laid against an isolated vehicle or a German column on Route 10. On August 27, the Germans learned that the Braconne camp was about to be bombed, so they evacuated the area and were rapidly replaced by maquisards preparing their attack on Angoulême.

"The city had been held by six or eight thousand men, Gildee recalled. Among them were many Russians, Hindis and Italians who weren't very keen about fighting. We had sent them tracts urging them to desert and some of them had joined the Bir-Hakeim maquis."

Once Angoulême was liberated, the Charente battalions pushed on towards Ruffec, Cognac, Barbezieux and Saint-Jean-d'Angely.

Thus Team Ian found itself on the outskirts of Royan on September 9, and left there a week later for London. Along the coast, pockets of German resistance had formed at the Pointe de Grave, La Rochelle, Royan, Saint-Nazaire. They were attacked by FFI groups from the

372

Centre and the South-West who had been chasing the enemy forces caught in the Allied trap.

To coordinate the surrounding of these pockets, an interallied mission code-named Shinoile was sent into the Vendée on September 8. It was directed by Commandant Villecourt, seconded by Alex Willk of the SOE, and with its twenty-five men and numerous radio sets, it was made up of a staff and signal center for the Saint-Nazaire and La Rochelle FFIs. At the same time Jed team George II [28] also jumped into the Gironde.

Through Berry from the Vienne to the Loire

Further north, in the Indre, the German garrison in Châteauroux had, as we have seen, evacuated the city early on August 20. Colonel Chomel, alias Martel, had just been named chief of staff of the FFI départemental command. His area of operations included the southern part of the neighboring Indre-et-Loire:

"The interallied mission, he indicated, informed me that my action was to remain regional and that I could not cross to the north bank of the Loire without their permission."

Jed team Hugh commanded the sector. But against the team's advice, the FFI had entered Châteauroux and relieved the prefect of his functions. BBC announced the liberation of the city.

By this time the enemy was having a hard time retreating through Tours, and it was tempted to shorten its route by crossing the Indre, and reduce the danger of airstrikes by using multiple routes.

To try to stop them, the Resistance forces considered simultaneously attacking all their columns, to force them to take roads where Allied aviation attacks would be easier and where the FFI, reinforced with mobile units from the south of the département, could lay ambushes.

---

28. Mission Shinoile controlled not only this team but also Harold and Tony who were already operating in the region, as well as fourteen Jeds who disembarked on September 28, 1944 from a destroyer in the port of Les Sables d'Ollonne with 50 tons of material.

West of Châteauroux, the FFI command could count on Colonel Martel's brigade: four battalions and a mobile reconnaissance group consisting of a mobile battalion and two squadrons. From Levroux to Reuilly, the two battalions belonging to the AS Francis group were operating with Team Julian. North-east of Châteauroux, the three battalions of the AS Robert group were working with Team Hamish.

The first phase of the operation was carried out as planned and, on August 24, the mobile troops started moving toward the main route into the Cher, where action was coordinated with Colonel Bertrand and Team Ivor. The southern flank was assigned to the FTP and the Le Blanc AS, and a battalion from the Robert group covered Châteauroux.

On August 25, the FFI launched an all-out attack between Tours, Loches and the Cher valley. The brigade was engaged between two routes and was forced to wage battle both to the north and to the south.

So Hugh asked London to send someone for liaisons:

"Unless you state definitely to contrary, the message indicated, Crown will return to England by Dakota to discuss several pressing subjects and will return here 48 hours later by next Dakota."

During the night of August 27, British Major Crawshaw and American Lieutenant Anstett, from Team Hamish, thus took off from Le Blanc. According to Crawshaw, they intended to inform the London EM FFI that 60,000 to 100,000 Germans were still remaining west of the Indre, and brief them on the operations they were planning, so as to obtain Allied air support, as well as an American column from the north bank of the Loire River.

"The purpose of our visit was threefold, Anstett explained. The first was to see if it was possible for an American armored column to come as far as Chateauroux to cut the escape road being used by the Germans along the valley of the Cher River. Next, we wanted a large supplies of arms and ammunition. We also hoped to set up some form of air assault to cover the Germans that were massing near Poitiers and Chatellerault. Only the third point met with any success."

Before September 4, the resistance increased ambushes and raids, inflicting in numerous enemy casualties. But the elements of the 16th ID managed to get out of the area, in spite of the FFI and the air forces which intervened, especially on August 29 at Grand-Pressigny.

The German troops had received strict orders:

The Resistance must be broken by all means, including heavy artillery. Any houses where shooting starts are to be leveled.

While Anstett was in London, the decision was made to pull Team Hamish out, since command was unified under Hugh. Meanwhile the two battalions of the Robert group, which had been sent north of Issoudun towards the Cher valley, were surrounded and only saved by American fighter bombers called in by Lieutenant Blachère.

Back in Limoges on September 9, Anstett left immediately for Aigurande and joined up with his team the next day at Issoudun. Crawshaw had come back earlier, bringing with him from Limoges Team Lee and two OGs. They set down to work as soon as they arrived, with sixty maquisards, blocking an important enemy column for several hours.

This action was undoubtedly the skirmish with the Le Blanc protection elements — the FTP Guy Lebon Battalion and Capitaine Nimetz' AS group — that cost the enemy column coming from Saint-Savin a lot of lost equipment and a hundred prisoners.

"During the first days of September, Hugh explained, traffic on the Châtillon-Levroux and Loches-Valençay axis being used by the 16th Division was badly cut up. Finally the Division abandoned these routes for the single Preuilly-Mézières-Châteauroux axis. That made Allied air attacks easier."

A bombing raid took place around Preuilly on September 1 and 2: reconnaissance units counted 150 cars and trucks destroyed four days later.

"On the 4 September, Hugh continued, the capture of Poitiers by the FFI hastened the end of the retreat, and on 9 September, a final lame German column of 20,000 men passed through Chateauroux, was courageously engaged by Major Clutton of Team Julian who was relieved by Lieutenant Magil and the tardy American column of the

83rd Division from the North of the Loire, who claimed and obtained much credit for neutralizing these forces."

The surrender of the Elster column was a subject of controversy from the start, concerning both the military honors granted and the attitude of the Americans. A diplomatic incident even broke out as to disposition of captured equipment, claimed by the FFI.

The Elster column was one of the Marschgruppen of the 159th ID which had assembled in Poitiers on August 31. Group A, made up of the mobile elements, started out on September 1. Group B included the cyclists assigned to the former commander of the city of Bordeaux. It travelled through Preuilly to Bourges and then Autun, where it arrived on September 4. Groupe C made up the rear guard. It was commanded by General Major Botho Elster and had left from Dax. It was composed of several units of foot soldiers, including the three regiments from the naval base in Bordeaux.

They were being followed by the XIX Tactical Air Command which had spotted the Elster group on photos taken at night. During the day, the columns were constantly harassed by P-47 Thunderbolts.

Undoubtedly the surrender of these nearly 20,000 Germans [30], was the most satisfactory operation undertaken by the FFI, advised and armed by the Jedburghs. Three teams played a major role: Hugh as the Indre départemental military deputy, Julian in the north Indre sector, and Ivor south of the Cher River.

"The negociations with Elster, Hugh explained, ended in an agreement signed on the 10th by Major General Robert C. Macon, commanding the 83rd Infantry Division, and Colonel Martel. In the Cher, Colonel Bertrand of the 1er RI requested that General Elster sign a second capitulation in Team Ivor's presence."

Movement towards the Loire from Orléans, Beaugency and Mer started on the 12th in three columns escorted by SAS jeeps and covered in the air by P-51 Mustangs.

Ivor joined up with Colonel Bertrand who was following one of the columns.

30. 754 officers, 18,850 men and two women.

Then the team decided to travel to Paris, where they contacted headquarters at the Hotel Cécil: it was told to return in three or four days.

"When we returned to Bourges on September 17, Ivor reported, we learnt of a message from London ordering an attack on La Rochelle. But we preferred to go to Orléans to attend the review of our maquis units before General de Gaulle."

As everywhere else, once the fighting was over, the unoccupied teams had to look for a new job or return to their base.

Alec had entered Bourges on September 6 with its FFI, and then took charge of getting the airfield back into shape. Four P-38 Lightnings, short on fuel, were to land there four days later.

"The day after, Alec explained, a B-17, badly damaged by flak over the Rhine, made an emergency landing. It took off again thirty-six hours later, repaired and refueled. Despite this parade of planes, the RAF still questioned the suitability of the field for Dakota operation."

After they had waited in vain for an airplane bringing medical supplies, the Alec team left for Paris on September 22.

On the other hand, in Châteauroux Team Hamish had better luck: a Dakota set down around noon on September 16 with medical supplies that were immediately transferred to the local Red Cross.

"This did much, Anstett commented, to alleviate the bad feeling which had arisen against the Americans as a result of the terms of the surrender at Issoudun. We entertained the pilots at a luncheon and showed them around Châteauroux. They left at approximately 18:00."

Team James, which had been operating in Corrèze, went to Limoges on August 28 to inform the DMR and the regional FFI chief about the situation in its département. Then it travelled to the Creuse where it joined up with Commandant Rewez of Mission Bergamotte. Since Guéret had already been liberated, the team continued on to Le Blanc where, early in the morning on September 1, contact was made with Commandant Legrand of Team Hugh.

Then the Jeds went back to Guéret where the DMR gave them permission to go to London to negociate the arming of a light column that could be formed from Hubert's battalion group.

Thus Lieutenant Singlaub took off from Limoges on September 10. In London he was received by Colonel Carleton-Smith and requested to be assigned to a new mission.

His request was granted so the light column project was abandoned and Singlaub took the next Hudson back to Le Blanc where a car was waiting to drive him to Limoges.

On the 20th, he was settled in Corrèze and busy recruiting the personnel he would need [31].

"While in the département of Corrèze, Singlaub added, we were approached by many individuals who implored us to make a report of the political situation there. They stated that the methods used by the political groups in power were just as frightening as those used by the Germans."

On September 25, Singlaub was in Paris with his radioman, where they found Lieutenant Leb already set up at the EM FFI. And on the 28th the whole team flew back to England.

"We left Châteauroux, explained Anstett, after a grand reunion dinner for all the Maquis during which Jed team Hamish said good-by."

He added nostalgically:

"We were extremely lucky to have excellent French officers with us. They were responsible for the success of our mission."

Further east, beyond the Allier River, on September 6, five thousand Germans were reported covering the Decize crossing-point.

The R.6 Auvergne light division [32] was the first element engaged near Digoin to try to stop the German columns turning east. What these precursors of Colonel Schneider's South-West mobile group

31. In its report, James was notably silent about this mission.
32. The Haute-Loire FFI received on August 17, 1944, Jed team Jeremy arriving from Blida: Captain Geoffrey M. Hallowes (Aimable) from the Gordon Highlanders, Lieutenant Giese alias Fontcroise from the Infanterie and Serjeant R.A. Leney (Ferme), Royal Armoured Corps.

(Groupement Mobile du Sud-Ouest - GMSO [33]) didn't know, was that the Kampfgruppe Bauer, composed of 5,000 German soldiers, was at that time advancing in the loop of the Allier River, followed at a two-day march by the Elster group, the rear guard of the retreating Atlantic columns.

On the 7th, the R.4 Toulouse light division was engaged towards Autun. The next day the R.5 Corrèze brigade intervened in Moulins in coordination with the Cher FFI. The R.3 Languedoc column was to arrive after the battle of Autun was over.

With the Dragoon Forces

Contact was soon made with the left wing of Armée B travelling north from Lyon and threatening the Germans in Autun. On September 9,

Oberst Bauer, commander of the 1287th Artillery Regiment, surrendered to the delegates of the CFP and the 2nd Dragoons, a tank-destroyer battalion from North Africa. Then the advance guard of the Elster column, unable to cross the Loire River in Decize because the bridges had been destroyed, turned around and gave up to the Americans. Team Quinine was marching with the GMSO from Toulouse. Their mission had been first to create the group, then to direct its use. Major MacPherson, in particular, participated in the destruction of bridges over the Loire and the negociations with General Elster.

Near Autun another team had contacted the 2nd Dragoons: it was Team Harry which had come down from the Morvan, bringing Bernard de Lattre, who had a foot injury, to the maquis field hospital installed in Anost.

"The following morning, said Captain Guthrie, since Autun was liberated, I passed through Macon, where I was re-directed to Lons-le-

33. Colonel Schneider arrived in Toulouse from Algiers with General Chevance-Berin, and took command of the GMSO at the end of August 1944: 30,000 men in five "columns" assigned to cover the western flank of the Allied forces invading through the South-East.

Saulnier, where the SFU-4 was. I reported to Colonel Head who sent me to G-2 Air to be debriefed. Our mission was over and Team Harry left for Paris, then London."

Team Quinine also — after accompanying the Schneider group east and, at Colonel Zeller's request, participating in Armée B discussions about the future of the FFI — made its way to Avignon and then joined up with the SF No. 1 in Italy at the beginning of October.

Of the 209,000 Germans who had retreated from the South-West, no fewer than 130,000 reached the safety of the Kitzinger line [34]. There they could regroup and create a more orderly plan of retreat. When they arrived in Bourgogne, they joined the 19th Armee troops moving north out of Provence.

For these troops, the retreat was somewhat different. Four army divisions had blockaded themselves in at Toulon and Marseille or covering the Alpine gaps leading into Italy.

The others, plus 20,000 soldiers from Toulouse, withdrew north through the Rhône River corridor, protected by the 11th Panzerdivision as rear guard.

The few roads leading through the valley of the Rhône were jammed with a disorderly crowd — fugitives, solitary vehicles, lost columns — trying to make their way north. They became the prey of fighter bombers or maquis ambushes and disrupted the patiently organized flow of the regular army units.

On August 31 a catastrophe was barely avoided. Disorder and confusion were the lot of the airmen, customs officers, railroad workers, female auxiliairies, French militiamen, Eastern European volunteers, Italians, etc. But the commander of the 244th ID, who had been in charge of picking up the stragglers since August 22, managed to save the day and reestablish a semblance of order. His mission terminated on September 2, just as the bulk of the German 19th Army arrived in the Chalon-sur-Saône region.

34. *Förderkorb-Linie* drawn up by Hitler on August 22, 1944, usually called the *Militärbefehlshaber in Frankreich*. The line passed through the Seine and Yonne Rivers, Dijon and Dôle.

Elements of this army also managed to escape destruction, in spite of the American and French troops on their heels, and the constant attacks by Allied air units and maquis groups supported by the special forces.

On the Mediterranean coast, Team Sceptre and Lieutenant Silvani's maquisards were among the first to meet the First Allied Airborne Task Force jumpers in Fayence. They joined them in attacking the La Roque radar installation, defended by the Germans. Six days later, after difficult negociations punctuated by artillery fire, the 182 occupants finally surrendered.

Fifteen miles to the south-west, Team Lougre was travelling toward Le Muy, by night, slowly in the darkness, without headlights.

"At 05:10, when we arrived in the little town of La Motte, recalled Capitaine Allain, we heard a sound that I easily recognized: the purr of the Douglas C-47, our training plane at the parachute school. The murmur became stronger and soon filled the air. There must have been a lot of them. Then white sails filled the sky, tens, hundreds, thousands of them, as we were able to see once the sun had risen, when we noticed a multitude of small white spots strewed about in the pastures, hanging from trees, high tension wires and on the housetops. My gendarmes couldn't believe their eyes."

Thanks to Captain Jones, contact was made rapidly and guides were assigned to the parachute companies. During the afternoon, Allain managed to reach Brigadier General Robert T. Frederick, the ABTF commander, who asked him to stay with the task force until they joined up with the invading troops landing on the beaches. A short time later, in Le Muy, he found his radioman and liaison agent who had jumped near Brignoles and crossed the enemy lines safely.

At the CP he also met Adjutant Schevenels, assigned, with fifteen men from the Shock Battalion as English and German interpreters. On the 16th he accompanied Company B, 551st Infantry, to Draguignan where the German garrison laid down their arms the next day.

That same day, Aspirant Lombard and Chasseur Aubry, who had jumped with the British paratroopers and patrolled from

Châteaudouble to Fayence, were assigned to the Americans to reconnoiter Lorgues. They then crossed over to the ABTF east flank and continued along with them to Cannes and Grasse where a liaison with Captain Jones was established.

Elsewhere, Captains Lécuyer and Gunn, travelling by car from Puget-Théniers via Saint-Auban, met the first Americans south of Callas on the morning of the 16th. They managed, with some difficulty, to find the ABTF command post north of Le Muy.

The two officers suggested to General Frederick the possibility of a rapid push towards the north and east as far as Nice through a region where the enemy was scarce. While he was waiting for an answer to the corresponding message sent to the Seventh Army, Lécuyer decided to observe the Allied invasion operations in Saint-Tropez.

He learned that General Cochet was there:

"I knew he had something to do with the FFI, but not exactly what."

When he finished his report on the situation in R.2, Cochet answered:

"*C'est très bien, continuez!*"

Back in Le Muy, he learned that the ABTF had been allowed to extent its territory to the Var, after checking intelligence reports.

"Bamboos and I were only onlookers, recalled Lécuyer. We were a bit irritated at not being included in what was going on."

The ABTF armed jeeps left on reconnaissance early on the 17th and crossed Fayence, Saint-Auban and Puget-Théniers safely to end up at Levens, fifteen miles from Nice. From there the detachment leader reported back by radio and then returned to Draguignan after spending the night in Beuil. That was when Lécuyer and Gunn abandoned the Allied paratroopers and returned to their former occupations!

Lécuyer had just missed the arrival of D'Astier de la Vigerie's Special Detachment, which had left secretly, in plain clothes, working for treacherous Albion.

This is partially true: the detachment had been trained at the Club des Pins, and joined the SFU-4 before boarding a skiff armed by Royal Navy sailors who looked more like buccaneers. He disobeyed General De Gaulle's orders to return to Algiers.

Openly, the Detachment undertook reconnaissance operations from August 20 on, in small groups dressed as civilians, beyond Castellane and towards Avignon. They were so successful that D'Astier managed to get his group assigned to the armored division in charge of the left bank of the Rhône, and thus continue his private war.

Near Toulon, where Capitaine Allain arrived on August 23, he met his men from Missions Gédéon and Sampan.

"I learned, Allain noted, of Ayral's death, accidentally killed in the western suburbs of Toulon, and of the mission undertaken by Sanguinetti to Armée B headquarters [35]. Even though the two teams didn't manage to stop destruction of the Toulon port, they were able to participate in the liberation fighting with the FFI and the storm chasseurs."

In Marseille and Port-de-Bouc, Mission Caïque also had its hands tied: the port installations were destroyed and the naval firefighters, who had been ordered by the Germans to move inland and had no weapons anyway, could do nothing but look on from their barracks.

Activity in the South-East evolved around the American march toward Grenoble via the Route Napoleon. The Faisceau plan — named with respect to Colonel Zeller, who had constantly pleaded the Allied command to choose the Alpine route, effectively controlled by the FFI — started on August 18, when Task Force Butler left Le Muy. The column, composed of three thousand men and a thousand vehicles, stretched over thirty miles: the 117th Cavalry Reconnaissance Squadron took the lead.

At Riez TF Butler was joined by nine members of SFU-4 who had been sent from Saint-Tropez by Colonel Bartlett to serve as interpreters. They were immediately dispatched to different elements in the column.

Lieutenant Brandes, from OG Ruth, also arrived and was assigned by Brigadier General Frederick B. Butler to protect the right flank of Troop B, 117th Cavalry. He had agreed to send these troops to Digne at the request of Capitaine Justin Boeuf, commander of the Valensole plateau FFI.

35. See Paul Gaujac, *La bataille et la libération de Toulon*, NEL, Paris, 1994.

The OGs had abandoned their Barrême bivouac, much to the delight of the maquisards who immediately picked up whatever they had left on the site. Of the thirteen original soldiers, only three had good enough boots left to be able to march. Fortunately Brandes was supported by twenty-five marquisards with a bazooka and a mortar.

The next day the B/117 started off up the Asse valley with the four OGs, some FFI and two British and French officers from SFU-4. At Mézel, on August 19, they met Capitaine Fournier of Mission Sorensen, who had arrived on foot from the Alpes-Maritimes, where, with Lécuyer and Gunn, he had been spotting possible dropping sites on the plateau. The soldiers easily destroyed the roadblock set up by the Germans and their light tanks rolled into Dignes. The FFI immediately called in all their units as reinforcement and the garrison, completely surrounded, finally surrendered to the Americans.

Ruth then turned east to join Gunn. But since the OGs couldn't find him, Sorensen and Lécuyer decided in Thorenc to assign them to defend the Plan-du-Var bridge against incursions by the Germans from Levens. When they were relieved on August 27 by an airborne anti-tank unit, the OG, completely worn out, reported to the 517th Infantry CP in Grasse where Captain Jones, who had arrived with a team from the ABTF G-2, managed to find them a vehicle to take them to the SFU-4.

As the Task Force moved on toward Sisteron, they met Team Chloroform which followed the column and took up position at the Bayard pass with the A/117 to protect Gap, liberated on August 20th.

Afterwards the Task Force was sent west to the Rhône valley, and then relieved by the 36th Infantry Division which quickly dispatched patrols to space out its front line. In Embrun they met Team Chloroform as well as Novocaïne, OG Nancy and the BLO mission. These irregular formations cooperated with the 36th Division and the ABTF in holding the region around Briançon and the Larche gap.

In the sector controlled by the 3rd Infantry Division, Team Cinnamon entered Saint-Maximin on August 19 before being met by the reconnaissance patrols. Two days later Citroën met the Americans at the Durance River.

The team was busy with the FTP and the advance elements of the 45th Infantry Division, skirmishing with the German rear guard stalled in Pertuis and Cadenet. Then with Team Graham it took part in the liberation of Apt the next day. After that the two teams separated: Citroën reached Avignon three days later, preceding the elements of the 3rd ID, while Graham headed for Barcelonnette and the Larche gap.

On the other side of the Rhône, in Languedoc, the retreating German columns from Perpignan, Toulouse, Albi or Rodez were made up of the regular units plus a variety of hangers-on. Their equipment was intact and all they wanted to do was to escape. So the skirmishes with the maquis were bloody and the retaliatory actions against the population correspondingly cruel.

In spite of the delicate problem of crossing the Rhône, and the relative weakness of the IV. *Lufwaffen-Feld-Korps*, the troops managed to make it to Dijon, even though pressure from the FFI forces around Lyon was considerable.

On to the Belfort Gap

By August 19 the garrisons of the Aude and the Hérault were evacuated, but the installations in the port of Sète were severely damaged in spite of the Schooner group's efforts. On the 21st, the Germans left Nîmes. Numerous convoys — often under more or less successful attack by the FFI or FTP —continued to pass through the area.

On the 24th, the rear guard of the Toulouse column, composed of Flak elements, went by. On the 26th it was the Rodez column, and the day after, one from Cahors. Each time Team Packard managed to get air support from the Allied air forces, which hastened the surrender of the German troops by devastating their columns.

Packard took part in the liberation of Alès, then watched the FFI and FTP squabble over Nîmes. Without warning and contrary to the advice of Team Minaret, the FTP dismantled the road blocks and took possession of the city once the Germans had left.

Then Captain Bank left to look for the French forces to ask them to come help the FFI. He arrived in Avignon on the 27th after crossing the Rhône in a rowboat, and reported to the G-2 of the French 1st Armored Division to give them all the necessary information.

When the Jeds got back to Alès on the 30th, it was easy to capture the few isolated elements left. Of the 60,000 Germans that crossed the Languedoc-Roussillon region, only 15,000 — German occupation or legion troops — were lost.

"On August 31, Bank noted, the French forces arrived in Nîmes, but it was too late to capture any more Germans in our sector."

Team Minaret was already in Nîmes, where it helped round up more than a thousand prisoners. When General De Lattre reviewed the troops, the team paraded with their maquis, then left to report to the SFU-4 in Brignoles. Team Packard followed on September 3, then went on to Briançon to take part in the attack on that city. Once the German columns had escaped from the Languedoc net, they had to cross the Ardèche and the Isère, where the same problems awaited them.

In the Ardèche, after the Privas garrison had been evacuated, the FFI thought the département was free. But all of a sudden the columns of the 716th ID appeared, marching towards Lyon along the Rhône or through Alès and Aubenas, stretched out over almost fifty miles. On August 22, OG Louise was the first to be alerted about the arrival of this western column in the Ardèche. An initial skirmish took place south of Aubenas and the 37-mm cannon performed brilliantly. But the second attack wasn't as lucky.

"On the morning of the 25th, Lieutenant McKensie said, the FFI informed us that there were one thousand five hundred Germans in Vallon. I immediately gave orders to set up the 37s in battery to protect the village and its outskirts. But when I got there I discovered to my surprise that — instead of the fifteen hundred Germans mentioned — there were ten thousand of them and they had no intention of surrendering."

A few vehicles, some half-tracks, were destroyed, and maybe two hundred men killed. But the enemy maneuvred quickly and the battle lasted until the end of the day, when the OGs and FFI had to withdraw, abandoning their two anti-tank guns.

At that time OG Lehigh-Simone, made up of five French-speaking paratroopers commanded by Captain Roger J. Morin, arrived on the Devesset site, with Major Alfred Cox, Company B commander, and Captain John Hamblet, its chief medical officer. Cox was in charge of the OGs at SPOC and was aware of the disagreement between McKensie and the Mission Pectoral chief (the DMD Vaucheret).

"By coming into the field, Cox explained, I hoped to be able to smooth over differences and improve coordination of the Special Forces actions."

This was right; he got along well with Commandant Vaucheret. They both went to the FFI CP in Vals, where Captain Montague, from Team Willys and British Major Carl Nurk [36] were waiting for them. Then Cox met McKensie and ordered him to withdraw south of Aubenas.

His idea was to assign each OG to a specific sector and constitute a central reserve squad. He knew that two or three other groups might be sent, but couldn't estimate how long it would take the Germans to cross through the Ardèche nor the date when the French troops would arrive.

Cox had a good chance to observe the enemy fire power when a column took four days to cross Tournon, without really being seriously hindered by the maquis. But on the 30th the group that had been previously attacked at Vallon arrived in Chomérac without its artillery. AS elements and OGs with a 37-mm cannon took advantage of this windfall.

"The commander of the column and his four thousand men were ready to surrender, said Cox, on condition that it be to the Americans. I was sent for and left Devesset hurriedly to help finalize the negociations. On the afternoon of the 31st, a tank from the French 1re DB arrived from the south just in time to fire a few rounds and convince the Germans to give up."

On the opposite bank of the Rhône, in the département of the Drôme, the Shock platoon left their Bourdeaux refuge to join the FFI in the Marsanne forest, from which it launched its attacks against

36. Nurk was of Russian origin and had been sent by SPOC to incite the numerous Poles, Cossacks and Ukranians serving in the German forces to desert.

convoys travelling up Route 7. On August 15th, with the AS 17th Company, it laid an ambush north of Montélimar.

It then hitched a ride with the 16th Company vehicles to Route Napoleon. From Clelles, sometimes marching, sometimes fighting, it reached Grenoble, and then went on to Voreppe on the 22nd.

That day Mission Union III and Team Ephedrin arrived in the Maurienne from Briançon, and installed their CP at the maquis led by Capitaine Gerlotto (Villon) in Montricher. On the road along the Arc valley, the German columns were pushing toward the Mont-Cenis gap.

They were followed by the Americans of the 45th Infantry Division, who didn't go beyond the Tarentaise, and turned north, leaving the valleys at the mercy of the Germans before the arrival of the advance elements of Armée B.

Ephedrin finally reported to SFU-4 in Grenoble on September 8, and Union III, with no news from London, decided to go to Lyon and Paris a month later.

During this time the Shock troopers had returned to the Drôme to take part in the last battles preceding the liberation of Montélimar and Valence.

OG Alice did not participate in the attack on Valence on August 24. TF Butler had arrived two days before, and the OG had moved to the north of the Isère, towards Lyon. Capturing the bridges over the Saône and the Rhône and liberating Lyon, City of the Gauls, was on everyone's mind at that time. Many teams from London or Algiers converged on Lyon to help the FFI.

On August 15, during a drop of equipment on the Saphir DZ in Saint-Martin-en-Haut, an American plane crashed. Twenty miles further north, that same night, Jed team Jude [37] was parachuted south-

37. Team No. 71: Captain W.L.O. Evans (Glamirgan), from the King's Regiment (Liverpool), Capitaine Larrieu alias Lavisme (Rence), 4th African Chasseur, and Sergeant A.E. Holdham (Guinea), Royal Armoured Corps.

38. Raymond Basset, like Vaucheret with Pectoral in the Ardèche, arrived in the field from London, to organize the Resistance groups in the département of the Rhône, with Mission Gingembre on July 9, 1944. Composed of an adjutant, a radioman, two sabotage and weapons instructors, the mission was more "maquis" than interallied.

west of Villefranche-sur-Saône along with the French SAS from Mission Jockworth. The Jeds joined the troops of Commandant Mary [38], FFI départemental leader in the Rhône, with whom they participated in entering Lyon from the north side.

On August 30, Lieutenant Paul Sheeline, of the USAAF, was dropped on Devesset to resolve the conflict between OG Louise and the Ardèche DMD. Since the problem had already been dealt with, Major Cox asked him to remain at his CP as liaison officer. The same night two OGs and two Jedburgh teams arrived on the Tandem site.

OG Lafayette-Sodium — an Italian group led by Lieutenants Odilon J. Fontaine and Leonard Rinaldi — was sent out to support Lieutenant McKensie and his 37-mm gun. The other OG — Helen-Bismuth with Captain L. Vanoncini and Lieutenant V. Ralph — was assigned to the Privas battalion, also involved in the attack on Lyon.

Jed team Scion [39] arrived too late to play its role as FFI instructor. The mission that the team had received before departure was to contact Commandant Noir in the Isère and proceed to the Vercors. Their flight from Maison-Blanche was delayed at first because of mechanical problems. Then, even though the weather was clear, the pilot, after flying over the Baleares and up the Rhône valley, couldn't find the Lee DZ in the Drôme, so finally dropped the team on Tandem, prepared by the Ardèche SAP.

When Major Grenfell arrived, Vaucheret let him decide whether he wanted to cross the Rhône River and try to find Noir, or work with Mission Pectoral.

The team, like Jed team Masque [40], which had been through the same adventures, decided to stay in the Ardèche, because it would take five or six days to cross the Rhône, and by then the fighting would be over. The DMD then suggested that they move on to Saint-Etienne to

39. Major P. Grenfell (Scintillating), Royal Tank Corps, Capitaine Gruppo alias Revard (Vif), 6th Algerian Tirailleurs, and Serjeant T.F. Cain (Vibrant), 1st Fife and Forfar Yeomanry.

40. Captain Nelson E. Guillot, Field Artillery, Capitaine Bertrand Bouvery alias Gramont, of the Infanterie, and Sergeant Francis M. Poche, USAAF.

establish liaisons with the FFI in the Loire, or into southern Ardèche where the maquisards were fighting the Germans. Of course the Jeds chose the second proposal and headed for Vals-les-Bains. That same evening they met Colonel Lecoq whose 2nd Algerian Spahis were acting as advanced echelon for Armée B.

Around Lyon on September 2, the maquisards were in position in the hills to the west and north-west of the city. The 13th Foreign Legion Demi-Brigade had arrived in L'Arbresle, and an officer came to their CP in Lentilly to make contact. In Devesset Lieutenant Sheeline had come to greet OG Williams-Mercury, but he had no transportation to get them to Lyon in time to participate in the capture of the city.

On the morning of the 3rd, section by section, the FFI entered Tassin and took up positions along the Saône.

Cox and Sheeline then crossed the excited city to the 36th Infantry Division CP in Satolas.

"The basic directive did not consider actions beyond Grenoble and Lyon, and the jurisdiction of SPOC over special operations extended no farther. Except for those involved in combat along the Italian frontier, the OGs, the Jedburghs, the inter-allied and liaison missions, and 4-SFU could consider their work completed [41]. But the war was far from over. North of Lyon at least twenty teams from the Special Forces continued, along with the SAS and the FFI, to harass the German columns retreating towards the Vosges and the Belfort Gap."

In Franche-Comté, eight teams carried out typical maquis missions, either alone or in groups [42]. Only one team — Stanley in the Haute-Marne between the Third and Seventh Armies — received a special intelligence mission for the Allied troops progressing toward it. Team Godfrey, intended for the Mulhouse region, decided to stay in the Haute-Saône where it had been dropped, and joined the other Franche-Comté teams.

41. Arthur L. Funk, Hidden Ally, New York, 1984.
42. Teams Basil, Brian, Norman and Maurice, Gregory, Cedric and Roderick, Bunny.

In Burgundy, only two teams were carrying out missions of the usual type [43]. On the other hand, several were involved in direct action [44], justified by the density of the German forces in the area, threatening the wings of the two Allied armies.

The interallied missions, often sent too late to be completely successful, had varying fortunes.

The results of Canelle — a maquis style mission — directed from London and sent out by Massingham into the Saône-et-Loire during the July moon period, remain unknown.

Etoile — dropped on September 5 in the Ain and affiliated with Jed team Gregory — was initially intended to coordinate the activities of the FFI and the SAS parachuted into the Vosges. The mission was rapidly overtaken by the regular forces and so joined up with the French SAS and the different Jedburghs operating in the Jura. It took the initiative of creating several Alsace-Lorraine battalions in October who were equipment parachuted from England on the Valdahon site.

Next came Sainfoin, which was part of a larger group code-named Mission Orgeat, designed to equip and organize the maquis in Regions C and D. Three Jedburgh teams were associated with this mission [45]. Sainfoin was dropped in Pontarlier, within the Allied lines, and understood immediately that it was not needed. Much to the disappointment of the French leader, the Allied mission members decided to leave Besançon and go back to London.

Another mission from Orgeat, Mission Pavot, was parachuted over the cliffs of the Vosges, much too late to have any significant effect. The three Jed teams intended to accompany the mission were sent to attack the German pockets along the Atlantic coast instead.

Finally, on September 15, Mission Cutthroat, composed of sabotage and weapons instructors, was parachuted near Rambervilliers. Its work

43. Teams Arthur and Paul, who were to be joined by Henry.
44. Teams Alan and Anthony in association with the French of the 3rd SAS, Desmond with the Americans from OGs Christopher and then Adrian.
45. Timothy with Sainfoin, Jim with Camomille and Douglas II with Serpolet.

consisted mainly in organizing the FFI who had already joined up with the American troops. One of the B-24 Liberators was shot down by the anti-aircraft fire, thus confirming the fears of some who had said that the code-name would bring bad luck.

Beyond the Burgundy Gate, the main occupation of the EM FFI in London was to regroup and equip the soldiers from Alsace-Lorraine who were spread out all over France and Switzerland, so that they could participate in the liberation of Alsace. A mission parachuted into the Vosges in July for this very reason, was responsible for organizing the maquis in the mountains and plains. However, because of the military operations underway, it was prevented from fulfilling its role of regrouping the soldiers of Alsace-Lorraine and getting them ready for action.

Two Jedburgh teams and an SAS mission were dropped in the Vosges in August [46], where they were very active.

The stiffening of the front during the month of September created a problem for the Vosges maquis groups, who were frequently attacked and dispersed by the German forces. However, information furnished by the Resistance, encouraged the Allied command to send two Jed teams to insure that it was relayed by radio. So Brian and Gregory infiltrated volunteers — either by crossing the lines or through Switzerland — toward Montbéliard and Belfort, then on into Alsace as far as Mulhouse, with orders to collect tactical information to be diffused to the French First Army [47].

In view of the success of this mission, the EM FFI decided to send two similar missions to the region around Nancy. But because of delays due to bad weather, Team Julian was only able to infiltrate the lines on November 16 toward Thann and the Haut-Rhin.

The second mission, Echalote, left London for Paris shortly after. At the end of November it was placed under the control of the Direction

46. Teams Alastair and Jacob, the latter in association with SAS Mission Loyton.
47. Armée B was initially placed under the control of the Seventh Army. When the two French army corps were activated, on September 19, 1944, Armée B became independant and French was designated First Army.

générale des études et recherches (General office of studies and research), which was now directing operations.

After the Special Project Operations Center, the headquarters of the French Forces of the Interior were also closed down. From November 23rd on, the staff in the London offices was reduced to a liquidating echelon, and the organization was officially dissolved on December 1st, 1944.

Epilogue

At the end of October 1944, the Allied forces invading through Normandy and through Provence linked up to create a unified front stretching from the mouths of the Escaut to the Swiss border. From that moment on, the Belgian and French Resistance groups lost their military importance.

In north-eastern France, especially, the stiffening of the front south-west of the Vosges wiped out any hope of activity by the maquisards, who were ruthlessly tracked by the enemy.

However, the participation of Resistance fighters in intelligence collection — and the corresponding role of the different Special Forces teams still in the field — became essential in preparation for the Allied offensive toward the Rhine. But this type of activity was usually the job of the Special Services, who soon took back control of operations.

In December the EM FFI was dissolved. Certain members of the SOE, the OSS or the BCRA were retrained to be sent to the Far East, others were sent into Germany and Austria. The last mission, infiltrated into Alsace in November, returned to its London base in March, 1945.

Of the 265 Jedburghs [1] sent into France, seventeen were killed and nine wounded, with only two teams destroyed: Jacob in the Vosges, whose two officers were taken by surprise with their maquisards, and Augustus in the Aisne.

---

1. 82 Britons, one Canadian, 76 Americans, one Belgian and 105 Frenchmen.

Compared to those of the SOE and OSS circuits, the losses may seem light. It is true that the work of the Jeds more closely ressembled the open war fought by the SAS or the OGs, than the underground war of the traditional secret agents.

Once operations were over, eight British officers returned to their units, thirteen remained for various reasons in the intelligence community, including four assigned to the Germany-Austria sector and one to the Foreign Office. About fifteen were sent to the Far East, along with 25 radio operators.

The vast majority of the Americans — 37 officers and 31 radiomen — were assigned to the Far East.

On the other hand, the French Jeds followed a variety of paths. Five officers reported to General Koenig's HQ or their unit in Paris, two to the 5th bureau of the Première Armée and the 1re Division Blindie, four others to their units in France or in North Africa. Two remained with the FFI in the South-West. Eight officers and operators joined the DGSS; seven were sent on missions to Alsace or Germany. But the largest number, retrained or not, were assigned to the Far East: 25 officers and 33 radiomen.

The American Operational Groups, whose numbers reached of 1,100 parachutists in August, 1944, were reorganized into a more coherent structure named the 2671st Special Reconnaissance Battalion, Separate (Provisional). After the defeat of Germany in the spring of 1945, the OGs returned to the U.S. and also underwent retraining to be deployed in the Far East.

Qualitative results of the actions undertaken by the different Special Forces teams — liaison missions, Jed teams and OGs — are difficult to establish. Their activities were rarely independent and their advisory role is difficult to evaluate. Moreover, and this is also true for the maquis or other armed movements, it is meaningless to try to judge their results by classical military criteria: their capacity for destruction had little relationship to their numbers.

As Stewart Alsop has written about the Jeds: No list of Germans killed, bridges blown up, trains derailed, information transmitted, can adequately reflect their activities. All the Jeds of all nationalities combined amounted to less than a half-battalion. It is clear that so few men could not play a decisive role. But the Resistance fighters who knew the Jeds and who received the parachute drops so vital to them, realize that it would have been much more difficult to fight the enemy occupying their country if they hadn't been helped by the Jedburgh operation [2].

As for the OGs, the official OSS report indicates:

'The actual record of OG operations is matter for the theater accounts. The OGs were not Rangers, an idea which Donovan had sponsored in early 1942. However, they did assume of the nature of commandos and of Rangers in some aspects of their operations. The distinction was simply that, while Donovan saw the Rangers as operating in the face of the enemy, the OGs fitted into the pattern of OSS activities behind the enemy lines [3].'

But beyond these expressions of official satisfaction, what was their real impact? The reports written up by the returning mission members speak for themselves.

In his comments, Captain Monahan, of Team Arnold, didn't mince his words:

"We were sent too late. Four days before the liberation were wholly inadequate for organising and arming the FFI in a region where they were little organised and very scantily armed. The parachuting operation requested for us by the 3rd Army also took place too late to be of any use."

In spite of repeated requests, no personal equipment or quartz crystals for the radio would ever be replaced. The impossibility of the team to transmit messages to London would be a serious handicap for them.

"Though we were dropped in civilian clothes we were given neither photographs nor false papers. The omission of at least photographs was grave ; papers could have been obtained in France but, we were told, not photographs. We had been told in London that such

2. Stewart Alsop - OSS, l'Amérique et l'espionnage, Fayard.
3. War Report, Office of Strategic Services - Volume 1.

photographs would not be necessary for us but this view was not endorsed by the FFI and agents with whom we worked."

The leader of team Basil, in his testimony, regretted that the team had not been notified, during the initial briefing, of the presence of a British agent in the maquis where they were to operate:

"His character was such that we found it difficult at first to see eye to eye with him. Luckily it worked out all right, but he could easily, and nearly did, cause the complete failure of our mission."

With respect to relations with the London base, he added:

"We received QSL to all our messages, but never any indication of whether our requests would be answered. In actual fact they never were. London instead expressed verbose sympathy for casualties which only wasted our time deciphering."

The criticisms contained in the Chloroform report are just as instructive:

"Why were Jed teams not dropped six months before? If equipment was not available why did the Headquarters not have the courtesy to notify us? Most drops had 25% breakage or damage. We feel it was sabotage."

And the report continued:

"The briefing was poor, inadequate and inaccurate. This was caused possibly by lack of information from the field, but more probably by poor coordination of information of the services. And why was information sent in by us not passed on to the higher headquarters? For example the bombing of Sisteron, Savine, and other cities of the Valence/Gap railroad."

OGs and Jeds, generally speaking, regretted the lack of information during the briefing about the political situation in their future sector of operations, and London's silence in response to their repeated requests for arms drops.

Actually each officer in the field reacted to the situation according to his personality, his tastes and his convictions. The case of Prince Obolensky and the FTP has been discussed, as well as the problems of the Morvan teams split between royalists and republicans. Things sometimes became more complicated when the personalities of the members within the team clashed. Alsop praised his French teammate, a Saint-Cyr career officer, who managed to get along with the maquisards, mostly armed civilians, and communists to boot.

It became embarrassing when London or Algiers put a stop to a team's activities. It is particularly difficult, for lack of syntheses, and especially open archives, to get an idea of SFHQ's, the EM FFI's or SPOC's policy toward the maquis groups and armed movements, and consequently toward the Special Forces teams that supported them.

We can only note the varying treatments of the different regions and try to imagine the reasons, which often appear contradictory. SFHQ generally followed the policy line indicated by the SOE circuits, with which the Jeds were often associated.

Then, after the formation of the EM FFI, operational necessities generally seemed to take precedence.

In southern France the two basic policies of the Allied forces were, for the Americans, support for the invasion of Provence, and, for the British, protection of the troops in Italy.

But as we have seen political preoccupations were never far from the surface, even though it is difficult to ascertain their importance. This is true for the Force C project in the Massif Central, which the Allies rejected for technical reasons while the French remained convinced of the contrary. The Vercors tragedy is another example of policital interference in military matters.

Almost all of France was covered by the Special Forces, but only certain regions received deliberate assistance from abroad. In this, deliveries of weapons, especially mortars, are an excellent indicator of the amount of political confidence or strategic interest manifested by the interallied command.

The example of the Morvan illustrates the conflict of interests, with efficient action by the interallied mission in the northern hills for the benefit of Patton's Army, whereas in the south there was no such deployment of activity against the columns threatening Patch's flank. It is true that the northern part of the region was controlled by London and the south more by Algiers.

Finally, interception of the German forces retreating from the South-West was not assigned to a liaison mission, as would seem logical, but to an efficient Jed team, that had managed to establish its supremacy over the other teams operating in the region. The messages exchanged on September 10 and 11, 1944 between London and Team Hugh reveal the climate of confidence existing between these partners that would result in the surrender of the Elster column:

"From Hugh. Departement of Indre and attached areas of Indre-et-Loire now entirely liberated. Franck is ill and tired. Propose establish liaison with Allied forces and then return. Do you consent."

" To Hugh. Congratulations liberation Indre and Indre-et-Loire."

All the members of the Special Forces — even those who intervened in the South where coordination was better than north of the Loire — agreed on one point: they were sent to France too late.

For men speaking French with a strong American accent, operating behind the lines before Liberation was usually considered suicidal. It was only possible once the worst dangers to these obvious foreigners had been averted by massive popular support. That was the reason for restricting the parachute drops before Overlord.

It is clear that those responsible for deployment policy were too cautious. Had Special Forces been engaged earlier, they would certainly have helped increase enemy insecurity, if uniformed and armed teams in large numbers had started to operate inside France during the months before D-Day. But in this specific case the risks were enormous, and only the rash can blame the Allied command for wanting to avoid them [4].

Another handicap for the Special Forces was that Allied generals did not consider their activity important. Patton, one of the least conformist, found the OSS efforts futile, and judged that the support given by the FFI was better than expected but less than advertised.

SHAEF disbanded the SF Detachments during the first week in September 1944. At the end of the year, most of the men from the Special Operations Forces had been transferred to Asia. No account was taken of a possibility of guerilla activity in Germany:

4. Michael Foot - *SOE in France*, HMSO.

That was no doubt a correct assessment, but one also senses a certain relief, as if unwanted house guests had finally departed [5].

But, as Captain Mynatt of Team Arthur hoped in the conclusions to his report, the experiment would not be completely in vain:

We can only hope that in any future tasks that may have to be accomplished in any scene of operations, greater vision will be possible, and that those who will be sent to the field, will not be left without help, and will be sent in a more useful time, and not at the last minute as was the case for us in France.

In spite of all this, we cannot dismiss the psychological impact on the French in occupied France: after years of occupation, the appearance, behind the enemy lines, of Allied soldiers in uniform was a harbinger of liberation and a call to action. Inversely, these operations proved that the call did not go unanswered. For the Jedburghs the ultimate triumph of the project was the successful formation of groups of soldiers, professionals or not, from different countries working together for a common cause. Many of these men would later pursue successful careers in diplomacy, politics or business.

Ironically, some would find themselves on opposite sides because of the political ideals of their respective governments. Thus in Indochina, American Jeds were to support Hô Chi Minh while French Jeds, with the help of the British, tried to maintain French sovereignty.

Appropriately, it is in France that the flame of the Special Forces was rekindled. At the beginning of May, 1947, in the somber courtyard of the Montlouis Citadelle, Capitaine Aussaresses passed under review the thirty-five men making up the core of the 11th Shock Battalion, which had inherited the missions and the methods of the SAS, the Jedburghs and the original Batallion de Choc. This 850-man unit formed part of the Action branch of the Special Services. They later fought successfully in Indochina and Algeria.

The arrival of the cold war would bring the same concerns and the same initiatives in Great Britain.

5. S.J. Lewis - Jedburgh Team Operations in Support of the 12th Army Group, August 1944, Combat Studies Institute.

The SAS, at first made up of reservists, soon participated successfully in Malaysia and on the Arabian peninsula. With the troubles in Ireland, it branched out into counter-terrorism, using methods of action similar to those used by the 11th Storm Battalion against the Algerian FLN.

The Americans were naturally reticent and forgetful of the lesson taught by the OSS, namely that a large population, speaking different languages and with different ties to other foreign countries, can, with intense training and audacious maneuvering, play an important role in modern non-conventional warfare. It took them longer to realize the importance of maintaining special forces on alert. It wasn't until the end of the 1950's that Aaron Bank, the former leader of Team Packard, suggested to the Secretary of Defense and the CIA the idea of creating guerilla units capable of working behind the Iron Curtain. This would be the starting point for the Green Berets in Germany and the numerous special forces units engaged in the Vietnam War.

Interallied missions

Mission code name	Date of arrival in the field	Area of operations	Region or FFI subdivision	Chapter(s) in which mission is mentioned
Aloes	August 4 1944	Brittany	M.3	5
Aube	August 8 1944	Ariège	R.4	9,10
Basses-Alpes	August 4 1944	Basses-Alpes	R.2	9,10
Benjoin	May 9 1944	Cantal	R.6	8
Bergamotte	June 27 1944	Creuse	R.5	7,10
Citronelle	April 12 1944	Ardennes	C.2	1
Cutthroat	September 15 1944	Vosges	D.2	10
Etoile	September. 5 1944	Franche-Comté (south)	D.2	10
Eucalyptus	June 29 1944	Vercors	R.1	8
Hautes-Alpes	August 7 1944	Hautes-Alpes	R.2	9
Isaac	June 10 1944	Nièvre	P.3	4
Isotrope	June 9 1944	Lozère	R.3	9
Michel	April 10 1944	Basses-Alpes	R.2	9
Musc	June 7 1944	Ain, Haute-Savoie	R.1	8
Pavot	September 11 1944	Vosges	C.3	10
Pectoral	June 13 1944	Ardèche	R.1	9,10
Sainfoin	September 10 1944	Franche-Comté (north)	D.2	10
Shinoile	September 8 1944	Vendée, Charente	M.3,B.2	10
Snow-White	September 16 1944	Hérault	R.3	9
Tilleul	July 7 1944	Corrèze	R.5	7
Toplink	August 1 1944	Hautes-Alpes	R.2	9
Union	January 6 1944	Isère and Savoie	R.1	3
Union II	August 1 1944	Savoie	R.1	9
Union III	August 13 1944	Savoie	R.1	9,10
Vaucluse	July 12 1944	Vaucluse	R.2	9
Verveine	July 6 1944	Morvan	P.3	4,6

Jedburgh teams

Mission code name	Date of arrival in the field	Area of operations	Region or FFI subdivision	Chapter(s) in which mission is mentioned
Alan	August13 1944	Saône-et-Loire	D.2	10
Alastair	August28 1944	Vosges	C.3	10
Alfred	August24 1944	Oise	P.1	6
Alec	August 10 1944	Cher	P.2	7,10
Alexander	August 13 1944	Creuse and Dordogne	R.5	7,10
Ammonia	June 10 1944	Dordogne	R.5	10
Andrew	August 15 1944	Ardennes	C.2	1
Andy	July 12 1944	Creuse	R.5	7
Anthony	August 15 1944	Saône-et-Loire	D.2	10
Archibald	August 26 1944	Meurthe-et-Moselle	C.1	6
Arnold	August 25 1944	Marne	C.1	6
Arthur	August 19 1944	Côte-d'Or	D.1	10
Aubrey	August 11 1944	Seine-et-Marne	P.1	6
Augustus	August 16 1944	Aisne	1.5	6
Basil	August 26 1944	Doubs	D.2	10
Benjamin	August 21 1944	Meuse	C.1	6
Bernard	August 21 1944	Meuse	C.1	6
Brian	August 28 1944	Doubs	D.2	10
Bruce	August 15 1944	Yonne	P.3	6
Bugatti	June 29 1944	Hautes-Pyrénées	R.4	10
Bunny	August 18 1944	Haute-Marne	D.1	10
Cecil	August 26 1944	Aube	P.3	6
Cedric	August 28 1944	Haute-Saône	D.2	10
Cinnamon	August 14 1944	Var	R.2	9
Citroën	August 14 1944	Vaucluse	R.2	9,10
Chloroform	June 30 1944	Drôme, Hautes-Alpes	R.1	8, 9,10
Chrysler	August 16 1944	Ariège	R.4	9,10
Collodion	August 7 1944	Aveyron	R.3	9
Daniel	August 6 1944	Côtes-du-Nord	M.3	5
Desmond	September 5 1944	Dijon	D.1	10
Dodge	June 26 1944	Drôme and Isère	R.1	8
Douglas	August 6 1944	Morbihan	M.3	5
Douglas II	September 10 1944	Ain, Jura and Doubs	D.2	10
Ephedrin	August 13 1944	Savoie	R.1	9,10
Felix	July 9 1944	Côtes-du-Nord	M.3	5
Francis	July 10 1944	Finistère (south)	M.3	5
Frank	September 27 1944	Vendée, Charente	M.3,B.2	10

Mission code name	Date of arrival in the field	Area of operations	Region or FFI subdivision	Chapter(s) in which mission is mentioned
Frederick	June 10 1944	Côtes-du-Nord	M.3	4
Gavin	July 12 1944	Ile-et-Vilaine	M.3	5
George	June 10 1944	Morbihan	M.3	4
George II	September 8 1944	Gironde	B.1	10
Gerald	July 19 1944	Morbihan	M.3	5
Gilbert	July 10 1944	Finistère (south)	M.3	5
Giles	July 9 1944	Finistère (center)	M.3	5
Godfrey	September 18 1944	Haute-Saône	D.2	10
Graham	August 13 1944	Vaucluse/Basses-Alpes	R.2	9,10
Gregory	September 5 1944	Doubs	D.2	10
Guy	July 12 1944	Ile-et-Vilaine	M.3	5
Hamish	June 13 1944	Indre	R.5	4, 7,10
Harold	July 15 1944	Vendée, Deux-Sèvres	M.3,B.2	6,10
Harry	June 6 1944	Nièvre	P.3	4, 6,10
Hilary	July 18 1944	Finistère (north)	M.3	5
Henry	September 10 1944	Belfort	D.2	10
Horace	July 18 1944	Finistère (north)	M.3	5
Hugh	June 6 1944	Indre	R.5	4, 7,10
Ian	June 21 1944	Vienne and Charente	R.5	10
Ivor	August 7 1944	Cher	P.2	7,10
Jacob	August 13 1944	Vosges	C.3	10
James	August 11 1944	Corrèze	R.5	7,10
Jeremy	August 17 1944	Haute-Loire	R.6	10
Jim	September 10 1944	Ain, Jura and Doubs	D.2	10
John	August 17 1944	Tarn-et-Garonne	R.4	10
Jude	August 15 1944	Rhône	R.1	10
Julian	August 11 1944	Indre	R.5	7,10
Julian II	November 17 1944	Haut-Rhin	D.2	10
Lee	August 10 1944	Haute-Vienne	R.5	7,10
Mark	August 17 1944	Tarn-et-Garonne	R.4	10
Martin	August 17 1944	Gers	R.4	10
Masque	August 28 1944	Ardèche	R.1	10
Maurice	August 28 1944	Jura	R.1	10
Miles	August 17 1944	Gers	R.4	10
Minaret	August 14 1944	Gard	R.3	9
Monocle	August 14 1944	Drôme	R.2	9
Nicholas	September 10 1944	Haute-Saône, Vosges	D.2,C.3	10

Mission code name	Date of arrival in the field	Area of operation	Region or FFI subdivision	Chapter(s) in whichmission is mentioned
Norman	August 28 1944	Jura	D.2	10
Novocaïne	August 7 1944	Hautes-Alpes	R.2	9,10
Packard	August 1 1944	Lozère and Gard	R.3	9
Paul	August 19 1944	Côte-d'Or	D.1	10
Philip	September 1 1944	Meurthe-et-Moselle	C.1	6
Quentin	September 27 1944	Vendée	M.3	10
Quinine	June 9 1944	Lot	R.4	10
Raymond	September 27 1944	Charente	B.2	10
Roderick	September 1 1944	Doubs	D.2	10
Ronald	August 5 1944	Finistère	M.3	5
Sceptre	August 14 1944	Alpes-Maritimes	R.2	9,10
Scion	August 30 1944	Ardèche	R.2	10
Simon	September 27 1944	Vendée, Charente	M.3,B.2	10
Stanley	September 1 1944	Haute-Marne	D.1	10
Timothy	September 11 1944	Jura and Doubs	D.2	10
Tony	August 18 1944	Vendée	M.3	6,10
Veganin	June 9 1944	Drôme and Isère	R.1	8
Willys	June 29 1944	Ardèche	R.1	9

Bataillon de Choc

Mission code name	Date of arrival in the field	Area of operations	Region or FFI subdivision	Chapter(s) in which mission is mentioned
Salvage	August 1 1944	Drôme	R.1	8

Commandos de France

Mission code name	Date of arrival in the field	Area of operations	Region or FFI subdivision	Chapter(s) in which mission is mentioned
Special Det.	August 17 1944	South-East France	R.2	10

Counterscorch Groups

Mission code name	Date of arrival in the field	Area of operations	Region or FFI subdivision	Chapter(s) in which mission is mentioned
Caïque	July 18 1944	Bouches-du-Rhône	R.2	9,10
Gédéon	August 12 1944	Var	R.2	9,10
Lougre	August 12 1944	Var	R.2	9,10
Sampan	June 14 1944	Var	R.2	9,10
Schooner	July 12 1944	Hérault	R.3	9,10

Operational Groups

Mission code name	Date of arrival in the field	Area of operations	Region or FFI subdivision	Chapter(s) in which mission is mentioned
Adrian	September 9 1944	Côte-d'Or	D.2	10
Alice	August 8 1944	Drôme	R.1	9
Betsy	July 26 1944	Ardèche	R.1	9
Christopher	September 3 1944	Côte-d'Or	D.2	10
Donald	August 6 1944	Finistère (north)	M.3	5
Emily	June 9 1944	Lot	R.4	10
Helen	August 30 1944	Ardèche	R.2	
Justine	June 29 1944	Vercors	R.1	8
Lafayette	August 30 1944	Ardèche	R.2	10
Lehigh	August 25 1944	Ardèche	R.2	10
Lindsey	August 16 1944	Cantal	R.6	10
Louise	July 18 1944	Ardèche	R.1	9
Nancy	August 13 1944	Hautes-Alpes	R.1	9,10
Pat	August 7 1944	Tarn	R.4	9
Patrick	August 15 1944	Indre	R.5	7,10
Peg	August 12 1944	Aude	R.3	9
Percy Pink	August 11 1944	Dordogne	R.5	10
Percy Red	August 1 1944	Haute-Vienne	R.5	7,10
Ruth	August 4 1944	Basses-Alpes	R.2	9
Williams	September 2 1944	Ardèche	R.2	10

Bibliography

Alsop, Stewart and Braden, Thomas, *Sub Rosa: The OSS and American Espionage*, New York, Harcourt, Brace & World, 1964.

Bigeard, *Pour une parcelle de gloire*, Paris, Plon, 1975.

Calvi, Fabrizio, *OSS, la guerre secrète en France*, Paris, Hachette, 1990.

Cave Brown, Anthony, *La guerre secrète*, Vol. 2, Le rempart des mensonges, Paris, Pygmalion, 1981.

Clayton, Anthony, *Forearmed, A History of the Intelligence Corps*, London, Brassey's, 1993.

Corta, Henry, *Qui ose gagne*, Vincennes, SHAT, 1997.

Destrem, Maja, *Les Commandos de France*, Paris, Fayard, 1982.

Foot, Michael R.D., *SOE in France*, London, Her Majesty's Stationery Office, 1966.

Funk, Arthur Layton, *Hidden Ally*, New York, Greenwood Press, 1992.

Hall, Roger, *You're Stepping on my Cloak and Dagger*, New York, W.W. Norton, 1957.

Le Clerq, Noël, *Détachement spécial*, Paris, Saint-Just, 1966.

Lewis, S.J., *Jedburgh Team Operations in Support of the 12th Army Group, August 1944*, Fort Leavenworth, Combat Studies Institute, 1990.

Lormier, Dominique, *Les FFI au combat*, Paris, Granger, 1994.

Muelle, Raymond, *Le 1er Bataillon de Choc*, Paris, Presses de la Cité, 1977.

Obolensky, Serge, *One Man in his Time*, New York, McDowell, 1958.

Ruffin, Raymond, *Ces chefs de maquis qui gênaient*, Paris, Presses de la Cité, 1980.

West, Nigel, *Secret War, the Story of SOE*, London, Hodder & Stoughton, 1992.

Le Bataillon de Choc en action, de Staoueli à l'Arlberg, Paris, Gilbert, 1947.

CONTENTS

410

411

ISBN : 2 908 182 947
Publisher's number : 2-908182
© *Histoire & Collections 1999*

ISBN: 2 908 182 91
Publisher number: 2 908 82
© Thierry & Cultures 1999

This book has been designed, typed, laid-out
and processed by Histoire & Collections,
fully on integrated computer equipment.
Lay-out : Sylvaine Noël
Editorial composition : FRT Graphic
Printed by KSG Elkar / KSG Danona. Spain.
European Union.
November 30th, 1999.